LITTLE IRELAND

An Irish Emigrant Family's Life in
Nineteenth Century Edinburgh

Patricia Delaney Dishon
and
Michael Delaney

Grosvenor House
Publishing Limited

The right of Patricia Delaney Dishon and Michael Delaney
to be identified as the authors of this
work has been asserted in accordance with Section 78
of the Copyright, Designs and Patents Act 1988

The book cover is copyright to
Patricia Delaney Dishon and Michael Delaney

This book is published by
Grosvenor House Publishing Ltd
Link House
140 The Broadway, Tolworth, Surrey, KT6 7HT.
www.grosvenorhousepublishing.co.uk

A CIP record for this book
is available from the British Library

ISBN 978-1-83615-122-7
eBook ISBN 978-1-83615-123-4

AUTHOR

Patricia Dishon (nee Delaney) is the great-granddaughter of Arthur and Cecilia Delaney. She has a BA (Hons) from the Open University. She lectured in Scottish Studies in the Centre of Continuing Education at the University of Edinburgh. Her first book *The Delaneys of Edinburgh* was a novel published in 2012 by

Grosvenor House Publishing Limited

www.grosvenorhousepublishing.co.uk

If you have any relevant information about this story the author can be contacted at

patricia@dishon.eu

DEDICATION

In memory of my beloved brother
Michael Delaney
who first began the journey into this story with me.

CONTENTS

PREFACE   ix

1   THE OLD COUNTRY   1

2   STRANGERS IN A STRANGE LAND   9

3   THE DELANEY SIBLINGS   15

4   THE BOYLAN CONNECTION   21

5   THE DELANEY BROTHERS   25

6   SARAH DELANEY   31

7   JANE DELANEY   39

8   THE MURRAY/MARTIN FAMILIES   45

9   THE TREGILGAS SISTERS   57

10   JOHN SYLVESTER DELANEY   95

11   "GLORY, GLORY TO THE HIBEES"   121

12   LUKE JOSEPH BOYLAN   149

13   LUKE TERENCE DELANEY   205

14   THE LOST CHILDREN   249

15   THE FIGHT FOR THE DELANEY CHILDREN   271

16   SEARCHING FOR THE DELANEY CHILDREN   309

CONCLUSION   329

ACKNOWLEDGEMENTS   331

LIST OF ILLUSTRATIONS   333

FAMILY TREES   337

BIBLIOGRAPHY   361

PREFACE

This history of the Delaney family came about through research into another.

In the summer of 1990, our mother's nephew James came to Edinburgh from England to search for his roots. His family had lived in the Old Town after arriving from Ireland, in the nineteenth century, so St. Patrick's Church in the Cowgate – at the hub of the old Irish ghetto - known as 'Little Ireland' – was the obvious place to go for information.

Since our family were friendly with Fr Stephen McGrath, the parish priest, they arranged for James to look at the church records of baptisms and marriages and went along to give him a hand. Searching through the dusty old volumes they came across the 1886 entry recording the marriage of our great-grandparents Arthur Delaney and Cecilia Clifford. We knew nothing about them.

Shortly afterwards, our aunts Margaret and Frances Delaney were looking through our late grandfather, Patrick Delaney's, personal papers when they came across a fragment of a legal document. It was a court case in which Arthur was trying to recover custody of three children he had fathered during his first marriage to a Mary Mowat. The children had been taken to Canada by an early version of the child migrant scheme.

At this point, our knowledge of the family history was scant, but the two discoveries set us off on a trail that led, eventually, to a village in Ireland. Along the road, we spent hours checking parish registers in churches, census returns in libraries and records of births, marriages and deaths in registry offices, this being in the days before such records were available on the Internet. Letters were written, telephone calls made, cemeteries tramped around and the journey finally made to County Monaghan where it had all began.

This is the story of what we found.

Michael Delaney

CHAPTER ONE

THE OLD COUNTRY

EMYVALE is a quiet village in an historically unquiet part of Ireland. Most people who have occasion to go there are usually just passing through on the road to the border, five miles distant, which has been the source of so much conflict since the years it was established to divide north and south. But, there is no sign of this troubled relationship on the roads that wind their way through a countryside where the small egg-shaped hills known as drumlins, for which County Monaghan is noted, are the main feature.

From one of these roads, east of the pleasant whitewashed houses that line the village's main street, a lane branches off and stops at the creaking, iron gate of Old Donagh Graveyard. Just inside is a well preserved grey headstone marking the last resting place of Arthur Delaney. Born in 1761, he is the earliest ancestor we can trace in Ireland.

The fact that we found him so easily was the result of one of the many coincidences that were to occur throughout our research. My brother, Michael Delaney, stepped off the bus in the village, on his very first visit to Ireland, in search of his roots. Seeing a small group of men standing beside the Emyvale village sign he approached and asked one man if he would kindly take a photograph of him beside the sign. Michael explained the reason for his visit and, after taking his photograph, the man introduced himself. He was Seamus McCluskey, retired village Headmaster, author, and historian of Emyvale, and he had known the last of the Delaneys to have lived in the village! He showed Michael around all the properties associated with the Delaney family, told him stories of how, as a young boy, he would jump on the back of the last Arthur Delaney's hay cart and hitch a ride into the village. He knew all about the last Delaney family to live in Emyvale and he gave him directions to the Old Donagh Graveyard, where Michael found our ancestor's gravestone.

Seamus, an incredibly gifted writer and historian, was to become a great friend to our family over the years that followed. He gave a warm welcome to many members of the family who subsequently made their pilgrimages to the Old Country and was a valuable source of information on all things Irish. Later, he was to tell us that the only reason he was standing beside the sign for Emyvale was that it was a brand new sign just erected that morning!

And that's how it all began.

Delaney, O'Dubhslaine in Irish, literally translating as 'black river', is not a name native to Monaghan. The clann's traditional heartland was in the counties south west of Dublin, particularly Laois and Kilkenny. But, over the centuries it spread out all over Ireland, although it is much less common than may be supposed, and found its way to Ulster. Monaghan, like Cavan and Donegal was cut off from the rest of this ancient province by partition in 1921, but in Ulster geographically if not politically, it remains. Ironically, Ulster was once the part of Ireland which provided the stiffest resistance to foreign domination and the Emyvale area was very much to the forefront of this epic struggle.

In ancient times, it marked the northern outpost of the lands of the Ui Meith, the tribe from which Emyvale probably takes its name. As the centuries passed, the area fell under the control of a variety of families in the intricate Irish clann system, chiefly the McKennas who were to fight a long rearguard action against both native rivals and English and Scottish settlers. This resistance effectively ended with the defeat of the Irish Catholic forces of James VII and II by the British Protestant followers of William of Orange at Drumbanagher, near Glaslough. The McKennas' once great fort at Tully, just south of Emyvale, is now just an earthen mound, but a more telling sign of their past importance can be found in the number of local people who bear the name. Seamus McCluskey, author of *Emyvale Sweet Emyvale*, the history of the village, says:

"If you go searching for a McKenna in or around Emyvale, you better first of all know their nickname."

While the power of the McKennas waned, that of the settlers increased and the dominant families came to be the Leslies and the Anketells, who gradually came to own most of the area between them. The Leslies, who ran their estates from their castle at Glaslough, east of Emyvale, were regarded as relatively good landlords who had fair dealings with their tenants. The family later lost Emyvale to their great rivals, famously over a game of cards, but took revenge for their loss by granting land at Corracrin opposite the gates of the Anketell estate for a Catholic church which was dedicated to St. Patrick. Corracrin graveyard is where many of the early Delaneys are buried and many other gravestones bear their name as sculptors. They were a family of stonemasons.

By that time, Catholics were just beginning to emerge from the dark years of oppression and persecution followed by William of Orange's victory after which they had been subjected to harsh penal laws which left them with little or no civil rights and affected every aspect of their lives, particularly land ownership.

"The penal laws and the land problems brought continuous strife and party fights during the 1700s, particularly in the second half of that century. Local fairs and race meetings, particularly those of Emyvale, were the centres of riotous gatherings and secret societies abounded." (McCluskey)

The situation blew up into a serious confrontation in 1763, but there were disturbances throughout the period involving factions like the Catholic Defenders and Protestant Peep O' Day Boys, which eventually became the Orange Order. Meanwhile the Protestants had successfully gained more control over Irish affairs from Britain, but some, inspired by the French Revolution, wanted to go further and set up a completely independent Irish Republic. The Society of United Irishmen, a revolutionary movement founded by Wolfe Tone in 1791, hoped to bring Catholics and Protestants together to achieve this and men were soon being recruited throughout the country.

The Society first made it's appearance in the Emyvale district about 1795 and in a very short time practically every man in the village and surrounding district became a member. It was little wonder that the young men flocked in their hundreds into the ranks of the United Irishmen as the cruelty of the Yeomen of the period against the Catholic population was of such ferocity that the Society provided their only hope of protection or redress.

The Society's members infiltrated the Monaghan Militia to such an extent that the authorities became alarmed and transferred the regiment to Blaris Moor camp, later known as Long Kesh, where four men from the Emyvale area were betrayed by a notorious informer, tried and shot.

Back in Monaghan, men were being tried at the assizes for arms raids, which led to more executions, but when open rebellion broke out finally in 1798 there was no rising in the county.

Ironically, the Monaghan Militia, purged of the United Irishmen, went into battle on the government side at Antrim and Ballynahinch where, on both occasions, the Republican side was mainly Protestant and the British mostly Catholic. Emyvale played a very minor role in the aftermath of the rebellion when the captive Wolfe Tone was brought through the area.

"It had been intended to spend the night at the village inn in Emyvale, but Tone's captors obviously felt it was much too risky. Instead, they spent the night at Achnacloy Church thus giving Emyvale a wide berth. The fears of the escorting party were probably unfounded, however, as all the local leaders and United Irishmen were either in prison or in exile by this time." (McCluskey)

These then were the times that our founding father, Arthur Delaney, whose grave Michael found in Old Donagh Graveyard, lived through. Would he have been a supporter of the United Irishmen? We have no way of knowing but, given what we now know about the Delaney families later political affiliations, I believe he probably was.

After the rebellion was crushed, the Irish Parliament was abolished, but union with Britain in 1801 did nothing to quell outbreaks of sporadic violence. At this time, monthly fairs were held in Emyvale on dates including New Years Day and St. Patrick's Day and, just as in the previous century, they provided the focus for conflict. In 1813, Catholics were shot down in cold blood by the Yeomen. Three years later our great-great-great grandad, also named Arthur Delaney, was born in Donagh parish, and when he was two years old, some of his family's Emyvale neighbours, attending the Auchnacloy races, were shot, in cold blood, at the hands of the town's Orangemen. In both cases, the killers were acquitted by the courts which enraged the Catholics and encouraged a steady flow of recruits into the secret societies. But, in 1826, a major breakthrough was made in Monaghan when Henry Westenra, a follower of the Irish Nationalist leader Daniel O'Connell, defeated Charles Leslie of the Glaslough landowning family in an election fought over the issue of emancipation which aimed to remove many of the disabilities still affecting Catholics from the penal laws.

That same year, the presence of the Delaney family was officially noted in the Emyvale area when the tithe applotment book, a land register drawn-up to assist the collection of taxes for the established church, the Protestant Church of Ireland, recorded that a Dunladdy (one of the many variants on the Delaney name) and a Caldwell jointly held a quarter-acre of land on which they paid two pence and three farthings annually. This they had to pay even though the Delaneys were Catholic and not members of the Church of Ireland.

By 1837, when the records for Donagh parish began, there were already several branches of the family in Emyvale and the surrounding area and more over in Tydavnet Parish to the west. These church returns of births and marriages give scant information and with no state registration of Catholics before 1864, the only way to make sense of the relationships between the people mentioned is to tie them together through common Christian name patterns. But it is only through the Scottish records, which started in 1855, that the jigsaw can really be pieced together. So the James Delaney, who we can identify as our forebear, through the records of his children who came to Scotland, was probably the son of the Arthur Delaney who is buried in Old Donagh Graveyard.

James Delaney was a stonemason to trade and it was this occupation which appears to have brought the Delaneys to Monaghan. According to an old man, Benny Hackett, who had been an employee of the Delaney family during Seamus McCluskey's time, the Delaney family had originated in Caledon in County Tyrone, just miles away across the present-day border. He told this to another descendant of our Delaney family from Emyvale, Leah O' Grady. Leah's branch of the Delaney family had emigrated to Prince Edward Island (PEI) in the early 1850s and her founding father there was called Arthur Delaney. The common continuous use of the Christian name, Arthur, marks us out as closely related. Seamus McCluskey put us in touch with Leah in PEI and she generously shared her findings with us. Benny Hackett told Leah that the Delaneys had been stonemasons on the construction of Caledon House (Castle), in County Tyrone. When building on the castle was completed the Delaneys moved to nearby County Monaghan (part of the county overlaps the large Caledon Estate) because they had bought a quarry just outside Emyvale.

In his *A Topographical Dictionary of Ireland* of 1837, Samuel Lewis describes Emyvale as a post town for the stage coaches which passed on the Dublin-Derry road, containing 123 houses and 571 inhabitants. He goes on:

> "This town consists principally of one street and is skirted by a stream, the Scarnageera River, tributary to the River Blackwater which descending from the mountains of the west frequently becomes a rapid and dangerous torrent after heavy rains. On its banks is a large flour mill and in its bed above the town is a quarry of greenstone. Freestone quarries also abound whence large quantities superior to Portland stone are procured and the great entrance to Caledon House was constructed of this stone."

We know the family were stonemasons so could the Delaneys have procured this stone to build the grand Portico of Caledon House and when the great house was finished and they heard that the Emyvale quarry was for sale had decided to move there? Whatever the reason move they certainly did and became a prosperous family from quarrying and building. As stone-cutters many gravestones in the Emyvale cemeteries, to this day, bear the family name as sculptors. They also farmed at least three parcels of land at Emyvale, Knocknagrave and Knockconnan townlands. Benny told Leah O'Grady that the Delaneys were a prosperous family until they took on a contract to provide the stone and labour to build the Bank of Ireland in Monaghan town. However, the bank reneged on the costs, on completion, and a court case ensued. The Delaneys were not paid what they were owed but the bank gave several decrepit houses, in Monaghan town, in recompense, which led to the family's economic decline. Benny Hackett said to Leah - "If you're a Delaney you're alright" - so the family must have been well respected in the area.

The land wars of the previous century were replaced by the tithe wars of the early 1830s. Catholics objected to having to pay one tenth of their meagre incomes to the established Protestant Church of Ireland. Stand-offs resulted between collectors and those liable and where belongings, if any were available, were seized when money was not forthcoming or, worse still, people were turned out from their homes onto the road. The land system, of which it was once said that there was no disadvantage which it did not possess, was a constant source of grievance and the narrow range of foods on which the people depended made famine a regular visitor.

With so much political unrest, insecurity and fear of further famine many Emyvale people decided to emigrate. Aided by their parish priest, Father Patrick Monaghan, they went to Prince Edward Island, in Canada. Leah's Delaney family were part of that exodus. Though the Delaneys of the area were not poor, they were a large extended family and even a prosperous business could not support them all. Leah's son, Thomas O'Grady, born on Prince Edward Island, grew up to become Professor of Irish Studies at the University of Massachusetts in Boston thus, fittingly, completing the circle.

James Delaney's son, Arthur, was one of those who left, but he did not make the journey across the Atlantic Ocean. Instead, he took the much shorter trip over the Irish Sea to Scotland and eventually he arrived in Edinburgh. Arthur had not worked in the family quarry, nor on the farms, he trained as a tailor, enabling him to take his skills anywhere. In time we think that three of his brothers joined him in the city then, two of his sisters and finally, when the Great Famine struck, two more of his sisters settled there in 'Little Ireland.

CHAPTER TWO

STRANGERS IN
A STRANGE LAND

EDINBURGH'S Royal Mile is one of the world's most famous streets. Visited by thousands of tourists each year who come to view the historic buildings which line its route and which have escaped the ravages of time and the town planners.

Two thirds of the way down it is joined by a road used since at least Roman times which once housed a convent dedicated to the Virgin Mary from whom it takes it's name, St Mary's Street, formerly St. Mary's Wynd. At the halfway point on the east side it gives way to a narrow opening called Boyd's Entry where, on 7 June 1841, Scotland's first census of the population recorded the presence of Arthur Delaney, his wife Helen Collins and their son James. When the census enumerator called at their home he noted only the briefest of details; that Arthur was twenty-five years old, that he had been born in Ireland and that he was working as a tailor; that Helen was tweny years old and had been born in Scotland; and that James was one year old and had been born in the city.

This was not the first mention of Arthur in the town. On 2 June 1838, he was named as god-father at the baptism of Elizabeth, daughter of John Gillespie and Sarah Stewart. Interesting that neither of the parent's names were Irish. Less than a year later, on 12 April 1839, Father George Riggs declared in his parish register that Arthur Delaney and Helen Collins were ' lawfully married persons'. The record states this took place at Brown's Square but no witnesses are given. This address was the priest's house for the church of St. Patrick in nearby Lothian Street, which later became St. Francis Church. The lack of witnesses given might suggest that Arthur and Helen had already married elsewhere, perhaps in Glasgow where we know Helen was born, and were simply giving their 'marriage lines' to their new church.

At this point the Catholic church in Scotland was just beginning to emerge from the centuries of official disapproval and sometimes outright persecution that had followed the Scottish Reformation. Emancipation had only been granted a decade before and there had been serious rioting, including the burning of a church, in protest at earlier measures aimed at relieving discrimination against Catholics in Scotland. So its activities tended to be low key and its churches kept from open public view, usually down side streets. Catholics were few and far between in Edinburgh and most of those in the city were immigrants, ranging from a few native Sots – most of them Highlanders who had held on to the Old Faith in remote Highland areas, out of the reach of the reformers - to exotic incomers from Europe, at one time including the exiled French royal family, and the Irish.

Though Irish farm labourers had come to Scotland for centuries, staying only long enough to work on the harvest before returning home with money to help pay their rents, feed their families over the winter and plant their own crops in the spring, it was the development of new transport links and industry which led to large-scale and permanent immigration from Ireland. Roads, canals, mills and mines provided employment and many of the migrants became immigrants and settled down in the cheapest parts of Scottish towns and cities where they found themselves.

In Edinburgh, this meant the Old Town, long since deserted by the aristocracy after James VI of Scotland became James I of England and by the middle classes who had found more desirable accommodation in the New Town. The houses left behind had been endlessly sub-divided by their landlords to fit in as many paying tenants as possible and the poor condition of the homes was often matched by those who lived in them. Outside, the wynds, closes and entries served as an open sewer for all types of waste and refuse and water was drawn from insanitary street wells. The closely-packed living arrangements combined with the lack of proper sanitation to provide a breeding ground for life-threatening diseases like cholera and typhoid which erupted in periodic outbreaks and sometimes reached epidemic levels.

Arthur Delaney arrived in this Edinburgh between the first wave of immigrants and the later deluge that resulted from the Great Famine of the 1840s. It is possible he spent sometime in the west of Scotland where he would have made landfall, either from a steamer or perhaps from one of the coastal traders which would take passengers steerage for a pittance, putting in at small ports along the coastline and at the great disembarkation point of the Broomielaw in Glasgow. Scotland was not necessarily the final destination for all the immigrants. Sometimes, it was merely a stopping off point allowing those who intended making the longer journey across the Atlantic to Canada or the United States to muster their fare. Likewise, those who did remain in Scotland were not confined to the Glasgow area but spread out east to find employment in everything from mill work in Dundee to mining in Fife. While later censuses show that Helen Collins, Arthur's wife, was born in Glasgow, and it may be possible that Arthur met her there, it is probable that he did not spend long in that city and he was bound for Edinburgh with a special purpose in mind.

The Irish in the capital had produced their own entrepreneurs who tended to operate in businesses shunned, for one reason or another, by the the native population, particularly the licensed trade and second hand clothes dealing. In his *The Life and Times of James Connolly* Desmond Graves explains:

> "A section of the Irish became petty pawnbrokers, then local dealers and finally established a substantial trade exporting second-hand clothes to Ireland. In the 1830s, three-quarters of the 250 second hand clothes dealers of the Grassmarket area were Irish. In time, a section of these entrepreneurs rose still higher in the social scale and acquired the small businessman's outlook."

Along the Cowgate, in St. Mary's Wynd, lived one of those highly successful Irish entrepreneurs, a man who would come to play an important part in the lives of the Delaneys. Philip Boylan was born in Ireland, possibly as early as 1795. He is first noted in Edinburgh in 1821 when he married Dorothy Warrick, daughter of an Irish hat maker, by whom he fathered at least six children all but two of whom died young. At the time of their wedding he was described as a tailor of East Common Close in the Canongate. He expanded his tailoring business and opened a shoemaker's shop and over the next decade he moved into other activities.

By the mid-1830s, the Register of Sasines, which details property transactions, was recording his purchases. On 23 April 1835, for example, he bought 17 St. Mary's Wynd, an address with which the Delaney family was to become closely linked, as well as a newly built tenement between Halyburton's and Gullan's Closes, behind Boyd's Entry, and a hayloft and stables at the Netherbow where St. Mary's Wynd met the High Street and Edinburgh gave way to the Canongate. We believe that Philip Boylan originated in County Monaghan, possibly even in Emyvale, and that he is the reason why Arthur Delaney did not remain in Glasgow when he landed but made his way to a job that awaited him in Edinburgh. Philip Boylan's tailoring business was thriving and since Arthur was a trained tailor he was given employment in the older man's long established business.

If the Edinburgh to which Arthur came was unwelcoming in terms of its foul environment, it was no less so in the hostility of some of its people. Although Ireland was part of Britain, its inhabitants were effectively second-class citizens widely regarded as lazy and stupid and prone to heavy bouts of drinking and fighting. Living memory could recall a time when the Irish had risen in rebellion and they were also marked out by their Catholic religion. But, of more immediate concern to the natives was the effect their arrival was having on jobs and wages. The poverty-stricken immigrants were desperate enough to work long hours for lower pay than might be expected by Scots and in many respects their country upbringing – clean air, hard physical work and, in all but the worst of times, a basic but healthy diet of potatoes and milk – had fitted them better for heavy labour. Occasionally, tensions between the two groups blew up into violence with Scottish labourers frequently invading what was already becoming known as 'Little Ireland', assaulting its inhabitants and wrecking shops and homes.

But, it was not only the working class who were hostile. Establishment organizations ranging from the Church of Scotland to the 'Glasgow Herald' newspaper were among the harshest critics of the Irish. By contrast the Free Kirk leader, Thomas Chalmers, and the novelist, Sir Walter Scott, had strongly supported emancipation and the newspaper of the Edinburgh establishment, 'The Scotsman', was a rare beacon of sanity and moderation according to Tom Gallagher in his story of the Irish in Scotland *The Uneasy Peace*.

"It frequently refuted the more extravagant or spiteful claims of their religious detractors and was prepared to highlight virtues among them such as the chastity of their womenfolk, even in the most reduced circumstances, or their low illegitimacy rate when compare with the native Scottish figures."

This was remarkable given the explosion of the Irish population in Edinburgh as a report in 'The Scotsman' as early as 18 June 1823 shows:

> "It may be mentioned, as an exact instance of the increasing numbers of Irish people within this city that Toddrick's Wynd which some years ago did not contain one is now entirely inhabited by them." (Gallagher)

So there was already a sizeable population of his compatriots around when Arthur Delaney and Helen Collins set up home at Geddes Entry in the Old Town. Their son, James, was born there in 1840, followed by a still born child who was buried in the Greyfriars Churchyard. The couple then moved to a house in St. Mary's Wynd where twin daughters, Mary and Rosanna, were born in November 1843 but both died, one after the other, within months of their birth and were also buried in Greyfriars. In December 1845, a son, Thomas, was born and in 1848 another son, John, completed their family.

CHAPTER THREE

THE DELANEY SIBLINGS

When Arthur Delaney and his wife, Helen Collins, settled in the Old Town of Edinburgh in 1839 they were the first of the Delaney family to do so. Indeed, there were no other Delaneys recorded at that time.

The records show they were later followed by a Joseph Delaney, a Michael Delaney and a William Delaney. We believe they were Arthur's brothers but, because those very early church marriage records do not give parents names unlike the later Civil Records from 1855, we cannot prove it.

Michael Delaney married Ann Brown on 14 May 1848. There are no further records of Michael and Ann Delaney. It is unlikely they returned to an Ireland gripped by famine, so perhaps they emigrated.

Joseph Delaney did leave further records. He married his wife, Isabella, on 7 February 1845, according to St Mary's Cathedral Registers. In one record he gave his occupation as 'goldsmith'. The couple had one child, named Catherine, but sadly she died as an infant. Two other daughters were born to them but, tragically, we think Joseph must have died soon after the birth of his third daughter because in the 1851 census Isabella declares she is a widow. The reason we think Joseph may also have been Arthur's brother is that when Arthur and Helen's son, Thomas, was born they gave him the middle name of Joseph.

Another possible brother of Arthur was William James Delaney who married a Margaret Monaghan on 5 November 1850. The couple had a son, Joseph William Delaney, born 31 August 1851. I think that baby may also have been named after the deceased Joseph Delaney. The repeat of the name of Joseph seems to suggest that Joseph, William and Arthur were all brothers. The fact that Arthur and Helen named their first son James and that William's middle name is James, also lends weight to the fact that they were all sons of James Delaney and Mary Hughes of Emyvale.

We have proof that the only other Delaneys recorded as living in 'Little Ireland' around that time were all Arthur's sisters. We are therefore looking at one single family of Delaneys settling in Edinburgh's Old Town from around 1838 to 1850 – there were no others.

The first to arrive, after Arthur, was his sister, Sarah Delaney, who had married John Skiffington. The couple must have married in Ireland because there is no record of their marriage in Scotland and they do not appear in the 1841 census. But they were certainly here by 1842 when their son, Arthur Skiffington, was born on 31 August at 42 St. Mary's Wynd. Arthur Delaney stood as god-father to their second son, John Skiffington, in 1844 in St. Patrick's Church in Lothian Street, which had been built to serve the growing Irish diaspora. Sarah Delaney and John Skiffington were god-parents to Arthur and Helen's twin daughters, Mary and Roseanna, on 15 November 1843, so the families were obviously close. It does not appear that Sarah Skiffington (nee Delaney) had any more children.

While searching the Registers at Mortonhall Cemetery, which holds the records of all the old Edinburgh graveyards, in one old register we came across a reference to a Mary Delaney, who had died of 'childbed' on 15 March 1848 aged twenty-five at St. Mary's Wynd and was buried in the Greyfriars Churchyard. It is likely that Mary Delaney died of childbed fever - Puerperal Fever. This fever killed many thousands of women in the eighteenth and nineteenth centuries. There were many medical theories about what caused this condition in women. One Hungarian born physician, Dr Ignaz Semmelweis, in 1844, was the first to come up with a diagnosis and a remedy. In his lying-in hospital in Vienna, he noticed that deaths were lower in the maternity wards where midwives delivered the babies than in the wards where doctors did. He came to the conclusion that it was a result of cross-contamination. Doctors would routinely carry out autopsies on women who had died in childbirth and then be called to a live birth. He realised that it was vital that such doctors (or anyone delivering a baby) should first wash their hands. It seems like common sense to us now but in those days doctors didn't understand about germs. Dr Semmelweis insisted that all his medical staff should wash their hands in a solution of chlorinated lime before and after attending to patients.

The results were dramatic – the maternal death rate fell to an incredible low in his hospital. When he published his findings a few doctors agreed with his thesis but the majority ridiculed him. One physician in Philadelphia, Dr Charles Delucena Meigs, protested - "Doctors are gentlemen and gentlemen's hands are clean". Because doctors had such a high opinion of themselves thousands of women were to continue to die. Dr Semmelweis was ridiculed, ostracised and hounded by the medical profession. Eventually, he had a breakdown, was committed to a mental institution and died. It was left to other pioneering doctors such as Oliver Wendell Holmes and Thomas Watson to carry on his work.

It is unlikely that Mary Delaney would have had a doctor attending her at her home birth. In the Old Town, experienced local women (known in Scotland as 'Howdies') would attend at the delivery of working class women in childbirth. It is likely that unclean hands was still the cause of the fever in these mothers. Living in poor housing, with no running water, would not have helped. None of the houses in Little Ireland at that time had plumbed water. All water had to be carried from street wells, two of which still survive in the Old Town, up the tall tenements and then heated on wood or coal fires. Hardly conducive to good hygiene. Though, of course, even higher class women in grander houses died as a result of childbed fever. One of the most notable was Mary Wollstonecraft, a famous Feminist and author of *The Vindication of the Rights of Women*. She died of childbed fever after giving birth to her daughter, Mary, who, under her married name Mary Shelley, was the author of 'Frankenstein'. Tragic that such a pioneering Feminist as Mary Wollstonecraft should die by reason of being a woman.

Of course, women died in 'childbed' for many reasons but, in the nineteenth century, the single most common cause of maternal deaths related to childbed fever. The reason I think that it was Puerperal Fever that killed Mary Delaney was that the infection also claimed the lives of many of those women's babies. Mary had given birth to a daughter, Mary Ann Cavana, shortly before she died. Mary Ann's god-mother was Jane Delaney. Sadly, the baby died in the week after her birth.

There were very few people named Delaney in the Old Town at that time so we assumed that Mary and Jane must be related to us.

We discovered later that Mary was indeed another sister of Arthur and Sarah. Mary Delaney had married Francis Cavana (Kavanagh) in 1847 and a year later she was dead. The child's godmother in St Patrick's Church in Lothian Street, Jane Delaney, was also a sister of Arthur and Sarah and was only fifteen years old at the time.

Jane Delaney, the youngest of the sisters, must have stayed on in Edinburgh after acting as godmother to her dead sister Mary's baby. Perhaps her parents had sent her to Edinburgh to escape the ravages that the Great Famine had wrought in Ireland. In the 1851 census, Jane is listed as a general servant in the home of the McLaughlin family in the Old Town. Jane Delaney was to marry a clothier, John Murray, on 1 January 1855 at 17 St. Mary's Wynd in 'Little Ireland'.

Another sister of Arthur had also moved to Edinburgh. Her name was Anne Delaney and she was born in County Monaghan in 1831. She also appears in the 1851 census, as a fruit seller, lodging with the MacKenna family in the Cowgate. Monaghan was known as 'MacKenna County', from earliest times, and so we assume Anne must have known the family from back home.

It seems that Anne was an outcast from her sibling's families. They all stand as godparents for each other's children, but Anne is never mentioned in any capacity within the family. Why so?

Perhaps the reason is that Anne gives birth to an illegitimate son in Edinburgh. The Delaneys, Skiffingtons and Murrays all appear to be respectable business people within the Irish diaspora in Edinburgh and also devout Catholics.

Had Anne put herself beyond the Pale? Sadly, she was not to have the consolation of her son, John, as he died of smallpox on 8 September 1856, after eighteen days illness, at Skinners Close, High Street in the Old Town, aged 6 months. Anne was present and on registering the baby's death she 'made her mark X' – meaning she could not write.

Smallpox was an ancient, highly contagious disease. The distinctive pustules (pox spots) have been found on an Egyptian Mummy from a tomb. It was caused by a virus, which was easily spread, and ranged across the ancient world killing millions of people throughout history. We can probably comprehend it better ourselves now having experienced a global coronavirus pandemic. It was difficult, indeed almost impossible, to contain once it took hold.

The first major breakthrough in Britain came in 1796. Edward Jenner had heard the folklore that claimed that milkmaids who had contracted a milder related virus, cowpox, never contracted smallpox. This is the origin in books and poems of referring to beautiful women as having a complexion 'like a milkmaid'. Jenner collected pus from a cowpox pustule on a milkmaid's arm and injected it into the arm of an eight-year-old boy, James Phipps, which made him immune to smallpox. But it was to be one hundred years later before the World Health Assembly signed a Resolution to eradicate smallpox and widespread vaccination became possible.

Sadly, it was much too late to save poor baby John Delaney. I wonder if his mother, Anne Delaney, had natural immunity, since the disease is so contagious and Anne would have been in close contact with her baby during his illness. The Delaneys in Ireland were farming people so it seems likely that Anne may well have milked cows back home on the family farm. Certainly, she survived.

In spite of the World Health Organisation (WHO) programme smallpox continued into modern times. The last 'natural' case reported was in Somalia in 1977, which resulted in fifty-four thousand people being vaccinated. The final reported case is even more shocking. It was agreed that all stocks of the smallpox virus in laboratories across the world should be destroyed, with the exception of one in Russia and one in the USA. In 1978 the last reported case of a death from smallpox was reported. The victim was a medical photographer who was accidentality infected while working in a laboratory in Birmingham, England. No one knows how this was possible.

When baby John Delaney died of smallpox he was was buried in the Canongate Burial Ground in the Old Town. We know from census entries that his mother, Anne Delaney, continued to live in Edinburgh but there appears to be no contact between her and the rest of her family. Then, on 18 July 1864, when she is thirty-three years old, Anne does marry. Her husband is Joseph Daly, aged thirty, who is a house-painter. Joseph's father's occupation is given as 'Lamplighter'. All the Edinburgh street lamps at that time were lit by gas. His father would have gone round lighting the gas lamps at night, using a light on the end of a long pole, and returned to snuff them out in the morning. Later, many lamplighters were employed as night-watchmen for the city - they were a kind of early police force.

When Joseph Daly and Anne Delaney marry, Anne gives her parent's names as James and Mary Delaney of County Monaghan but states they are now deceased. Anne Delaney and Joseph Daly have no children registered to them. Perhaps Anne is too old by then. We know from census returns that they continue to live together but then Anne Daly (nee Delaney) disappears from the Scottish records. There are no further census entries for her and no death certificate. So what has happened? Could she have gone home to Ireland? A later census for Joseph Daly states that he is married but lives with another woman as 'man and wife'. So Anne is still alive - but where? We can find no further trace of her so Anne is our mystery Delaney sibling.

CHAPTER FOUR

THE BOYLAN CONNECTION

Tragedy was to strike the Delaney family when, on 8 May 1850, Arthur Delaney died of Inflammation, aged just thirty-four, at his home on St. Mary's Wynd, leaving his wife, Helen Delaney (nee Collins), to bring up their three surviving children alone. James was ten, Thomas five and John just two years old. Arthur was laid to rest in a private plot in the old Greyfriar's Churchyard alongside his stillborn child, his twin daughters, Mary and Roseanna, and his godson, John Skiffington, who had died when he was just two years old.

Three months later Arthur's wife, Helen, married old Philip Boylan.

At first, this seemed to us quite shocking. Philip's own wife, Dorothy Warrick, had died just six months earlier. Helen was twenty-nine years old and Philip was almost twice her age. But, on reflection, it seems understandable. With the family breadwinner gone Helen and her sons faced the Poorhouse. There were no public benefits then, no widow's pension. Philip Boylan was a very wealthy man with a large house at 17 St. Mary's Wynd. He was highly respected among the Irish diaspora and was a devout Catholic. Certainly, the priests at St. Patrick's Church in Lothian Street appear to have raised no objections to this hasty marriage when they married the couple there on 18 August 1850. Perhaps they had seen too many children left destitute by the loss of a father to be worried about the religious niceties. Nor did Arthur's sister, Sarah Skiffington. She obviously appreciated what this would mean for her late brother's children and was pragmatic enough to stand as Helen's bridesmaid at the wedding.

What then are we to think about Philip's motives? He was, for the times, an old man. He had been married to his wife Dorothy for thirty years when she died. Together they had built up a highly successful business and she had given him six children. There seems no doubt that it was a long and happy marriage. But the couple had suffered the loss of four of those children when they were young. Only two children survived, daughters, Eleanor and Agnes. Eleanor was married to John Lennon and Agnes to John O'Connor. Philip had no sons to pass on his business and his extensive property portfolio to. Married women's inheritances would come under the control of their husbands. An astute man like Philip would understandably object to the fruits of his years of hard work passing to another man who had done nothing to earn it.

Philip needed a son.

Helen had produced three healthy sons for Arthur, perhaps he might have thought she could produce a son for him. If that was his thinking he thought right. Helen gave him three healthy sons to replace his lost children. He even gave the boys his dead son's names, Luke, Philip and James Boylan. Sadly, they did lose one son, John, in infancy, but Helen also produced another daughter, Mary Boylan, for him and they seemed to have had a long and happy life together. Helen wanted for nothing and when Philip died he left her an annuity of her own.

The only person who seems to have disapproved of the marriage was Philip's daughter, Eleanor. She had grown up just as astute a business person as her father and had built up a very large portfolio of property in Edinburgh and Leith which she rented out. When John Lennon married her he married money. Eleanor owned a mansion house in South Fort Street in Leith. In the Valuation Rolls it states that it had seventeen windows and I have seen from a drawing of the site that it stood in a large plot of land, detached from surrounding properties. She called it Warrick House after her beloved late mother. Sadly, the house was long ago demolished as the Port of Leith expanded.

Such a devoted daughter could hardly be expected to approve of her father replacing her mother, so soon after her death, with a much younger wife. Certainly, when Helen died in 1890 just a year before Eleanor herself, she refused to allow Helen to be buried in the same extensive private plot in the Canongate Churchyard where her mother and father both lay.

Instead, Helen's first son by Philip, Luke Boylan, laid her to rest in a new cemetery at Morningside. She could not have been laid beside her first husband, Arthur, because Greyfriars Churchyard had long ago been closed for burials by Sir Henry Litttlejohn, Edinburgh's First Medical Officer of Health. Littlejohn was concerned at the hygiene implications of continuing burials in old Greyfriars. It was so overcrowded that bones were beginning to appear above the ground! In recent times an eminent Edinburgh historian has caused offence, to some, by suggesting that 'Greyfriars Bobby', the little dog made famous for keeping watch for years on his dead master's grave, was actually in there looking for bones! A statue of the dog stands outside the gates of the Graveyard.

If Helen Delaney had married Philip Boylan to secure her three son's futures it also was a sacrifice that paid off. Philip Boylan proved to be a caring, supportive and devoted stepfather to Arthur Delaney's sons. They grew up in the large house at 17 St. Mary's Wynd, with servants, alongside their half-siblings. They would want for nothing. Philip, a master tailor, would ensure they were extremely well dressed. He made sure they received the same education as his own children, even permitting young James Delaney, a gifted artist, to work as a professional artist – a rather precarious profession. Thomas, he apprenticed as a brass-founder, so he would have a good trade. Then later, when Thomas married Margaret Maguire and produced six children, he allowed Thomas to take over the Boylan shoemakers business on St. Mary's Wynd. John Delaney, he apprenticed to the Printing Trade and he qualified as a compositor. You had to have good connections to enter the world renowned Edinburgh printing and publishing industry in those days. Prejudice against Irish Catholics, in Edinburgh, remained strong and few businesses were open to them. They were completely barred from the Police Force, which took instead Protestant Scottish Highlanders as recruits. The printing trade was the only large industry which accepted Catholics in the city. This continued into modern times when successive generations of Delaneys entered the printing trade. Philip must have been indulgent indeed when his stepson, John Delaney, announced he was giving up his good job in the Printing industry to go on the stage!

CHAPTER FIVE

THE DELANEY BROTHERS

When Arthur Delaney died on 8 May 1850 and his wife, Helen, married Philip Boylan on 18 August of the same year, Arthur's son, James Delaney, was ten years old, his son, Thomas Delaney, was five years old and his son, John Delaney, was just two years old. The three boys and their mother moved into Philip Boylan's large house at 17 St. Mary's Wynd in the heart of 'Little Ireland'. Since the death of his wife, Dorothy, six months earlier, Philip had been living there alone except for a cook and a housemaid. It was to prove a very comfortable childhood but one wonders what ten-year-old James thought of it all. He would remember his father, Arthur, very well, as would his brother, Thomas, but, in time, two-year-old John would remember little of Arthur. Philip Boylan would be the only father John would ever know. There seems little doubt that Philip was a caring, even indulgent, stepfather to the Delaney brothers. Being so young, John was also closest to the children born to his mother, Helen, and Philip. In particular to the couple's first-born, Luke Boylan, born in 1851, when John Delaney was just three years old. Luke was followed by brothers, Philip, James, John and a sister Mary Boylan. Sadly, baby John Boylan was to die of Encephalitis, when he was just months old and was buried in the large Boylan family plot in the Canongate Churchyard.

From their later lives we can tell that the Delaney brothers received a good education. Schooling was not compulsory in the 1850s but we know that there was a Catholic school attached to St. Patrick's Church in Lothian Street, and the church placed great importance on education as a way of improving the lot of their poor Irish children.

When James Delaney grew up he was shown to have a talent for painting. In later census returns he gives his occupation as artist.

On the 9 August 1859, young James Delaney married in unusual circumstances. The wedding took place in Viewfield House, the

Catholic priest's home, in Dunfermline, across the River Forth from Edinburgh. His bride was Ann Maloney, who was described as 'a spinster of Dunfermline' and gave her age as nineteen. James, who said he was 'an artist of Dunfermline' claimed to be twenty-two when, in fact, he was nineteen years old. Ann states she is Irish born, that her father, Patrick Maloney, was a carter and that her mother, Catrine Gorman, was deceased. Since James lived in Edinburgh we have no idea how they ended up marrying in Dunfermline. One slight possibility is that there was a Drawing School in the town. Could James have been studying there? The incorrect age, the fact that no address in Dunfermline is given, the witnesses who appeared - none of whose names are familiar, and the likelihood that Ann was pregnant, all point towards a marriage that did not have parental approval and may even have been the result of an elopement.

If James did try to hoodwink his parents, they were back under Philip Boylan's roof and apparently back in favour by the following year. James and Ann's son, Arthur Philip Delaney, was born in the Boylan house at 17 St. Mary's Wynd on 20 April 1860 and baptized in the new St Patrick's Church, in the Cowgate, where Philip Boylan stood as his godfather.

The immigration resulting from the Great Famine had led to a huge increase in Edinburgh's Catholic population and, in 1856, a new church was provided in the heart of 'Little Ireland' to meet the increased demand.

The building was bought from the Presbyterian United Seceders though it had been built eighty-five years before for the Episcopalians and as such can claim to have served the three main religious denominations in Scotland. The church was dedicated to St. Patrick, replacing the small chapel of the same name in Lothian Street which was then used wholly as a Catholic school. Until the 1872 law making primary education compulsory, the church was already providing schooling for the youngsters of the parish. We know from the 1851 census that James and Thomas Delaney were listed as 'scholars' to be joined later by their younger brother, John.

Once their schooling was complete the Delaney brothers, Thomas and John, were apprenticed into solid trades. Thomas as a brassfounder and John as a printer. But James followed a less conventional path earning his living as an artist.

In the 1861 census, after his son Arthur's birth, James is describing himself as 'an artist and photographer'. Many artists had switched to photography which had been invented twenty years earlier. In fact, photography in Scotland had been pioneered by the painter David Octavious Hill and his partner Robert Adamson, based in Rock House on the slopes of Calton Hill in Edinburgh. Their work is now considered as an art form and is highly collectable. Octavious Hill had turned to photography after being commissioned to paint a massive painting of all the members of the General Assembly of the Church of Scotland. Unable to gather all the members together more than once, he hit on the idea of taking a photograph of them and painting from that. It was an amazing achievement and the finished painting is a wonder to see.

So, when James Delaney turned to photography he was following in the footsteps of famous painters like Hill. When James was earning his living as an artist it is possible that he was doing portraiture. His clients would have to be monied people, so a limited market, but now the new photography opened up having your image captured to everyone. There were soon several studios in the city following the establishment of the first one on a Princes Street rooftop. Practical photography classes were being held from the late 1850s onwards, but most learned by trial and error and mastering the new skill quickly began to replace miniature painters and silhouette makers. But photography needed cameras and glass plates and chemicals – an expensive business to begin with. We suspect that Philip Boylan again came to his aid by providing the initial capital and James himself seemed to take other employment to set up a studio. In one census, Anne and their son, Arthur, were living at 13 High Street and she declares she is a "clerks wife." James himself is absent from the house, providing, perhaps, a foretaste of what was to come. The next year the couple had a second child, Ellen, at 43 High Street, an address better known today as John Knox House. Her father, James Delaney, stated on her Birth Certificate that he was working as a photographer.

On 19 April 1863, Ann gives birth to a second daughter, also named Ann, at 327 Canongate and on 1 May 1865, a second son, James, was born at 8 St. Mary's Wynd. James was still working as a photographer at the time of these births. All seems to be going well for the family. Then everything changes on 6 February 1866, when wee Ann, who was not yet two years old, died of croup at the Edinburgh Royal Infirmary and was buried in the Canongate Kirkyard. On her death certificate James states that he is working as a General Labourer. What has gone wrong?

Over the next few years, James and Ann's marriage appears to come under increasing strain. In the 1871 census, Ann and her daughter, Ellen, are lodging with a woman in a house in the Cowgate. At the same time, James, now back to working as a photographer, was living in a large Boarding House for professional people at 17 High Street, just across from St. Mary's Street where his mother, Helen, and stepfather, Philip, were still living. Within a short space of time he seems to have left Edinburgh altogether. Certainly, his marital problems would not have been viewed kindly, particularly in the strict Catholic community from which he came. Divorce was forbidden by the Church and, regardless of religion, the cost kept it out of the reach of all but the very wealthy. Couples were simply expected to make the best of a bad situation, but separation and even desertion seem to have been common.

We do not know where James went when he left Edinburgh, nor do we know if he sent any money back to his wife to support his children in Edinburgh. Throughout this period, travelling photographers abounded, often transporting themselves in horse-drawn wagon studios and setting up in town squares, railway stations and other central locations. Others simply hired hotel rooms as makeshift studios and dark rooms for the day.

Some found areas in which they could make a steady living and that seems to be what happened to James Delaney. He settled in Wigan, a Lancashire town, which had a large Irish immigrant population working in the mills and mines. But he began to suffer ill health and he died there in the hospital of the Union Workhouse on the 19 December 1886, aged forty-eight, of a variety of medical conditions, including dropsy and heart disease which killed so many members of the Delaney family over the years. He was alone. The Workhouse Master registered his death. A sad end to a wee boy from 'Little Ireland' who had shown such promise.

When following his trail I picked up a hint that he may have died in Wigan so I phoned the town's Register Office to see if I could find out anything about him. When the Registrar asked his name and I told him, 'James Delaney', he burst out laughing. He explained that in Wigan, with a high immigrant population at the time, it would be like looking for a needle in a haystack! On the off-chance, he asked what his job might be in an attempt to narrow it down. When I said – 'photographer' – there was a pause - "A well now you're talking" he said, "there was only one James Delaney whose death was registered as – ' a photographer of Wigan.'" I had found my great-great grandfather and he was still working at his profession fifteen years after leaving Edinburgh.

While his brother, James, left Edinburgh, Thomas Delaney barely moved outside 'Little Ireland', but he was to be a great support to James' son, Arthur Philip, in the trials and tribulations that were to come, after his father, James, abandoned him and his mother and left for England.

Thomas Delaney had fathered an illegitimate son named James, born 2 August1869, to a Helen McIntosh but the couple did not marry. Instead, he married Margaret McGuire, daughter of a second-hand clothes dealer. They married in St. Patrick's Church and Margaret was already pregnant with their first child, Mary Helen, who was born on the 2 October1869 - two months later! She would bear her husband ten more children, many of whom died in infancy including two daughters, Catherine and Joan, who died of Scarlet Fever within a fortnight of each other in 1880. 'Little Ireland' was a dangerous place for children with epidemics of Measles, Whooping Cough and Scarlet Fever carrying off hundreds of them before they were five years old. Thomas had many jobs, including brassfounder and leather worker, before taking over the Boylan's shoe-making business. His younger brother, John Delaney, was to have a very different life. He became a professional actor.

CHAPTER SIX

SARAH DELANEY

Sarah was born to James Delaney and Mary Hughes in Donagh Parish in Co. Monaghan in 1820. We do not know when, or where, Sarah married John Skiffington but we suspect it must have been in Ireland as there is no evidence of the marriage in the Scottish records. We believe John Skiffington was also from the county. Within a short time after he and Sarah arrive in the Old Town in 1842, they open a grocer's shop in the High Street so they must have had some capital. They arrive three years before the Great Famine struck.

We know that Monaghan was one of the counties in Ireland worst affected by the Great Famine. In Irish, *'an Gorta Mor'*, *'The Great Hunger'*, raged in Ireland from 1845 to 1849, with 1847 being described as *'the Black Year'*. By the end of that period around one million Irish people had died and another million had emigrated. It is sometimes described as the 'Great Irish Potato Famine' as it was the failure of the potato crop, due to blight, that triggered mass starvation in Ireland. However, the causes of the tragedy run much deeper than that. Ireland, in the 19th century, was a conquered country ruled by Britain and dominated by a British land-owning class, many of whom were absentee landlords. The Irish themselves had no land rights and were reduced to impoverished tenant status or cottars. Ireland was a fertile, prosperous land that exported huge amounts of cattle and grain to Britain at the time that the potato blight struck. But the Irish themselves had been utterly dependent on the potato crop to feed themselves. There was more than enough food to feed the people in Ireland when the blight struck. Historians now claim that 'The Great Hunger' was the result of political inaction by the British Government to address the problem. They argue that this potato blight did not just affect Ireland. It spread, possibly from Mexico, through North America and across Europe. Some suggest that it was actually brought into Ireland from potatoes, carried in Clipper Ships, to feed passengers and crews. It was a virulent crop disease that affected many countries but, only in Ireland did it result in a million deaths in the population and mass emigration. Throughout the period of the Famine shiploads of food were exported to Britain while the Irish people starved. In previous times of famine, on a smaller scale, different British governments closed the ports to food imports from Ireland to keep food in the country until the problem eased. Neither the Tory party, or later, the Whigs adopted that policy arguing that it was against their belief in 'Free Trade' and so a people starved.

It left a bitter legacy in Ireland and among those forced to emigrate, and their descendants, to this day. Mass emigration took place to Australia, Canada and most notably to America, where the numbers of citizens of Irish descent runs into millions. But the first impact of Famine emigration was felt in English ports, especially Liverpool, where by the 1850s half the population were Irish or of Irish descent - and in Scotland.

The vast majority of Irish emigrants to Scotland settled in Glasgow, but there were large numbers in Dundee, in the mining areas of Ayrshire and Fife and, of course, in Edinburgh.

Of course, Irish people had been settling in Scotland for hundreds of years but not in any great numbers.

When I first began researching my Delaney family roots, I consulted St. Mary's Roman Catholic Cathedral's records of Births, Deaths and Marriages. It was a real eye-opener. The earliest record showed very small numbers of Catholics in Edinburgh. In the years following on from the 16th century Protestant Reformation there were few Catholics in Scotland. Hardly surprising when attending mass became a punishable offence, and priests were hunted down, imprisoned and, in one notable instance, executed. John Ogilvie was a Scots priest who was hanged and drawn in 1615, in Glasgow and canonized as, St John Ogilvie, in 1976. The religion went underground, especially among the Catholic aristocracy and gentry who continued to hide priests and hear mass in their private homes. In many of these grand houses you can still see the 'Priest Holes' where priests could hide in the event of danger.

But in the Lowlands generally the Reformation was writ large. The same was not true of the Scottish Highlands and Islands were the old Faith clung on, in pockets, remote and far from the reach of the authorities. This was brought home to me when I searched those early records. Nearly every family name of Catholics, then living in Edinburgh and in the congregation of the Cathedral, was a Highland Scottish one. This continued until the middle of the 19th century when, as I turned each page, nearly every name in the record was Irish. A whole social history in one volume. One early entry has always intrigued me. It was from the Deaths record and it stated simply - 'Mrs Delaney killed when her house fell on her'. I have never been able to find out who this poor woman might have been. It predates the arrival of our family. It sounds very like the woman had been living in slum property which collapsed around her. Who she was I don't suppose we will ever know but after the Famine, when many hundreds of Irish arrived in Edinburgh, those were just the kind of slum housing conditions they were forced to endure.

The Old Town of Edinburgh had been a walled city stretching downhill from Edinburgh Castle to The Netherbow, the original location of the City Gate in the wall. The street that ran along the junction between that and the Burgh of the Canongate was called St. Mary's Wynd and it was in that area, that became known as 'Little Ireland', that the Delaney, Skiffington, Murray and Boylan families were to live out their lives.

The Royal Mile, which is the name by which the area is now best known, housed everyone from the rich and famous to the poorest of the poor. They all lived crowded together in tall tenements known as 'Lands', the name being given, apparently, because in this vertical city, restricted within the walls, they provided living space where there was little. Many of them rose six or seven storeys high, more when you counted the stories below ground. The poor lived at basement or ground level, where the smell from the garbage was strongest. Everyone threw their food waste and the contents of their chamber pots into the streets and closes, those at higher storeys shouting a warning of 'Gardyloo' - *Gardez l'eau* – 'mind the water' - to the unwary passer-by. Better-off poor lived in the attics where, though the climb was steep, the air was fresher – sometimes too fresh. The wealthy lived in the floors in between, at different levels depending on just how wealthy they were. Everyone rich or poor met on the common stair. It was a very democratic way of living. All of that changed with the development of a New Town of Edinburgh, in the late eighteenth and early nineteenth centuries, across the Nor Loch to the North. Gradually, the wealthy and the middle classes moved to the fine Georgian buildings rising on the meadowlands across the new North Bridge. Their handsome apartments and houses in the Old Town were bought by speculative landlords and sub-divided to be let to the working classes and the poor, leading to horrendous overcrowding.

Like Philip Boylan, John Skiffington became a very successful businessman. We can follow his progress through the entries in Edinburgh's Street Directories. Beginning in 1852, he is listed at various addresses in the Old Town, over the years, as an owner of grocer's shops, spirit merchants, a china shop and, finally, a rag merchant's store at 105 High Street. The latter business was to prove highly lucrative as it supplied rags to the paper-making industry throughout Scotland and down into England, as far as Yorkshire. Paper made using cotton rags produced a high quality paper much in demand for legal documents and art, as it did not deteriorate. Following Philip Boylan's example, John began to speculate by buying up properties and renting them out. His main business of China Shop and Rag Store was a five-storey building at 105 High Street in the Old Town, where he also lived with his wife, Sarah Delaney. He also owned a spacious flat in a handsome stone tenement at 6 High Street, on the corner of the Netherbow and St. Mary's Wynd. Both these properties still survive some two hundred years later.

When the Great Famine sent many hundreds of their fellow Irishmen into Edinburgh's Old Town seeking work and accommodation, both Philip Boylan and John Skiffington were well placed to reap the benefits. I have found no evidence that either Philip or John were slum landlords, as far as I can judge. According to the Valuation Rolls, held in Register House, their properties seem to be in decent addresses and none had multiple occupants as tenants. In the worst of slums, poor people were crowded in large numbers in one room accommodation.

John Skiffington and Sarah Delaney had two sons. Arthur, named after Sarah's brother, was born in 1842 and lived until he was twenty-four before dying of Bronchitis and Tuberculosis in1867. Their second son, John, was born on 6 November 1844. His godfather was his mother's brother, Arthur Delaney, and his godmother was Sarah

McLachlan. Sadly, John died on 25 January 1847 and was buried beside his twin cousins, Mary and Roseanna Delaney, in the Greyfriars Churchyard.

The Skiffington family continued to live and trade at 105 High Street. On Sunday, 24 November 1861, in the early hours of the morning, a tenement between Bailie Fyfe's Close and Paisley Close collapsed. As it fell it narrowly missed the Skiffington's building.

A report of the disaster in '*The Scotsman*' newspaper noted:

"A broken gas pipe on the corner of Mr Skiffington's premises on the west was lighted and cast a bright light to help in the rescue attempt. About nine o' clock yesterday morning, the workmen on raising some flooring, discovered a small black and white dog. It was taken care of by Mr Skiffington, china merchant, and by good treatment soon recovered. We understand that the present guardian (Mr Skiffington) has expressed his intention to sell the animal which would probably be valued by many, as a memento, for behoof of the relief fund."

The newspaper report went on to decry the appalling condition of the old buildings in the area. John Skiffington obviously took umbrage at the coverage and made a complaint to the newspaper. Later, *The Scotsman* printed a clarification of the previous story it had carried.

"A remark made by us yesterday as to the wretched-looking homes which these dilapidated buildings contain seems to have been understood in some quarters as having special reference to the tenement on the west side of the ruin, which is owned and partly occupied as a shop and dwelling house of Mr Skiffington. The reference however, as might be seen by what followed was general and the remark was introductory to the description of some of the dwellings in the 'back land' by a gentlemen who had inspected them the previous day."

John Skiffington was obviously proud of his business and home, which was indeed in excellent condition, and did not want it compared to slum housing. The proof is in the fact that the building still stands to this day. As a prominent merchant he also did not want his reputation damaged.

The old tenement, between the Closes, housing over one hundred people had simply collapsed. Those on the lower and ground floors made their escape as the building shook, but the residents on the upper floors fell from a great height and were swept forward and buried in the debris as the building fell on top of them. Thirty-five people were killed and many more seriously injured.

A twelve-year-old boy, named Joseph McIver, was buried in the rubble. His call of "Heave awa chaps, a'm no deid yet"- was heard by the rescuers and he was pulled, alive, from the wreckage. His survival was later commemorated, when the entrance to Paisley Close was rebuilt, by an ornate carved sculptural image of his head surrounded by his cry. Locally, the Close is usually referred to as "Heave awa" Close and the carving can still be seen. John Skiffington took the chance to add an Oriel window to his building in the subsequent repair. The collapse of the building made newspaper headlines. Even *The London Illustrated News* displayed a drawing of the scene and in it the Skiffington's building can be clearly seen. It was reported that the author, Charles Dickens, who was visiting the city to perform one of his famous Book Readings, made a visit to view the disaster site. Dickens, a great social justice campaigner, would no doubt be appalled at the human loss.

The great tragedy is that the disaster could have been avoided.

A workman wheeling his barrow down Paisley Close one day noticed that it stuck where it hadn't done before. He noticed there was a bulge in the wall of the old building. He reported it to his boss who told him to ignore it. But residents were complaining to him that their doors were sticking. The man grew more concerned and each day, for a week, as he passed along the Close he measured the bulge in the wall of the house and each day it grew larger. Seriously worried, he travelled over to the the South Side of the city where one of the landlords lived and reported his findings. He was sent away with a flea in his ear and warned that his job was at risk if he alarmed the residents. At the inquiry that followed the disaster his boss was asked why he had ignored the man's warnings. He replied that - "Jamie was a strange man, always havering". The inquiry found that several years before, a man who owned the basement of the building and used it as a workshop had removed a supporting wall to accommodate his machinery!

The collapse of the tenement caused a huge outcry about the overcrowding and the perilous state of many of the buildings some of which were over two hundred years old. This led to Edinburgh appointing a Medical Officer of Health, the first in any city in the UK. The man appointed was Henry Littlejohn, a doctor and forensic scientist. He worked closely with Edinburgh's Lord Provost, William Chambers, to improve the living conditions for working people, and the poor, living in the Old Town.

Littlejohn's Report – 'On the Sanitary Condition of the City of Edinburgh' led to the Improvement Act of 1866. Dangerous buildings, in the most congested slum areas, were swept away, narrow closes and streets were widened by a large scale demolition project, letting light and air into previously rundown areas. One side of St. Mary's Wynd, which was particularly notorious, was reduced to rubble out of which grew the new, wider St. Mary's Street. Philip Boylan's properties at Nos.15 and 17 and the other building on the west side survived,

Littlejohn also arranged to have public conveniences and public washhouses built, where women could do their washing with copious amounts of hot water available, and street cleaners (Scaffies) were employed to keep the streets free of filth and debris. He introduced the first laws requiring people to notify any cases of infectious diseases and established hospitals to isolate such patients. Henry Littlejohn was knighted for his Public Health work, becoming Sir Henry Littlejohn. He served as Edinburgh's Medical Officer of Health well into his old age, and later gained fame as being one of the doctors who were said to have inspired his former student, Sir Arthur Conan Doyle's famous character, Sherlock Holmes.

Sadly, John Skiffington himself was not to live to see these momentous changes take place in the Old Town. He died of Epilepsy aged just forty-four on 27 December 1863. He was buried in the grand new graveyard of the Grange cemetery. His wife, Sarah Delaney, erected a tall Celtic Cross monument over his grave, inscribed proudly - 'John Skiffington – Merchant of Edinburgh'.

John Skiffington's Will makes interesting reading. He was a wealthy merchant and obviously a very astute man. He leaves his moveable Estate to his wife, Sarah Delaney, on the proviso that, if she remarries, she forfeits her claim! The money will then pass to the

Catholic Archdiocese of St. Andrews and Edinburgh, the funds to be used to support the church's Orphanage for Boys. John and Sarah still had a surviving son, Arthur Skiffington, but I have not found any provision being made for him in his father's Will. We know that John Skiffington owned several properties, not least 105 High Street, housing their home and thriving businesses. Perhaps the law that stated that properties would pass to the oldest son would ensure Arthur's inheritance. This would explain why his son, Arthur, is not mentioned in the Will. Another explanation may have been the state of his son's health. Young Arthur Skiffington dies in 1867 just three years after his father, aged just twenty-four, of Bronchitis and Tuberculosis. Was Arthur always delicate and so his father realised that he might not live long?

After taking a DNA test, my sister Frances Connolly (nee Delaney) made online contact with a cousin of ours, Maureen Macneil (nee Martin), who had emigrated to Canada and who, though born in Edinburgh, we hadn't known existed. She is the great-granddaughter of Jane Delaney. In 2022, Maureen came on holiday to Edinburgh and to our great joy we were able to meet up. On that visit Maureen remembered that when she was a child, in Edinburgh, her family owned an old Bible. She managed to track it down and to her amazement the old Bible, dating from 1848, had a cover inscribed in gilt with the names – John Skiffington and Sarah Delaney! Maureen held history in her hands. She has had it beautifully restored. It was an approved Catholic Bible, finely illustrated with religious scenes and personally inscribed. It would have been a very expensive item at that time. Further investigation proved that it could only have been owned by very wealthy Catholics. This confirmed what John Skiffington's Will had already indicated, that those early immigrants from County Monaghan made good!

Sarah Delaney was to outlive her husband John Skiffington by fifteen years, dying in 1878.

CHAPTER SEVEN

JANE DELANEY

With Sarah Delaney's husband, John Skiffington, and her son, Arthur Skiffington, dead, Sarah came to rely on the support of her sister, Jane Delaney, who had married John Murray. John had, in fact, worked as a Manager in the Skiffington family business at 105 High Street and so was well placed to come to Sarah's aid.

John Murray was born in Letterkenny in Donegal in Ireland. He had come to Edinburgh as a young man and set up as a Clothier in the Old Town. The couple married on 1 January 1855 at 17 St. Mary's Wynd, the home of Philip Boylan and Helen Delaney. Their marriage entry is an historic one as it is the very first one recorded when Statutory Records came into force in Scotland in 1855. It provided a major breakthrough for us because, though census records had told us that the Delaney siblings had been born in Ireland it hadn't said where in Ireland. Jane's marriage certificate stated she had been born in Donagh Parish in County Monaghan in 1833 and it gave her parents names as James Delaney and Mary Hughes. Now we had documented proof of our Irish ancestry and we had gone one step back on our family tree. We think that Jane is the youngest daughter of James Delaney and Mary Hughes. She was born in 1833, therefore seventeen years after the birth of her brother, Arthur. She is twenty-two years old at the time of her marriage and states that her parents were both still alive in Ireland.

Thereafter, the lives of the Delaney, Skiffington and Murray families are inextricably linked.

Whereas Anne Delaney appears to have been estranged from her sisters throughout her life in Edinburgh, Sarah, Jane and their sister-in-law, Helen Delaney, remained extremely close all their lives. John and Sarah Skiffington owned the spacious flat at 6 High Street, (today above The World's End pub) on the corner of St. Mary's Wynd, where Jane and John Murray later lived with their family.

A daughter, Ellen, (named after Helen Delaney) was born to Jane and John Murray in 1856 a year after their marriage. She was born at 17 St. Mary's Wynd, the home of Philip and Helen Boylan. Then there are no more children born to the couple for over four years. This seems very strange. Did the couple separate? This would have been a very unusual occurrence in a Catholic family. Perhaps Jane lost babies in those years. Then six further children follow in rapid succession, John (1860), Sarah (1863), Mary (1865), Arthur (1867), James Charles (1869) and Jane (1872). Another curious fact is that their son, John Skiffington Murray, was born in May 1860 at 105 High Street, the home of John and Sarah Skiffington (nee Delaney) and it is John Skiffington who registers the birth. Where was John Murray that he didn't register his first son's birth? Whatever the explanation, Jane and her husband are living together at 105 High Street in the 1861 census, with their daughter, Ellen, and ten-month-old baby, John.

John Murray is listed as a 'Salesman Clothier' in the 1861 census which was the same occupation he had in 1855 when he married Jane. According to the Valuation Rolls, John Murray held the tenancy of two Clothier shops on Niddry Street, in the Old Town, at one time and we also know from John Skiffington's Will that he employed John Murray as his Manager in the Rag Store.

After John Skiffington died, John Murray helped his sister-in-law, Sarah Skiffington, run the business. As the Murray family grew, John and Jane's first child, Ellen Murray, moved to live with her aunt, Sarah Skiffington, in the house above her business at 105 High Street to keep her company. Ellen Murray became like a daughter to her widowed, childless aunt, Sarah Skiffington.

At this stage, Jane and John and their six other children were living in a spacious flat at 6 High Street on the corner of the Netherbow and St. Mary's Wynd.

Tragically, John Murray was to die in 1874 aged forty-one of Dropsy, in their home at 6 High Street leaving Jane a widow with seven children to support, the youngest of whom, Jane, was only two years old. Fortunately, she had a live-in servant named Isabella McInnes to help. Isabella had been with the family for a long time and she is still with them when she is fifty-seven years old, up until Jane Murray dies. It surprised me that live-in servants were common in the families' lives.

John Murray was buried in the Grange cemetery beside his brother-in-law, John Skiffington. A simple stone marks his grave.

The two widowed sisters were left to run the businesses together. It seems that they make a very good job of it as the businesses continue to prosper.

In 1877, Ellen Murray, aged twenty-one, marries Joseph Tregilgas in St. Patrick's church. Unusually, he was not a Catholic. He was born in England to a family of Cornish descent. When he was about fourteen years old he came to Edinburgh and was apprenticed to his uncle, William Tregilgas, as a Tailor. His uncle, at that time, appeared to be a very successful businessman operating Tailoring and Outfitting shops, at various times, in very upper class shopping areas in town, like Princes Street and George Street. He was married to Sarah Lewis but they had no children. It looked like young Joseph might be his uncle's heir.

We later learned, from a codicil to Sarah Skiffington's Will, that she gifted £100 to her niece, Ellen Murray, for a 'wedding outfit' on the occasion of her marriage to Joseph. That was a considerable sum, at that time, and we wondered if the money was actually for a trousseau, or even a dowry, for her favourite niece.

Sadly, Sarah Skiffington died in 1878, one year after her niece's wedding. She was sixty-two years old and died of Jaundice and Liver Disease. Her Will was very revealing. She left her entire Estate to her widowed sister, Jane Murray - "On condition that she did not remarry". If she did so she was to be "considered as dead for the purpose of the Will" and Sarah's Estate was to pass to Jane's children. And Sarah's Estate was a large one. Her executors were named and Sarah testified that they had read the Will back to her, "since she could not read or write, never having learned". Here was a woman who had run a very successful business, over many years, yet had been unable to read or write.

The codicil to the Will stating that she had given her niece, Ellen Murray, £100 for her 'wedding outfit' went on to say that therefore that amount was to be deducted from Ellen's share of Sarah's future Estate.

My sister, Frances Connolly, is an expert online genealogist and she started to investigate William Tregilgas and his wife. As a result of those investigations she made contact with Matt Lunn, who was also investigating his Tregilgas family roots. Matt, while trying to put together his own story, was wondering were the Murray family came into it. He very generously shared his findings with us. At the same time, Frances made contact with Beth Barry who was also researching her husband's Tregilgas ancestors. In an act of serendipity our three stories were to come together even though we were living in three different countries!

Frances discovered William Tregilgas' Will and was surprised at how little money he had left on his death, considering how long and at what prestigious addresses he had been operating apparently successful businesses. He left his Estate to his wife Sarah Tregilgas and though Joseph Tregilgas registered his uncle's death he received nothing from his Estate. In truth, there was not a great amount to inherit and since Joseph Tregilgas was an executor of his uncle's will he would have known that the Estate was willed to his aunt. But, in a strange twist, the lawyer handling the Estate wrote that though Joseph Tregilgas was named as executor he had declined to fulfil that role on his uncle's death. How very mysterious – had there been a family rift?

Another interesting discovery was that when we had previously found Sarah Skiffington's Will among her list of creditors was Joseph's uncle William Tregilgas. He had borrowed a large sum of money from Sarah Skiffington in 1877 the year that her favourite niece, Ellen Murray, had married his nephew, Joseph Tregilgas. Curiouser and curiouser.

Further examination of Sarah Skiffington's Will revealed the fact that her sister, Jane Murray, who was Ellen Murray's mother, held the equivalent of Power of Attorney and therefore had control of Sarah's bank book. This may have been because Sarah Skiffington could not read or write, or it may have been that Sarah was in mental decline. Which ever, it raises the interesting point that Jane Murray may have given the loan of the considerable sum of money to her son-in-law, Joseph's uncle, with or without Sarah's knowledge. Perhaps William Tregilgas had offered his nephew a partnership in his business and was intending to expand using the loan from Sarah Skiffington.

And now, one year after the wedding, Sarah was dead. Is that the reason that William Tregilgas left so little when he died? Had he been forced to pay back the large loan to Sarah's Estate in such a short time? Or had he been unable to pay back the loan? Is that why Joseph refused to fulfil his role as executor in his uncle's Estate? Had William Tregilgas reneging on the loan caused a large bad debt in the amount Sarah had thought she was leaving?

We know that Jane Murray continued to run the Rag Store business she had inherited, after her sister's death, with the help of her son, John Murray. Sarah had stated in her Will that she wished Jane to continue the long established business at 105 High Street. Indeed, in the 1881 census Jane is living at that address as well as all her children except Ellen Tregilgas. She is also running the Rag Store from there, employing a workforce of seven women and one man, Patrick Delaney, born in Ireland, who is listed as a van man. Business appears to be booming.

However, things do not appear to be going so well for her daughter, Ellen, and her husband, Joseph Tregilgas. Matt Lunn's cousin, David, also searching for his Tregilgas roots, found a newspaper entry headed – *Notice to Creditors* – dated 4 November 1881. It states that 'Mr J H Tregilgas, Tailors and Clothier, 227 High Street, Edinburgh' has gone bankrupt. It appears that Joseph had attempted to set up a Tailoring business on his own but he hadn't made a success of it. We had wondered why, in the 1881 census, Jane has her granddaughter, Sarah Tregilgas, born on 23 February 1878, living with her.

We discovered that Ellen Murray and Joseph Tregilgas had a baby son, John Murray Tregilgas, born on 25 October 1881. Sadly, baby John dies on 1 August 1882. So was Jane helping her daughter, by looking after little Sarah while Ellen was pregnant and while her husband's business was on the rocks? The couple had another daughter as well as Sarah. Emma Tregilgas was born on 25 August 1879 and after the death of baby John another daughter, Ellen Clarke Tregilgas, was born to them on 16 April 1884. Emma was named after Joseph's mother and his daughter Ellen's middle name comes from Joseph's paternal grandmother, Grace Clark.

One other incident reported in the Edinburgh newspaper, and found by Matt Lunn's cousin, was that Ellen Tregilgas, Joseph's wife, had been the victim of an unprovoked assault by a man. It reports 'John Donnolly, a young man, was charged at the City Police

Court, with having assaulted Helen Murray or Tregilgas in High Street, last night. The prisoner took hold of the complainer as she passed, and when she threw him off he struck her. He pleaded guilty, and was sentenced to ten days imprisonment'. The Old Town was a very rough place in the nineteenth century so Ellen sounds like she was a feisty lady well able to take care of herself.

In 1883, Jane Murray died, aged fifty, of Valvular Disease of the Heart at her home at 105 High Street. Her son, John Murray, registered her death. She is buried beside her husband, John Murray, in the Grange Cemetery and the gravestone bears her name.

She was the third of the Delaney sisters, born in County Monaghan to James Delaney and Mary Hughes, to have died in the Old Town of Edinburgh.

Jane was the only one of the four Delaney sisters to leave children who would continue the Delaney blood line.

CHAPTER EIGHT

THE MURRAY/MARTIN FAMILIES

Jane left behind her daughters Ellen (Tregilgas), Sarah, Mary and Jane and her sons, John, Arthur and James Charles. We can find no Will for Jane and yet we know that she had inherited a large sum of money, plus the Rag Store business and rented out property from Sarah Skiffington's Estate. We know, from the 1881 census, that the business was a going concern, so why no Will? We also know that Sarah Skiffington had intended to leave her Estate to her nieces and nephews in the event of Jane remarrying, which Jane did not do. So we have to assume that Jane's Estate was passed to, and divided among, her children, informally.

We know that Jane's son, John Murray, carried on with the business at 105 High Street and the family continued to live there for seven years after Jane's death. The siblings were looked after by their sister, Sarah Murray, who was a Tailoress. Sarah married James Joseph MacMahon, a Hotel Waiter, on 28 January 1884 in St Patrick's Church. The wedding was conducted by Canon Hannan. They are both twenty years old. Their witnesses were John Murray, Sarah's brother, and Mary Murray, her sister. Strangely, Sarah states on her marriage certificate that her father, John Murray, had been a Shoemaker. Certainly, Sarah was just a child when her father died and over the years the story might have got confused, but we have no record of John Murray ever having been a Shoemaker. Her siblings, Mary, Arthur, James and Jane continued to live with her and her husband. Sarah Murray would have inherited her share of her mother's large estate and she was a trained Tailoress, so James Joseph McMahon made a good match! In the 1891 census, seven years after they married, Sarah, her husband and her four siblings are all still living together but have moved to 7 Hill Place on the Southside, and Sarah and James Joseph also have a daughter and son of their own. The property was in a handsome stone terrace and it must have been a big flat to accommodate six adults and two children.

Sarah's sister, Mary Murray, was a Dressmaker, her brother, Arthur Murray, a waiter, her brother, James Charles, a Billiard Ball Maker and her youngest sister, Jane, was a Drapers Shop Assistant.

By the 1901 census Sarah and her husband have moved to 195 Dalkeith Road in the Newington district. Her husband, James Joseph MacMahon, is now a Billiard Room Manager and the couple have another child, Sarah, as well as their daughter, Jane, and son, Robert. When the census was taken, Sarah's sister, Jane Murray, was the only one of her siblings still living with her. She was twenty-nine years old and was now a Confectioner.

Sadly, Sarah MacMahon (nee Murray) died on 6 August 1901, the same year the census was taken. She was just thirty-eight years old and she died of Cardiac Disease. Her mother, Jane Murray, had also died of heart disease, aged fifty, and we have discovered that there is a history of a congenital heart condition causing Delaney family members to die young. Even when heart disease is not mentioned on the death certificate, the fact that these people died so young, of other conditions, may suggest a weakness from an underlying undiagnosed heart condition.

Sarah and Jane Murray's sister, Mary, had married John Martin, a Cabinet Maker, in St Patrick's Church on 28 January 1893. Their witnesses were Thomas Fullam and Isabella Leydon. John Martin was the son of John Thomas Martin and Mary Ann Mercer. His father was a Carpenter and also a Restaurant Keeper, born in Liverpool in 1824. It appears John had a shop at 4 South Clerk Street in the Newington area called 'John Martin & Sons, Cabinet Makers'. This would be where John was his father's apprentice. The business had obviously prospered as his father and mother, Mary Ann, who had been born in 1834 in Kelso in the Scottish Borders, also had a Restaurant on Rose Street in the New Town. However, by the time that John married Mary Murray both his parents were dead. His father died on 21 June 1880 at 12a Rose Street and his mother, Mary Ann, at the Restaurant at 63 Rose Street on 4 April 1882.

John Martin appears in the 1881 census, living as a boarder, at 22 Mid Arthur Place and gives his occupation as a 'Cabinet Maker' – 'living on own means'. The woman who owns the house and lets out rooms is a widow earning her living as a Dressmaker. One of her daughters, also living there, is a Tailoress and another Boarder is a Tailor. Since Mary Murray was also a Dressmaker we wondered if that is how she met John Martin.

When John Martin and Mary Murray marry they are both recorded as living at 6 Ingliston Street in the Pleasance area. Mary was pregnant when they married and gave birth to their first son, John Murray Martin, on 23 May 1893 at 19 West Crosscauseway. Two other sons followed. James born 27 June 1895 at 1 Hill Place and William Ferguson Martin born 19 July 1897 at 19 West Crosscauseway. In the 1901 census the couple say that - 'They are living of their own means'. This could give some credence to the idea that Mary Murray had inherited money from her mother's Estate and John Martin from his father's Estate. John Martin is thirty-eight years old and his wife, Mary Murray, is thirty-six years old.

The family later move to 4 St Patrick's Square on the Southside and, sadly, Mary died there, aged forty-five, of Tuberculosis in 1910.

Next to childbed fever, Tuberculosis was the second greatest killer of women. Edinburgh was rife with Tuberculosis and men and children also died in huge numbers. Sir Robert Philip was a pioneer of the treatment and control of Tuberculosis in the city. He was born in Govan in 1857, the son of a minister of the Free Church of Scotland. In 1866 the family relocated to Edinburgh. Philip was educated at the Royal High School and studied medicine at Edinburgh University. He lived for most of his life at 45 Charlotte Square in the New Town. He qualified to practise medicine in 1882, the same year that Robert Koch discovered the Tuberculosis bacillus. It became Philip's life-long crusade to control the spread of Tuberculosis. In 1887 he founded the first Tuberculosis dispensary clinic in Edinburgh, at 13 Bank Street.

This had previously housed The Institute for the Destitute Sick and, coincidently, a friend and colleague of mine later bought the flat in which it had been housed. She left the brass plaque, with the name of the Institute, on her front door and in her main living room a large medical cabinet still stood, with many little drawers, taking up the whole of one wall. This, too, she preserved having a sense of the importance of the piece in medical history. A blue plaque commemorating Sir Robert Philip is attached to the outside of the building.

In 1894 Robert Philip founded the Victoria Hospital for Consumption (Tuberculosis) at Craigleith House, in Edinburgh, as a sanatorium to work in conjunction with the Dispensary Clinic. Prior to the discovery of medication to treat Tuberculosis, his focus was to isolate patients from family and friends to prevent cross-infection and offer sun, fresh air and exercise. Robert Philip was at at the forefront in the fight against the scourge of Tuberculosis. In the 1950s, Dr Crofton and his colleagues used and expanded Sir Robert Philip's pioneering system of 'trace and contact' in the treatment of Tuberculosis. They were able to use the charitable funds raised by Sir Robert Philip's Endowment to develop the world-changing 'Edinburgh Method' which was adopted world-wide.

Tragically, in spite of having lived in such a pioneering city for the treatment of Tuberculosis, Mary could not be saved. The numbers in her time were just too great - with a high percentage of Edinburgh's population infected.

We have learned that Jane Murray moved to 4 St. Patrick's Square, Edinburgh to help care for her dead sister Mary's sons and housekeep for their father, John Martin.

And what of the family that this devoted 'Aunt Jane' cared for and kept house?

It seems that Jane Murray continued as her brother-in-law's, John Martin, Housekeeper and brought up his sons. His youngest son, William Ferguson Martin, lived on at St. Patrick's Square until he joined up to fight, as a Private, with the 2nd Battalion of the Royal Scots Regiment, in WWI.

When the First World War broke out in 1914 thousands and thousands of young British men rushed to volunteer to fight. This was partly for patriotic reasons and partly from a sense of adventure, a spell away from their humdrum lives. After all they were told it would all be over by Christmas. None of them could have imagined the horror of the trenches.

My grandfather, Patrick Delaney, gave me another reason why many Edinburgh boys from the Old Town joined up – poverty. They took the 'King's shilling' because there was widespread unemployment in the town and the government would send the 'shillings' home to their mothers. He did exactly that for exactly that reason. The money was sent home to his widowed mother, Cecilia Delaney, then caring for her other five children in St. James' Place in the New Town. My grandfather joined up, aged twenty, as a Private but was quickly promoted to Corporal rank. He was a smart boy but, as he said himself, he was also a 'wild laddie'. His father, Arthur, had died when Patrick was only thirteen and after that he ran free in the Old Town without a father to control him. The result was that in spite of his promotion he was thrown out of the army for "fighting with a fellow soldier and insubordination to an officer"! We have always been amazed that, considering how desperate the army was for recruits, as the casualty rate rose that anyone was thrown out of the army! But for Patrick the need to support his mother was still there and so he enlisted again, under a false name, (Joseph Clarke), and off he went to serve. Later in life he would say to me - "Patricia never volunteer for anything!" He served in France and in Egypt, where he was wounded, but he survived the war albeit with what we now recognise was Post Traumatic Stress Disorder.

Tragically, the same was not the case for his 'cousin' William Ferguson Martin. (Patrick was descended from Arthur Delaney and William Martin was descended from Arthur's sister, Jane Delaney).

William Ferguson Martin - "Died of his wounds" - in France, aged just nineteen, on 14 July 1917.

The number of Scots who died in the First World War was over one hundred thousand. Scotland lost the largest number of all the nations of the United Kingdom. Their names are commemorated in the great War Memorial built in Edinburgh Castle to honour their sacrifice. Our grandfather Patrick's medals were displayed in a fine oak case, in our grandparents house, all through our childhood.

Mary Murray and John Martin's oldest son, John Murray Martin, also lived on at 4 St. Patrick Square, being cared for by his Aunt Jane. We do not know if he also served during the war but it seems likely. World War I started off with the army calling on volunteers but, after the horrendous losses on the Western Front, conscription was introduced. You would only be exempt if you worked in a 'reserved' occupation (something vital to the country) and since John was a silversmith it is unlikely he would have been exempt. When next we find him he is marrying Wilhelmina Thomson, aged twenty-four, of 60 St. Leonards Hill on 1 September 1923 at the Church of the Sacred Heart at Lauriston. John's address is still

4 St. Patrick's Square, he is aged thirty and he is a Silversmith. She is a Bookseller's Assistant. Her father, Robert Thomson, is a Plasterer and her mother, Mary Webster, is deceased. After the marriage John moves in to 60 St. Leonards Hill and he remains there until he dies in 1933. He died of a Duodenal Ulcer in the Royal Infirmary, aged just thirty-nine, leaving Wilhelmina a widow with a young son, William Desmond Martin, named for John's dead brother. William Desmond Martin died in1984. They also had two daughters. Mary Anthony Martin was born in 1924 and died as a baby and her sister, Myra Wilma Martin, was born in 1928 and died in 2013.

By the time that John Murray Martin's father, John, died in 1936 he had lost his wife, Mary Murray, and two of his sons, John Murray Martin and William Ferguson Martin. What an unfortunate family, yet their losses were not unusual. Many hundreds of Edinburgh families lost loved ones to Tuberculosis or in World War I.

Mary Murray and John Martin's sole surviving son was James Martin. He also was cared for by his Aunt Jane, at 4 St. Patrick's Square, until he enlisted in the army in WWI. On 30 January 1915, presumably when home on leave, he marries a Mary Sharpe apparently by Special Licence. It is Mary alone who registers the marriage afterwards, presumably because James has to return to his Regiment. The reason for the haste is that Mary is pregnant. When the baby is born on 11 March 1915 she is registered as Margaret Martin, but known thereafter as Peggy. James is just twenty when he married in 1915 and the war dragged on until 1918. When James returns he discovers that his wife, Mary, in his absence, has given birth to a son whom she named James Martin. Since her husband, James Martin, had been away serving in the army he disputed the boy's parentage. They divorce in 1921 and it is believed that Mary goes on to marry the child's real father. Sadly, the baby boy died. James Martin obtained full custody of his daughter, Peggy, and raised her apparently with the help of his aunt Jane (Jeannie) Murray. Peggy Martin married a William Dickson in July 1936 in St. James Episcopal Church in Leith. Apparently, her father did not approve of his daughter marrying outside the Catholic Church and they became estranged.

Strangely, when James remarries it is in the Church of the Sacred Heart. This is odd because the Catholic Church did not allow divorcees to marry in the church. However, Annulments could be given and there is a family story that James was given a Papal dispensation. If a Catholic had married outwith the Catholic Church, the marriage was not recognized by the Church and considered 'null and void'. Since James and Mary's marriage appears to have been a civil one this is a possible explanation. James Martin's second marriage was to Jessie Harper Farmer. At that time James Martin gives his occupation as Goldsmith, like the ancestor, Joseph Delaney, who settled in 'Little Ireland' in the 1840s - artistic genes seem to run in the Delaney family.

James was living at 43 Nantwich Drive, Edinburgh when he registered his aunt Jane Murray's death on 2 October 1943. Jane died of Colon Cancer in Leith Hospital, aged seventy-two. Her 'occupation' is given as 'Housekeeper' (Retired) so she had cared for the Martin family for all those years. Obviously, after all those years, (his mother Mary Murray died in 1910) James Martin was a bit vague on the Murray family history. He records on Jane's death certificate that her father, John Murray, was a 'scrap metal dealer' when in fact he was a clothier and salesman. He also records that Jane's mother was 'Sarah Skivington', when it was Jane Murray. Since we now know that the old Skiffington Family Bible was in Jane Murray's possession when she died and James Martin inherited it, perhaps that confused things. James Martin himself died, aged seventy-one, in 1966. His wife, Jessie Farmer, lived on until 1991 dying at the grand old age of ninety-four.

Jane Murray, who cared for the three brothers after their mother's death, never married.

So what happened to Jane Delaney and John Murray's sons, John, Arthur and James?

In the 1891 census, Arthur Skiffington Murray is living with his sister, Sarah, and her husband, James MacMahon, at 7 Hill Place. He is a waiter aged twenty-four but, sadly, he dies aged thirty-one on 13 December 1898, of Pneumonia, at 7 Hill Place. Pneumonia is often associated with Tuberculosis. His death is registered by his brother-in-law, John Martin, his sister Mary Murray's husband, who gives his address as 19 West Crosscauseway. It must have been a terribly sad Christmas for the family that year.

His brother, James Charles Murray, is also living with their sister, Sarah MacMahon, and her husband at 7 Hill Place in the 1891 census. He is twenty-two and is a Billiard Ball Maker but by the 1901 census, when he would be thirty-two, he is no longer with them. But, curiously enough, James MacMahon, Sarah's husband, is a Billiard Hall Manager in that census. We can find out nothing further about James Charles Murray, Jane and John Murray's youngest son. Perhaps he emigrated.

We know that John Murray, Jane Delaney and John Murray's oldest son continued in the family business and continued to live at 105 High Street with his siblings after his mother's death in 1883. He had been very close to Helen and Philip Boylan's son, Luke Boylan, growing up together and when Luke married Patricia Campsie, in 1881, John was his Best Man and his sister Sarah was Patricia's Bridesmaid. However, when John married Jessie McGee on 23 October 1884, in St. Patrick's Church, he did not return the honour. The marriage was conducted by Rev Canon Hannan and John and Jessie's Best Man was a Peter Reilly and the Bridesmaid was Bridget Hand. By this date John was living at 109 High Street. He was twenty-four and he was still a Rag Merchant. The couple's first child, whom they named Arthur, was not born until 1887.

In the 1891 census they are living at 295 Cowgate and they also have a baby daughter, Mary Jane, aged four months. John's occupation is given as a Mason's Labourer. It appears that the family business and house at 105 High Street has been sold and the money shared among the Murray siblings as this coincides with Sarah Murray taking her younger siblings to live at 7 Hill Place – a good address on the Southside.

By the 1901 census John and Jessie Murray are living at 4 Piries Close. Interestingly, John has returned to his old trade and is a Rag Store Foreman. Sadly, little Mary Jane did not survive but they have another daughter, Maggie Murray, aged five. Their son Arthur is now fourteen and working as a 'Messenger Boy' and they also have a six-year-old boy living with them named, George Lavin.

It is stated that George is their 'adopted son'. My sister Frances Connolly found George Lavin's Birth Certificate which shows he was born on 24 June 1894 and that his father was dead at the time of his birth.. His mother was Maggie Lavin (nee Bryce) and they were living at 16 High Street in the Old Town. It seems as if Maggie Lavin also dies and so John and Jessie Murray adopted her son.

They must have had kind hearts. I wonder if Maggie was a close friend of Jessie and that perhaps John and Jessie named their daughter after her.

Sadly, Jessie Murray died of Pulmonary Tuberculosis on 12 September 1902 in the Edinburgh Royal Infirmary. She was thirty-seven years old. Her usual address is given as 246 Canongate and her husband, John Murray, is a Labourer.

John was left to bring up the three children on his own.

Tragically, five years later, John Murray also dies of Pulmonary Tuberculosis, aged forty-seven, on 2 June 1907 at the Craiglockhart Poorhouse in Edinburgh. Unlike his mother, Jane Murray, John does leave a Will, dated 1907. His Estate totalled £21.12 shillings. This does not seem like much but it was worth more in those days. It also shows that he was not admitted to the Poorhouse because he was destitute but because he was ill. The Poorhouses always had a hospital attached, in those days before the National Health Service. This proved problematic later when, after the NHS was established, they continued to use these hospitals. Many older people refused to go into these hospitals because of the stigma of the previous association with the Poorhouses.

It is heart-breaking to think of the children John left behind. Arthur Murray was now twenty years old so may well have already been out on his own. However, Maggie would only be eleven years old. Could she have gone to live with her brother, Arthur? We next find her living in the Pleasance district of Edinburgh in 1913. She is seventeen years old and she is marrying a man named Simpson Begbie. Maggie and Simpson have a daughter in 1920 whom they name Elizabeth. Sadly, Simpson Begbie died young, in a pithead accident, and Maggie later married the man who had been best man at her first marriage! Maggie's daughter, Elizabeth Begbie, married a man named William Wastle but, tragically, he died at sea during the war in 1941, aged just twenty-one, leaving Elizabeth a young widow with a baby son also named William Wastle. And, in one of the many coincidences that occur in the Delaney story, we find Elizabeth living, in 1947, at 17 Niddrie Mains Terrace the same street that our maternal grandmother was living in at that time!

Poor George Lavin. John Murray's adopted son's childhood had just been a disaster. His parents die, but he is adopted by John and

Jessie which must have given him some sense of security. Then Jessie, his adoptive mother, dies and finally, when he is just twelve, his adoptive father John dies. The surname Lavin is quite uncommon so Frances Connolly was able to trace him in the 1911 census. He appears to be living in some kind of 'Industrial School', with lots of other boys, learning a trade.

My sister, Frances Connolly, has done a lot of research into the Murray children. They seem to have been an exceptionally close-knit family. Certainly, Sarah MacMahon (nee Murray) looked after her siblings until the day she died and her sister, Jane Murray, looked after their sister Mary's sons, when their mother died, and gave hospitality and support to her sister Ellen Murray's daughter later.

The only other information we have turned up on John and Jessie's son, Arthur Murray, is in a worksheet from Rosyth Naval Dockyard in Fife. Arthur is working as a Labourer there in 1919. However, his employment is being terminated because of 'absence'. We later find him as a patient in a hospital in a census. Could he be suffering from Tuberculosis like his parents? He is thirty-two years old and is a Shipyard Plater with the The Sunderland Shipbuilding Company. We can find no other record of him.

Unfortunately, because Jane Murray (nee Delaney) does not appear to have left a Will we have no way of knowing how much she left. But we know that Jane herself had inherited a considerable sum from her sister, Sarah Skiffington, a few years before as well as all Sarah's property. Could the fact that William Tregilgas, Joseph's uncle, had borrowed the equivalent today of thousands of pounds from Sarah Skiffington have affected how much Sarah left behind? It may be that William Tregilgas had reneged on the debt but he left a rather sparse Estate, given his successful businesses, so this seems unlikely. Or perhaps the fact that Jane's Estate was divided between seven siblings had affected how much they had all received? None of the siblings were rich but they seemed to be reasonably comfortable in later life. All are living at good addresses in nice areas. Only John Murray seems to have struggled a bit, since it appears he continued for years with the family business at 105 High Street and then it had to be sold so that his siblings could receive their shares. So John lost his home, his job and his income and though he also would get his share it would not have been enough to start up a new business.

Because Jane left no Will we do not know if the money that Sarah Skiffington gave to her niece, Ellen Tregilgas, for a 'wedding outfit' was removed from any monies that Ellen may have inherited from her mother. However, given the business was so profitable, we imagine that Ellen would at least inherit some share of the balance after her siblings had received their share, as Sarah had stipulated.

If so, it was not enough and, given that her husband, Joseph Tregilgas, was a declared bankrupt he and Ellen decided to emigrate to Canada with their daughters to make a new start.

CHAPTER NINE

THE TREGILGAS SISTERS

After their mother Jane Murray (nee Delaney) died, her children, John, Sarah, Mary, James Charles, Arthur and Jane continued to live together in the family home at 105 High Street in 'Little Ireland', above the family Rag Store and China Shop. However, their sister, Ellen, who had married Joseph Tregilgas was about to embark on a far more uncertain future.

Ellen Tregilgas had given birth to their third daughter, Ellen Clarke Tregilgas, just one month before her husband Joseph Tregilgas set off to Canada. Presumably, her birth was the reason that Joseph went on ahead without his wife and family. He sailed on *The Vancouver* via Belfast and Liverpool, arriving in Quebec on 18 May 1884. He is listed on the ship's manifest as a 29 year-old labourer.

Joseph Tregilgas' recent bankruptcy had made the need for a new beginning seem imperative.

His wife, Ellen, set sail with her three daughters one year later on board *The Carthaginian*, the same ship on which, the next year, Emma Stirling was to take young James Delaney to Nova Scotia as a child migrant.

The fate of James and his cousins from 'Little Ireland' was to prove equally traumatic.

The ship sailed with Ellen and her daughters on board from Glasgow, via London, and docked in Quebec on 13 May 1885 - and that is the last piece of official information we have on Ellen Tregilgas (nee Murray) - she was just twenty-nine years old.

As far as the official records go Ellen disappears into thin air. No census records show her thereafter in Canada. We have found no death certificate for her.

On the ship's manifest it states that Ellen was booked through to Winnipeg to rejoin her husband, Joseph Tregilgas. However, Matt Lunn has uncovered evidence that Joseph was not, in fact, living in

Winnipeg. He found him in a State census at that time living and working in Minnesota, USA.

So, if Ellen did make it to Winnipeg, with their three daughters, it would appear that she would not have found her husband Joseph Tregilgas there.

It was also Matt Lunn who set us on the road to discover what had happened to the three Tregilgas sisters, Sarah aged six, Emma aged five and one-year-old Ellen.

Matt had spent many years researching his Tregilgas family history. His mother was a St. Clare-Tregilgas, who had herself been searching for her family roots. Her son, Martin, had spent much time and energy helping her search but without success. It was not until Matt, her other son, decided to do a DNA test that they began to make a breakthrough.

His DNA revealed that his elusive great-grandfather, William Tregilgas, was the brother of Joseph Tregilgas, Ellen Murray's husband.

Gradually, Matt began to put the pieces of his ancestry together but one crucial fact eluded him for years. He learned that his great-great-grandmother disappeared from the official records, around 1860, and he could find no trace of her anywhere thereafter. The Tregilgas family had remained tight lipped about this disappearance. Matt was sure she was not dead in 1860 because her husband continued, in every census, to describe himself as 'married' – not as a widower. Matt's great-grand-father, William, as a child, continued to be listed with his father in London but his 15-year-old brother, Joseph Tregilgas, was sent to Edinburgh to be apprenticed to his uncle, William Tregilgas, in his Tailoring business.

Matt's mysterious great-great-grand-mother's name was Emma Tregilgas and so when his research turned up an Obituary of an Emma Tregilgas, in Canada, he was intrigued. Could this be why he had been unable to find his great-great-grandmother. Had she run away to Canada? However, the Obituary was in French so, first he had to translate it and this is what he discovered.

SISTER SAINT ELPHEGE

Emma Harvey Tregilgas
1879–1953

"My eyes have been constantly fixed on you Lord, you have lifted up my soul, in you I have entrusted myself and I will not be confounded."

(Deuteronomy, Liv.5, V.18)

May our dear Sister Saint Elphege, freed from all suffering of whom this poor life made, rest in peace.

This is the thought that comes to mind in front of the tomb of one who is borne towards the house of the Father.

In the world she was named Emma Harvey Tregilgas; she was born in Edinburgh, Scotland, to the marriage of Joseph Harvey Tregilgas and Ellen Harvey both of Scottish origin. The father belonged to the Anglican religion and the mother was of our belief. However, Mr Tregilgas, although not a Catholic, had an exemplary moral conduct, he was in good faith, had a righteous spirit and his religion he practised with all the sincerity of his soul. Seven children were born of their union, five girls and two boys.

Emma and her older sister were still very young when Mr Tregilgas, then secretary to Lord Richardson, president of the Hudson Bay Company, had to travel with his family across the ocean to settle in America.

Through a young priest, met in Port Arthur, who had just been appointed for Winnipeg, Mrs Tregilgas decided to settle in this city and, according to the advice of this excellent counsel, Emma and her sister were placed with the Gray Nuns in St. Boniface, Manitoba. Entrusted to these nuns the two girls received an excellent bilingual education in this boarding school. Emma was twelve years old when she made her First Communion. It was a day of intense joy for her that of her first contact with Jesus.

In the personal notes of our Sister St-Elphege we have found this, among her childhood memories, "I had," she says, "a disposition and playful nature," I searched for rather flashy companions. They thought that they were mischievous and gave me this beautiful qualifier ; "Queen of good humour", and she added; "My father, in view of his position, has travelled a great deal, even to Australia and other countries. Although not of our faith, he was a man of integrity and loyalty."

At the age of eighteen, having no attraction for the transient pleasures of the world, Miss Emma thought she recognized in her inclinations for the religious life, in order to better serve God and secure her salvation. She frequented the world without loving it. Without finishing her studies, although she loved her father and mother, she confided to her director, Rev. Father Elzir Gravel, her desire to become a nun. After the advice of this enlightened director, she chose our community and, in concert with her older sister, she asked for her admission to our postulate on Dorchester Street.

Many trials waited these generous souls, but they were too indecisive. The homesickness began to torment them, the nostalgia at certain hours was such that the temptation returned them to the world. The letters they wrote to their parents were full of illusions. But alas, human friendship resembles a flame that recurs, but eventually devours and consumes. And so, wanting to fill the emptiness of their hearts with a more stable and stronger love, the two girls say goodbye and are admitted to our novitiate on Dorchester Street on September 10, 1899. Kindly welcomed they had their place at the postulate of our old fold. The years of probation continued in bursts of generosity, despite the inevitable small failures and minor incidents in which weakness is revealed. But finally, the radiance of the good example fertilizes the seed and the two Sisters move towards the blessed day of the garment, the first under the name of Sister St-Elise and the second under that of Sister St-Elphege.

Then it is then the emission of their temporary wishes. For the two new professed sisters who had the pain of losing their beloved mother, the religious life appeared as a complex reality to the point that the elder realised she was not in the life she had dreamed of and returned to the world to resume secular living. As for her Sister St-Elphege, the enigma of her inner struggles are difficult to decipher. The departure of her sister, as well as the disappearance of her mother, were for her like lightning bolt blows.

Exceptionally talented, in any field where obedience placed her, she made her functions a success, however she found herself being at home as a sort of duplication, it seems that she lived behind a fog of reflection and secrets of her heart, it is difficult to do justice by explaining. We will not undertake to enumerate the mutations which were many.

In turns jobs of secretarial, pharmacy, economist in charge of guests and Haileybury's little Christmas stocking, Sault au Recollect. Sister Elphege also had notions of music and could accompany the services of the chapel.

In short, if in the course of her religious career she had many difficulties, there were also magnificent hours of which she feels the need to sing her gratitude to the Lord. She praises him for the great benefit of the conversion of her beloved father, who was baptized a few days before entering eternity when she went to visit him in St. Paul, Minneapolis, with Sister St. Catherine of Sienna as companion. Mr Tregilgas, after the death of his wife, was going to settle down with his son in that populous city. It was there that God was waiting for him to open the gates of heaven. What an indescribable moment for our dear Sister to see the surrender and abandonment, the author of her days for which she had offered so many sacrifices.

Under the influence of the grace of a retreat our dear Sister St-Elphege felt more than ever in a climate of fervor unknown until then. Her soul is stripped to better hold God. Here is what she had written in her personal diary, found after her death. "My God, I desire only one thing, it is always to pray to you better, to love you better. Give me the grace to desire with love what is pleasing to you. Give me the patience to suffer and to fulfil in all your Holy Will.

This phase of her life is intensely lived, a prelude to the last term of her sanctification and purification.

A health maintained in good balance, at least apparently, foreshadowed for our sister a longer existence. The inexorable disease that was to prevail took its toll without our knowledge.

Following several severe seizures, thrombosis; coronary, doctor's diagnosis after diagnosis, her condition worsened. The prospect of death finds her helpless. She hesitates before her act of complete abandonment but the encouragement of our Father Chaplain pacifies her and her courage strengthens. The Blessed Virgin whom she loved so much came to extend her arms and heart with an open soul that our dear Sister St-Elphege went to the Supreme meeting. It was August, 29, 1953.

Once Matt read his translation it was obvious that he had not found his missing great-great-grandmother, Emma Harvey Tregilgas, but, amazingly, he had found her grand-daughter and namesake. Sister Saint Elphege was Emma Harvey Tregilgas daughter of Joseph Tregilgas and Ellen Murray. Emma had emigrated to Canada with her mother and sisters in 1885 and we had found no trace of them thereafter. The Obituary was to throw open an astonishing story but it was to conceal as much as it revealed.

Alerted by the name Tregilgas in Matt Lunn's online translation of the Obituary, my sister Frances Connolly contacted Matt seeking further information on this Tregilgas connection. He, very generously, shared his family research with us. Matt was to continue to share and research further information for us. His help proved to be invaluable and we had many a laugh in the process!

Prior to Matt putting his translation of the Obituary online my sister Frances had come across a photograph on *Ancestry*. The photograph, which dated from 1948, showed a mother in a hospital bed with her newborn baby. The mother was Jeanne Barry and grouped around the bed were her husband Charles Barry, her small son Michael Barry, and three women. The caption stated that the women were Constance Lussier and her daughter, Gabrielle, and the woman, in a nun's habit, was Emma Tregilgas (Sister St. Elphege). The newborn baby was Charles (Chuck) Barry. It was Chuck and his wife, Beth Barry, who had posted the photograph online. Alerted again by the name Tregilgas, Frances made contact with Chuck and Beth Barry. It was the beginning of a lovely friendship and one in which we were to discover we were family related. Not only that but Matt Lunn was also related to Chuck and Beth and we were able to reunite the three families! Chuck Barry's great-grandfather was Joseph Tregilgas and Matt's great-grandfather was Joseph's brother, William Tregilgas.

We were not to know after these initial contacts the incredible story that was about to unfold.

Matt Lunn had previously made contact with Tregilgas 'cousins' in the United States through his online research. They had shared their family trees with him. One name that recurred in various of these trees was Blanche Tregilgas. The trees claimed that Blanche was a daughter of Joseph Tregilgas and his wife Frances Boland, born in Minnesota. Matt's subsequent investigations led him to think that this could not be true. The trees also stated that this Blanche had died in 1919.

Beth and Chuck Barry's research had also included a Blanche Tregilgas. Their family 'story' was that Chuck's mother, Jeanne Auther, had been orphaned aged eight in 1927 and been raised until that time by Blanche Tregilgas, initially in Chicago, Illinois, and later in New York City. When Blanche died in 1927, Jeanne was sent to live with Blanche's sister, Constance Tregilgas, who was now married to Joseph Lussier and lived in Montreal. Beth did wonder if perhaps Blanche was a single mother. The true story was to be much more complicated than that. Since the Tregilgas tree stated that Blanche Tregilgas had died in 1919 how could Chuck's mother, Jeanne Auther, have been living with her in New York until Blanche's death in 1927? It was not until Chuck's mother, Jeanne Barry (nee Auther), died, and Beth was helping him sort through his mother's papers that she came across Jeanne's birth certificate. It stated that Jeanne's mother was Ellen Auther (nee Tregilgas)! Now the couple were seriously puzzled. If Jeanne's mother's name was Ellen then who on earth was Blanche? Or who on earth was Ellen when Jeanne only knew Blanche as her mother? For a while Beth and Chuck wondered if Blanche was actually Jeanne's aunt but this was a theory not shared by the rest of their family. But Beth and Chuck can now say that they have an answer to this particularly perplexing question, thanks to the new found friendships across the ocean and the sleuthing skills of my sister Frances Connolly.

Matt Lunn was suffering similar confusion. Who on earth was Blanche Tregilgas and who was Ellen Tregilgas? The two women never seemed to appear in the records at the same time.

With all this new information Frances and I tried to piece the story together. Several years previously, Frances had found a census entry for a Joseph Tregilgas living in Minnesota whose age seemed to fit the Joseph who had married our Ellen Murray in Edinburgh. We knew they had emigrated to Canada but this Joseph was living in the USA, was married to a Frances Boland and there was no mention of his three daughters Sarah, Emma and Ellen in the census. Where were the girls and where was their mother, Ellen Tregilgas (nee Murray)? We assumed that Ellen must have died in Canada but

Frances could find no census giving Ellen's name. Neither could she find a death certificate nor, indeed, could she find any information on what became of the three Tregilgas girls.

EMMA HARVEY TREGILGAS – 1879–1953

Mat Lunn's discovery of the Obituary for Sister St Elphege (Emma Harvey Tregilgas) was the key that unlocked the mystery. But the information in the Obituary was deeply flawed.

So let us return to that Obituary and examine the information it contains. But before we do that we have to bear several points in mind. Self-evidently, Emma Harvey Tregilgas was dead when it was written. She entered the convent when she was 18 years old and she was 74 years old when she died. It appears she had been very unwell for two years prior to her death. From the tone it is obvious that the Obituary was written by another nun who may not have known Emma for long, perhaps only when she was old, and it seems to be cobbled together from the convent records.

The Obituary states correctly that she was born in Edinburgh. But it names her parents as Joseph Harvey Tregilgas and Ellen Harvey both of Scottish origin. Of course, Emma's mother's name was Ellen Murray not Ellen Harvey and, though she was born in Edinburgh, Emma's father, Joseph, was born in England not Scotland. It goes on to state that seven children were born to them - five girls and two boys. This is wrong. Joseph and Ellen had four children – Sarah, Emma and Ellen and one boy, John Murray Tregilgas - who sadly died as an infant in Edinburgh. But Joseph had another two daughters and a son with his second wife, Frances Boland, meaning he had seven children in total.

It then goes on to state that, when Emma and her older sister were very young, her father and the family had to travel across the ocean to settle in America. This also is wrong. We know from the passenger list that Joseph Tregilgas sailed to Canada alone in 1884 aboard *The Vancouver*. His wife Ellen and his three daughters sailed to join him a year later on board *The Carthaginian*. The reason given for the emigration, in the Obituary, was that Emma's father, Joseph Tregilgas, was Secretary to Lord Richardson, President of the Hudson Bay Company.

We knew from the passenger list of *The Carthaginian* that Ellen and her daughters were booked all the way through to Winnipeg.

When we began this research we found that, indeed, the H.Q. of The Hudson Bay Company, at that time, was located in Winnipeg so the story of Joseph's position rang true. My husband, Brian, searched the records online for The Hudson Bay Company. He could find no record of Joseph Tregilgas ever having been employed by the company. Stranger still, he could find no record of a Lord Richardson ever being President of The Hudson Bay Company. Separately, Matt Lunn had also made a search of the Company with the same outcome. When we looked again at the passenger list for *The Vancouver* we found that Joseph Tregilgas' occupation is given as a labourer. Alarm bells began to ring. There was obviously something very strange going on here.

The Obituary continues - 'Through a young priest, met in Port Arthur, who had just been appointed to Winnipeg, Mrs Tregilgas decided to settle in that city'. According to the ship's manifest, Ellen and the girls were booked through to Winnipeg anyway because that's where Joseph apparently lived.

Alarm turned to dread when the Obituary stated that, taking the advice of this young priest, Ellen placed Emma and her sister with the Gray Nuns in St. Boniface, Manitoba. It goes on -'Entrusted to these nuns the two girls received an excellent bilingual education in this boarding school'. Emma was six years old at that time and she was still living in the 'boarding school' when she was twelve years old and made her First Communion.

Why would their mother, Ellen, put her daughters into a 'boarding school' when she had just brought them across the ocean to begin a new life with their father? And why only two of the girls? Where was the third sister? Matt Lunn contacted the Gray Nun's convent in St. Boniface to ask for information about the Tregilgas girls but has received no reply. Matt also discovered that when Ellen and her daughters arrived in Winnipeg, expecting to meet Joseph, he was no longer living in Canada. He found him, at that date, in a State census living in Minnesota in the USA.

This is a very unhappy scenario. Why was Joseph not there? Why did Ellen put (at least) two of her daughters into what sounds, in fact, like a Children's Home? Why does Ellen never appear in any Canadian census records and why can we find no death certificate for her? If Joseph did, in fact, travel back to meet Ellen and the girls in Winnipeg, intending to take them to where he was living in Minnesota, then why would his daughters be left in a Children's Home in Manitoba?

Emma's Obituary states that it was Mrs Tregilgas who placed the children so, if we can believe it, she must have been alive then. However, it seems very likely that if she was, Ellen must have died soon after. The girls stayed in the Home until they were around 18 and 19 years old so their father never came back for them. That their mother, Ellen, died, either on board ship or soon after she arrived in Winnipeg, seems likely because, just over two years later, Joseph Tregilgas marries again. He must have known that Ellen was dead.

We had learned that two of the girls were admitted to the 'Boarding School' and we assumed it was the two oldest, Sarah and Emma. We wondered if Joseph Tregilgas had taken the baby, one-year-old Ellen Clarke Tregilgas, into his care. We can find no evidence that that happened. Even after he marries his second wife, Frances Boland, young Ellen does not appear in any census living with them. We are now pretty certain that it was a Children's Home, run by the Gray Nuns, and that baby Ellen was admitted with her sisters. Later findings seem to bear this out.

In the Obituary one gets the sense that Emma constructed an alternative reality for herself – perhaps to increase her status -or perhaps someone told her to give her a more comforting sense of herself. We now know that the notion that her father had a high position in The Hudson Bay Company is untrue. She also claimed that -'My father, in view of his position, has travelled a great deal, even to Australia and other countries'. We now know, from census records, that is just make-believe - Joseph did no such travelling, held no such position. I wonder perhaps if Emma just made it up to explain why her father never visited his daughters.

We learn from the Obituary that when she is about eighteen years old Emma decides to embrace the religious life and become a nun. Then there is a curious sentence - 'Without finishing her studies, although she loved her father and her mother....' she decided to enter a convent. Well, Emma's mother, Ellen, was long dead so could she be referring to her father and her stepmother? But we know that Emma was still living with the Gray Nuns in the Children's Home, in

St. Boniface, where she had been for eighteen years, so what difference would it have made to her father, or stepmother, if she went into a convent? Was she again constructing an imagined reality?

It is at this point that we have confirmed that it was her sister Sarah who decides to enter the convent with her – 'She chose our community and, in concert with her older sister, she asked for admittance to our postulate on Dorchester Street (Montreal). Sarah Skiffington Tregilgas was Joseph and Ellen Murray's first-born child, named after Ellen's beloved aunt, Sarah Skiffington.

Sarah and Emma decide to enter a different Order of nuns (from the one they had been raised by) and choose The Sisters of Misericorde - and travel from Manitoba to Montreal and enter the convent on 10 September 1899. However, they don't seem to settle and decide to return to the world and again there is a reference to 'letters they wrote to their parents'. Were they really in touch with their father or was it just part of Emma's constructed reality? We have no evidence of any contact between them. Again, they don't settle and -'wanting to fill the emptiness of their hearts with a more stable and stronger love, the two girls say goodbye' and are readmitted to the novitiate back in Dorchester Street in Montreal on 19 March 1900. The sense of two lost and lonely girls is just heartbreaking.

Emma and Sarah are listed as living in the convent in Montreal in the 1901 census aged 20 and 21. From the records that Matt Lunn obtained from the Archives of the convent in Montreal, it seems that the two girls served successfully in several positions in the Order over the following years, Emma as Sister Saint Elphege and Sarah as Sister Saint Elise. They were obviously bright girls.

On 16 January 1902 both girls make their Profession of temporary vows. Between 1902 and 1904 Emma is serving in the Misericordia Hospital in New York and for five months her sister Sarah (Constance) is also there. Then Sarah (Constance) leaves and is listed as serving at St. Mary's Hospital, Green Bay, Wisconsin until 1904 when she returns briefly to the Mother House back in Montreal. Emma also returns to the Mother House in 1904 but she continues serving there until 1907. Between 1904 and 1907 Sarah (Constance) returns to serve at St. Mary's Hospital, Green Bay, Wisconsin. It seems that the two sisters were spending very little time together in the convent.

As they moved towards 'taking the garment', their final profession, everything seems to go 'pear-shaped'. The Obituary states that - 'For the two new professed Sisters who had the pain of losing their beloved mother, the religious life appeared as a complex reality to the point that the elder sister realised that she was not in the life that she had dreamed of, returned to the world, and resumed secular living.'. It seems from this account that the trauma of losing their mother so suddenly, in childhood, in a strange land, finally caught up with them. It also confirms their mother, Ellen, suffered a sudden death.

It seems that in the Children's Home, Sarah Tregilgas became known as Constance Tregilgas. We have no idea why her name was changed. As one can imagine this did not make family researchers's task easy and led to further confusion. Sarah (Constance) Tregilgas left the Order on 7 January 1907.

On 16 January 1907, her sister, Emma Tregilgas, took her Profession of Perpetual vows as Sister Saint-Elphege at the Mother House in Montreal.

Emma, left behind in the convent without the support of her older sister, appears to go into a deep depression. The writer of the Obituary states - '.....for Sister St-Elphege, the enigma of her inner struggles is difficult to decipher. The departure of her sister, as well as the disappearance of her mother were for her like lightning bolt blows.' She goes on to state that Emma was 'Exceptionally talented, in any field where obedience placed her, she made her functions a success'. But it is obvious that Emma continued to suffer severe mental health issues for the rest of her life.

Matt Lunn obtained a resume of Emma's subsequent positions within the Order. Between 1907 and 1908 Emma served at St. Mary of the Angels, Hartsdale, USA. Between 1908 and 1911 she served in St. Mary's Hospital, Greenbay Wisconsin, the same hospital that her sister Sarah had served in before leaving the Order. Between 1911 and 1912 she was moved to Misericordia Hospital in Milwaukee, USA. Between 1912 and 1913 she was back serving in Montreal but then she was moved to Misericordia Hospital in Edmonton, Alberta and served there until 1916. She served at Asylum Ritcher, St. Norbert, where she stayed for two years. She returned to the Mother House in Montreal where she held several positions until 1923 when she moved to St. Mary's Hospital, in Ottawa to take up the post of Mistress of the Guest House. A year later she was moved again, this time to St. Mary's Home and Hospital in Toronto where she was in charge of the Nursery. In 1926 she returned to the Mother House in Montreal where she served in various positions until 1935. She was then moved to Misericordia Hospital, Haileybury, Ontario to work in the Admissions Office and as Sacristine. In 1942 she was on the move again back to St. Mary's Home and Hospital in Toronto. In 1947 she is posted back to Montreal to work in the Pharmacy of Saint Janvier House. Between 1948 and 1952 she is back serving at the Mother House in Montreal where on 16 January 1952 she celebrated the Golden Anniversary of her Profession. She had been a nun for fifty years. One wonders why she was being constantly moved around the various establishments run by the Order. Poor Emma doesn't seem to be in any place long enough to make friends which could not have been conducive to her mental health.

Towards the end of the Obituary there is a strange paragraph which seems to suggest that Emma visited her father, Joseph Tregilgas, on his deathbed in St. Paul in Minneapolis, in the USA. The writer states that 'after the death of his wife' (Frances Boland) Joseph was going to settle down with his son in that city. That is certainly where his son, Richard Harold Tregilgas lived. But the story takes on the aura of another of Emma's constructed reality scenarios. We know that Joseph Tregilgas was not a Catholic, he was an Anglican. According to Emma's story her father underwent a conversion, and was baptised a Catholic, during her visit, while on his deathbed. Now this could well be true but it seems very strange that Joseph Tregilgas had married two Catholic women, Ellen Murray and Frances Boland, and had brought up two sets of children as Catholics without feeling the need for conversion himself. But apparently this was the miracle that Emma had prayed for all her religious life and it brought her great consolation. Her father died in 1927, the same year as her sister and his daughter, Ellen Clark Tregilgas, died in NewYork. It must have been another trauma for Emma losing them both in the same year.

Emma was obviously a devout woman of strong religious faith. She also seems to have been a woman of many abilities, as the Obituary states - but I can't help feeling that her life was lived under a cloud of sadness. This is hardly surprising given the trauma of her childhood. As seems likely, her mother suddenly disappears from her life when she was just six years old and she and her sisters are left in a Home, in a strange country, where another language is being spoken. She must have clung to her sister Sarah who was only a year older.

Did any of the girls ever see their father again? We have no way of knowing but certainly he was never a constant presence in their lives during all the years of growing up in the Children's Home. She obviously sought solace in her religion and at least had the support of Sarah when they first joined the Order. When Sarah decided to leave the convent in 1907 the bottom must have fallen out of Emma's world.

Sadly, the year after the 50th Anniversary of her Perpetual Profession, Emma Harvey Tregilgas, grand-daughter of Jane Delaney, daughter of Ellen Murray and Joseph Tregilgas, the wee girl born in Edinburgh's 'Little Ireland' fell ill and had to be admitted to the Infirmary at the Mother House in Montreal. She suffered a period of ill health, a series of seizures and a coronary thrombosis.

As the Obituary states, she - 'went to the Supreme Meeting' - on 29 August 1953, aged 72 - obviously, a woman of great Faith. Fr Hannan of St. Patrick's would have been so proud of her!

SARAH SKIFFINGTON TREGILGAS

So, what happened to her sister, Sarah Skiffington Tregilgas, who became Sister Saint Elise and who, when she left the Order in 1907, went out into the world bearing the name of Constance Harvey Tregilgas? This would surely have broken her mother Ellen's heart. Her Christian name of Sarah and middle name of Skiffington had been given in honour of her mother's beloved aunt, Sarah Skiffington (nee Delaney), who was like a second mother to Ellen, and who had given her £100 to buy a wedding outfit when she married Joseph Tregilgas.

Both my sister, Frances, and Matt Lunn had found a Border Crossing document (between Canada and the USA), which stated that a woman named Blanche Tregilgas had travelled from Montreal to New York in 1907. In it Blanche stated that she was travelling to visit her sister, Sarah Tregilgas, living at 12 W 129th St., New York. Blanche gave her last contact in Montreal as a Fr Gerald McShane.

Our next big breakthrough came when Frances discovered a marriage certificate for a Constance Tregilgas, who had married on 20 September 1914 in Montreal. The certificate was in French but, using school-book French, we were able to discern the relevant facts. Constance was marrying a Joseph Lussier and she gave her name as Marie Constance Eliza Sarah Tregilgas. But the proof of identity came when the document stated that her parents were Ellen Murray and (Joseph) Harvey Tregilgas. We had found our lost Sarah Skiffington Tregilgas, the seven-year-old girl who had arrived in Winnipeg in 1885 with her mother Ellen Tregilgas and her sisters Emma and baby Ellen!

We now know that when Sarah (Constance) had left the convent in Montreal in 1907 she had ended up in New York and we suspect that she worked as a nurse from then onwards. The reason for this is that when we look at Sarah/Constance's convent record, on where she served as a nun, all the placements were in hospitals run by the Order in Canada and the USA. This is given credence by the fact that Joseph Lussier, whom she married, gives his profession as doctor. Did the two meet as medical colleagues at some point? We have no proof, as Sarah (Constance) leaves no evidence of what she was doing between leaving the convent in Montreal in 1907 and marrying in 1914. We only know that she was living in New York in 1907, when Blanche (who we now realised was her youngest sister, Ellen) travelled to join her.

The Obituary had helped us find out what happened to Emma Harvey Tregilgas after arriving, aged six, in Winnipeg in 1885. We now knew that she had entered the convent in Montreal when she was 18 years old and had remained with the Order until her death. It also told us that her elder sister, Sarah (Constance), had joined the same Order of nuns but had left in 1907 to 'return to the world'.

But we knew nothing at all about what happened to their baby sister, Ellen Tregilgas, until Frances and Matt found the 1907 Border Crossing. Frances found the marriage certificate that proved that Constance was, in fact, Sarah Skiffington Tregilgas, daughter of Ellen and Joseph Tregilgas, and that therefore the Blanche Tregilgas who travelled to join her in New York was, in fact, her sister Ellen Clarke Tregilgas.

ELLEN CLARKE TREGILGAS

Where, we wondered, had Ellen Tregilgas been all these years since arriving as a one-year-old baby in Winnipeg in 1885 with her mother and sisters?

We have no documented proof until Ellen (Blanche) leaves Montreal in 1907 to travel to New York to join her sister, Sarah (Constance) Tregilgas. But we have one clue. In the column asking her to declare the closest friend or family member she is leaving behind, she gives the name of a priest, Fr Gerald McShane, of 66 Rue Notre Dame Avenue West, Montreal.

Beth Barry researched Fr Gerald McShane and found that where he was living had previously been a Children's Home. We began to wonder if baby Ellen had been placed in the same Catholic Children's Home where we knew her sisters, Sarah and Emma, had been placed in St. Boniface in Manitoba. Could it be that, when Sarah and Emma moved to Montreal to enter the Order of the Sisters of Mercy, the nuns arranged for Ellen to move to a Children's Home in Montreal to be near her sisters?

Another curiosity revealed in the Border Crossing document is that though Ellen (Blanche) states she is 23 years old at the time, in the column asking for 'occupation' she states 'none'. What on earth had she been doing all this time? During her time with Fr McShane did she help out in the Children's Home? Or is it possible that Ellen (Blanche) was still a student, perhaps at University? The fact that Emma's Obituary states that she and Sarah – 'without finishing their studies' – decided to enter the convent, though they were 18 and 19 years old at that point, suggests they too were in some form of higher education.

What, we wondered, did Ellen (Blanche) do once she went to live with her sister Sarah (Constance) in New York?

We are certain that she trained as a nurse. In a later newspaper interview Ellen (Blanche) states she trained as a nurse in the USA. We think that Sarah (Constance) was already nursing, possibly in a hospital run by the Order of the Sisters of Misericordia in New York, where she had previously served when she was a nun. We do not know when or why Sarah (Constance) leaves New York but we know, for certain, that she did.

SISTERS AT WAR

Next we come to the significant year of 1914.

We know where Sarah (Constance) was that year. She was marrying Dr Joseph Adonis Lussier in Montreal and her bridesmaid was her sister, Ellen (Blanche).

Of course, 1914 is not just significant in the life of these two Tregilgas sisters, it is the year that World War One broke out, 'The Great War', the 'War to end all wars'!

Canada was still a Dominion of the British Empire and as such did not have the power to claim neutrality.

These facts were to have a significant influence on the lives of the two Tregilgas sisters, who had left the Old Town of Edinburgh and travelled as children to Canada 28 years earlier.

When Britain declared war on Germany, Canada, as a Dominion within the British Empire, entered the war.

The Canadian Minister of Militia and Defence, Sam Hughes, asked for volunteers and within two days 33,000 men, from every province, enlisted at the recruitment centres. Within a few weeks Hughes had formed the First Canadian Expeditionary Force at Camp Valcartier in Quebec, for basic training before shipping the troops off to England in 32 transport ships. Over the next four years the Canadian Corps grew to almost one million men (and women).

One of the volunteers in this First Contingent was a doctor, John MacCrae from Montreal, who wrote – 'On Flanders Fields' – inspired by his experiences in the trenches. The poem was to become the unofficial war anthem.

Shortly after the First Contingent of Canadian volunteers was shipped to the war, the McGill University in Montreal began to organise the No.3 Canadian General Hospital (McGill) to serve in France. The Dean of the Faculty of Medicine, Dr Henry S. Birkett, became the Commanding Officer, with the rank of Colonel, recruiting the majority of his staff from the University. Many of the nurses were drawn from hospitals in Montreal.

Following the example of the McGill University plan for its No.3 Canadian General Hospital (McGill) the University of Laval, in Montreal, set up the No.4 Stationery Hospital to offer medical service in France. This hospital was intended, exclusively, for the care of wounded French-speaking Canadians on the battlefields.

Its founder was a colourful French Canadian, Arthur Mignault, who had graduated from medical school at the University of Montreal in 1888. He practised as a physician in the USA before returning to Canada in 1896 and starting a pharmaceutical business from which he made his fortune. He became a philanthropist and in 1909 offered some of his lands in downtown Montreal to establish a playground for poverty-stricken children. In the same year he was granted a militia commission in the rank of surgeon lieutenant with the 65th Regiment "Carabiniers Mont-Royal". Before WWI Canada did not have a regular army, only a permanent militia force of some 3,000 men.

When war broke out in 1914, Mignault suggested to Prime Minister Robert Borden that a solely French-Canadian battalion be formed within the Canadian Expeditionary Force. He argued that this would allow Canadians of French extraction to overcome the language barrier of volunteering for the English-speaking battalions. To support his idea Mignault offered a donation of C\$50,000 towards its formation. The Canadian Prime Minister had committed to raising half a million volunteers to the Allied cause, in spite of Canada's modest population, and so accepted Mignault's offer. On 14 October 1914 the exclusively French-Canadian 22nd Infantry Battalion was formed.

It seems that Mignault had hoped he would be given a command in such a battalion but when he realised this was not going to happen he proposed founding and financing a war Medical Unit. He argued that such a Unit would improve Canadian medical services, as their French-speaking personnel would be a better fit within French lines on the Western Front than their English-speaking counterparts. This was agreed to and the No.4 Canadian Stationery Hospital (Laval) began its recruitment campaign in early Spring 1915. Mignault was put in command and promoted to the rank of Lieutenant Colonel.

One of the recruits to volunteer for the No.4 Canadian Stationery Hospital (Laval) was Ellen (Blanche) Tregilgas, daughter of Ellen Murray and Joseph Tregilgas.

My sister, Frances Connolly, found an Enlistment Document for Blanche Tregilgas. She is described as a Graduate Nursing Sister and she was joining the Canadian Army Medical Corps. Could the term 'Graduate' mean that she had graduated from a University – perhaps Laval? Certainly, Nursing Sisters in the Canadian Army Medical Corps had to have had a higher education background. On enlisting they were given the rank of Lieutenant. They had higher status within their Canadian Expeditionary Force than British nurses serving in the British Expeditionary Force, and they were better paid.

Another curious fact was that, apparently, Canadian Army Nursing Sisters had to hold a British passport. Was this because Canada was still a Dominion of the British Empire?

When Ellen (Blanche) enlisted on 11 March 1915 in Montreal, she stated that she was born in Scotland, was of Scotch Nationality and was 25 years old. She was not 25 years old, she had been born in Edinburgh in 1884. We have no idea why she lied about her age. It is not as if it would have prevented her enlisting, the Army accepted nurses up to the age of 38. Could it be possible that having been placed in a Children's Home as a baby she did not know her exact age? That she could pass for 25 is not in doubt. Chuck and Beth Barry have generously shared a photograph with us of Ellen (Blanche) Tregilgas in her nurse's uniform. The fact that she was slim and only 4ft 11in tall would also have helped her to appear younger. Ellen (Blanche) had been nursing in the USA and America had not yet entered the war so, in travelling back to Montreal to enlist meant that she was answering the call from her motherland and her adopted country.

Once the No.3 Canadian General Hospital (McGill) was established, staffed and trained, it set sail on board the *SS Metagama* from Montreal on 6 May 1915. The No.4 Canadian Stationery Hospital (Laval), with Nursing Sister Ellen Tregilgas aboard, shared the same sailing.

The *SS Metagama* was built by Barclay, Curle & Company Ltd., Glasgow in 1914, for the Canadian Pacific Service. The River Clyde in Glasgow was world renowned for shipbuilding. Its many shipyards, on both sides of the river, built some of the world's most iconic ships. The *SS Metagama* was intended as a luxury Cruiser for tourists on the British-Canadian route. There was accommodation for 520 Cabin passengers and 1,200 3rd class passengers. Most of the 3rd class passengers would likely be emigrants heading for a new life in Canada. She was launched on 19 November 1914. Britain had entered the war on 4 August 1914. The ship's maiden voyage took place on 26 March 1915. She sailed from Liverpool to St. John's, New Brunswick, on 26 March 1915. Thereafter, it would appear, she was requisitioned as a troop carrier. With the danger of mines and German U-Boat activity there would be little appetite for tourists to take unnecessary sea voyages during the war. It was not until after the Armistice that the SS Metagama resumed her original role. She sailed from Liverpool on 20 November 1918 for St. John's New Brunswick. Later, she started Glasgow to St. John's sailings and then, throughout the twenties, sailings from Antwerp to Canada. However, with the arrival of the 'Great Depression' in the 1930s, the demand for luxury sailings dried up. The SS Metagama was laid up in Southend, England from 1931 to 1934 and then sold for scrap. She was broken up at Bo'ness, on the Firth of Forth, not far from Ellen's birthplace in Edinburgh. A sad end to one of the great ships of the era that had served all through the war years.

But that was to be in the future. When Ellen (Blanche) Tregilglas, and the No.4 Canadian Stationery Hospital (Laval), set sail on her from Montreal on 6 May 1915, to the strains of 'O Canada', the SS Metagama was a brand new luxury ship.

The ship sailed first to England to enable the hospital staff to receive further training and make preparations before arriving in the active theatre of war in France. Ellen (Blanche) Tregilgas stepped back onto British soil for the first time since leaving as a one-year-old baby 28 years before.

The ship had berthed at Plymouth and the Canadian Army forces and hospitals' staff were taken by train to the long-established British Army Camp at Shorncliffe, near Folkestone in Kent.

Shorncliffe was chosen for the Second Canadian Expeditionary Force as it was a purpose-built garrison recently vacated by Kitchener's British Army recruits.

In her fascinating and well researched academic Paper –' En-route to Flanders Fields: The Canadians at Shorncliffe During the Great War' – Diane Beaupre, of Canterbury Christ Church University, gives an excellent insight into the experiences of the Canadian forces.

She explains that, when the Second Expeditionary Force arrived from Canada initially, the camp at Shorncliffe was not large enough to accommodate all the force. The rank and file were housed in 'tent cities' while the officers were billeted in private homes across the Folkestone and Hythe area. Later, wooden huts with corrugated iron roofs were hurriedly constructed and these new 'tin towns' were sited among the surrounding hills.

The newly arrived Canadian medical staff were housed at the old Moore Barracks with the Nursing Sisters housed in the Somerset Barracks on the site. An old photograph of Canadian Nursing Sisters outside the barracks, where Ellen would have stayed, shows they were of solid brick construction.

When the First Contingent of Canadians had arrived in 1914 they had been housed in tents on Salisbury Plain, for three months, while they underwent basic training. As Diane Beaupre relates, it proved a disastrous decision. As winter descended, the weather deteriorated and it rained continuously for months. Eventually, wooden huts holding 40 men were erected. Inadequately ventilated they became breeding grounds for infections. In addition to influenza and chest problems, a fatal strain of meningitis killed 28 Canadian soldiers and left many more seriously ill.

They were determined at Shorncliffe camp not to repeat that mistake. All new arrivals were kept in isolation in Dibgate Plain barracks for 28 days after arrival, to avoid the spread of any diseases they may have brought with them from Canada.. Only four men were allowed in a tent, as compared to eight, there were no parades and the food was of the best. As one soldier recalled - "all you had to do was enjoy yourself!" After the period of quarantine the soldiers were allowed a short leave to explore the surrounding villages or travel to London for a short visit.

However, no soldier was left in any doubt about what lay ahead after training. The boom of the big guns in Belgium could be clearly heard across the water from the camp. So close was Folkestone to the Front that it was said that a soldier could eat his breakfast at Folkestone and be fighting in the trenches by lunchtime.

The area around Shorncliffe had been a popular tourist destination and so was well used to catering for the needs of many people, but the sheer number of Canadian forces threatened to undermine the infrastructure. Damage to roads was a problem and supplying the camps with water could be a challenge at times but the locals seemed to welcome the Canadians, appreciating that they were fighting for the Mother Country.

The soldiers were well catered for, especially by the Young Men's Christian Association (YMCA) who supplied them with free necessities as well as religious worship opportunities. Their canteen huts provided a place for the soldiers to relax and enjoy food and drink at reduced prices. They also provided entertainment and sports activities. As the war intensified the Canadian YMCA took over responsibilities for their own troops. They also opened theatres and a cinema at the camp.

The Canadian Salvation Army and other church denominations also offered support. Shorncliffe was also the base for the Canadian Welfare HQ, administered by the women of Canada who sorted donations of 'comforts' to send in packages to the men at the Front.

But perhaps the most outstanding innovation for war-time soldiers was the 'Khaki University'. As Diane Deaupre relates, this educational facility was set up in 1917 as a joint venture between the Canadian YMCA and the Chaplain Service of the Canadian Army. It offered the young recruits, many of whom were illiterate, the chance to educate themselves for their future after the war was over and they returned to Canada, and it gave them an interest and a focus away from the mundane tasks at the camp. It proved a highly popular idea and successfully prepared men for Higher Education, on their return, but it also offered practical courses such as bricklaying and farming which increased their opportunities and employment prospects back home after the war. The College at Shorncliffe was headed by Major William Wallace of Toronto University. The camp at Shorncliffe was nicknamed a 'suburb of Toronto'!

However, it does not appear that Ellen (Blanche) Tregilgas had long to enjoy the relative comfort of the Somerset Barracks or sample any of the entertainments or opportunities on offer.

Though Ellen's No.4 Canadian Stationery Hospital (Laval) settled in for further training at Shorncliffe she appears to have been seconded to the No.1 British General Hospital in France.

The First Contingent of the Canadian Army was already serving in France, having arrived with the first volunteers in 1914. Badly wounded Canadian soldiers were already being shipped back across the Channel to England for treatment as Shorncliffe was now the main Canadian Depot.

It appears from her army record that, before her No.4 Canadian Stationery Hospital (Laval) Unit was deployed, Ellen (Blanche) was sent across to France on 28 May 1915, just 12 days after arriving in England. Obviously, quarantine regulations didn't apply to nurses!

She was based in Le Havre where there was a large tented hospital run by the No.1 British General Hospital. Its purpose was to care for seriously wounded troops awaiting return to England for further treatment. It is strange that she was sent here before her Unit deployed. Could it be that, since she was a French-speaker, she was sent to support wounded French-Canadian soldiers being shipped back to England? After all, that was the founding purpose of the No.4 Canadian Stationery Hospital (Laval). In later life, during a newspaper interview, Ellen (Blanche) revealed that she had been decorated for bravery by the British Government after she had won a lieutenancy by her work in France.

Unbeknown to either of them, when Ellen (Blanche) was tending the wounded at Le Havre, her cousin, Luke Terence Delaney, was driving armoured car chassis from Paris to the British Base in Dunkirk.

Ellen Tregilgas' Canadian Army record states that on 27 July 1915 she was transferred back to No.4 Stationary Hospital (Laval) still at Shorncliffe. She had been serving in France for two months but we don't know if she was travelling back and forth with the wounded.

It was not until November 1915 that Arthur Mignault, and the first 100 men, arrived in the commune of Saint Cloud in suburban Paris and began to set up the No.4 Canadian Stationery Hospital (Laval) and it was not until March 1916 that the first convoy of wounded French Canadian soldiers arrived there.

The hospital's capacity was initially set at 250 beds but increasing cases of venereal disease among French-Canadian soldiers led it to expand its capacity to 600. Treating venereal disease was to be a major problem throughout all the forces serving in the war. It took up a high proportion of medical beds on the battlefields and resulted in separate specialist isolation hospitals having to be set up at base camps. They were a massive drain on medical resources. One imagines that when Ellen (Blanche) and the other Nursing Sisters volunteered they expected they would be nursing wounded casualties, not such huge numbers of venereal cases. To meet this increased demand the hospital was re-organized and re-designated as No.8 Canadian General Hospital of the Canadian Army Medical Corps and Arthur Mignault was promoted to Colonel.

Long before this Ellen (Blanche) appears to have left the staff of No.4 Canadian Stationery Hospital (Laval) because, on 12 August 1915, she is transferred to the Duchess of Connaught's Red Cross Hospital at Taplow in Buckinghamshire. This hospital was concerned mainly in caring for wounded Canadian soldiers. The land for the hospital was a gift from the wealthy Astor family and was located on their country Estate of Cliveden. The hospital was built by the Canadian Red Cross. An old photograph shows a temporary, purpose-built, hutted hospital laid out in rows. The Duchess of Connaught was the wife of Prince Arthur, the Duke of Connaught, who had been Viceroy of Canada, before the war, and continued to take an interest in the Canadian Army of volunteers.

While still serving at the Duchess of Connaught Hospital, Ellen (Blanche) was struck down with a serious eye infection. She later declared - "a syringe with which I was treating a dangerous wound in a French field hospital broke and the poison got into my eye, gradually this disfigured me". On 5 October 1915 her Medical Leave was extended for six months. At this time she remained in the UK. Then, on 25 October, she was granted Leave to return to Canada. It is obvious her war service is over.

So what did Ellen (Blanche) do during the time she was on medical Leave in the UK? It is my belief that some of that time was spent with her aunt, Jane Murray, in Edinburgh. Jane Murray was Ellen's mother's youngest sister. Jane would have last seen one-year-old baby Ellen when she left Edinburgh to emigrate to Canada with her mother, Ellen Tregilgas (nee Murray), in 1885. So much had happened to that baby since then. Her mother had died on arrival in Canada, she and her two sisters were put in a Home run by nuns, her sisters became nuns and Ellen (Blanche) herself had become a nurse. Now, her profession had brought her back, aged 31, to her Edinburgh birthplace via the battlefields of France.

What must her aunt, Jane Murray, have felt to see her dead sister's daughter on her doorstep at 4 St. Patrick's Square, Edinburgh? In the time that had passed, Jane had not only lost her sister, Ellen, but also her sisters, Sarah and Mary. Indeed, she was still keeping house for her sister Mary's widower, John Martin, and his sons. Though it would appear that all her nephews were themselves soldiers serving in the Great War, when their cousin, Ellen (Blanche), arrived in the city.

We do not know how long this visit lasted nor do we know the date that Ellen (Blanche) returned to Canada. The conditions of her medical exemption would have allowed her Leave for six months, which would have taken her up to March 1916, but we do not know if she spent all of that time in Edinburgh.

The idea that Ellen (Blanche) stayed with her aunt, Jane Murray, for a time, comes from a Border Crossing document from Canada to the USA dated January 1917. In the column which asks name and address of - 'nearest relative or friend from whence she came'- Ellen (Blanche) gives the name of her aunt, Jane Murray, at 4 St. Patrick's Square, Edinburgh.

On the basis of previous declarations on these documents it is obvious that the person is meant to give their last contact in a country before crossing into the USA. It is not asking for the person's next of kin. This would suggest that Ellen (Blanche) had arrived in Canada directly from the UK. Did she go home to Canada on a troop ship without being resident in Canada before travelling on to the USA? We just don't know, but it does give credence to the idea that she spent some time, prior to her return, in Edinburgh with her aunt, Jane Murray. This also tells us that, despite the death of their mother and their long years of residence in Canada, the Tregilgas sisters knew of their Edinburgh family.

Ellen's official discharge, on medical grounds, from the Canadian Army is given as 29 September 1916 but other evidence suggests she was retained by her Unit in Canada. Her discharge payments did not commence until November 1918 by which time she was living at 426 W 23rd St. New York. She also continued to be listed as serving in the British Army's List of overseas dominions and colonies until 1918. However, it is obvious she never served overseas again and I think her war duties ended on her official discharge date.

The Canadian Government paid all the expenses of sending its troops to the war. Canada did not have a regular army of its own in 1914 and insisted that all its soldiers were volunteers, initially, who were paid by the Canadian Government. A massive contribution of troops and money from the Dominion of Canada. There is evidence also that Ellen (Blanche) received a war gratuity from the government of some C$2000 and that they paid her a disability pension until her death in 1927.

I wondered why Ellen did not go back to her sister, Sarah (Constance) Lussier, in Montreal, on her return from her war service. We later discovered that Sarah (Constance) was actually living in France at that time where her husband, Dr Joseph Lussier, was an eminent neurologist serving in the Canadian Army.

Dr Joseph Lussier had become the medical officer of Le Regiment de Chateauguay at Beauharnois and in 1915 was promoted to Captain and attached to No.6 Stationery Hospital, Royal Canadian Army Medical Corps.

Sarah (Constance) and Joseph Lussier's first child, baptised Marie Fernande Helene Lussier, was born late 1915 or early 1916 in Quebec. Presumably, the name Helene was after Sarah's mother, Ellen Murray. The family were living in Berri Street in Montreal when Joseph departed aboard the SS *Baltic* for England on 23 March 1916.

On his arrival in England on 8 April 1916 he was promoted to Major and his Unit was attached to the hospital at Shorncliffe, the same army camp that his sister-in-law, Ellen (Blanche) Tregilgas, had arrived at on 15 May1915. Although Joseph was attached to a 'Stationary Hospital' these did in fact move about. Unlike his sister-in-law, Ellen (Blanche), Joseph had four months at Shorncliffe to enjoy the facilities on offer.

He was posted to France on 8 July 1916 and, until the end of the war, his Unit operated at hospitals in St. Cloud, a suburb of Paris, Joinville le Point and Troyes.

During his research into Dr Joseph Lussier's army records, Matt Lunn discovered that Joseph's wife, Sarah (Constance) joined him in France at some point. We were astonished! We had never heard of anyone being allowed to take their wife to war!

We do not know exactly when Sarah (Constance) travelled to join her husband but it appears it must have been sometime in 1916 as her sister Ellen's army discharge documents, of the same year, give her next of kin as Sarah (Constance) Lussier living in Joinville le Point in France. Joseph and Sarah (Constance) move, at some point, to Troyes in France and that is where their second daughter, Gabrielle Lussier, was born on 16 July 1918.

Matt Lunn found that the No.6 Stationery Hospital was based in Troyes between 1917 and 1918. We know that Joseph was a highly-qualified neurologist and his services would have been much needed in caring for soldiers suffering from 'shell-shock', or Post Traumatic Stress Disorder as we would call it today. It makes me wonder if, perhaps, Sarah (Constance) had actually been a nurse in a neurology department during peacetime. Maybe that is where she and Joseph met. Surely, she must have possessed some specialist skills to be allowed to be with her husband in a war-torn country (complete with two young children!). The family were to continue serving in France for the rest of the war and beyond. In 1919 their address is Nogent sur Marne, a suburb of Paris.

So when Ellen (Blanche) was given her medical discharge and returned to Canada, from the UK, on board the troop carrier SS Corsican, there would have been no point in her disembarking in Montreal because her sister, Sarah (Constance), was still in France.

Instead, as the Border Crossing documents show, Ellen (Blanche) returned to New York where she had lived before the war.

It was a decision that was to ruin her life.

MARRIAGE AND MAYHEM

In 1918 Ellen (Blanche) married Pierre Paul Auther in New Jersey. She married using the name Ellen H. Tregilgas even although her name was actually Ellen Clarke Tregilgas. Perhaps she never knew that.

Pierre Paul Auther was, allegedly, born in France about 1887 making him about 31 when they married. He gives his occupation as a chemist. We wonder where he and Ellen (Blanche) met and there is a suggestion that they both worked for the Du Pont Chemical Company. It is unlikely that Ellen (Blanche) would have been able to return to nursing because of the eye condition that had resulted in her medical discharge from the Canadian Army Medical Corps. She had her army gratuity and also a disability pension from the army but it seems unlikely that would have been enough to live on.

Pierre Paul and Ellen's daughter, Jeanne, was born on 3 August 1919 in Cook County, Illinois. Her full baptismal name was Marie Jeanne Blanche Frances Helen Anne Auther! In the 1920 State Census Ellen and Pierre Paul were living with their baby daughter at 419 East 45th Street, Chicago, and Pierre Paul is working for the University. Later they move to the Highland Park area of the city. Here, Pierre Paul was known locally as the 'Spanish Grandee' since he claimed to be descended from Spanish aristocracy. Beth and Chuck Barry have a photograph of him, at that time, and he is a handsome, scholarly-looking man, at his desk, wearing a tweed suit and holding a pipe.

Every inch the gentleman.

But appearances can be deceptive.

Chuck Barry's mother, Jeanne Barry (nee Auther), had always wondered what had happened to her father. She only had memories of being raised by the woman she knew as her mother, Blanche. When Ellen (Blanche) died in 1927, eight-year-old Jeanne was sent to live with her aunt, Sarah(Constance) Lussier, in Montreal. There she was brought up by Sarah (Constance) and her husband, Dr Joseph Lussier, alongside their two daughters, Helene and Gabrielle.

Jeanne herself always spoke of her mother as Blanche and never mentioned the name Ellen. It was not until we began to research the Tregilgas sisters that we were able to identify Jeanne's mother, Blanche, as Ellen Clark Tregilgas and her sister, Constance Lussier, as Sarah Skiffington Tregilgas, both daughters of Ellen Murray and Joseph Tregilgas from 'Little Ireland. Their name changes to Constance and Blanche having confused other family researchers for years.

Jeanne told her daughter-in-law, Beth Barry, that her childhood with the Lussiers was a classic 'Cinderella' story. She was sent to a French-speaking school, which must have been traumatic for an eight-year-old girl who only spoke English. She was made to do all the chores, had to sleep on top of a trunk and never had nice clothes to wear. On one occasion she took a sheet off her bed and made herself a new dress with it! This was a forerunner of Jeanne's great skill as a dressmaker which was, in later life, to allow her to build up a very successful business making dresses for wealthy women in Montreal.

It was not until Jeanne died and Beth Barry was helping Chuck sort through his mother's papers that they found her birth certificate declaring that Jeanne's mother was, in fact, Ellen Tregilgas. The couple had tried to find out more about Jeanne's father, while she was still alive, but it wasn't until after Jeanne's death that Chuck went online and a whole cascade of newspaper articles tumbled out. When Chuck and Beth had read them they were both astonished, and grateful, that Jeanne never knew the story of her father.

In 1920 it seems that Ellen (Blanche), Pierre Paul and baby Jeanne Auther, were living happily in Highland Park and doing well in Chicago.

However, on 1 January 1921 Ellen (Blanche) Auther reported her husband, Pierre Paul, missing.

Then on 7 January 1921 matters took a dramatic turn.

A warrant for Pierre Paul's arrest was issued after a man named Philip Franzen had made a statement to the police that Pierre Paul Auther had stolen his wife, Charlotte, at gunpoint, and forced him to hand over $100 for a 'honeymoon' they intended taking! Franzen reported that Pierre Paul had stated that his real name was Pierre Devoy and he claimed he had married Franzen's wife some 13 years previously in Australia. They had become separated after two years and he had been searching for her ever since. He had travelled through Australia, Europe and America and now that he had found her he did not intend to lose her. Pierre makes Charlotte go out and cash a cheque while he holds a gun to her husband's head warning him to say nothing or he will kill him. He states that -"He has come for his woman and he will not leave without her". He then made Philip Franzen sign a piece of paper declaring he was surrendering all rights to Charlotte – a real quickie divorce! Charlotte tells her husband -"he can keep the brat." She is referring to their child, whom they had actually adopted but, whom Charlotte had led her friends to believe she had given birth to by hiding him in the house for months!

The couple then made off.

When Pierre Paul first went missing there was some suggestion of foul play, that his life was in danger as he had previously claimed that, as a chemist, he had a secret formula for an aniline dye developed by the Germans.

However, once Ellen (Blanche) was informed of her husband's antics she expressed little surprise. She said - "*I have felt that ever since he disappeared that he had not met with an accident but had gone to some other woman. I have found several love letters signed 'Charlotte', some from Madison and some from Milwaukee.*" She also stated that a will left by her husband urged her to marry the day after he died and left an estate of $2 in cash, to her and her daughter! The will also states that his daughter, Jeanne, must be taught to spend money well and that she must be brought up to respect all women, even those of the so called low class. Jeanne must also be taught to love her husband, heart, body and soul! You just could not make it up!

Ellen (Blanche) further reported that Pierre Paul had begun spending her $2,000 dowry (probably an army gratuity) on other women immediately after their wedding. She also comments that she thinks the reason her husband chased after other women was because she was disfigured by the infection she suffered to her eye during her medical war service.

Our Poor Ellen, who had already suffered so much in her life. Leaving her home in Edinburgh, being abandoned in a Children's Home in Canada after the death of her mother, volunteering and serving on the battlefields of France as a nurse, before suffering a nasty eye infection as a result of her nursing duties, and returning home alone after her medical discharge. One can't help wondering how different her life might have been if her sister, Sarah (Constance), had been in Montreal when she returned instead of still being in France with her doctor soldier husband. How lonely Ellen (Blanche) must have been and how very vulnerable to the charms of a 'con artist' like Pierre Paul.

We do hope that the period of Leave she seems to have spent in Edinburgh with her aunt, Jane Murray, was a happy time for her. It seems to have been because, when she gives birth to a child, she names her Jeanne, the French for Jane, presumably after her kindly aunt in Edinburgh.

During the newspaper reporting of Pierre Paul's case Ellen (Blanche) states that she does not believe his claims that he had ever been married to Charlotte, or anyone but herself. She is reported as saying - "*Why, Australia is the only country he has not been in so he couldn't have married anyone there thirteen years ago. That story..... sounds too much like one of his romantic yarns*".

So it appears that Ellen (Blanche) has come to realise that her husband is a fantasist. But she does not realise the extent of his deception.

Beth Barry has traced some information on the early life of Pierre Paul Auther that seems to cast doubt on his much travelled claims and, more importantly, on his marital status before marrying Ellen (Blanche).

Beth and Chuck discovered that he was indeed born in France, in Guerande. He may have some claim to Spanish ancestry. He claims his full name was - Pedro Paulo Hernandez Gnimemez Rosario y Martinez y Castet y Errotaberria De Casteleurgas!

However, it seems that he was dis-inherited by his family and excommunicated by his local church. He told Ellen (Blanche) that he spent some time in an asylum in France as a result of some obsession with a woman. He leaves France in 1914 and we know he sails to Canada, thus avoiding serving his native country in WWI. Beth Barry's research uncovered the fact that, once in Canada, Pierre Paul marries a woman named Elza Liebscher, in Toronto in 1915. But he hasn't escaped being called up for the war. He avoids the Draft by claiming that he has to care for a dependent wife. My friend, Sarah Ryan-Frost, discovered that the woman he had married was in receipt of a war disability pension. This made us wonder if Pierre Paul made a habit of targeting vulnerable women in possession of army gratuities.

Beth next picks up on Pierre Paul and his first wife requesting entry to the USA on a Border Crossing document. In it he states they are intending to join his brother-in-law in New York.

The mystery now is – what happened to his wife? Given the dates between him arriving in the USA and marrying Ellen (Blanche) in 1918, there would hardly have been time for them to divorce. So could she have died? Or, can we add bigamy to Pierre Paul's crimes? It is quite obvious, from her comments, that Ellen (Blanche) did not know that Pierre Paul had been married before. Nor, given his age and the timescale, does it seem likely that Pierre Paul did much world travelling before sailing to Canada in 1914. In a later interview, Pierre Paul claims that his and Ellen's was a battlefield romance - but again the dates just don't fit. He made sure he kept well away from any battlefields!

There seems no doubt that Pierre Paul Auther was a complete fantasist.

After fleeing with Charlotte he learns that a warrant has been put out for their arrest. They try to flee the country but a country-wide search is being made for them. They had made a pact to die together if they could not live together and intended escaping over the border into Mexico. However, they book into a hotel in St. Louis under assumed names, but are recognised, arrested and held in adjoining cells at the police station.

Pierre Paul tries to put the blame for his behaviour onto Ellen (Blanche). He said she nagged him about staying out late and accused him of having affairs with other women. He goes on to say he met Charlotte in Milwaukee (so not Australia then!) and liked her from the start.

Charlotte, meanwhile, announces she has left her life to fate and she will now seek to capitalize on her recently gained publicity through an engagement in the Movies or on the Vaudeville stage. In the meantime, she will write a book containing the history of her life's love romance!

Sounds like they deserved each other!

Numerous Court appearances follow and newspapers across the entire USA have stories on the gun-toting 'Spanish Grandee'. Pierre Paul waived his right to extradition to France and hoped to clear his name. Philip Franzen seems to drop his larceny charges leaving Pierre Paul facing the charge of abandonment of his wife and child.

He and Charlotte both end up being sentenced. One newspaper reports they both got three years in the State Penitentiary. The judge who sentenced them told Pierre Paul - "he was a bad egg" and declared Charlotte - "a disgrace to womanhood". That was them told!

When Pierre Paul was led away he declares - "The world will hear from me again". One newspaper reported that Ellen (Blanche), with Jeanne in her arms, attended the trial in the packed courtroom.

But after the high drama of the trial, information in the

newspapers becomes scanty and confusing. One newspaper reported that, on the way to Court, Pierre Paul hit the accompanying Detective on the mouth leaving an imprint of a ring he wore. This resulted in him getting a longer sentence. Another stated that Pierre Paul was held in default of bail on his grand larceny charge and he was to be sent to a hospital for the insane for observation. If Physicians there pronounced him insane he would be sent to the asylum. Another news story said deportation proceedings would likely be initiated and an investigation under the Mann Act instituted.

And then the trail goes cold. We have been unable to find out what became of Pierre Paul Auther. When he was released from prison was he deported back to France? If not, did he stay in the USA and change his name – again? One thing seems certain, after his trial, Ellen (Blanche) and Jeanne never saw him again. We must be grateful for small mercies.

The family believe that while the trial was ongoing Ellen (Blanche) took Jeanne to Montreal to live with her sister, Sarah (Constance) Lussier. The Lussier family had returned to Montreal in 1920, two years after the end of the war. Presumably, Dr Joseph Lussier's neurology skills were still needed to treat traumatised soldiers. His army record shows that on several occasions during those years he also had to go to the UK himself for treatment for severe haemorrhoids. There is no evidence of whether Sarah (Constance) and their daughters travelled with him or not.

The one certainty is that, in the 1921 census, Jeanne is living with her aunt, Sarah (Constance), at the Lussier family home on Berri Avenue in Montreal. She would be two years old at that time.

Quite apart from all the trauma of Pierre Paul's bizarre behaviour, and the ordeal of the trial, it appears that he had left Ellen (Blanche) and Jeanne destitute. He had spent her army gratuity which would have provided a safety net until Ellen found work.

The records are incomplete but it seems that Ellen (Blanche) returned to New York, where she had previously lived and worked, leaving Jeanne to be looked after by her sister in Montreal until she could get settled. A Border Crossing document for Jeanne shows that, after her mother's death in 1927, she crossed from the USA to Montreal. On the same document is the statement that Jeanne had previously lived in Montreal from 1923 to 1926.

So did Jeanne live with her mother in New York for a time between 1921 and 1923? Then, because Ellen (Blanche) was having to work as well as look after four-year-old Jeanne, did she send her daughter back to live with her sister, Sarah (Constance), until Jeanne was old enough to go to school?

We know from a census that Matt Lunn found that, at one time, Ellen (Blanche) was living in a Rooming House, in the 'Hell's Kitchen' area of New York, and was employed as a 'powder packer' in a factory that made gun-powder for the mining industry. It must have been so hard for this lovely, caring, highly intelligent woman, who had qualified as a Graduate Nurse, to be living in these conditions.

According to a Border Crossing document Jeanne would be nearly seven when she returned to live with her mother in New York. From conversations with Jeanne, Beth Barry believes that, for some of that time, Jeanne was placed in a Boarding School or Childcare Facility, presumably because her mother had to work. Perhaps she returned home at weekends because Beth Barry said her mother-in-law, Jeanne, was adamant that it was Blanche who 'mothered' her, that she spent a lot of time with her and she had fond memories of her mother. Another possible reason for Jeanne being put in a residential facility, of some sort, was that perhaps Ellen (Blanche) was ill.

Tragically, Ellen Auther (nee Tregilgas) died in New York in 1927, aged 43, leaving behind her beloved daughter, Jeanne. We do not know the cause of death. She is buried in St. Michael's Cemetery in New York under the name of Blanche Auther.

A sad end for a wee girl from Edinburgh's 'Little Ireland' who had shown such intelligence and bravery.

When Ellen Tregilgas died and her daughter, Jeanne, was left alone in New York, aged just eight, a surprising person came to her aid.

Richard Harold Tregilgas (always known as Harold) was Ellen's half-brother, son of her father Joseph Tregilgas and his second wife Frances Boland.

As far as we can tell, Joseph Tregilgas played no part in his three daughter's lives after the death of their mother Ellen Tregilgas (nee Murray) on their arrival in Winnipeg. The sole mention of any interaction is when his daughter, Emma Tregilgas (Sister St.-Elphege), claims she visits him on his deathbed in St Paul, Minnesota, in 1927.

So how could Ellen (Blanche) know this half-brother who was ten years younger than her?

Chuck and Beth Barry have in their possession, from Jeanne's effects, a photograph of Harold in his forces uniform. There is no evidence that Harold and Ellen (Blanche) ever met as children so Beth and I speculated that perhaps they met during the war. However, we ruled that out on the basis that Ellen (Blanche) was serving in the Canadian army, whereas Harold, having been born in the USA, was serving in the American army. By the time America joined the war against Germany and Harold enlisted, Ellen (Blanche) had already served in France and England, suffered her eye condition and been invalided home. It was highly unlikely their paths would have crossed.

Beth then turned sleuth again and investigated the life of Richard (Harold) Tregilgas. She discovered that at the end of the war he had gone to University to study medicine. I wondered if perhaps he took the opportunities offered to those who had served in the war to be granted scholarships. He qualified as a doctor and Beth discovered that in 1921 he was doing a year's internship at a hospital in Chicago. Could that be how they came to meet? As we know, the newspapers were full of the Pierre Paul Auther scandal playing out in Chicago at that time. Beth also noted that, in the articles, Pierre's wife is always referred to as Ellen and her maiden name of Tregilgas is given. Also, in an interview Ellen (Blanche) mentions that she was born in Scotland, was 'orphaned' and put in a Children's Home on her arrival in Canada. Did Harold Tregilgas read the reports and take note of the name Tregilgas (which was not a common name) and put two and two together? Or, perhaps he already knew that his father had been married before and had three daughters. His father, Joseph Tregilgas, was still alive in 1921 so perhaps he asked his father if Ellen (Blanche) was his sister. We will never know, but when we look over the dates of Ellen's (Blanche's) and Harold's lives, this seems to be the only point at which they intersect.

However the connection was made there is no doubt that Harold kept in contact with his half-sister, Ellen (Blanche), after she returned to live in New York and for the rest of her life. How else would he know when she died and make the arrangements to have Jeanne escorted to Montreal into the care of Jeanne's uncle, Dr Joseph Lussier? Harold himself was living in St Paul in Minnesota at that time, as was his father, Joseph Tregilgas, who died the same year as his daughter, Ellen (Blanche), but it was Harold who came to the aid of little Jeanne. One of life's good guys!

Jeanne's experiences living with her aunt, Sarah (Constance) Lussier, and her cousins, Helene and Gabrielle, after her mother's death in 1927 do not appear to have been happy. We wondered how this could be as her uncle, Joseph Adonis Lussier, was a renowned neurologist and assistant professor in Montreal – a respectable pillar of the community – and presumably an empathetic man. Chuck's older brother, Michael, told them that indeed Dr Joseph Lussier was very kind to their mother, Jeanne. Possibly trying to compensate for his wife, Sarah's (Constance's), treatment of her. Michael described him as the kindest man, very wise and cultured.

He had a distinguished war record. He had volunteered to serve as a doctor in France during the war. He was a member of the Royal Canadian Medical Corps and he set sail for England on 23 March 1916 aboard the *SS Baltic*. On arrival in England, on 8 April 1916, his Unit was attached to the hospital at Shorncliffe, Kent and he was promoted to Major. He arrived in France on 8 July 1916 and his Unit operated until the end of the war at St Cloud, a suburb of Paris, Joinville Le Point and Troyes.

As already mentioned, sometime in 1916, his wife Sarah (Constance) Lussier, joined her husband in France, presumably accompanied by their first-born daughter, Helene. A second daughter, Gabrielle, was born on 16 July 1918 in Troyes. So she must have been conceived around November 1917 when we know that No.6 Stationary Hospital was based in Troyes.

It is a mystery why Sarah (Constance), his wife, was allowed to join him in France during the war. We can only speculate that she had relevant nursing experience. At first I thought that, as Joinville le Point and Troyes being near Paris and well back from the trenches, Dr Joseph Lussier was based in a 'proper' hospital. However, when I researched the history of both places during WWII found that was far from the case. Both communes housed large army camps and the conditions were atrocious. Poor drainage and lack of sanitation caused huge medical problems. The accommodation blocks were wooden and ramshackle. Apart from wounded soldiers, the camps also treated large numbers of cases of venereal disease in soldiers which stretched the number of beds to the limit.

Dr Lussier's war service was far from a 'cushy' number. It is not surprising that he was a highly decorated soldier. He, his wife and his daughters arrived back in Canada aboard the *SS Grampian* on 20 January 1920, two years after the war had ended. In November 1920, Dr Joseph Lussier received the French Medalle d'Honneure avec Glaives from the President of the French Republic. He was also awarded a Medal of Gratitude by the British Government which was sent to him straight from No.10 Downing Street!

He went on to have a successful career as a neurologist and as an Assistant University Professor. He remained attached to the Royal Canadian Medical Corps and attained the rank of Lt. Colonel, serving in France and also working in hospitals in Paris until 1927, before returning to Canada permanently.

There does not seem to be any suggestion that Sarah (Constance) accompanied her husband on these trips back to France.

We know Sarah (Constance) was living in Montreal at the time of the 1921 Census and also when Jeanne was with her between 1923 and 1926. So, perhaps, Joseph was not around much at these times and, also, we have to factor in that men did not take much part in household affairs or the raising of children. Sarah (Constance) would rule the roost. However, it is curious that Dr Lussier appears to return finally to the family home in Montreal in 1927. The same year that Ellen (Blanche) died and that Jeanne went to live with them permanently.

Dr Joseph Adonis Lussier, eminent Neurologist, Professor, and decorated war hero, died on 14 November 1955 in Montreal.

His wife, Sarah (Constance) Lussier (nee Tregilgas), raised their own two daughters and also her sister Ellen's daughter, Jeanne Auther. Jeanne's relationship with her Aunt Constance remained fraught even after Jeanne married Charles Barry and had five children of her own. Jeanne's eldest son, Michael, related that Constance was always hard on his mother.

Constance's own daughters also married. Helene Lussier became the Editor of a French edition of a magazine in Canada. She married

Joseph Auguste Giles Laurent Julien in 1940 in Quebec. The younger daughter, Gabrielle Lussier, married Arthur James Spiers in 1945 in London, England.

Sarah Skiffington Tregilgas (Constance), daughter of Joseph Tregilgas and Ellen Murray, wife of Dr Joseph Adonis Lussier, died on 4 June 1968 in Montreal, aged 90, and is buried in the Cote des Neiges Cemetery. The wee girl from Edinburgh's Little Ireland' had led a long challenging life full of adventure that she could never have imagined as a child living in the Old Town of Edinburgh.

The photograph that Beth and Chuck Barry posted online that set my sister, Frances Connolly, on the trail to us finding our lost Tregilgas sisters was a treasure indeed. It is an amazing icon to one family that had its origins in Edinburgh's 'Little Ireland'.

CHAPTER TEN

JOHN SYLVESTER DELANEY

John Sylvester Delaney was born in St. Mary's Wynd, in Edinburgh's Old Town, on 1 July 1848. The street lay at the heart of 'Little Ireland' where the Irish diaspora had settled both before and after the Great Famine. John was the last of the five children of Arthur Delaney and Helen Collins. His siblings were, James (1840), twins Mary and Roseanna (1843) and Thomas (1845).

After his father's death on 8 May 1850, his mother, Helen, married Philip Boylan, three months later on 18 August, and John and his brothers moved, with their mother, to Philip Boylan's large house at 17 St. Mary's Wynd. John was only two years old.

In 1851, a son, Luke Joseph, was born to Helen and Philip, followed by Philip, James, John and Mary Boylan. John Delaney and Luke Joseph Boylan, with just two years separating them, appear to have grown up very close. In fact all the Delaney boys, being young, would not see Philip and Helen's children as half siblings, but just their brothers and sister. John was also close to his Aunts, Sarah and Jane Delaney, and his Skiffington and Murray cousins.

The church of St. Patrick's, which had been built in Lothian Street in 1834, could not accommodate the growing Irish population in the town and so, in 1856, Bishop Gillis bought a large former Episcopalian church in the Cowgate. They named it St. Patrick's and the former church in Lothian Street became the school. In time the 'new' church also had to be extended to house the growing congregation.

We do not know if John Delaney was educated in the school in Lothian Street but it seems likely.

When he was old enough John was apprenticed in the Printing Trade. Edinburgh was world famous as a centre for Publishing and Printing and jobs in the industry were highly sought after. It is interesting to note that prejudice against the Irish Catholic community in Edinburgh was fierce and many trades and professions were closed

95

to them. But, for some reason, the Printing Trade accepted Irish Catholics, and several family members, as well as John, worked in it.

The parish of St. Patrick's continued to boom and it was decided that they needed to build a Church Hall. St. Mary's Wynd had been widened, on the instructions of Edinburgh's first Medical Officer of Health, Henry Littlejohn, under the first City Improvement Act. One side of St. Mary's Wynd was demolished and the street widened, thereafter to be renamed as St. Mary's Street.

St. Patrick's Church took the opportunity to feu a large plot of land and on it they built a most impressive Catholic Institute, known by the parishioners as St. Mary's Street Halls. A beautiful piece of architecture that survives to this day, though no longer as Church Halls. The building was a warren of rooms, suitable for every purpose, and at its heart was a magnificent Main Hall, capable of seating 1000 people, with a stage suitable for performances.

St. Patrick's Church had the great good fortune to have appointed a young, energetic, Irish priest, Fr (later Canon) Edward Hannan, in 1861, as a curate. He was to serve the parish for 30 years.

Fr Edward Hannan was born in Ballingary, Co. Limerick, in Ireland, on 21 June 1836. He was ordained as a priest on 13 May 1860 and was appointed a Professor of Classics, in the church. However, while on holiday in Scotland, he was persuaded by Bishop Gillis, of the Archdiocese of St. Andrews and Edinburgh, to move to Edinburgh to serve the Irish community. In October 1861 he was appointed as junior curate at St. Patrick's. Thirteen-year-old John Delaney would come to know the priest very well.

Fr Hannan decided to tackle the many social ills of the area known as 'Little Ireland' and especially among the youth. His uncle, the Right Reverend Monsignor Richard B. O'Brien, Dean of Limerick, had founded the Catholic Young Men's Society in Ireland in 1849. On 5 October 1865 Fr Hannan founded a St. Patrick's branch of the CYMS, which provided both educational and social opportunities in the parish for young men. John Delaney, at seventeen, became one of it's first members, and it was the Dramatic Association of the Catholic Young Men's Society that caught his interest. He soon became one of it's leading lights.

Fr Hannan was instrumental in the project to build the Catholic Institute to take forward his plans. On the 2 April 1869, the foundation stone of the building was laid by the Lord Provost of Edinburgh, William Chambers. An amazing achievement, given the hostility to the Irish in the town. Even after all this time, the Irish in 'Little Ireland', were still regarded as inferior aliens. The main vitriol against them was led by the Church of Scotland fearing that Catholics would dilute the purity of Presbyterian Scotland. In the west, the Glasgow Herald newspaper was equally sectarian, and adept at stirring up hatred against the Irish but, in Edinburgh, The Scotsman newspaper held a much more balanced viewpoint. The Lord Provost's address, at the laying of the Foundation Stone for the Catholic Institute, hints at the prejudice that existed.

"Through my whole life I have never taken part in any proceedings calculated to exalt one sect above another. My wish is to see fair play and toleration to all, and since I have the honour to be raised to the Magistracy of this city I have studiously, and in a particular manner, adhered to that line of conduct... ....From the enquiries which I have latterly made, I find conclusive evidence that the Catholic Young Men's Society is one worthy of support. It began about four years ago and has done much good. Its particular object, I am told, is to raise the moral and intellectual status of its members, who now amount to about 800 in number ...... We are told that up to the present time the society has exerted a remarkable beneficial influence over its members. Youths, formerly degraded and intemperate, have been reclaimed. Those who were once ragged and dissolute are decently clothed and now a creditable part of society. Through the energetic effort of the society a very conspicuous improvement has been effective in the Cowgate."

The whole speech was reported in The Scotsman newspaper.

None of those achievements would have been possible without the energy and commitment of young Fr Edward Hannan and his supporters in 'Little Ireland'.

Fr Hannan had started the Dramatic Association of the Catholic Young Men's Society. Later he was also instrumental in helping to found the Hibernian Football Team. The football club was launched on 6 August 1875 as part of a celebration at St. Mary's Street Halls to mark the centenary of the birth of Daniel O'Connell, the champion of Catholic Emancipation. Michael Whelehan, a parishioner, became the team's first Captain and Fr Hannan became the Club's Manager and

Life President. The team, bearing the name of their Irish homeland, Hibernia, went on to great glory, winning the Scottish Cup in 1887 and bringing great acclaim to 'Little Ireland'. The team still plays in Edinburgh and is still a force in Scottish football to this day.

But that was for the future.

The Catholic Institute had been expensive to build and fund-raising was on-going. One of the first reviews we found of John, in an acting role, was for a fund-raising event held in the Church Hall, on 29 October 1870. The Hall was filled to overflowing, with all of the 1000 seats taken, and The Scotsman newspaper said the audience was 'enthusiastic'. Interestingly, the leading actor in the production was P. Niven, who was a professional from the Theatre Royal in Edinburgh. The reviewer states that - "Mr J. S. Delaney made a smart *Gaiters,* and looked as foolish and absurd as any Cockney could have done in kilts". An early indication that John's forte was going to be in comedy.

John's experience in the Dramatic Association of the CYMS was to lead to a whole new career. He was 22 years old at this point, now a fully-qualified printer with a well-paid job, but he threw it all up and decided the stage was for him. Amazingly, old Philip Boylan, his mother Helen, and the family appeared to support him because up to the late 1870s, though John travelled the world in starring roles, and toured extensively in the UK, he gave his permanent address as Edinburgh. We can only assume that early on the family realised John had real talent and would go far.

Because of this early foray into comedy, when I first began researching John Sylvester Delaney's life on stage, I assumed he had been a performer in the Music Halls. I have found no evidence of him ever being in 'The Halls'. And although he is often referred to as a 'Comedian' or even an 'Irish Comedian,' in publicity materials, John was, in fact, a dramatic actor, a 'character' actor, who played serious roles as well as comedy and pathos, and did it very well. As any actor will tell you, comedy is much harder to pull off than tragedy, requiring perfect timing, and John was a very good actor indeed.

Before his appearance at the St. Mary's Halls fund-raiser, John had already appeared, in 1868, at The Edinburgh Theatre, as *The Landlord* in *The Lady of Lyons.*

The next year he appeared in productions at the Theatre Royals in Liverpool and in Dundee.

On 23/24 May 1869, he is again appearing in The Edinburgh Theatre, in *Romeo and Juliet,* where he plays *Gregory,* and on 25/ 26 in *The Hunchback,* as *Peter,* and later, in *Never Reckon your Chickens until they are Hatched.*

On 11 March 1870, the Dundee Advertiser's Reviewer wrote -

"As *Bailie Nicol Jarvie,* MR DELANEY, deserves favourable mention. Although rather youthful in appearance he had evidently made a study of the part, his Scotch dialect being capital."

He was youthful, being only 22, and having been born and raised in Edinburgh it is hardly surprising he spoke with a good Scotch accent!

On the 18 April 1870 The Scotsman Newspaper Theatre Reviewer wrote -

"Still another surprise prepared for the public by Mr R.H. Wyndam, was the *debut* of Mr J.S. DELANEY, who appeared, for the first time, in Edinburgh, in the particularly thankless and ungracious part of *Michael Feeney.* MR DELANEY was very careful not to overdo the part. And having a capital *brogue*, succeeded in rendering to the life the character of the vindictive yet sneaking process server."

The fact that his father, stepfather and aunts and uncles were all Irish born may have gone some way to his having a good ear for the '*brogue*'!

Also, in 1870, he is appearing in the Theatre Royals, in Edinburgh and Liverpool, with Mr E.D. Davis' company, and in 1871 he returns to The Theatre Royal, in Edinburgh, with Mr R.H. Wyndham's Company.

A Reviewer notes -

"*Rob Roy* has been put on the boards of the theatre this week after a lapse of about two years.....it has been warmly greeted with well-filled houses. Rob Roy is played by Mr Frank Kilpack, Major Galbraith's character well sustained by MR J S DELANEY."

These are all important theatres and John is working with big name Theatre Managers. R.H. Wyndham later became part of the highly successful Howard & Wyndham Partnership who owned and ran several Theatres including the Royal Lyceum in Edinburgh. They were to continue to give John leading roles over the following years.

Janet Croome (nee Delaney) told of how a painting of her great-grandfather, John Sylvester Delaney, in his famous role as *Greppo*, in *The Black Crook*, hung in her grandmother Amy's hallway when Janet was a child. The painting was captioned - "Upwards of 300 consecutive performances in America" and shows a dark-haired man, with brilliant blue eyes, in stage costume and makeup.

This caught my interest and I decided to investigate *The Black Crook*, and a fascinating story unfolded.

It opened on 12 September 1866 at the 3,200 seat Niblo's Garden on Broadway, in New York City, and ran for a record-breaking 474 performances. The revenues exceeded a record shattering one million dollars. The production featured state-of-the-art special effects, elaborate scenery and a Ballet Troupe of 70 ladies in skin-coloured tights and scanty costumes – a great attraction!

It continued as a Touring production for many years and was revived on Broadway in 1870-71, 1871-72 and many more times after that. "It is often considered a prototype of the modern musical in that its popular songs and dances are interspersed throughout a unifying play and performed by the actors." Some theatre historians claim it is the world's first musical.

Whatever the truth, there is no doubt it was a big deal and made theatrical history.

So where does JOHN SYLVESTER DELANEY fit in to all this?

In the 1871 census, he is still living with his mother and Philip Boylan at 17 St. Mary's Street, aged 23, but by May 1871, he has gone to America to seek fame and fortune and appears to have had instant success.

In the Troy Daily Times, in New York, USA, on 21 May 1871 it announces -

"Benefit of J.S. Delaney – The well known and popular comedian of the *Griswold Opera House* took his benefit last night to one of the best houses of the Season. - *"Robert Macair – Jones' Baby* and *Handy Andy* formed the programme. We are pleased to announce

that MR DELANEY'S benefit was a complete success, both financially and artistically. We hope to see him again among us"

Another Review on the Benefit states -

"J S DELANEY'S friends rallied in large force last night, at the Opera House and testified their appreciation of his **personal** and professional merits in the most substantial and satisfying manner. Pecuniarily the entertainment must have been a gratifying success to MR DELANEY and the performance appeared to please the audience.... and elicited great applause. MR DELANEY himself was called twice before the curtain but declined to make a speech beyond a brief expression of thanks. In the course of the evening he was made the recipient of a gold finger ring. The benefit was a complete success from first to last and we congratulate MR DELANEY upon it."

It appears that a 'benefit' is where one member of the cast receives the entire proceeds of an evening performance, as a sort of bonus, after performing for some time in a role. A Benefit night is usually attended by the more famous and fashionable members of a community, usually paying top dollar for the tickets. John seems to be doing very well financially. It also appears that he has been performing in New York for some time if, "he is well known".

John has gone from his appearance, in the Catholic Institute, in St. Mary's Street, in 1870, to leading roles in a New York theatre in 1871.

The boy done good!

John Sylvester Delaney's family have, in their family archives, a Contract from a Broadway Agency, Canning & Lowell's International Dramatic Agency, 678 Broadway, New York City. John is being hired by the Bidwell & Macdonagh Theatrical Company, for the role of *Greppo,* in the *Black Crook,* for a term of six or more months. It is a touring production of the show, made possible because the development of the railways enabled all the scenery, special effects, costumes and actors to be transported around the USA. The Tour is to start in Kansas City in September 1872, and to run for over 300 consecutive performances in cities and towns across the States. John has struck gold! He is to be paid $20 a week plus full board and travel costs. A quite amazing amount for a young actor. A skilled craftsman would take six months to earn what John was making in a week.

On 4 September 1872 the Kansas City Journal reports -

"There is a world of fun in the face of DELANEY, which had the effect of setting the house in a roar when he appeared as *Greppo*, the patient drudge, (in *The Black Crook*), and in a comic duet with, Miss Annie Mack, they received numerous encores".

The Black Crook is a long, dramatic play (It's original performance ran for 5 hours!), lightened by the servants roles, which provide the humour and comic songs. John excelled at both and received rave notices for his role as *Greppo* every time he performed. It made his name and it made him a great deal of money.

Because of it's popularity the Production ran beyond the performances contracted for, so in 1873, John is still in America.

On 5 April 1873 the New Orleans Picayune, USA reported -

"MR J S DELANEY, the gent of the theatre, takes his annual benefit tomorrow night when he will appear as *Joe Bright* in *Through Fire and Water* and in *Barney O'Toole* and *Peep-o-Day*.

MR DELANEY has hosts of admirers and we expect to see a bumper house."

Another Benefit adding to John's financial success.

In 1874 John has joined Mr Ben De Bar's company of Canada and is appearing in Montreal.

He has been away from the UK for more than three years and he has not finished travelling yet.

He moves on from Canada to the West Indies on a tour with Mr W. M. Holland's Company and on 23 November 1874 a Review appears in the Kingston Times, Jamaica -

"Mr W. M. Holland's Company appeared last evening in the *Serious Family* and *Handy Andy*.

MR J S DELANEY, the comedian of the company, is undoubtedly the most versatile artist that has appeared here for many years, and his performance of the pious charlatan, *Aminadab Sleek,* was a rare piece of acting whilst as *Handy Andy* he convulsed the audience."

The West Indies Tour continued and he didn't return to Edinburgh until 1875, co-incidently, the year that Fr Hannan founded Hibernian Football Club. No doubt John, like the rest of his family in 'Little Ireland', became a life-long Hibernian supporter! He had been touring abroad continuously since1871, including his run of over 300 consecutive performances in *The Black Crook* between 1872 and 1873 in the States, then a tour in Canada and straight into the West Indies tour.

He must have been exhausted, but on his return he is advertised as appearing in The New Edinburgh Theatre with Mr Wybert Reeves' Company. From there he went straight into Pantomime in Edinburgh in December 1875.

Pantomime was, and continues to be, a hugely popular theatrical entertainment, and one that seems to have been a particularly British theatre tradition, usually lasting from before Christmas and into the New Year

The Scotsman, in Edinburgh, of 4 January 1876 has the following Review -

"Mr Wybert Reeves' successful Pantomime of *Blue Beard* still attracts crowded houses.

MR DELANEY deserves special notice for his very funny impersonation of *Rusti Fusti*, Head Cook and Bottle Washer to the great *Bashaw.*"

After the pantomime he is advertised as appearing in The Grand Theatre, Edinburgh, with Mr Wilson Barrett's Company.

The Edinburgh Athenian of 17 May 1876 states -

"MR J S DELANEY, agreeably surprised us as *Old Pete*. It is the best rendering of the part since Dan Leeson played it. His dialect and make-up were artistic and deserve special mention."

John has been living with his mother while back performing in Edinburgh, but soon he is to set off touring again, where he will be living in theatrical digs.

The same year, of 1876, saw John Sylvester Delaney embark on a long tour with Mr Wilson Barrett's Company around the UK in the play that was to cement his status as a leading UK performer. He played the leading role of *Conn* in - *THE SHAUGHRAUN.*

The Shaughraun was written by Dion Boucicault an Irish actor and playwright. He was born in Dublin on 26 December 1820. His mother was Anne Darley, sister of the poet and mathematician, George Darley. The Darleys were an important Dublin family well known in many fields and related to the Guinnesses by marriage. Anne Darley was married to Samuel Smith Boursiquot, but it appears that Dion's father was actually Dionysius Lardner, who lodged at Anne's house at a time she was newly separated from her husband. Dion's full name was Dionysius Lardner Boursiquot and Lardner was known to have given him financial support until about 1841 so it seems the rumour was correct.

Lardner was elected as professor of natural philosophy and astronomy at University College, London in 1828 and Anne followed him to London taking all but one of her children with her.

Dion attended various schools in London and Dublin. In 1837 he attended Wyke House, a school at Brentford, where he appeared in a school play and wrote his own first play. However, he took up an apprenticeship as a civil engineer to Lardner in London.

But the stage had captured him and he gave up his apprenticeship to take up an acting offer adopting the stage name of Lee Morton. Thereafter he is known as Dion Boucicault. He continued to act and write plays and, in 1841, he had a big success as a dramatist with *London Assurance* at Covent Garden with a cast of well-known actors. Many other successful plays followed including the hit *The Corsican Brothers,* in 1852.

In his play, *The Vampire,* also in 1852, he made his debut as a leading actor. From1854 to 1860 he took up residence in the United States where he became a popular favourite and, with his second wife, the actress Agnes Robertson, toured America.

From around 1855 his business manager and partner in New York was William Stuart, an expatriate Irish MP, and together they leased and ran Wallack's Theatre in New York and also put on a short season at the Washington Theatre in Washington, D.C.

In 1859 they became joint lessees of Burton's New Theatre on Broadway. After extensive remodelling, he renamed his new showplace the Winter Garden Theatre and there, on 5 December 1859, he premiered his new play, *The Octoroon,* in which he also starred. This was a sensation – with an anti-slavery theme, it is considered to be the first play to appeal to the African-American population.

He fell out with William Stuart over money matters and went back to England.

On his return to England, he produced, at the Adelphi Theatre, a dramatic adaptation of Gerald Griffin's novel, *The Collegians,* which he renamed *Colleen Bawn.*

Colleen Bawn was one of the most successful plays of the times and was performed in almost every city of the United Kingdom and the United States. Although it made Dion Boucicault a fortune he lost it in the management of various London Theatres.

His next marked success was at the Princess Theatre, London, in 1864, with, *Arrah na Pogue*, in which he played the part of a County Wicklow Irish car man. This, and his outstanding creation of *Conn* in his play, *The Shaughraun*, first produced at Wallack's Theatre in New York City in 1874, then at the Theatre Royal, Dury Lane in London in 1875, won him the reputation of being the best "Stage Irishman" of his time. He even gets a mention in Gilbert & Sullivan's operetta, *Patience,* in the line "The pathos of Paddy, as rendered by Bouccault."

He was an excellent actor, especially in pathetic parts. His uncanny ability to play these low-status roles earned him the nickname "Little man Dion" in theatrical circles, and his plays, often ingenious in construction, had great popularity. They still have a cult following and have been staged, in Ireland, in recent times.

In 1875, after the success of *The Shaughraun,* he returned to New York City, where he made his home. Boucicault had eloped to New York, originally, with his second wife, Agnes Robertson. This caused a huge scandal back in 1853, because Agnes was Charles Kean's ward, and the juvenile lead in his company. She was an actress of unusual ability and toured with him for many years in the USA. She also bore Boucicault six children, three of whom became distinguished actors in their own right.

However, between July and October 1885, Boucicault toured Australia and, towards the end of the tour, he suddenly left Agnes to marry Josephine Louise Thorndyke, a young actress, aged 21 (He was now 65.) on 9 September 1885 in Sydney. This caused a huge scandal as his marriage to Agnes was not finally dissolved until 21 June 1888, by reason of "bigamy with adultery".

The rights to many of his plays were later sold to finance alimony payments to Agnes.

His final play, *A Tale of a Coat,* opened at Daly's Theatre in New York on 14 August 1890 and closed on 13 September 1890. Dion Boucicault died in New York five days later, aged 69, on 18 September 1890. A sad end to a brilliant career.

By the later part of the 19th century, Boucicault had become known, on both sides of the Atlantic, as one of the most successful actor-playwrights then in the English-speaking Theatre.

He was a big influence on the famous Irish playwrights who were to follow him. His plays were also later made into films so his fame spread beyond his times.

Sean O'Casey and his brother, Archie, put on performances of Boucicault's plays in their family home in Ireland in the 1890s. O'Casey even got a small part in a production of *The Shaughraun* in the Mechanics' Theatre, which stood on what was to become the site of the famous Abbey Theatre in Dublin.

Boucicault was also an influence on the work of famous Irish playwright and film maker, John Macdonagh, born in Tipperary in 1880. He was a republican and participant in the 1916 Easter Rising in Dublin. During the Rising he served alongside his brother, Thomas Macdonagh (one of the seven leaders of the Rising). After the surrender, Thomas, aged thirty-eight, was court-martialled and executed by a British Army firing squad on 3 May 1916. One of the other leaders of the Easter Rising was the Republican Socialist James Connolly, and co-incidently, he was born in the Cowgate in 'Little Ireland' just around the corner from St. Mary's Street, on 5 June 1868. There is no doubt the Delaney and Boylan families would know Connolly's parents in that close-knit community around St. Patrick's church, as they too came from Co. Monaghan.

John Macdonagh, himself, was initially sentenced to life imprisonment and sent to Fronoch Internment camp but he was released in August 1916, just five months after the Easter Rising. This would be as part of the general amnesty given to those who had taken part in the Rising but were not part of the leadership.

Before the Easter Rising, the republicans did not have widespread support among the Irish people. That all changed after the manner of the execution of the leaders by the British which caused support for Irish Independence to soar. James Connolly's execution was a major contribution towards this. He was a leader and Commander on the day, but he was shot and seriously wounded in the battle at the GPO. He was taken to hospital and declared to be within days of death. However, the British government ordered him to be returned for execution, with the other leaders, at Kilmainan Gaol. He was unable to stand and so was tied to a chair to be shot. The huge outcry that followed this action alarmed the British government who realised that it was encouraging support for the Irish Independence cause.

And so John Macdonagh was spared a life sentence. He later became involved with the Film Company of Ireland and directed many significant documentaries relating to the Cause. He also later filmed the funeral of his brother Thomas' wife, which was said to be one of the largest funerals Ireland had ever seen. He continued to be involved in the Irish Independence cause.

John Macdonagh directed Boucciault's *Colleen Bawn* in 1920, during the Irish Wars of Independence. It was shot in the grounds of St Edna's in Rathfarnham, where his brother, Thomas, and Patrick Pearse, (another executed leader of the Easter Rising), had founded a school to promote Irish education. John also acted in the film but he and the other actors used false names in the credits to protect themselves during those politically troubled times.

The Easter Rising and the wars that followed were very much a product of the Irish need to promote their own culture and language, after years of oppression. They would look back to Dion Boucicault's Irish work on that basis. The Great Famine, which led thousands of Irish to flee to America, had given Boucicault his audience, with his plays referencing the Fenian movement, transportation and landlordism.

John Sylvester Delaney had come to know Dion Boucicault during his time in America and had even acted with him, in a supporting role in *The Shaughraun,* when Dion was performing as *Conn* in a production at the Gaiety Theatre in Dublin.

Boucicault took up permanent residence in the United States and he became an American citizen in 1873. He was now 53, too old to convince in some of his most famous 'Irish' roles, and so John Sylvester Delaney took on his mantle. John also inherited Boucicault's Irish audience throughout the UK, where other Great Famine victims and their descendants had long been settled.

John announced to the UK theatregoers that "he begged to inform them that he had been specially selected, while in America, by Mr Boucicault" to take on these famous roles.

John Sylvester Delaney had a hugely successful career playing these iconic 'Irish' roles to a large Diaspora. Having watched the original actor at close quarters, he was able to present authentic portrayals that satisfied the audiences who had seen the great Boucicault.

Between 1876 and 1877 he undertook a *Shaughraun* Tour with Mr Wilson Barrett's company, playing the leading role as *Conn,* for upwards of 400 nights in theatres throughout the UK.

He also performed in the other Irish roles of "Myles", "Shaun the Post", "Barney O Toole" and "Terence O Moore".

The Delaney family have in their possession a scrapbook of Reviews on John Sylvester's performances over the years showing how popular he was and what an incredible work ethic he must have had. There seems to be no obvious periods when John is 'resting' between parts.

It is announced that -

"MR J S DELANEY will perform in, *The Shaughraun,* for six nights only, in Wakefield from 16 October 1876"

The Theatre Royal at Middlesborough announced -

"From 6 November 1876 and every evening **until further notice.** *The Shaughraun.*

On 10 November a Grand fashionable night under most distinguished patronage, being for the Benefit of MR J S DELANEY."

The Shaughraun at Hartlepool -

"The weightpiece necessarily falls upon *"Conn"* whose eccentricities are admirably captured by MR J S DELANEY the scenes received hearty applause which they so richly merit."

The Theatre Royal Hull -

"The performance of the drama this week is especially noticeable for the circumstances that a new *"Conn"* has been introduced to us in the person of MR J S DELANEY who, a few weeks ago, made his appearance in Hull as *Terry Rooney* in Manville Fenn's '*Land Ahead*'.......His acting in the part met with the entire approval of the audience."

The Corn Exchange, Derby -

"MR J S DELANEY was specially engaged as *"Conn"* and the enthusiastic, not to say boisterous, applause of a crowded house showed that his efforts were appreciated."

The Plymouth Theatre shows John in a different role in *The Shaughraun* -

"The production has afforded MR JS DELANEY a capital opportunity for distinguishing himself as the sneaking, cringing rascal, *Harvey Duff*. As a piece of what is called character acting this impersonation deserves great praise and is decidedly the feature of the play."

Adelphi Theatre, Oldham – The Shaughraun -

"MR J S DELANEY played *Conn* and completely established himself ere he had proceeded far in the delineation of the character. He seemed to carry the audience entirely with him and their roars of laughter testified to their appreciation of his racy and humorous rendering of *Conn*. Mr Barrett is lucky to have selected so able an exponent of this difficult character."

The Reviewer of the Leeds Express on 28 May 1877 reported -

"The leading character of '*The Shaughraun*' *is played by MR J S DELANEY* in an admirable manner. His brogue is excellent, just the thing without the slightest exaggeration and indeed the same might be said of the entire impersonation. It is a thoroughly natural and humorous sketch, full of spirit, humour, and rollicking fun, highly coloured, as is necessary, but not overdrawn. Mr Boucicault is the original, and we congratulate Mr Wilson Barrett for having secured so excellent a substitute."

By 11 July 1877 John is back playing in *"The Shaughraun.* This time in London.

The London Chronicle of 11 July 1877 reports – *The Shaughraun* -

"MR J S DELANEY made his first appearance in London last night as *"Conn"* and made a decided hit, receiving a special call after each Act."

In the Era magazine of 15 July 1877 the Reviewer states -

"MR J S DELANEY is a capital comedian, full of humour, pathos and activity."

A Reviewer in Leeds reported -

"Last night we found an old favourite in Leeds in possession of the part of *"Conn"* and a better representative we could not desire. MR DELANEY has the proper conception of *Conn's* character and places his idea before the audience with rare talent. Throughout he was followed by the heartiest laughter and applause, and we were glad to see was warmly welcomed on his very first appearance."

The Theatre Royal in Leeds also proudly proclaimed a 'Farewell Benefit' for J S DELANEY.
   He had obviously captivated the theatre-going public of Leeds.

The Theatre Royal, Leeds -

"Farewell Benefit for J S DELANEY after his performance of upward of 400 nights, as *Conn*, in *The Shaughraun*. Acknowledged by the Press and Public of Leeds to be the original and best representative of the character witnessed on the stage of the Theatre Royal. On this his last appearance as *Conn*, in Leeds, MR DELANEY stated he had been specially selected for the part by Mr Dion Boucicault, while in America......and that his *Conn* was approved of by -"The great author of the play". J S DELANEY also appeared as *Barney O Toole, in Barney the Baron.*"

It sounds like the Benefit was another huge financial and artistic success for John.

Next he is playing *The Shaughraun* at the Theatre Royal at Grantham - "With Mr Wilson Barrett's talented London Company". The Reviewer comments -

"We may however, besides commending generally the manner in which the piece has been produced, refer in terms of the highest praise to MR DELANEY'S excellent impersonation as *"Conn"*......it revealed a great amount of talent and ability on the part of the actor. MR DELANEY, indeed gave immense satisfaction."

Next he is appearing at the Theatre Royal in South Shields where the Reviewer states -

"Special engagement of MR J S DELANEY. The celebrated Irish Comedian to enact the part of *Conn* in *The Shaughraun* and admirably did he play the character. His impersonation being received with hearty applause."

Next to The Cardiff Theatre – a Production of *The Shaughraun* -

"MR J S DELANEY as *"Conn"* his acting produces immense effect, creating roars of laughter."

Though John Sylvester Delaney is obviously the 'go to actor' to play *Conn,* he also had great success with Boucicault's other iconic plays.
    On 12 May 1877, the Theatre Royal in Sunderland announces that MR JOHN S. DELANEY will take the role of, *Shaun the Post*, in a production of, *Arrah na Pogue.*

The Sunderland Times of 15 May, 1877, reported -

"*Arrah na Pogue* was the attraction last night, being excellently mounted. MR DELANEY's, *Shaun the Post,* was a charming piece of acting – full of pathos, wit and humour."

In December 1877 he is appearing at the Theatre Royal, Plymouth, in the pantomime, *Babes in the Wood,* as *Paddy Whack.*
    This is followed by an appearance in a production of a play, *Youth.*
    Between 1878 and 1879 John is appearing in a Season at Astleys and Duke's Theatre, London.

A Reviewer writes - "that the Dukes Theatre, London, is housing a production of *The Colleen Bawn*, which serves to introduce to the public, as *Myles na Coppaleen,* MR J S DELANEY. He is a gentleman who has a distinctly Hibernian appearance, and speech, and who acts the part with due regard to the traditions concerning it transmitted from its first exponent the author "(Boucicault)"".

The Colleen Bawn was, perhaps, Dion Boucicault's most successful play. It made him a fortune, was turned into several movies after his death, and the play was hugely influential in inspiring future Irish dramatists. It was first performed at Laura Keene's Theatre, New York, on 27 March 1860, with Boucicault playing the role of *Myles na Coppaleen.* Its most recent production was at the Lyric Theatre, Belfast, in 2018.

He was inspired to write the play after reading Gerald Griffin's novel, "The Collegians", written in 1829. The novel was based on the true story of Ellen Scanlan (nee Hanley), a fifteen-year-old girl who was murdered on the 14 July 1819. She had married John Scanlan, but he tired of her and persuaded his servant, Stephen Sullivan, to kill her and dump her body in the River Shannon. Both men then fled but Scanlan was traced first, found guilty, and then hanged at Gallows Green. Sullivan was found shortly afterwards, confessed and was also hanged.

Boucicuilt's dramatic adaptation of the true story thrilled and captivated audiences with its interwoven character plots and story, and continued to play to huge houses in every theatre in which it was produced.

So when John Sylvester took on the leading part of *Myles na Coppaleen,* the part that Boucicault himself had played in the original production, it showed his status as an actor of note, at the top of his game.

A Reviewer in The Times newspaper commented -

"MR DELANEY made his *debut* on Thursday night (at the Duke's Theatre) representing, *Myles*, the traditional Irish peasant with characteristic nationality. His face and brogue gave pleasant token that he was to the manner born. And his high animal spirits and racy Hibernian humour helped to complete the picture which was not the less acceptable to the general audience because in general outline it had evidently been copied from the original by the author."

Other Reviews were also complementary -

"*The Colleen Bawn* introduced a good comedian in MR J S DELANEY who, with a good brogue, and a sympathetic style, played *Myles na Coppaleen* forcibly winning abundant applause from the audience."

"MR J S DELANEY, who made his first appearance here at this theatre as *Myles na Coppoleen* in *The Colleen Bawn*, proved himself in full possession of the qualification necessary to give effect to the genial Irishman, who is always sure of enlisting popular sympathies on his side."

This is a significant point in the Delaney family history because it appears that when John is starring in *Colleen Bawn*, at the Dukes Theatre, London, this is where he met, and married, Elizabeth MacAlpine.

They married on 28 November 1878 at The Register Office in Lambeth, London. John is 30 years old, an Actor, and Elizabeth is 21 years old, a Spinster, but with no profession given. They are both living at the same address - 7 Crosier Street, Lambeth. Could these be theatrical digs or are the couple already living together? John gives his father's name as James Delaney whereas it was, of course, Arthur. But perhaps it is not surprising. John was two years old when his father died. He grew up thinking of old Philip Boylan as his father. Perhaps he thought that since his oldest brother's name was James, that that was his father's name too. He noted correctly that his father was a 'clothier'. Elizabeth's father is given as William John MacAlpine and he is a carriage painter.

John has spent the past 10 years on the road, travelling the world, and appearing in all the top theatres in Britain. He has never married.

One can't help but feel that Elizabeth must have been a very special woman indeed.

Sadly, we know very little about her life before she married John.

She was born on 3 May 1857, and baptised at St. Philip's Church, Bethnal Green, London. This was a Church of England Church. Her father was John William MacAlpine, a coach painter, and her mother was Catherine Macarthy. They had married in London at the same church on 27 May 1857, a few weeks after Elizabeth's birth. John William's father, George MacAlpine, was a labourer, Catherine's father a farmer. It is believed that the MacAlpine's were from Belfast and both the couple's families originated in Ireland, and indeed, if Catherine's father was a farmer it seems likely he remained in Ireland.

Neither John William nor Catherine could read or write and had to make their mark(X) on the marriage certificate. Elizabeth herself, being a different generation, was able to write. She had a younger brother, George, born 19 October 1859.

Tragically, Elizabeth's mother, Catherine, became ill with tuberculosis and had to be admitted to the hospital attached to the Workhouse, in Southwark, where she died on 31 October, 1868, aged just 29. Elizabeth was eleven years old at the time, her brother George just nine so they must have had a very sad childhood.

Elizabeth's father later remarried and it is believed she had two stepbrothers and a stepsister.

We wonder how John Sylvester and Elizabeth MacAlpine met and one possibility is, that since Elizabeth was a seamstress, perhaps she worked as a wardrobe mistress in the theatre. But that is speculation, we just don't know. The one photograph the family have of her, in her younger days, is when she is 26 years old. It shows a striking, attractive woman, well-dressed in a bonnet and furs, looking very prosperous.

The couple stay on in London after the run of *Colleen Bawn* finishes with John appearing in the Theatre in Holborn.

They then move to Plymouth where, on 3 November 1879, Elizabeth gives birth to their first child, Luke Terence Delaney, at 15 Buckingham Place, Plymouth.

John is probably in Plymouth to play in the pantomime in which he had performed there before.

He is still in the town in 1880 appearing at the Theatre Royal with Mr J R Newcombe's Company.

A Review from the theatre states -

"That excellent character comedian, MR J S DELANEY took his Benefit last night. That MR DELANEY is popular with Plymouth audiences was demonstrated by the well filled house and hearty reception accorded to him. The entertainments commenced with *The Break of Morn* and concluded with the comic play of *Handy Andy*. As *Peery Connolly* in *Break of Morn* and as *Handy Andy* in the Irish Drama of that name MR DELANEY sustained the reputation he has deservedly won here for genuine comic power, and kept the audience in a continual roar for the whole of the evening.

The fact that he performed in Plymouth regularly was shown in another Review from the Theatre Royal -

"In the farce of *The Happy Man*, MR J S DELANEY (an old favourite) sustained the title role."

Another mention is in a playbill for the Theatre Royal in Plymouth where he is appearing in Holt and William's production of the play - "*Youth*".

John named his first born after his half-brother, Luke Boylan, in Edinburgh. This is not surprising as John and Luke were very close in age and grew up together at 17 St. Mary's Street. Also, Luke married late so, when John returned to Edinburgh between tours he would stay with his mother, Helen. Luke and Helen lived together for many years until Luke married Patricia Campsie. Luke Boylan was a very successful pawnbroker in the Old Town, then, when his father, old Philip Boylan died, Luke, as his eldest son, inherited all his property. He was a very wealthy young man. When his half-sister, Eleanor Lennon (nee Boylan), died in 1890, Luke also inherited all her property. She owned over 45 houses and shops in Edinburgh and Leith, and lived in a mansion house (with 17 windows!) in Leith, which she named Warrick House after her late mother, Dorothy (old Philip Boylan's first wife). Perhaps John thought his half-brother would look after his namesake in the future. It may well be that Luke Boylan did that but we have no way of proving it.

The Delaney family have a wonderful photograph of John Sylvester Delaney taken in Plymouth at the time of Luke Terence's birth, showing a handsome man with clear eyes (We know they were a startling blue because of the *Greppo* painting, and because the trait has continued in John's descendants) and slightly receding dark hair.

Like Elizabeth, in her photograph, John is very well dressed in a smart wool suit, with shirt and tie and he also looks very prosperous indeed.

In the 1881 census John, Elizabeth and Luke Terence, are living at 11 Upper Marsh Street, Lambeth, London.

On 27 August 1881, John is reprising his role for a Season at the Greenwich Theatre, playing in *The Shaughraun*, *The Factory Girl* and Boucicault's famous anti-slavery play, *The Octoroon*.

Earlier that year, John is appearing at Astleys and Dukes Theatre, London in a Starring Tour of "*Land Ahead.*" This play was written by George Manville Fenn and John is playing the part of *Terry Rooney.*

A Reviewer writes -

"In *Land Ahead* the best rendered part was the *Terry Rooney* of a thoroughly experienced Irish comedian, MR DELANEY.......who, to the delight of the Gallery, introduced a live pig on the scene".

Another Review comments -

"The major part of the acting in *Land Ahead* falls to the share of MR DELANEY......who acted the dreamy poetic Irishman to the life."

Earlier in his career, when John was beginning to make a name for himself, he had appeared in a production of *Land Ahead*. A very snooty Reviewer wrote -

"The bills inform me that MR.J.S. DELANEY, Irish comedian, has been specially engaged for the part of Terry Rooney. The name of the gentleman is not a very familiar one (to him!) and I am sure it would puzzle me to tell where he acquired the fame which should entitle him to a 'special engagement'. Let me however do him the justice to say that he is a very good actor indeed".

George Manville Fenn, born 1831 in London, is now a largely unknown literary icon and educationalist of the Victorian era, but he was hugely successful in John's time. His main fame rests in his novels, especially books for young adults. He published over 100 such books, plus political journalism. He was an important Socialist writer, and his writing was much lauded by Charles Dickens.

He wrote just a few plays of which *Land Ahead* was the most popular so his name would prove a big draw to John's theatre production. He lived until 1909 by which time he had built up a library of 25,000 books in his home, Syon Lodge, in Isleworth.

In 1882, John is appearing with the Dion Boucicault Company, on tour, with a programme of plays, including roles as *Feeney*, *Harvey Duff* in *The Shaughraun*, and *Larry* in the play, *Youth*.

In the same year their second child, a daughter, Kathleen, presumably named after Elizabeth's mother, is born to them on 19 November 1882. They are living at 38 Hastings Street, Pancras, London. Elizabeth registers the birth on 18 December, presumably since John was working away. A week later he opens in the pantomime, *Mrs Sinbad*, playing the leading role at the Theatre Royal in Bradford. Elizabeth must have been a very resilient woman to cope alone.

In 1883, he is again touring as *Conn in The Shaughraun*, appearing in theatres in London, Leeds and throughout the provinces leaving Elizabeth at home with the two children.

Later that year, John is back home when he plays the part of *Job A. Croggs* in *Child of Charity* at the Elephant & Castle Theatre. The couple are living nearby at 31 The Palatinate, Rodney Place, off the New Kent Road. This unusual name was given to two six-storey blocks, erected in 1875, and designed "to provide convenient and healthy dwellings at moderate rents" to enable those "of a grade higher in the social scale" to live nearer their work. At the time the flats were put up they were an experiment in housing, with shops on the ground floor. So the couple were living in fairly upmarket accommodation.

When John and Elizabeth were first married she travelled around with him to wherever he was appearing. Depending on how long the run of his production was they would live in theatrical digs or rented accommodation. Their first child, Luke Terence Delaney, was born in rented accommodation in Plymouth, during John's run at the Theatre Royal there. Obviously, since John had to go where the productions were being staged, there would have been no point in buying a property, even though John's earnings at that time would have made it possible. Luke Terence was also baptised at the Catholic Church in Plymouth. In later life he was to describe himself as 'a lapsed Catholic'.

On 18 June 1883, a third child, John William, presumably named after Elizabeth's father, was born to them at 31 The Palatinate,

Rodney Place, Newington, London. (When John William Delaney was baptised on 30 March, 1884, in St. Patrick's Church in Edinburgh, he was nine months old.)

Tragically, not long after his birth, his sister, Kathleen, died of convulsions, from a baby form of tuberculosis, aged almost two, at 31 The Palatinate, Rodney Place, Newington, London. John registers Kathleen's death on 13 October 1884, and states he was present at her death. This must have been a traumatic experience for the couple watching their little daughter die in such a distressing manner, and Elizabeth was also nursing a four-month old baby.

It must have been with a heavy heart that John had to leave Elizabeth, and his sons, to travel to Oldham. He was hired to appear in the same part that had won him such acclaim previously at the Theatre Royal, in Bradford, in the leading role in *Mrs Sinbad*.

In December 1884, just before Christmas, he had booked into theatrical digs at 3 Coronation Street, Oldham, and had begun rehearsals for the pantomime. But it was a role he was never to perform.

A newspaper cutting, kept by the family, reported -

"MR J S DELANEY, the popular Irish comedian, who had been rehearsing the character of *Mrs O Sinbad* for the Oldham pantomime was taken ill in that town, immediately preceding that production, and was at once conveyed to the local infirmary. We regret to state that he expired on Saturday last."

It goes on to say - "His part has been filled by Mr F. Kenward." - The show must go on!

In another co-incidence, Frank Kenward, had played the lead role of *Rob Roy* to John's supporting role of *Major Galbraith*, in the play, in John's first year of theatrical performances in Edinburgh in 1870.

John Sylvester Delaney's death certificate states that he died on the 27 December 1884 of Alcoholism, aged 36, at the Union Workhouse, Municipal, H.S.D. Oldham. He had been admitted on the 23 December with Delirioum Tremens and died 4 days later.

I was not shocked when I learned that John had died of Alcoholism, but I was surprised.

The world of Victorian Theatre would, no doubt, be a hard drinking one.

But what surprised me is that nothing in the rest of John's story, that I had researched, gave any hint of excessive alcohol abuse.

He had worked continuously since his days in Edinburgh. He had achieved success very early in his career, touring America in the role of *Greppo,* for over 300 consecutive nights, and continuing without any break, or suggestion of 'resting,' into tours in Canada and the West Indies, before returning to Britain and becoming a famous actor, especially in his Irish roles. Working through his collection of glowing Reviews, his work ethic and his energy levels seem phenomenal. One would imagine, considering how expensive it was to mount these theatre productions, and especially the tours, that any of the famous Theatre Managers he worked with would be wary of giving him these major roles if there was any danger of him letting them down through alcohol abuse. Yet they continued to use him, year after year, and even his last part in *Mrs O Sinbad* was a starring role.

On a personal level I can't imagine that Elizabeth would have married an alcoholic when she was only 22 with her whole life ahead of her. Then there is the photographic evidence. The photograph of John in Plymouth in 1879, the year his son Luke Terence was born, shows a man with clear skin and clear eyes, no suggestion of excessive alcohol abuse on his face.

Something just didn't add up.

During my research into the wider Delaney family tree I was surprised at how many of them died young. Time and again the cause of death was a heart condition that we now know to be genetic. John's parents lost three infants shortly after birth. His brother James, who was an artist and a photographer, and who is my great, great grandfather, died at 45, of the same genetic heart condition as did three of his grandchildren, and John's aunt, Jane Delaney, and his cousin, Sarah Murray.

When John was rushed from his theatrical digs to the hospital attached to the local Workhouse the doctor would not know who he was. Could it have been that the symptoms John was displaying had been caused by a cardiac attack? A doctor, attached to a Workhouse, in those days would hardly be an expert on genetic heart disease. Indeed, little was known anywhere, at that time, about the causes and treatment of heart disease.

However, further confusion arises because of his death certificate.

It states that he died in the Workhouse. (He didn't. He died in the local Infirmary which, in those pre-NHS days, was the public hospital which was always attached to the Workhouse.)

The connotation of the Workhouse suggests he was destitute. (He wasn't. He was about to appear in a starring role in the pantomime and was living in theatrical digs in Oldham, while Elizabeth and his sons were living in good accommodation in London).

Because of the circumstances, and place, of John's death, normal procedures were followed and, three days later, he was buried in common ground in the local cemetery in Oldham. Before Elizabeth could even make arrangements for his funeral John was already buried.

The apparent circumstances around John Sylvester Delaney's death always troubled us, so many years later, as more records went online, my brother, Michael Delaney, who was a journalist, started to investigate the town's burial records.

He discovered that, in the haste of burial, it appears that John's death was confused with the death of an inmate of the Workhouse, around the same time, and John was buried under the other man's name!

Michael and I felt pretty sure that the cause of death on John's certificate, was in fact that of the other man. In the chaotic conditions of the workhouse the two men had been confused for how else could John have been buried under another man's name?

But, long after the event, there is no way that we could prove our theory regarding his death.

However, the existence of that death certificate has cast a shadow over the life of John Sylvester Delaney, that I hope has now been lifted by the true details of his remarkable life.

If we had to find a word or a phrase that would sum up John Sylvester Delaney they would be 'laughter' and 'He was a very good actor indeed.'

Not a bad epitaph for the boy from Edinburgh's 'Little Ireland', who brought such joy and happiness to so many people living all around the world, and in grim, industrial towns in Britain.

John Sylvester Delaney was one of the biggest stars to grace the stage of the Victorian Theatre.

CHAPTER ELEVEN

"GLORY, GLORY, TO THE HIBEES"

After John Sylvester Delaney gave up his secure job as a printer and set forth to find fame as an actor, Fr Edward Hannan launched another initiative for his Catholic Young Men's Society (CYMS). The CYMS, founded on 5 October 1865, met in St. Joseph's Hall on Horse Wynd in the Old Town, and it was there that John Sylvester Delaney honed his skills in their Dramatic Society.

Another member of the CYMS was Michael Whelehan. He had been born in Co. Roscommon, in Ireland, in 1854, and moved with his family to Edinburgh's Old Town, when he was four years old. Like John Sylvester Delaney he was apprenticed to the Printing Trade. Leaving school, aged ten, Michael went to work in the Miller & Richard type foundry behind Nicholson Street.

In this chapter I have drawn heavily on the research and writing of the late Alan Lugton. He was kind enough to give me his permission to quote from his book. Having known Alan, and his love for Hibernian Football Club, I know he would be happy to see these accounts from his Magisterial book – 'The Making of Hibernian' – which was published in 1995, receive another airing.

It would be impossible to tell the story of 'Little Ireland' without telling the story of the Hibernian Football Club – the two are inextricably linked.

In his book Alan Lugton tells of how Michael Whelehan and two friends from the St. Patrick's CYMS were watching the increasingly popular game of football being played on The Meadows, just a short walk from where he worked. His friends, Malachy Byrne and Andy Hughes, had already played a couple of games for a street team named White Star but this did not last long when it was discovered they were Irish Catholics. Prejudice against the Irish was rife in Edinburgh – they were regarded as undesirable aliens.

As Michael watched with his friends from the sidelines he determined that the CYMS should form their own football team. When he approached Fr Hannan with his idea it met with the priest's approval. When the proposal was put to the CYMS at a meeting in St. Mary's Halls it was greeted with enthusiasm. Intense discussion took place on what the name of the team should be and it was again Whelehan who came up with the name -'Hibernian'. This was the Latin name for an Irishman – and thus an appropriate one for the Edinburgh Irishmen.

Alan Lugton tells how a special occasion was about to be celebrated by St. Patrick's CYMS – the centenary of the birth of Daniel O'Connell - the champion of Catholic Emancipation. The date was Friday 6 August 1875. It was thought to be an auspicious date on which to launch Hibernian Football Club. It also shows that Ireland's concerns were still followed closely by the exiles in 'Little Ireland'.

"The day started with Holy Mass in St. Patrick's and in the evening in St. Mary's Street Hall there were speeches on the life of Daniel O'Connell and a concert of Irish song and dance. In the middle of the evening, amidst great excitement, Father Hannan officially launched Hibernian Football Club and by popular acclaim Father Hannan was elected 'Manager' and life President. Fr Hannan, in turn, handed over a set of strips, white with green trimmings and a harp on the breast. Michael Whelehan was then elected to be the first captain of Hibernian Football Club." (Lugton)

All seemed fair then for Hibernian to enter into the world of Scottish Football but they had underestimated the virulent prejudice they were to meet. When they applied to join the Scottish Football Association, which would have allowed them to play competitive games with other clubs, they were curtly dismissed, out of hand, with the words - "We are catering for Scotsmen not Irishmen".

Such prejudice seems astonishing to us given that the Irish had been living in the town for some 75 years.

With the SFA's rejection the Edinburgh Football Association then issued instructions to all member clubs that under no circumstances should they play any matches or have any contact with Hibernian.

"It could not have been made any clearer to the Irishmen that like all the other spheres of their lives they were just not welcome." (Lugton)

122

But the Hibernian team were resolute and they continued to play games on the Meadows early on Saturday mornings. It was first come first served so the Irishmen would carry their goalposts to the Meadows at about six in the morning to mark out their pitch. They had to mount guards because other teams were liable to dispute their chosen spot. At first it was members of the CYMS who acted as guards but anti-Catholic mobs often attacked them, not wishing the Irishmen to have the use of the Meadows, which was a public space open to all. Things got so bad that eventually the young guards were reinforced by other men from 'Little Ireland' who were navvies and coal-heavers - the mobs disappeared like magic!

The Chapel of Ease (the first St Patrick's Church) had been built in 1835, on Lothian Street, just a short walk from the East Meadows. It was now used as St. Mary's School and Fr Hannan allowed the Hibernian Team to use it as changing rooms.

These practice matches continued in the hope that another team would be prepared to defy the Edinburgh Football Association and give the Irishmen a match.

The first team to do so, of all teams, was Heart of Midlothian who were later to become Hibernian's great rivals! They played on Christmas Day 1875 – the score was a 1-0 win for Hearts. Other teams broke the ban. The XI of Thistle played Hibernian on 15 January 1876 – Hibs winning by one goal. Another game, between the two first teams, played on Saturday 1 February, resulted in a no-scoring draw. Then on the 4 March the 2nd team of Hibernian and the 2nd team of highly rated Hanover met in a no-scoring draw. The Edinburgh Football Association was not pleased and though Heart of Midlothian had agreed to play another game against Hibernian they did not turn up. Shortly afterwards Hearts went out of existence due to lack of support. They were later to reform.

Fr Hannan and Michael Whelehan continued to canvas support among the other football teams for their new application to the football authorities. The response from the leading teams was favourable and the breakthrough came when Mr Frank Watt, a leading light of the Edinburgh Football Association, assured them of his support. He had the vision to foresee the crowd-pulling potential of matches involving an Irish team. This time their application to join the Scottish Football Association was accepted.

Over the years Hibernian grew into one of the most successful football teams in Scotland winning trophies and shields along the way. They also built their own football ground near Easter Road.

On St Patrick's Day 1885, some ten years after they had been formed, the CYMS gave their football team an official Reception. In a speech Fr Hannan said that "Hibernian are a credit not only to the Irish of Edinburgh but the whole of Scotland". Michael Whelehan replied - "Hibernian are pledged to become the best in the country, not for personal glory, but to increase the charitable work of the CYMS and to give a real sense of pride to all of Ireland's exiled children in Scotland.".(Lugton)

One of the CYMS's aims was to raise funds for charitable causes and Hibernian Football team were attracting such huge crowds to their matches that the takings going to charitable causes were considerable.

They played an incredible number of matches for charity. The miners of Loanhead were on strike for better pay and conditions and the families were beginning to experience real hardship. They asked Hibernian if they could arrange a charity match with Heart of Midlothian to raise funds. Fr Hannan agreed because he thought their cause was just, but Heart of Midlothian refused to take part so Hibernian made a generous direct contribution from their own funds.

"On September 25th 1886 Hibernian played two games, one after the other, at Easter Road. The first against Middlesborough they won by ten goals to two. Immediately afterwards they played Vale of Midlothian, in the Edinburgh FA Shield first round, and won by five goals to nil. At the same time, a mile away on Leith Links, a junior player, Willie Davidson, collapsed and died in the middle of a match. His family had been dependant on his wages and so his friends arranged a charity match between Edinburgh Thistle and Woodburn. Knowing Hibernian's willingness always to help a worthy cause, the Irishmen were approached to see if Hibernian Park could be used for the match. They agreed and they also made a generous contribution to the family." (Lugton)

Amazingly, to help boost the charity match takings, Hibernian allowed their star player, Willie Groves, one of the best footballers in Scotland, to play in the match! This, despite the fact that Hibernian themselves were playing away that same afternoon, so Groves went from one match to the other.

The Davidsons and their friends were Protestant so it was interesting that it was Hibernian they approached for help rather than any other club. A sign perhaps that, at long last, the Irish team was gaining acceptance in Edinburgh. The CYMS's ethos was that charity was their moving force and any gate money, after the teams expenses, went to good causes. The players were not paid.

The afternoon match that Hibernian played that same day was against Mossend Swifts, in West Calder, in the Scottish Cup second round, and the score was a one-one draw. Hibernian won the replay by three goals to nil.

In spite of their many successes, and rising status in Scottish Football, Hibernian had never won that Cup. The Scottish Cup was the Holy Grail of Scottish Football.

On Saturday 23 October, at Easter Road, Hibernian faced Heart of Midlothian in the third round of the Scottish Cup and won the match five goals to one.

The fifth round of the Scottish Cup was played against Queen of the South Wanderers at Hibernian Park which Hibernian won seven goals to three. On Christmas Day they met Third Lanark in the sixth round, quarter final, of the Scottish Cup, at Cathkin Park, which Hibernian won two goals to one.

New Year 1887 came in cold and frosty. In January Hibernian played former Scottish Cup winners, Vale of Leven, in the semi final at Easter Road, which Hibernian won three goals to one.

The date was now set for the Scottish Cup Final between Hibernian and Dumbarton, the best team in Scotland at that time.

"Saturday 12th February 1887 was to be a day long remembered by the Irish in Scotland. Hibernian, remember, were playing more than just a game of football. No other Irish organisation in any field had reached such prominence in Scottish affairs and the pressure on Hibernian to win was tremendous. A victory would be an affirmation of Irish pride a chance to say to Scotland, we've really arrived at last, we are part of your country and we're here to stay. Defeat was unthinkable" (Lugton)

In his book – 'The Making of Hibernian' – Alan Lugton gives a vivid description of that momentous day.

The game was to be played at Hampden Park in Glasgow and special trains were laid on to transport the huge numbers expected to attend. A special train carried the Hibernian players and club officials. There were still not enough seats to meet the demand, and so the rail company laid on freight carriages, normally used to transport goods, and even cattle! The Irish navvies and miners could not afford even those fares and so they set off early, walking all the way to Glasgow. The club had come up with the novel idea that everyone attending should wear something in the Hibernian colours and so most men wore a green tie, or a green hankie in their top pocket. Strange to think of it today when supporters of every team turn up at matches wearing replica strips often costing nearly one hundred pounds.

When the team and club officials arrived in Glasgow they were met by politicians, clergy and prominent businessmen from the Irish community in Glasgow and were escorted to their train onwards to Hampden. The Hibernian team officials and guests from the Glasgow community took their place in the stand. And then the singing broke out in the crowd - the Dumbarton supporters had never heard the like! 'God Save Ireland' the supporters sang and the team joined in from the dressing room below. The Irish navvies and miners, having walked all the way from Edinburgh, arrived just before the kick-off. Hearing the singing they rushed the gates and broke into the park - the police were powerless to stop them.

According to Alan Lugton - "Fifteen thousand paid for entry, but over twenty thousand attended, the biggest crowd to date for a Scottish Cup final".

When play began it was obvious it was going to be a rough game and the referee was kept busy!Dumbarton scored first, then Hibernian equalised – the crowd was in an uproar. Then 'Darlin' Willie Groves, the famous Hibernian player who had played in the charity match for Willie Davidson's family to boost the takings, went on one of his famous dribbling runs up the park and put the ball in the net. For the last ten minutes the noise from the terraces was indescribable. With the score at two goals to one for Hibernian the players were carried shoulder high from the pitch.

"There was an air of disbelief about what had just happened. Hibernian had done the impossible and won the greatest prize in Scottish football. The team from Edinburgh's poor Irish neighbourhood had actually won the Scottish Cup!" (Lugton)

The Hibernian team and officials were then taken to St. Mary's Hall, in the east end of Glasgow, to receive the official congratulation from councillors and dignitaries of the Irish community there and treated to a fine meal.

Alan Lugton quotes an extract from a speech given, at the meal, by a Dr Conway. Glasgow had a much larger Irish community than Edinburgh but Celtic had not yet been formed so Hibernian carried the hopes of all the Irish in Scotland

Reading the speech you can get a sense of just where the Irish in Scotland stood.

".......Their (Hibernian's) conspicuous success today was no doubt mainly due to their own heroic exertions, but if the ardent hopes and fervent prayers of large numbers of their countrymen on the field, and a multitude of them unable to be present, had any efficacy at all they must be credited with helping towards the good result. The performance of Hibernian evidences that they must be possessed of the greatest pluck, skill and perseverance to have achieved such a glorious result amongst a host of competitors animated not only by rivalry which is the usual concomitant of the game but, I am sorry to say, by a bigotry so great as to be a much stronger incentive to exertion than any mere desire for victory could possibly be. Now we all desire to give Hibernian that high commendation that they have so well earned, and it has become proverbial that imitation is the sincerest form of flattery, I think we could not please them better than by following their example each in our own department and seeking by the exercise of those same good qualities that have placed them so high among the football fraternity to place ourselves among the best men in our respective vocations. The effect of this upon our own happiness will not be the only good result derived, for each advance will increase vastly the weight of our influence, and so enable us to render more efficient assistance towards obtaining for our country that the united political sagacity of our trusted leaders has indicated as the first essential to her happiness, namely Home Government for Ireland. I have now, gentlemen, the greatest pleasure in proposing the health and continued success of Hibernian football club."

From this it is obvious that Hibernian's success extended far beyond the football field and into the wider experience of the exiled Irish in Scotland and further still into their aspirations for their mother country.

While Hibernian were being feted in Glasgow, back home in Edinburgh those who had not travelled to the game had been receiving updates on the score, by telegraph, at Irish shops in Edinburgh including Paddy McGraill's shop at 266 Canongate (The premises still exist to this day.) and Higgins Football Arms, Hill Place, on the south side. The news of the victory spread like wildfire through 'Little Ireland'.

Word was received that the team would arrive at Waverley Station at 10pm. The streets of the Old Town were filled with wildly celebrating Irishmen (and women). When the team arrived the station was thronged with supporters who carried the players, shoulder high, to a waiting horse-drawn brake draped with large banners one proclaiming "Welcome to Hibernian – Winners of the Scottish Cup 1886-1887" and the other "God Save Ireland". Two flute bands, that of the CYMS the other Leith Harp, led the procession up onto the Waverley Bridge, then along Princes Street and over the North Bridge to the Tron Kirk.There a huge crowd, of what must have seemed the entire population of 'Little Ireland', lined the High Street as the Young Ireland Flute Band led the brake down to St. Mary's Halls.

As the Delaney family were, and are by tradition, lifelong Hibernian supporters, I have no doubt every member of the extended family would have been in the crowd to welcome their heroes home.

In St. Mary's Street itself, where all our Delaney family ancestors had first settled fifty years before, green limelights had been placed in every window of every tenement, casting a green glow over the whole street.

The doors of St. Mary's Halls stood wide open as Michael Flannigan, the President of the CYMS, welcomed the team home. Inside, a Reception was held with over one thousand attending.

The unbelievable had happened, the team from poor 'Little Ireland' had won the Scottish Cup!

The celebrations continued out on the streets as the Irish danced and sang and, also unbelievably, the police announced there had been no arrests!

Hibernian continued to go from strength to strength, attracting huge crowds wherever they played and winning cups and shields. They had a huge support, not just from 'Little Ireland,' but throughout Scotland from all the Irish immigrants who saw Hibernian as 'their team'.

On 13 August 1887, as Scottish Champions, Hibernian played Preston North End, the English Champions, for the title of 'Champions of the World,' at Easter Road, and beat them two goals to one. Hibernian were the 'Champions of the World'!

The following Saturday Glasgow Rangers opened their new ground at Ibrox Park. Their opponents for this Gala occasion were Preston North End. With the score standing at eight goals to one, in favour of the English team, the fans invaded the pitch and the match had to be abandoned. This shows just what an amazing team Hibernian were at that time to have beaten Preston North End.

But the team's fortune was about to change. Ironically, their decline began as a result of football, religion and politics.

Brother Walfrid had appealed to Hibernian on many occasions for donations towards his 'Poor Children's Table' charity which he ran in Glasgow's East End. Hibernian had been generous supporters of the charity and had given the proceeds of charity matches to Brother Walfrid. He realised he could not expect to rely on the Edinburgh Team's charity forever as they also had to support the poor in 'Little Ireland'. The idea grew in his mind to form an Irish Catholic Team in Glasgow. Many in Glasgow's Irish community disapproved. They were all loyal Hibernian supporters, as were many elsewhere in Scotland, and felt it was disloyal to the team who had brought such credit to Scotland's Catholic Community.

However, after several stormy meetings, at a final meeting on Sunday 6 November 1887, in his Church Halls in Glasgow, Brother Walfrid and his supporters formally founded their own football club. It was to be called Glasgow Celtic. Though instrumental in founding Celtic, Brother Walfrid was never more than a figurehead, unlike Canon Hannan in Edinburgh. The real influence lay in the hands of a group of Irish businessmen who had been quick to spot the financial rewards that football could bring to them. They quickly saw the potential of professional football. Five days after that meeting the Celtic Committee leased six acres of wasteland for £50 per annum, to create the first Celtic Park, in the Parkhead area of Glasgow.

On St. Patrick's Day 1888, the usual parade had taken place through 'Little Ireland' followed by mass at St. Patrick's Church. That afternoon Hibernian played Hearts at Easter Road, the game ending in a three all draw. To celebrate St. Patrick's Day, Hibernian donated their share of the gate money to the Edinburgh Corporation Poor Children's Fund - one of their favourite charities. In the evening St. Mary's Street Halls were packed for a concert to celebrate the Irish patron saint's Day. Speeches were also given on Charles Stewart Parnell's new 'Plan of Campaign and Boycotting' in Ireland which St Patrick's CYMS openly supported.

"The Catholic Church authorities, and even the Pope himself, were closely considering the implications of this new Irish initiative and the consequences of this were to damage Hibernian as much as the rise of Celtic." (Lugton).

Charles Stewart Parnell was a Protestant Irish Nationalist politician who served as a Member of Parliament (MP) in the British House of Commons from 1875 to 1891. He agitated for Land Reform in Ireland as Leader of the Home Rule for Ireland Land League.

In 'Little Ireland' memories of the oppression of the Irish peasantry, famine and exile remained very strong. After all, that was how most of the Irish came to be in the Old Town anyway. From the beginning of settlement Irish politics remained of continuing importance in 'Little Ireland'.

Hibernian decided to go on a tour to Belfast that Easter. The purpose of this tour was to raise funds to aid Catholic victims of Orange Party pogroms which had been orchestrated by Unionist politicians, against Irish Home Rule. An excited Hibernian party departed for their first ever trip to Ireland. The team was warmly welcomed in the city. They won their first match, against Belfast Distillery, by three goals to one and at their second, an even bigger crowd turned out to see them defeat United Belfast by four goals to one. They left Belfast with a multitude of invitations to return. All seemed fair for continuing success.

"Since leasing their six acres of ground, Celtic had put in an enormous amount of work and now had an excellent ground with a well-grassed, level pitch surrounded by a cycling track and a grandstand that could hold a thousand spectators. Beneath the stand was a pavilion, dressing rooms, committee rooms and all modern conveniences. This was a fine achievement in only six months. The money Hibernian and countless others had donated had been well spent. Finally, Celtic Park was ready to be opened –but Celtic were missing the most important thing – a team" (Lugton)

Again the Glasgow Irish turned to their fellow-countrymen, Hibernian, for help. Again, like so many times in the past, Hibernian came to their aid. A match took place on the 8 May and was advertised as 'An Exhibition Day' featuring Hibernian against Cowlairs. The match ended in a no-scoring draw but the crowd went home satisfied at a fine display of football. Celtic were delighted, as well they might, as they benefited from the whole of the gate money.

After the match the team were given supper in the Royal Hotel in George Square at which Celtic's Honorary President, Doctor Conway, proposed a toast to Hibernian. John McFadden, Secretary of Hibernian, replied, wishing the Celtic club well and hoping that some time in the future they would see Celtic Football Club presented with the Scottish Cup.

Hibernian had no problem with a team from the Irish community in Glasgow being formed, especially since Celtic had stated they would draw players from the west of Scotland Irish. A week after Hibernian had played at the opening benefit match at Celtic Park they played Mossend Swifts in the final of the Rosebery Charity Cup, at neutral Tynecastle, and won by a single goal.

"This was to be the last Hibernian victory in a prominent competition for several years and the star studded squad of players that had been painstakingly put together would soon be no more."(Lugton)

On 21 May, His Grace, Archbishop William Smith, of the Diocese of St. Andrews and Edinburgh, attended a meeting in St Mary's Street Halls. The meeting was held by the St Patrick's branch of the St.Vincent de Paul Society. This charitable Society existed to care for the poor. It is still in existence to this day, still supporting those in need in many parishes throughout Scotland. The Archbishop used the meeting to launch a blistering attack on

St. Patrick's CYMS for their support of Charles Stewart Parnell's – 'Plan of Campaign and Boycotting in Ireland' - which Pope Leo XIII had condemned in a Papal Rescript.

"The Archbishop was furious that a Catholic organization, in Catholic premises, was flaunting the Papal Rescript and warned that - "Politics could not be put before faith."."(Lugton)

Perhaps, as a Protestant convert to Catholicism, the Archbishop could not be expected to know that, for Irish Catholics, their religious faith and their involvement in the politics and history of their persecuted homeland could not be separated. After all it was because of their faith that the Irish had suffered throughout their history.

"The writing was now on the wall for the men of St. Patrick's, and though they did not realise it then, they were, within a few short months, aided by the rise of Celtic and the wrath of Archbishop Smith, to be plunged into a deep crisis from which Hibernian would never fully recover." (Lugton)

On the 28 May, 1888, Celtic played their first game at Celtic Park, in their own right, and ironically, it was against Glasgow Rangers!

Celtic had still not managed to put together a full team so, once again, Hibernian came to the rescue and loaned them seven players who regularly played for Hibernian and John McFadden accepted Celtic's invitation to referee the match. This seems very odd to us now but, of course, we have to remember that none of these teams were professionals. On this occasion Rangers lost by five goals to two against what was basically a 'Hibernian 'Select.' On 16 June, Mossend Swifts played at Celtic Park against a Celtic team that had five Hibernian 'guest' players.

"Rumours had begun circulating that Celtic were trying to poach some of these players and others as well, but the Hibernian Committee disregarded the gossip completely, deciding it was so fantastic it did not merit attention." (Lugton)

Two weeks later Hibernian brought the Season to an end playing Clydebank, at Dalmuir, and losing two goals to one.

"Very few of Hibernian's Committee travelled with the team that day as, along with the rest of 'Little Ireland', they were attending a mass demonstration in the Queen's Park in support of the imprisoned

Irish MP, John Dillon, a staunch supporter of the 'Plan of Campaign and Boycotting'. Despite warnings from Archbishop Smith and the calming influence of Canon Hannan, Michael Flannigan delivered a strong speech in the MP's defence at this very public meeting" (Lugton)

In Glasgow, Celtic did not have any problems with the Church. Their parishes did not have a Catholic Young Mens Society branch nor did the businessmen who founded Celtic support the Irish Home Rule Movement. This seems strange to us today when Celtic is considered the Premier Catholic team in Scotland, wears green strips, and has been criticized for flying the Irish Tricolour at Parkhead. Ironic too, that years of sectarianism in Scotland has resulted, pitting 'Protestant' Glasgow Rangers against Celtic, a club that, according to a commentator, at that time, was neither very Irish nor very Catholic.

"In fact John Glass, and his influential partners on the Celtic Committee, deliberately steered Celtic clear of direct involvement with the Catholic Church or Irish politics as they needed complete independence of action to develop their business plans." (Lugton)

Meanwhile Celtic did not have a team and it was at this point that John Glass and his partners, unknown to the rest of the large Celtic Committee, made direct financial inducements to the top players in the Hibernian team to come and play for Celtic.

"During the summer of 1888, 'Little Ireland was rife with rumours that some of Hibernian's top players had been enticed to join Celtic with financial inducements." (Lugton)

Hibernian refused to believe the rumours, they could not believe that their Irish 'brothers' in Glasgow could betray them in this way, after all the support the team had given them and all the considerable donations they had made to Brother Walfrid for his 'Poor Children's Table' charity. But by early August, just before the Season started, they found it was true. Six Hibernian players plus four others who had agreed to play for Hibernian that Season also joined Celtic.

Hibernian were shocked.

"To be fair the vast majority of Celtic's numerous committee were equally shocked for this had been the work solely of John Glass and his cohorts" (Lugton)

"The summer of 1889 saw the unhappy members of Celtic's Committee at fever pitch as their fellow committee men were reneging on every principle on which the club had been founded. Brother Walfrid had quickly been swept aside by John Glass and his business partners, who were not following the principles the malcontents thought they should, and on top of that, they were paying the players and buying them public houses, which the Catholic Church had strongly condemned" (Lugton)

Many of the Celtic Committee were disgusted at this betrayal and they broke away and tried to form an alternative team, calling it Glasgow Hibernian. They tried to get Hibernian to join them but the Edinburgh team were committed to 'Little Ireland' and the team's charitable ethos.

Hibernian, of course, was a team run strictly on amateur lines with all profits, after the teams expenses, going to charitable causes.

"......even if they had wanted to try and match Celtic, they wouldn't have been able to, since all their gate money went to charity with only enough kept back for the basic running of the club and travelling and player expenses. In other words, for all their success and popularity, Hibernian were broke. Professionalism was on the horizon and John Glass had quickly grasped the financial possibilities of an instantly successful Celtic" (Lugton)

The press were quick to pick up on the ramifications of Celtic's actions.

"During the past few months, the prospect of a rival Irish Catholic football combination in Edinburgh and Glasgow, Hibernian and Celtic, have been freely talked about and the probable composition of the elevens having given rise to speculation in football circles. Since the publication of the Hibernian card, the opening match against Celtic in Glasgow, has been anticipated with more than ordinary eagerness..... The interest is highlighted by the very uncertain situation that prevails at Hibernian's Headquarters in St. Mary's Street Halls as many of their top players have gone over to Celtic........The encounter with Celtic will indeed be interesting as will be Hibernian's future"

A report from a Glasgow publication was more open and honest about the situation and the names of the players that Celtic intended to field, told it's own story.

"It is seldom that an "amateur" club commences it's career under such favourable conditions as the Celts, a team who will not have to begin at the bottom and fight their way up, but enter the area with a team composed for the most part of players who have already made their name in the football world, picked from the best Catholic football players in the country...........They begin the season with a match against Edinburgh Hibernian at Celtic Park.........The Celts will play the following team: Dunning, MacLachlan, McKeown, Gallagher, Kelly, McLaren, McCallum, Coogan, Groves,Coleman and O'Connor."

Celtic did indeed have the best of starts. Unlike Hibernian, at it's founding in 1875, it did not have to battle prejudice and sectarianism to gain acceptance in football in Scotland. Hibernian's ideals and behaviour, as well as the huge contributions the team had made to a wide range of charities, had won them friends and respect from all sections of Scottish society. They had trained and brought on a pool of footballing talent of young Irishmen from the community of 'Little Ireland' and built their own stadium at Easter Road. Over more than ten years,they had built up their young team to the point that they had risen to the very top of Scottish Football. They had won the coveted Scottish Cup and became the 'Champions of the World', competing against top teams in England. They had made generous donations towards the building of Celtic Park and allowed their players to 'guest' for Celtic at matches to raise funds for the new club.

A report on the Hibernian v Celtic game stated -

"The meeting of Hibernian and Celtic at Glasgow on Saturday ushered in another football season. The fixture had an interesting aspect as before the event the decision to play the match divided the Hibernian camp, and whether they will stand or fall is a question that must be discussed because of its great bearing on local football in the future.....Hibernian had helped Celtic get started in every possible way, even allowing their best players to guest for them in early matches, while they tried to put a team together. Hibernian of course did not wish to cut their throats and it appears there was an unwritten agreement that Celtic would not interfere with their players. During the summer months it appears that several Hibernian players became located in Glasgow and from appearances of friendly encouragement they assisted Celtic in some matches. Appearances as weeks went on proved to be deceptive with six top Hibernian players going over to Celtic. What the players had to gain in a football sense by their new steps is difficult to imagine, but many will suggest the answers to be the fleshpots of Egypt and cynics will explain the defection by quoting a proverb about rats deserting a sinking ship. It can be imagined that Hibernian were in dire straits to put together a decent team to cope with the hand picked eleven of Celtic on Saturday. Although beaten, it was the scratch Hibernian team that had the bulk of the support at Parkhead showing they still have many friends in Glasgow."

Of course, Hibernian were in no way a sinking ship - until the six players deserted.

Still reeling from the betrayal they had experienced Hibernian were now to receive a further shattering blow.

"It took place at a meeting of St Patrick's CYMS on 7th August 1888. The Society had continued it's political support for the Irish Home Rule 'Plan of Campaign and Boycotting', particularly at St. Mary's Street Halls, which were, of course, Catholic premises, despite the Papal Rescript's condemnation of the Plan as a vehicle of possible violence which the church would never tolerate."(Lugton)

Archbishop William Smith was determined to enforce the Papal Rescript and despite meetings and pleading from Canon Hannan, who argued that their was no evidence that this attempt to bring justice to the oppressed people of Ireland would have a violent outcome (Remember he was Irish born himself and an educated man who knew well the history of his poor country.) he also pointed out that the Plan was supported by Ireland's most respected MPs. It was all to no avail despite no such action being taken by any other Catholic Archbishop in Britain or Ireland he was determined to punish St. Patrick's parish.

At the next meeting of the CYMS Canon Hannan rose and read out a letter from the Archbishop.

"Dear Canon Hannan,

In your capacity as spiritual director of the Edinburgh CYMS you are requested to read to the members of the said Society at their next meeting the following announcement: Considering that respect for the authority of the Holy See is the foundation of Catholic order and organisation, and in disregard of that authority, Michael Flannigan, President of the CYMS, has given scandal by presiding at public meetings, where without protest on his part, the Plan of Campaign and Boycotting, were defended, in spite of their condemnation by the Holy Father, and considering moreover, that he has not embraced the opportunity afforded him of expressing regret for such conduct and so repairing the scandal given, the said Michael Flannigan is hereby declared to be deposed from the office of President of the YCMS

Signed by William
Archbishop of St. Andrews and Edinburgh"

There was absolute uproar in the Hall. Canon Hannan made a statement to the meeting -

"that during the considerable time that he had known Michael Flannigan, he found him to be a good Catholic, a good citizen, and a man of impeccable character and that he regretted that such things had come to pass".

Michael Flannigan defended himself stating he was a loyal Catholic and a loyal Irishman but he had no intention of giving up his political activity so he would forthwith tender his resignation from the CYMS to save the Society from further controversy.

There was pandemonium in the Hall. Michael Flannigan was not the only supporter of Home Rule for Ireland, all the rest of the CYMS members were also committed to the Cause. A number of people immediately resigned in protest at the Archbishop's action, including some who were members of Hibernian's Committee.

Meanwhile, the Hibernian Football team itself showed it's contempt for the Archbishop's actions when, before making it's way to play Dundee Harp on 11 August, to raise funds for Catholic charities, they attended an open-air meeting in Dundee in support of imprisoned Irish Home Rule MP, John Dillon.

"After the match, Hibernian were entertained to tea in the Dundee CYMS Headquarters in Tay Street Hall, where speeches defending Hibernian against the attacks by Celtic and Archbishop Smith were delivered" (Lugton)

Hibernian continued to battle on using replacement players for those who had deserted to Celtic but the results were not good.

"Hibernian's fortunes had never been at such a low ebb. Replacing the players they had lost was proving impossible; Celtic had stemmed the flow of top class players from the West of Scotland 's vast Irish Catholic community and Edinburgh's much smaller community was not producing anyone of any great promise. Hibernian's decline had been swift and sure, but bad fortune had not finished for them yet, not by a long way" (Lugton)

The start of 1889 saw Hibernian in a precarious financial position and criticism of the Committee was loud. But the truth was there was no way the club could win back its previous status given its lack of funds, and looming on the horizon was the threat to Hibernian Park, off Bothwell Street, with rumours that the site's owners were planning to develop the area for housing.

The only light in the gloom was the visit, on the 19 July, of Charles Stewart Parnell to the St. Mary's Street Halls to thank St. Patrick's CYMS for their unswerving support for the cause of Ireland's freedom and the Irish Home Rule Movement. A support that had cost the Society, and Hibernian Football Club, dear, at the hands of Archbishop William Smith.

Parnell was in the town to receive the Freedom of Edinburgh Honour, at the City Chambers. He was at the height of his fame because just a few months earlier he had been cleared of complicity in acts of violence in Ireland. A group from Hibernian Football Club had attended Parnell's Trial in London.

"His total vindication in Court also cleared his 'Plan of Campaign and Boycotting', and the CYMS had already written to Archbishop Smith to have Michael Flannigan reinstated to the Society" (Lugton)

Canon Hannan had been invited to attend the ceremony of awarding the Freedom of Edinburgh to Charles Stewart Parnell, in the City Chambers. It must have seemed incredible to him that the long years of supporting his congregation in St. Patricks, and his creation of the CYMS, to uplift the poor boys of 'Little Ireland' to respected citizens, his creation of Hibernian, with all the prejudice and sectarianism he had faced, that now the Leader of the Irish

Home Rule Movement could receive the highest honour the city could bestow, in what had previously been such a hostile environment. To round off his visit, Charles Stewart Parnell, held a huge political rally in the Corn Exchange,in the Grassmarket, one of the most densely populated Irish areas of 'Little Ireland'. Parnell's visit was to be the last opportunity for Hibernian's supporters to celebrate their Irishness before the long decline into near football oblivion began.

Though not the team they had been Hibernian soldiered on, still putting on creditable performances, in the circumstances, until a further deadly blow was to strike the club.

Sadly, on Saturday 27 September 1890, Hibernian played their last game at the 'Holy Ground' (as the stadium was known) at the foot of Bothwell Street. It had been the scene of so many Hibernian triumphs since it had been acquired in 1880. The house building had continued in the area and the access to the ground was becoming dangerous. Also, the matter of the club's legal tenure was now in doubt.

Back in the Old Town the community was in shock! Though the ground was in Leith, in the hearts and minds of it's supporters it had never truly left 'Little Ireland'.

The Club was now in a healthier financial position and attempts were made to obtain land at Powderhall and at Logie Green, but their offers were turned down.

Incredibly, in spite of having no home ground, both the first and second teams continued to function, but questions were asked about how Hibernian Football Team could continue under these circumstances.

"Hibernian were in disarray and action was demanded, but it was too little and too late." (Lugton).

As far as playing was concerned the first team ceased to function and all their fixtures were cancelled. The players were told they would not be playing for many months.

It was at this point that St Patrick's CYMS received support from their friends in Our Lady, Star of the Sea Church's CYMS, in Leith. Leith had a huge Irish Catholic community, and, in the nearby fishing village of Newhaven, it was Irish families like the Croans and the Kellys that dominated the fishing trade. Both communities had been enthusiastic supporters of Hibernian.

The Chaplain, Father, J.J. O'Carroll, OMI, held meetings urging his CYMS committee to do what they could to help Hibernian get back on their feet. Led by Charles Perry and the Farmer brothers, they began to get themselves organised.

"They were determined to lead in the fight for the survival of Hibernian" (Lugton)

Stella Maris (The name by which the church was known.) had a young energetic branch of the CYMS. They also had the support, in their efforts to save Hibernian, of Michael Whelehan, Hibernian's first Captain, who was a close friend of Charles Perry.

At a meeting in St Mary's Street Halls in 'Little Ireland', on 4 February 1891, Charles Perry announced he had obtained the use of Hawkhill for Hibernian's home matches and had the support of all the Hibernian players. He further suggested that for legal reasons the 'new' club should be known as Leith Hibernian. The meeting approved his plans and a new Committee was formed giving 'Little Ireland' hope that their beloved Hibernian could be saved.

"On Saturday 29th February 1891, Leith Hibernian played their first, and as it turned out last, home match at Hawkhill Recreation Grounds" (Lugton)

For some reason the terms under which Hibernian were using Hawkhill came into question a few days later and again the team had nowhere to play their home matches. Charles Perry was determined the team would play on and announced that, for the present, Hibernian would play on their opponent's grounds until a new homed could be found.

Inspired by Leith's motto - "Persevere' – Hibernian struggled on but defeat followed defeat until the close of the Season.

Then, perhaps the most grievous blow of all struck 'Little Ireland', St Patrick's parish, their CYMS, Hibernian and their supporters in Stella Maris, in Leith.

In the middle of May 1891, Canon Hannan was laid low by a severe bout of influenza. He was ordered to rest and went to recover his strength in Dunfermline, in the parish house of Canon Smith and Father Mullin. Everyone hoped that removing him from the demands of his large parish, in the slums of the Old Town, in the heart of 'Auld Reekie' would soon restore his health. At first the enforced rest and fresher air appeared to do the trick and he began to recover.

But suddenly on 19 June he was struck down with pneumonia. His condition deteriorated rapidly and his good friend, Father Whyte of the Sacred Heart Church, off the Grassmarket, was sent for. He administered the Last Rites and Canon Hannan's condition did seem to improve with the Sacrament. But again he began to fail. St. Patrick's was packed all day on Sunday with his people in 'Little Ireland' praying for their beloved priest, who had served them so well for so many years. By Monday his condition was critical and his brother, Father Joseph, was sent for. He mounted a prayerful vigil at the bedside, but at ten minutes after midday, on Wednesday 24 June 1891, the good priest went to his heavenly reward. The death of Canon Hannan at the age of just 55 was felt in every Catholic home in Edinburgh and Leith.

But it was not just the Catholic community that mourned the passing of Canon Edward Hannan. He was respected by many in Edinburgh who had come to know him as an energetic, committed priest, with a fine intellect. A Professor of Classics who could have made his mark in academia but instead chose to devote 30 years of his life to serving his poor parishioners in the worst slums in Edinburgh. A man who, through his founding of the Catholic Young Mens Society (CYMS), had saved the young men in his parish from the dangers of the Old Town and turned them into well regarded citizens of the city. A man who had so impressed the City Councillors that the Lord Provost himself had laid the foundation stone of the Catholic Institute (St. Mary's Street Halls) – something that would have been unthinkable in the early days of hostility to the Irish community.

Next to his religious duties education had been Canon Hannan's driving force. He had built several schools making sure that the poor children of 'Little Ireland' would not grow up in ignorance but would have the chance to be all they could be. He served on the Edinburgh School Board for fifteen years where he impressed everyone with whom he came in contact. It is often said that Irish Catholic parents, in Edinburgh, were the first of the Irish in the Scotland to be aspirational for their children. This becomes obvious when one looks at the Irish names of many descendants of 'Little Ireland' who entered the professions and made a name for themselves in Commerce, Medicine, Education and the Law, a pattern that continues up to the present day, and a far cry from the early experiences of Father Hannnan's flock, excluded from serving in the City Police Force.

The great Crusade of his life was founding the CYMS with its 'Total Abstinence from Alcohol Society', known as the League of the Cross, which had a membership of five thousand, and the founding of Hibernian Football Club, and inspired their charitable activities that had helped so many good causes, and not just Catholic ones, gaining the team widespread respect.

Canon Hannan's body arrived on 25 June by train at Waverley Station, from Dunfermline, made possible by the building of the Forth Rail Bridge, across the Firth in 1890, that had been constructed by many Irish labourers who had supported Hibernian. A guard of honour carried his coffin from the station to a horse-drawn hearse. It was formed by members of the CYMS. His brother, Father Joseph, led a large group of priests in the procession to St. Patrick's Church.

'Little Ireland' ground to a halt as the bells tolled from the church.

That evening a special meeting of the Edinburgh School Board gathered to pay tribute to the priest.

"We could not begin the business of the evening without referring to the great loss we have all sustained in the death of Canon Hannan. We might say for the members of the old board and of the present board, that we feel we have sustained a personal loss. In the removal of Canon Hannan the city itself has suffered a severe loss, a loss that will not very soon be replaced. Canon Hannan took a great interest in all social questions.

"He was a great power in the community and he was very greatly beloved by a very large number of people in the city who most require sympathy and help. Among the poor of Edinburgh, he will be missed for many a long day. We can only say that we trust Canon Hannan's place will be filled by someone who will take as much interest as he has done in the welfare of the poor in the City of Edinburgh."

The funeral took place on Friday 26 June 1891 and, not surprisingly, St. Patrick's Church was packed for the mass with others standing out in the grounds and the crowd even stretching into the Cowgate as 'Little Ireland' came to bid farewell to their beloved priest.

What was surprising was that the front pews were full of prominent Protestant members of Edinburgh's establishment.

"Liberal MPs, Edinburgh City Councillors, high ranking Police Officers, leading members of the legal profession, eminent businessmen, members of the Edinburgh School Board and officials from football clubs." Not one of them Catholic. Even more astonishing was the fact that six local Protestant clergymen were present in the church – in a Catholic church!

"All of this bears testament to the high esteem in which Canon Hannan was held by every section of the Edinburgh community - of course the CYMS were there with all the Hibernian players and officials old and new; all had turned up to pay their last respects to their old 'Manager'." (Lugton)

At the end of the mass the coffin was carried shoulder high, in the old tradition, by six members of the CYMS out the side door of the church onto South Grays Close. A different six members then took over and carried Canon Hannan up the Close to the High Street where a horse-drawn hearse waited. The twelve members of the CYMC, acted as pallbearers walking in front of the hearse. Thirty carriages full of mourners led a procession of over two thousand people on foot along the South Bridge, where thousands more lined the route all the way to the Grange Cemetery.

It must have been a subdued and sad meeting of the CYMS that took place on the 28 June, in St. Mary's Street Halls, to discuss the raising of funds for a suitable memorial for Canon Hannan. The Hibernian Committee gave the last of their small funds towards the memorial.

In truth there seemed little point in carrying on. Without a home ground to play on Hibernian would be reduced to playing on Public Parks. The committee decided that the club would take a break until they could find a new ground, sort out their finances and, hopefully, return Hibernian to their original stature.

"A strong Hibernian would rise again. It was the least that could be done, for the memory of Canon Hannan." (Lugton)

Fundraising continued to raise a suitable Memorial to Canon Edward Hannan which finally resulted in a plaque fixed at the back of St. Patrick's church and later, a tall Celtic cross was erected over his grave in the Grange Cemetery, but the Memorial that best captured the essence of this dedicated priest was 'The Canon Hannan Memorial Fund for Orphans'. This Fund was used to feed, clothe and house the orphans of 'Little Ireland' and Leith, in St. Joseph's Industrial School in Tranent.

As for Hibernian Football Club, it was to take a year and a half of difficulties and disappointments to see light at the end of the tunnel. It was again Father J.J. O'Carroll of St. Mary's Star of the Sea church who stepped in and urged his Leith congregation to save Hibernian.

"Some of these Leithers were old Hibernian committee men – all were staunch supporters and plans were formed to resuscitate Hibernian." (Lugton)

The leader of this group was Philip Farmer. He, and his brother, John, had served on the old Hibernian committee for some years. They were part of a well-known Irish Catholic family in Leith. The group that formed around the brothers were all Irish Catholics (or of Irish descent) and all were members of St. Patrick's or Star of the Sea CYMS. They were all forward looking men and they determined that the reformed Hibernian would be open, players and supporters alike, to all, with no religious conditions, and also that they would be a Professional football club.

The months that followed were hectic for Philip Farmer and his colleagues – who remember were all volunteers – and had pledged some of their own money to the cause of resuscitating Hibernian. Eventually, it was decided that a public meeting should be held, in St. Marys Street Halls, on the 21 October to announce their plans to the residents of 'Little Ireland' and report on their progress. The group received the wholehearted support of those present and it was agreed that the first priority was to secure a new ground for Hibernian.

Philip Farmer and Tom McCabe negotiated with the Trinity Hospital Committee who owned the land at Drum Park, just across the rail tracks from Hibernian's old ground, and successfully concluded a deal for a new 'Holy Ground' to rise at Easter Road. Philip Farmer, as Treasurer, also made sure that Hibernian's accounts were correctly kept and always open to scrutiny. It was the first time that the Farmer family of Leith were to come to Hibernian's rescue, but it wasn't to be the last.

On Monday 12 December, 1892, a reformed Hibernian Football Club held their first meeting back in their old stomping ground in St. Mary's Street Halls and elected a committee which had a good cross section of men from 'Little Ireland' and Leith.

The date for the opening match was set for 4 February 1893 and weeks of activity followed to get the new Hibernian Park fit for purpose. On the day, the old green flag with the gold harp and motto – *'Erin go Bragh'* - proudly flew above the stand. The opponents were Clyde Football Team and a carnival atmosphere prevailed with Clyde finally winning by four goals to three. The Hibernian support gave their team a great reception as they left the field, the score scarcely mattered – Hibernian were back!

On 6 May 1893, Hibernian Football Team became professional as professionalism had now been legalised. In a meeting at the Hibernian Park Pavilion it was agreed that players would be paid per match. The fees were ten shillings for weekday matches and £1 on weekends. The players had first to pay a signing-on subscription of one pound!

Over the years that followed, gradually, Hibernian Football Club again became a force in Scottish football.

Particularly noteworthy was the tenure of Leither, Dan McMichael, who served as treasurer, secretary and manager of the club for a period of 22 years.

Through all those years of trials and tribulations, as well as great successes, Hibernian had never again won the 'Holy Grail' - the Scottish Cup.

So when they made it through to the semi-finals, in the 1901/1902 Cup, where they were to meet, Rangers, the hot favourites, the tension must have been unbearable. They travelled to Ibrox Park, in Glasgow, and in front of a crowd of 30,000 they beat the mighty Rangers by two goals to nil!

And who were their opponents for the Scottish Cup Final? None other than the mighty Celtic!

The Press described it as -'Scotland's All Irish Final' – but, in truth, back in 'Little Ireland', Celtic's betrayal of their fellow countrymen, Hibernian, lived on in the memories of that Irish community, still living in the Old Town.

The final was to be played at the neutral ground of Ibrox on 12 April 1902, but the week before a great tragedy had befallen

Rangers, and the football community. During an international match between Scotland and England, at Ibrox, part of a new stand collapsed and many people were killed and injured. A period of mourning followed with football at a halt.

When the final was played, two weeks later, it was held at Celtic Park. Celtic, were the favourites as they had a first class team – money had never been a problem for them. But Dan McMichael had a great talent for spotting promising young players and Hibernian was a team of strength and talent.

Hibernian won the Scottish Cup, defeating the mighty Celtic by one goal to nil, on their own ground, in front of a 16,000 crowd. Revenge must have tasted very sweet to the old guard back in 'Little Ireland'!

Afterwards the team made their way to the Alexandra Hotel in Glasgow, where the SFA presented the Scottish Cup to the Hibernian president, Philip Farmer, who declared - "Hibernian have attained their hearts' desire and I am the proudest man in Great Britain".

Then the team made their way to Queen Street Station for the train home, surrounded by singing supporters, with Dan McMichael clutching the Scottish cup.

The Hibernian party alighted at Haymarket Station where a horse-drawn brake awaited them and, led by the Newhaven Brass Band, they made their way along Princes Street.

"Princes Street was ecstatic as Bobby Atherton (Hibernian's Captain) held the cup aloft, and to the popular Music Hall tune – 'Dolly Gray' he sang "Goodbye Celtic we must leave you."(Lugton)

The procession made it's way down Leith Street, with the town at a standstill, turned on to London Road, with crowds lining the route, several deep, and made their way home, down Easter Road to the Holy Ground in 'scenes of affection never witnessed before in Edinburgh for a football team'

After much rejoicing the crowds made their way into the pubs to continue celebrating and the Hibernian party followed their example retiring to "Philip Farmer's pub on Leith Walk where toasts were drunk from the Scottish Cup." (Lugton)

It was a golden era for Hibernian. They won the Rosebery Charity Cup, beating Heart of Midlothian, they also won the Glasgow Charity Cup beating Rangers and Morton on the way, before again defeating Celtic at Hampden – this time by six goals to two. The following season 1902/1903, Hibernian won the Scottish League First Division Championship. They defeated Rangers scoring five goals, at Ibrox, and defeated Celtic by four goals at Parkhead. They won the East of Scotland Shield and for the second year running, the Rosebery Charity Cup.

"Charity games were still a hallmark of Hibernian and they played a benefit for the Edinburgh Corporation Poor Children's Holiday Fund and benefits for the families of old players. It is of particular interest that Rangers accepted an invitation from Hibernian to play them at Easter Road in a match for the building fund for St. Mary's, Star of the Sea, RC School, Leith on the evening of 5 May, 1903 where they shared four goals. Six days later Celtic accepted an invitation from Hibernian to play them at Easter Road in a match for the Little Sisters of the Poor. Hibernian won by three goals to one. Through all Hibernian's fortunes, good and bad, they never forgot in these days their charitable birthright." (Lugton)

Looking back, these sound like halcyon days. Who would have thought that before long the world would be plunged into World War I, - "The war to end all wars" - except it wasn't – the Second World War followed in 1939. Many of those promising young footballers from all Scotland's teams, in both eras, never came home. In the Church of St. Patrick, in 'Little Ireland,' the Memorial Chapel, built to honour their dead, from both wars, displays the names.

After the Second World War football returned and Hibernian continued to be a force in Scottish Football. Between 1948 and 1952, Hibernian were Scottish Champions in three seasons out of five. Much of their success was due to their well acclaimed forward line of Gordon Smith, Bobby Johnstone, Lawrie Reilly, Eddie Turnbull and Willie Ormond, known as the 'Famous Five'.

Through good times and bad, their supporters stayed loyal to the old team founded in the squalor and poverty of 'Little Ireland ' in the nineteenth century. And when Hibernian were under threat from a hostile takeover bid, in 1991, the supporters mounted a fightback with their 'Hands off Hibs' campaign – and again a member of the Farmer family from Leith – Tom (later Sir Tom) Farmer – came to the rescue and bought the club.

And, amazingly, after 114 years, on 21 May, 2016, Hibernian again won the Scottish Cup and waiting for them returning, this time on an open top bus, not a horse-drawn brake, were all those descendants of the Delaneys of 'Little Ireland' – not in St. Mary's Wynd this time, but in Hibernian's second home in Leith.

There was certainly 'Sunshine on Leith' that day!

CHAPTER TWELVE

LUKE JOSEPH BOYLAN

When Charles Stewart Parnell was given the Freedom of the City of Edinburgh in 1889 one of the people who had campaigned to have the honour awarded was Luke Joseph Boylan, son of Helen Delaney and Philip Boylan. The couple had married on 18 August 1850 in 'Little Ireland' only three months after Helen's husband, Arthur Delaney, died and only six months after the death of Philip's wife Dorothy. Helen was thirty years old and Philip was sixty-one. What seems to us a bit unseemly was probably only pragmatic. Since arriving in Edinburgh at the beginning of the 19th century Philip had built up several successful businesses and the poor Irish emigrant was now a wealthy man.

The only thing that Philip Boylan lacked was a male heir. He was probably reluctant to see his large business empire pass to his two daughters' husbands – as under the marriage laws, at that time, it would have done. For Helen the choice was simple. Though her husband, Arthur Delaney, would have been in a comfortable financial situation as a tailor, (and indeed he had opened a brokers business with his profits and was trading in the Old Town) without his earnings Helen would have been unable to continue the business. As a thirty-year-old widow with three young children to support and only the Poor House to look forward to, marrying Philip would come as a godsend. Her sister-in-law, Sarah Skiffington (nee Delaney), obviously agreed as she was Helen's bridesmaid when the couple married in St. Patrick's Church on Lothian Street, even though her brother, Arthur Delaney, was only three months dead.

Helen kept her side of the arrangement as she gave Philip four sons, as well as a daughter. In 1851 their first son, Luke Joseph Boylan, was born. His god-parents were, Sarah Skiffington and James Boylan. He was followed in 1853 by their son, Philip Boylan, whose god-parents were Anne Boylan and John Skiffington (Sarah Delaney's husband). In 1856 their only daughter, Mary Boylan, was born. Her god-parents were John Lennon and his wife Eleanor Boylan (Philip's daughter by his first marriage). In 1858 another son, James Boylan, was born, his godparents being Eleanor Lennon and William Devlin. In 1860, when Helen was aged forty, their final child, John Boylan, was born, whose god-parents were John Skiffington and Margaret Lennon. Tragically, John died as a baby of encephalitis.

With the birth of Luke Joseph, Philip Boylan had his longed for heir and had secured his business empire. All of the children, as well as Helen's sons - James Delaney, Thomas Delaney and John Delaney from her first marriage - lived together in the large house at 17 St. Mary's Wynd. When Luke Joseph Boylan was born his half-brother, John Sylvester Delaney, was only three years old. As a result, they grew up to be very close and when John Sylvester Delaney, the actor, had his first son he named him Luke after his half-brother.

Throughout our research we found that Philip and Helen's house, at 17 St. Mary's Wynd, became the hub of family life, with extended family members marrying there, giving birth to children there and, in old Philip's case, dying there in 1875 of chronic bronchitis. He and Helen had been married for twenty-five years and in his Will he left her an annuity.

Philip appears to have been an indulgent stepfather to his three stepsons throughout his life and a devoted father to Luke Joseph, Philip, Mary and James, his own children by Helen.

His son, Luke Joseph Boylan, registered his father's death and stated Philip was eighty-seven years old. Philip died the year that Fr Hannan founded the Hibernian Football Club. His son, Luke Joseph, was an active member of St. Patrick's Catholic Young Men's Society (CYMS) and closely involved with the work of Fr Hannan and the Irish politics of the time.

Luke Joseph Boylan, as Philip's eldest son, inherited all his father's properties, making him a very wealthy young man at twenty-four. He set up as a pawnbroker which was a lucrative business in those times when many suffered financial difficulties. Luke's shop, displaying the traditional three golden balls sign of a pawnbroker, was at 240 the Canongate. Unredeemed pledges went on sale in his attached Saleroom. Money makes money!

After his father's death, Luke bought his mother, Helen, a newsagent and confectioner shop at 29 the Canongate. (On Helen's death, in 1890, her son, James Boylan, took over the business.)

Luke and his mother, Helen, remained very close throughout her life. After moving from 17 St. Mary's Street, the house having become too big for her, Helen moved into a flat in Chessel's Court behind Luke's shop in the Canongate and he lived there with her. It was in a lovely 17th century building. It was restored in the 1960s and still stands. Indeed a friend of mine lives there!

Luke Joseph was thirty years old by then so his mother probably thought he would never marry. It must have come as a shock when, in 1881, he announced his engagement. Even more of a shock was that his intended bride, Patricia Campsie, was only seventeen years old!

Of course, Helen herself had married a much older man, but she was a thirty-year-old widow at the time, not a teenager.

The wedding of Luke Joseph Boylan and Patricia Campsie took place in St. Patrick's Church, on 8 August 1881, their witnesses being John and Sarah Murray, Jane Delaney's son and daughter. Luke declared on the marriage certificate that he was twenty-eight years old, when in fact he was thirty. Patricia's father, James, a Wine Merchant, was deceased but her mother, Jane Campsie (nee Kay), was still alive.

She must have thought that it was a great match for her daughter, in spite of the age difference, as Luke Joseph was a very wealthy man. In the event it appeared to be a very unhappy marriage - proving that money isn't everything. The couple had no children.

After the wedding, Luke Joseph installed his mother, Helen, in a flat in a gracious stone building on George IV Bridge – co-incidentally, overlooking Greyfriars Churchyard where Helen's first husband, Arthur Delaney, was buried. The building still stands today. He and Patricia moved into a house at 5 Thirlestane Road, on the south side of Edinburgh.

Luke Joseph Boylan was a well known businessman in the Old Town and very involved in local politics, serving as Chairman, in the Calton Branch of the Liberal Party. The Liberals were the party of choice for most of the Irish Catholics in the Old Town. This was because of its leader, William Ewart Gladstone. He was M.P for

Midlothian, the County in which Edinburgh stood. Gladstone declared his support for Home Rule for Ireland in the British Parliament. The Labour Party had not yet been formed and the main opposition to the Liberals was the Unionist Party.

The Irish in the Old Town later had another political option - Socialism. This was the creed embraced by a son of 'Little Ireland', James Connolly, born in the Cowgate on 5 June 1868 to Irish immigrant parents, John Connolly and Mary McGinn, from County Monaghan.

The Delaneys, who were also from County Monaghan, would have known the Connolly family in the congregation of St. Patrick's Church. James Connolly would later in life reminisce fondly of his days as a Hibernian supporter, when, as a boy, he would carry the football team's bags from St. Mary's Street Halls to Easter Road, gaining him free entry to the match!

He was educated at the local Catholic Primary school, probably St Mary's in Lothian Street, leaving at the age of eleven to work in casual labouring jobs. He and his family were very poor so, when he was fourteen years old, he lied about his age and in 1882 enlisted in the British Army under a false name. He was then able to send money home to his parents in the Cowgate. He served in Ireland with the 2nd Battalion of the Royal Scots and the Kings Regiment (Liverpool) for seven years during the Irish 'Land Wars'. His experiences were to give him a lifelong hatred for the British Army. On hearing that his regiment was to be posted to India, he deserted in 1889 to marry Lillie Reynolds. They married in Edinburgh in April 1890 and he settled back in the city.

He became involved in the socialist movement and took the job of Secretary with the Scottish Socialist Federation. As a result he joined the Independent Labour Party which Keir Hardy had formed in 1893. In that same year he heard that the Dublin Socialist Club was looking for a full time Secretary with a salary of £1 a week. He, his wife and their three daughters moved to Dublin. Under his influence the club quickly evolved into the Irish Socialist Republican Party. In later years James Connolly was to become famous in the Irish Republican Cause and people were always surprised to hear him speak in a broad Scot's accent, from his years in the Cowgate!

It was to be some time before either the Labour Party or Irish Republicanism was to have any place in 'Little Ireland' where the Liberal Party continued to hold sway.

The background of James Connolly and another political agitator, Charles Stewart Parnell, could not have been more different. Parnell was born in Ireland in 1846 into a powerful Anglo-Irish Protestant landowning family in County Wicklow. His father was John Henry Parnell a wealthy Anglican landowner and his mother was Delia Tudor Stewart, of New Jersey, USA. They had eleven children in all, five boys and six girls. Parnell's father was a cousin of one of Ireland's leading aristocrats, Viscount Powerscourt. Parnell's grandfather, William Parnell, was an Irish Liberal Party MP for County Wicklow yet it was as a leader of Irish Nationalism that Charles Stewart Parnell was to find fame.

His parents separated when he was six years old and he was sent to different schools in England where he spent an unhappy childhood. His father died in 1859 and Parnell inherited his birthplace, Avondale House, in Wicklow, and its declining Estate. The Estate was in financial difficulties but Parnell was regarded as an improving landlord who opened the Wicklow area to industrialisation. The theme dominating Irish politics in the 1870s was the Home Rule League formed by Isaac Butt, in 1873, to bring about a degree of self-government.

A writer on Charles Stewart Parnell argues - "that the primary reason Parnell joined the Irish cause was his 'implacable hostility towards England' which probably was founded on grievances from his school days and his mother's hostility towards England." (Flynn 2005)

Flynn also reports - "When William Ewart Gladstone came to know him in later years, he was astonished to find that Parnell was ignorant even of the basic facts of Irish history. The romantic vision that characterised Young Ireland and the Fenians escaped him completely. He knew little of figures like Sarsfield, Tone or Emmett and even appeared unsure of who won the Battle of the Boyne."

In this battle the forces led by James VII and II (known in Protestant circles as 'The Old Pretender') was the brother, and successor, of King Charles II. He fought against his son-in-law, William of Orange, who had seized the throne of the United Kingdom in the name of his wife, Mary, James' daughter. The problem arose because James VII and II was a Catholic and was accused of imposing his beliefs on Protestant Scotland and England. William of Orange was a Protestant and therefore more acceptable as ruler. In the event James was defeated at the battle and fled into exile abroad. His son, Prince Charles Edward Stewart, (known in Protestant circles as 'The Young Pretender' but to Jacobites as Bonnie Prince Charlie) tried, unsuccessfully, in1745, to regain his father's kingdom.

The Battle of the Boyne in 1690 is often quoted as the starting point of all Ireland's troubles but, in truth, they go back beyond that time to James VI (King of Scotland) and I (of England) when he inherited the throne of England on the death of Queen Elizabeth. It was he who began what is known as 'The Plantation of Ulster'. This plan settled Protestants from England and also, notably, from Scotland on the lands of Ireland. The lands that were held and farmed by the Catholic Irish themselves. From that time onwards Irish Catholics were barred from owning any land in their own country. Their lands were given to Protestant gentry, many of whom were absentee landlords never living on their Estates. These landlords charged the Irish Catholics rent to farm their own pieces of land. In times of a poor harvest, if they could not afford to pay their rents, the Catholic Irish were evicted and cast out on the road. The Delaneys themselves, in County Monaghan, had three farms, but they too were only tenants and could have been evicted at any time.

Parnell, as a Protestant and member of the gentry, was probably insulated from what was going on around him in Ireland and, of course, he was educated in England where he would not have been taught about Ireland's history.

It appears that it was the injustice of the Irish land system, of which it was said - "there was no disadvantage which it did not possess" - that most inflamed his passions. He stood for election several times but was finally elected to the House of Commons at a By-election on 17 April 1875, as a Home Rule League MP for County Meath.

In time, this land passion of Parnell was to bring about great improvement in those land laws. In the autumn of 1879, while campaigning on the issue, he addressed Irish tenants after a long economic depression had left them without income to pay their rents - "You must show the landlord that you intend to keep a firm grip on your homesteads and lands. You must not allow yourselves to be dispossessed as you were dispossessed in 1847.".

This would have struck home powerfully as 1847 was the *Black Year* of the Great Famine - a famine in which over a million Irish people starved to death. A famine that led to hundreds of Irish people settling in Edinburgh's Old Town.

In February 1880, while on a tour in America, Parnell addressed the United States House of Representatives on the state of Ireland and asserted that to abolish landlordism would be to undermine English misgovernment and allegedly added -

"When we have undermined English misgovernment we have paved the way for Ireland to take her place amongst the nations of the earth. And let us not forget that is the ultimate goal at which all we Irishmen aim. None of us - whether we be in America or in Ireland – will be satisfied until we have destroyed the last link which keeps Ireland bound to England."

For Parnell the land issue and the Home Rule issue were always inextricably linked and in America, where most Irish fleeing the effects of famine eventually settled, he would get a warm welcome.

Parnell's American tour was brought to a halt when a general election was set in the UK for April 1880 and he returned to fight it. The Conservatives were defeated by the Liberal Party and Gladstone was again Prime Minister. Parnell stood in three seats in Ireland and won them all. He chose to sit in Parliament for the Cork City seat. This success resulted in him becoming leader of the new Home Rule League Party with Ireland faced with a threatened Land War.

Gladstone was alarmed at the growing power of the Land League at the end of 1880 and he attempted to defuse the Irish land question with dual ownership and introduced the Land Law (Ireland) Act in1881. This established a Land Commission that reduced rents and enabled some tenants to buy their land - this halted arbitrary evictions but not where rent was in arrears.

Parnell and other members including Michael Davitt, John Dillon, James J. O'Kelly, William O'Brien and Willie Redmond spoke out against the Land Act. They were all arrested and in October 1881 put in Kilmainham Gaol for 'sabotaging the Land Act'. While imprisoned Parnell, and the others, issued the 'No Rent Manifesto' – the Land League was immediately suppressed.

While still in gaol in April 1882 Parnell moved to make a deal with the government. Provided the government settled the 'rent arrears' question, allowing one hundred thousand tenants to appeal for fair rent before the land courts, he would withdraw the Rent Manifesto and move to stop agrarian violence. Parnell had come to realise that violent action would never bring about Home Rule. He was released from prison on 2 May1882 following the, so called, Kilmainham Treaty.

From then onwards, Parnell, Davitt and the others, would follow purely constitutional paths to Home Rule leaving them as the leaders of the nationalist movement in Ireland. Parnell resurrected the suppressed Land League on 17 October 1882 as the Irish National League (INL). The informal alliance between the new INL and the Catholic Church revitalised the National Home Rule Cause after 1882. Parnell saw that only with the support of the Catholic Church could Home Rule be achieved.

By the end of 1885 the INL had over a thousand branches around Ireland. Parnell left its day to day organization in the hands of his supporters, Timothy Harrington, William O'Brien and Tim Healy. The INL's continuing agrarian agitation led to the passing of several Irish Land Acts that over the course of the next thirty years changed the face of Irish land ownership, replacing large Anglo-Irish estates with tenant ownership.

"Parnell played a large part in the process that undermined his own Anglo-Irish caste; within two decades absentee landlords were almost unknown in Ireland."

On the 8 April 1886, William Ewart Gladstone introduced the first Irish Home Rule Bill, its object being to establish a devolved Irish Assembly. But the split between pro and anti Home Rulers, in the Liberal Party, caused the defeat of the Bill at its Second Reading.

Parliament was dissolved and elections called with Irish Home Rule the central issue. But the result of the July 1886 General Election was a Liberal defeat. Lord Salisbury formed his second government – a minority Conservative government with Liberal Unionist support.

(A second Home Rule Bill was later to pass in the House of Commons in 1893 only to be overwhelmingly defeated in The Lords).

From 1886 to 1890 Parnell continued to pursue Home Rule, striving to reassure British voters it would be no threat to them.

He pursued moderate and conciliatory tenant land purchase and, optimistically, still hoped to retain a sizeable landlord support for home rule.

All that remained, it seemed, was to work out details of a new Home Rule Bill with Gladstone. In the early part of 1890 he still hoped to advance the situation on the land question with which a substantial section of his Party was displeased.

Parnell reformed the Home Rule League and named it the Irish Parliamentary Party. He was its Leader from 1882 to 1891. His party held the balance of power in the House of Commons between William Ewart Gladstone's Liberals and Lord Salisbury's Unionists, during the Home Rule for Ireland debates of 1885 to 1886.

This balance of power was partly the reason that William Ewart Gladstone came to support Home Rule for Ireland and this explains the reason for 'Little Ireland's support for the Liberal Party.

Luke Joseph Boylan, as President of the National League branch in the Old Town, and the other members of the committee of the United Liberal Association along with the Working Men of Edinburgh Association, banded together and used their influence to persuade Edinburgh Town Council to present the Freedom of Edinburgh Award to Charles Stewart Parnell. It seems incredible after all the years of hostility to the Irish in Edinburgh that this became a possibility. However, the Irish were now a numerous presence in the city, a large part of the work force and their votes could be influential.

In spite of these facts, campaigning to have Charles Stewart Parnell being given the Freedom of Edinburgh had not been easy. The Liberal Party was in the majority on Edinburgh City Council but there was strong opposition from the Unionist/Conservative Councillors. These councillors tapped into the anti-Irish element in the town. They organised a 'plebiscite' – and went round the doors asking residents to sign a card saying they opposed the awarding of the Freedom. When the results came in, the majority against Parnell's award was so overwhelming as to be ludicrous and voter fraud was suspected. The Town Council ignored the unconstitutional plebiscite and as a result many of the Liberal Councillors suffered great personal abuse and threats. At the later Demonstration on Calton Hill, one of them, Councillor McPherson, a Highlander, not himself Irish, spoke of what they had suffered. He stated -

"As you well know........the majority of the Town Council had to go through a trial of no mean order. We have been slanderously vilified day after day for months past. I take it that tonight's demonstration was an answer to those slanders."

The Scotsman newspaper was totally opposed to the idea of awarding Charles Stewart Parnell the Freedom of Edinburgh and was at the forefront of the vilification.

Mr. A.L. Brown, MP was also to mention the newspaper's attitude at the demonstration. He mocked

"We know that *The Scotsman* is our political barometer. It is a barometer turned upside down. For whenever it said it was fair, we knew it was always wet; and whenever it said it was raining cats and dogs, we were sure that the sun was shining brightly."

To give *The Scotsman* credit, their reporter also reported the outbreaks of hissing and booing from the crowd anytime the newspaper was mentioned! Of course, back in those days, reporters saw their job as accurately reporting the news, or maybe the newspaper believed, even then, that there is no such thing as bad publicity!

Despite this opposition, or maybe because of it, Parnell's visit to accept the Freedom of Edinburgh award was covered extensively in reports in *The Scotsman* newspaper. I have used these reports to describe the scenes in Edinburgh when he arrived.

On the 19 July 1889, Luke Joseph and his mother, Helen, travelled down by train with the rest of the welcoming committee to meet Parnell's train at Carlisle. Councillor Pollard and Mr Gray had been deputed to represent Edinburgh Council and when Parnell's train drew into the station they boarded the train to welcome Charles Stewart Parnell and his Private Secretary, Mr Henry Campbell, MP for Fermanagh, on behalf of the Town Council and the United Liberal Committee.

In *The Scotsman* report it says that Luke Joseph Boylan was with the welcoming committee and was introduced to Charles Stewart Parnell in Carlisle rail station and he, in turn, introduced his mother, Helen Boylan. On reading this we wondered why Luke did not take his wife, Patricia, to meet the great man.

The welcoming party then boarded the train to travel back to Edinburgh. Carlisle Station was packed with cheering Irish men and women, there to welcome their hero. When Parnell appeared at the carriage window the noise was deafening and there were calls for him to speak but he declined, saying, that after his post lunch nap he had not had time to collect his thoughts and also he doubted the station master would approve if they held up the train any longer!

As the train approached Edinburgh, Irish flags flew from many windows and people hung out the windows waving their handkerchiefs.

Arrangements has been made to control the crowd at the Caledonian Station. The Chief Constable ordered that fifteen minutes before Parnell's train was due to arrive the platform would be cleared.

Only those with official passes would be allowed and that number would be restricted to fifty. But in the event a huge crowd covered the platform, shouting and cheering. The kind of welcome that only a pop group might expect today – certainly not a politician!

An official Reception Committee stood ready to greet the great man, consisting of Bailie Steel and Bailie Walcott, chairman of the United Liberal Committee. There were two Members of Parliament and several town Councillors alongside solicitors, Thomas McNaught and Ainslie Brown, and Mr McKie, the Advocate, and Mr McKay, the Justice of the Peace. The clergy were represented by Canon Hannan and his curate, Father George Culhane, and Father Steven Culhane, a priest from Dunfermline who was very supportive of the cause.

Canon Hannan must have seen it as a dream come true. All his work to uplift the young men of his poor slum parish and make them respectable citizens had come to fruition. The Irish were now a force to be reckoned with in the city and commanded respect from the 'great and the good'.

The Reception Committee were lined up in an orderly line but, as Charles Stewart Parnell stepped down from the carriage, the line broke and amid a great deal of jostling and loud cheers the crowd pushed forward to the edge of the platform. Enthusiastic admirers tried to reach forward to get within hand-shaking distance of their hero.

It took a group of burly policemen to clear a passage to allow the party to exit from the side entrance of the station into Rutland Street. Parnell was clutching his 'Gladstone Bag' as the porters could not get through the crowd to help carry his luggage to the horse-drawn carriage which waited at the station door. When he stepped out on to the pavement a huge roar went up from those waiting to greet him. He was trying to step into the carriage but was held back by the numbers wanting to shake his hand and hampered by the fact he was carrying his bag.

A group of stewards from the Arrangements Committee, wearing rosettes of white, orange and green ribbons, stood waiting at the end of Rutland Street. They were accompanied by the brass band of Miller and Richards Type Factory – the same company that Hibernian's first Captain, Michael Whelehan, had been apprenticed to, all those years ago. The stewards held up a banner proclaiming -'Welcome to our city, leader of the Irish people'. The inscription was surrounded by thistles. An acknowledgement that the Irish in Edinburgh now saw themselves as having a dual Scots/Irish heritage. On the other side the inscription read - 'Self government is true unity' above an illustration of clasped hands, while below it read -'We shake hands across the gulf of misrule.' In those sentiments we see the very beginnings of hopes being expressed of Home Rule for Scotland.

Eventually, Parnell got into the carriage and it set off with four mounted policemen riding ahead. The carriage belonged to Mr Buchanan the MP and the horse was dressed with green rosettes. Seated beside Parnell in the carriage was Mr Buchanan, his wife, his elderly mother and Bailie Walcott.

Waiting on Lothian Road was the St. Patrick's Catholic Young Men's Society Flute Band which took up position behind the carriage. When the carriage turned into Princes Street and Parnell was spotted, a huge cheer went up from the waiting crowds that lined the route. The Rose Street Flute Band followed the next carriage containing the town councillors, followed by the Leith Nationalists Flute Band with the carriage containing the Reception Committee. Bringing up the rear was the Musselburgh Brass Band.

The Magistrates had ruled that all traffic on the route should cease after six o' clock and it was a wise decision. The Irish Planning Committee had sent out word to all the Gladstonian and Irish Associations in the surrounding area to turn out and show support and they had turned out in force.

There had been a rumour that two thousand Orangemen from the West had intended to disrupt the Procession and so five thousand

Leaguers set off in pursuit. In the event nothing happened and the Parade went ahead peacefully, but it is a reminder that not everyone in the country approved of the decision to award Parnell the Freedom of Edinburgh or of the growing acceptance of the Irish.

The unbroken lines of people extended along both sides of Princes Street but the behaviour was orderly. Several banners were held aloft bearing the names of Trade Unions and Friendly Societies and one bore an image of William Ewart Gladstone, inscribed - 'Ireland's Friend' and another -'Scotland and Ireland United.'

The procession travelled along Waterloo Place, crossed the Regent's Bridge and then turned at the Calton Jail to make it's way up the Calton Hill. As the last carriage turned the crowds thronged behind and followed them up the driveway.

A platform had been erected at the Gate of the New Observatory building and Parnell and the party mounted and took up their seats. The position of the platform had been deliberately chosen. It was on the same spot that Daniel O'Connell, known in Ireland as 'The Liberator' for his campaign for Catholic Emancipation, had addressed a huge open-air meeting in 1835. The Delaneys had not yet arrived in Edinburgh at that date but old Philip Boylan, already a respected businessman in 'Little Ireland', would surely have been there and now, some fifty years later, his son, Luke Joseph Boylan, was still fighting the fight for Irish Home Rule.

The huge crowd covered the Hill, some gathered in front of the platform, others climbed the steps of the National Monument and took up position there – some even ascended the Nelson Monument to get a good view though it's doubtful they would have heard a word that was said from inside that Tower.

The noise on the Hill must have been deafening, great outbursts of cheering and much waving of hats. By now the rear of the procession had arrived and there were thousands of people on the Hill.

The Platform Party consisted of the two members of Parliament, town councillors, Liberal Party leaders and a number of priests. There were also the two ladies, Mr Buchanan's wife and his mother and, of course, the main attraction – Charles Stewart Parnell. He was used to attracting huge crowds in Ireland but such a turn out in Scotland must have exceeded his expectations.

The gathering was to be chaired by James Lochead who was the Chairman of the Working Men of Edinburgh Association. He began by saying that the people of Edinburgh had shown they were in complete sympathy with the Cause to which they were met there that evening and that was met by a burst of loud cheering. He then invited the Association's Secretary, Mr Scott, to read the address that had been prepared for Parnell. It read -

"To Charles Stewart Parnell, Esq. MP Leader of the Irish People.

Sir,

We, the working men of Edinburgh, take this opportunity of publicly testifying our appreciation of your high character, personal worth and the great ability you have displayed in guiding the great constitutional movement of which you are the head.

We have watched, with the greatest interest, the way in which you have hitherto conducted this movement. The judgement and firmness you have displayed calls forth our warmest admiration, while the calmness and dignity with which you have borne the calumnies and vituperation of your political opponents is beyond praise.

We desire, further, to express through you, to the people of Ireland, our heartfelt sympathy with them, in their long continued struggle, for the right of self-government, which must at no distant date triumph, however bitter and unrelenting be the opposition offered to their demand. We ask them to rest assured that the great mass of the people of Scotland, are with them in their struggle, believing that the consummation of their desires, will be the means of more firmly cementing a true and lasting unity of the people of these islands.

In conclusion, we would express the hope that you would have health, strength and a long life to guide the destinies of your country, we feel that Ireland, truly free, her energies at liberty from the distraction of political agitation, has great industrial possibilities, and we believe that the proper development of these would be the means of preventing so many of her sons being compelled to leave the soil which is so dear to them; to seek, in other lands, the liberty and security they cannot find at home. We declare this in the name and by the authority of the Working Men of Edinburgh."

As can be seen from this speech, The Working Men of Edinburgh Association was not a specifically Irish group and you can hear in the address the undertones of what had been a problem for the Scottish working class of desperate Irish immigrants being prepared to work for less and thus lowering the wages of Scottish workers. It had been at the root of much anti-Irish feeling over the years. The working men were beginning to organise themselves to force employers to raise their wages. Professor Tom Devine has pointed out that wages in Scotland were lower than in the rest of the United Kingdom. The influx of Irish had not caused this situation but the surplus of cheap labour made the demand for fair wages harder to enforce. It was this unrest that not long afterwords was to lead to the creation of the Labour Party under Keir Hardie. The Working Men's Association was expressing the hope that if Ireland had control over its own affairs it would improve the condition of its people, stemming the flow of cheap labour into Scotland.

James Lochead then presented the address to Charles Stewart Parnell on behalf of the Working Men of Edinburgh Association.

It is obvious from the response of some in the crowd that James Lochead and his members and, indeed, those on the Platform had no idea that they had -'a tiger by the tail'! Home Rule for Ireland was just the beginning of the long struggle towards Independence for Ireland and, in time,was to inspire the movement for Scottish Independence.

After accepting the scroll, Charles Stewart Parnell, said -

"People of historic Edinburgh, in thanking the working men of this great city for the very beautiful address that has just been presented to me and also for arranging this magnificent demonstration, I shall use but a very few words. It would be impossible for me in the compass of my voice to attempt to reach even a fractional proportion of this vast meeting; but it has given me the greatest pleasure and encouragement to come among the people of Edinburgh and to see that they understand that justice for Ireland, so far from weakening the greatness of the Empire, must surely consolidate and increase its strength. Ireland has never been rebellious save under the presence of bitter misgovernment and oppression ....

It is not the way of peoples to rise against good government – and Ireland would never have risen against England had you done what you did in1886 had you followed in the footsteps of your great leader – and offered to Ireland the hand of friendship. I am thankful to think that the old bad times have gone by and that we shall never again see a return to the evil days.

I trust we will henceforth be united in the bonds, the strong and enduring bonds, of friendship, mutual interest and unity. We know that Ireland will prove a source of strength to the Empire instead of a source of weakness, and you will have the knowledge that you will have helped Ireland to become prosperous and that giving her her legitimate liberty you have benefited yourselves as well as us.

There is a part of this address that says truly that the material resources of Ireland can be developed. That is one of the things that we wish – that we ardently long to devote our energies to - to finding for our people, employment at home - so that they may no longer flood the labour markets in Scotland and England - so that they may no longer lower the wages of your working men by their competition, but that they may remain at home – that those of them who are here may return to Ireland and help us with the knowledge they have acquired in your workshops and in your factories in developing the industrial resources of our own country.

Believe me, for many years to come, we will be fully occupied in the march of progress in promoting the happiness and welfare of our own people, and that Ireland will thankfully, and in good faith, accept the settlement which Mr Gladstone has offered to it – as an end to the strife of centuries – as a real treaty of peace between the two nations, which will bring comfort and happiness to many an Irish house, and which will leave you with the knowledge and the satisfaction that you no longer oppress a people who do not really feel any ill will against you, and that you have been able to do something to settle this great question, and to bring Ireland, Scotland and England into harmony with each other.

I thank you from the bottom of my heart for this magnificent reception and demonstration. I know that it has not been given to me personally. I know it is partly because you desire to help your great leader, Mr Gladstone, to settle this question, and because you desire to encourage us to remain in the peaceable and constitutional attitude we hold today – because you desire to encourage us to refrain from returning to the provocation of the Tory Government........which it daily inflicts on our people in Ireland – and also because you are convinced from inquiry and reason that this settlement which Mr Gladstone has proposed is a just settlement – that it can be accepted honourably by us, and that you can yield it to us,without fear that it will hurt your own interests – but in the confident belief that it will increase and strengthen the unity of the Empire – and enable this great country - this great Empire - to face her foes abroad - if they should ever arise – and I trust that they never will - with the confidence that she has unity and harmony at home – and there is no oppression towards anybody in any part of these great dominions.

I am pleased that this demonstration has come from the working men. I shall always be glad to help the working men of Scotland to obtain their just rights and to maintain their privileges – and whenever the united voice of the Scottish representatives demands a reform believe me that there and then you will have no firmer supporters for Scotland, no men then will walk into the division lobby more united and more firmly on behalf of the liberties of Scotland, than will the Irish representatives whom I have the honour to lead."

The Scotsman report describes how the vast crowd on the Hill erupted into loud cheering and that hats were flung in the air!

It is very clear from Parnell's speech that he is well aware that many of those present are not Irish, nor primarily concerned with Home Rule for Ireland, but that they have pinned their hopes on the Liberal Party led by William Ewart Gladstone to bring about social reform and improvement in the conditions of the working class in Scotland.

The day after the huge Demonstration on Calton Hill, Charles Stewart Parnell received the Freedom of Edinburgh in a ceremony in the City Chambers in the High Street of the Old Town. A ceremony attended by Canon Hannan. Afterwards, accompanied by Luke, he took Parnell down to St. Mary's Halls on St. Mary's Street, where Parnell thanked St. Patrick's Catholic Young Men's Society for all their support over the years for the Cause of Ireland's freedom and all it had cost them, and Hibernian Football Club. Parnell then went to a huge rally of supporters in the Corn Exchange in the Grassmarket, one of the Irish in Edinburgh's most populous areas.

It is almost unbearable to read the speeches from that day - so full of hope - knowing all that was to befall the people of Ireland in the long years of struggle that were to follow. All the betrayals, the hopes dashed and the blood that was to be shed in Ireland's name.

The long, tortuous, bloody history of Ireland is way beyond the scope of this book which seeks only to tell the story of one Irish family who lived through those times.

The story of the two political activists, Charles Stewart Parnell and James Connnolly, were also to end in tragedy.

The granting of the Freedom of Edinburgh in 1889 was to be the peak of Charles Stewart Parnell's life. From there it was all downhill.

The Irish Parliamentary Party, which Parnell founded, split in 1890 after the revelation that he had been conducting a decade long adulterous affair with Kitty O'Shea, the wife of Captain William O'Shea MP, and had fathered three children with her. This revelation led to many British Liberals, some of whom were Non-conformist Protestants, refusing to work with him. It also led to strong opposition from Catholic Bishops who had previously supported him.

"For the first time in Irish history, the two dominant forces of Nationalism and Catholicism came to a parting of the ways." (Larkin 1961)

Captain William O'Shea had separated from his wife in 1875 but did not divorce her then because Kitty was in line to receive a large legacy should her wealthy aunt die, from which he would benefit legally if he was still her husband. When Kitty O'Shea's aunt died in 1889 she did not receive the expected legacy, instead her aunt's money was left in a Trust. Denied the money, William O'Shea divorced Kitty the next year on 17 November 1890 and was awarded custody of her children, including the two surviving children she had with Parnell.

Charles Stewart Parnell married Kitty O'Shea eight months later on 25 June 1891 and they went to live in Brighton. She was the great love of his life for whom he was prepared to risk his dream of Home Rule for Ireland. On the day of the wedding, the Irish Catholic hierarchy, concerned by the number of priests who still supported

Parnell, published a condemnation - "by his public misconduct, (Parnell) has utterly disqualified himself to be...leader."

Even William Ewart Gladstone turned against him warning - "that if Parnell retained the leadership it would mean the loss of the next election, the end of their alliance, and also of Home Rule for Ireland."

Parnell refused to withdraw and his alliance with Gladstone and the Liberal Party collapsed in bitterness.

When Parnell refused to step down from the leadership, the other prominent members of the Irish party tried to reach a compromise suggesting that Parnell would temporarily withdraw. Parnell refused.

"He vehemently insisted that the independence of the Irish party could not be compromised either by Gladstone or the Catholic hierarchy."

As chairman he blocked any motion to remove him.

After five days of fractious debate, a majority of those present, led by Justin McCarthy, walked out to found a new organisation. This created new Parnellite and anti-Parnellite parties.

The minority Parnellite group continued as the Irish National League. But the majority of the important members including Michael Davitt, John Dillon, William O'Brien and Timothy Healy deserted him.

These, and the vast majority of the anti-Parnellites, formed the Irish National Federation, under John Dillon, which was supported by the Catholic Church.

The bitterness of the split tore Ireland apart and impeded the cause of Irish Home Rule for more than twenty years.

But Parnell fought on desperately despite his failing health. On 10 December 1890, he arrived in Dublin to a hero's welcome but most rural nationalists turned against him. Eventually, deposed as leader, he fought a long and fierce campaign for reinstatement. The party sustained one loss after another but Parnell, ever optimistic, looked to the next General Election of 1892 to restore his fortunes.

On 27 September 1891, he addressed a rally in pouring rain at Creggs and received a complete soaking, but he continued on an exhausting campaign trail. His health was deteriorating and he was suffering from kidney disease. When, on 30 September 1891, he arrived back in Dublin he was a dying man.

Six days later he died of pneumonia at his home at 10 Walsingham Terrace, Hove in England, in the arms of his beloved wife, Kitty. They had only been married for four months and he was just forty-five years old and he never achieved his dream of Home Rule for Ireland.

(Two years later, in 1893, a Second Home Rule Bill did pass in the House of Commons but was defeated overwhelmingly in the House of Lords).

Parnell was buried in the non-denominational Glasnevin Cemetery in Dublin on 11 October 1891. His funeral was attended by more than two hundred thousand people.

William Ewart Gladstone was later to say of him -

"Parnell was the most remarkable man I ever met. I do not say the ablest man; I say the most remarkable and the most interesting. He was an intellectual phenomenon."

In his book, *Charles Stewart Parnell,* published in 1973, the writer, F.S.L. Lyons, summed up Parnell thus -

"He gave his people back their self-respect."

"He did this.......by rallying an inert and submissive peasantry to believe that by organised and disciplined protest they could win a better life for themselves and their children. He did it further, and still more strikingly, by demonstrating. .... that even a small Irish party could disrupt the business of the greatest legislature in the world and, by a combination of skill and tenacity, could deal on equal terms with ......eventually, hold the balance between – the two major English parties."

The historian, A.J.P. Taylor says -

"More than any other man he gave Ireland the sense of being an independent nation."

In 2002 an amazing artefact was found in St. Patrick's Church in the heart of 'Little Ireland' that appears to commemorate the Parish's strong support for Parnell's fight for Ireland's freedom.

At Sunday Mass, I listened as Fr Richard Reid a priest of the parish of St. Patrick's Church told of his exciting discovery! A friend had been visiting him in the parish house and he had commented on a painting that hung on the dining room wall. I knew the painting well, as a friend, Fr Stephen McGrath, had been parish priest at St. Patrick's some years before and I had often admired it while visiting him. Fr Richard realised he knew nothing about the painting and after his friend left he decided to google the artist to see if he could find some information.

The painting was titled '*Mass in a Connemara Cabin*' and the artist was Aloysius O'Kelly.

An article and a list of O'Kelly's paintings came up and included was that painting. But it was captioned -'Missing Mass in a Connemara Cabin'. Fr Richard was a bit puzzled at that because, as he said, the people were obviously NOT missing mass – they were there. It took a minute or so for him to realise that it was the painting that was missing! The article had been written by an Irish Art Historian, Dr Niamh O'Sullivan and Fr Richard managed to get a contact number for her. Her husband answered the call and said that his wife was working away from home but could he help? When Fr Richard said that he had the missing painting there was a pause and then the man said - "Is this some kind of a joke?" The painting had been missing for more than one hundred years! Fr Richard was alone in the parish house and he described how he paced up and down until his fellow priests returned and he could share the news with them. After another excited telephone conversation, this time with Niamh O'Sullivan, she was able to confirm that the painting was indeed the missing '*Mass in a Connemara Cabin*'. The painting was valued at £500,000. After discussion with Cardinal Keith Patrick O'Brien of the Archdiocese of St. Andrews and Edinburgh, the people of St. Patrick's Parish agreed that the safest, and most appropriate, home for the painting was in the National Gallery of Ireland in Dublin and gave it on loan. Fr Richard told of the stress he felt until a professional packer and courier arrived to transport the painting to Dublin.

The discovery of the painting had made the news. The night after the painting was sent safely on its way to Dublin the parish house was broken into!

A reproduction of '*Mass in a Connemara Cabin*' by Aloysius O'Kelly now hangs at the back of the church.

So how had this painting ended up in the priest's house of St. Patrick Church in 'Little Ireland'?

Aloysius O'Kelly was born on 3 July 1853 in Dublin to John O'Kelly and Bridget Lawlor. His father ran a blacksmith's shop and dray making business in Dublin. The O'Kelly and Lawlor family became part of a group of artists and political activists in 19th century Irish cultural history.

Aloysius' father died in 1861 and his mother, Bridget, took her children to London where her brother, John Lawlor, was a successful sculptor. He took Aloysius and his brothers James, Charles and Stephen on as apprentices in his studio.

Aloysius O'Kelly became an artist and moved to Paris to study at the Ecole des Beaux-Arts in 1874. In 1876 he moved to Brittany and painted many works featuring the region's scenery. By the time that 'Mass in a Connemara Cabin' was painted in 1883 he was already an established artist. The painting was exhibited at the *Paris Salon* of 1884. It was the first painting by an Irish artist to be selected by the *Salon*.

"In the early 1880's O'Kelly returned to Ireland having been appointed Special Artist to the *Illustrated London News*. This position 'allowed him to visually capture the bleak existence of working class people on the west coast of Ireland in the aftermath of An Gorta Mor (the Great Hunger) and the subsequent agrarian unrest, rise of the Irish National Land League and political and social upheaval. It was during these turbulent times that O'Kelly produced *Mass in a Connemara Cabin.*' "(Jim Slaven -Art and the Revolution)

O'Kelly had lived for a time in Connemara and it is thought that the Cabin in the painting may have been his own. "Both an artist and a Fenian, O'Kelly's painting is about the harsh reality of tenant farmers' lives in the West of Ireland at the time and their faith." It is not just a religious painting, it is also political. The Irish Land League had been founded in Castlebar in 1879 to try and undo the injustices inflicted on Irish Catholic tenant farmers imposed during penal times.

At the heart of the Land League stands Charles Stewart Parnell. So could there be a connection?

In October 1881, Charles Stewart Parnell, Member of Parliament and leader of the Irish Party, was arrested and imprisoned in

Kilmainham. Two days later, Aloysius' brother, James J. O' Kelly, John Dillon and other Party members were also arrested. They were held for seven months. Many of Aloysius O'Kelly's drawings during this period dealt with his brother's incarceration. He also painted and drew members of the Land League. Parnell, James J. O'Kelly and the others were released on the terms of the so called 'Treaty of Kilmainham'.

There seems no doubt that Aloysius O'Kelly's Irish paintings were political. They include – *'Opening of the New Irish Land Court in Connaught'* (1881), *'The State of Ireland -Tilling the Farm of an Imprisoned Land Leaguer (1881), An Eviction in the West of Ireland (1881), 'The Irish Land League:Recreation time in Kilmainham Prison'* (1881), *'Distress in Ireland:Waiting for Relief Outside the Priest's House in Kilronan'* (1886) and right in the middle of these paintings – *'Mass in a Connemara Cabin'* (1883). No wonder Art Historians see links between 'religious practice and the Land War' in the work. In those times Mass in rural areas was often followed by gathering socially and (the masses) 'almost seamlessly facilitate the transition from socializing to politicizing'. (Niamh O'Sullivan)

Given this strong political aspect it is perhaps not so surprising that a painting by Aloysius O'Kelly should end up in St. Patrick's Church in 'Little Ireland'. Nowhere, outside Ireland itself, showed more support for Charles Stewart Parnell and the Land League. Charles Stewart Parnell being awarded the Freedom of the City of Edinburgh gave a huge boost to the Home Rule for Ireland Movement. It generated a great deal of publicity at the time. It brought the Cause to the attention of people throughout Britain who had taken little interest before in what was happening in Ireland. The significance of the Award and the publicity around the Parade along Princes Street, when thousands lined the street, and the mass Rally on Calton Hill in Scotland's capital city got widespread attention. Its importance cannot be underestimated. The fact that it happened in Edinburgh and not Glasgow, with it's much larger Irish immigrant population, was entirely due to the support of one man, Canon Edward Hannan, and the people of St. Patrick's Church in 'Little Ireland'. The priest had endured censure from Archbishop Smith and the church hierarchy. Michael Flannigan had been stripped of the Presidency of the Catholic Young Men's Society in St. Patrick's parish and ordered by the Archbishop not to speak in support of Parnell's Land League. Both priest and people suffered greatly for their support.

There is a tradition in the parish that the painting was a gift to their parish priest for the congregation's support for Ireland. If that is true then the priest had to be Canon Edward Hannan. His unstinting support for the Land League and for his Catholic Young Men's Society and his parishioner's campaign to have Charles Stewart Parnell presented with the Freedom of Edinburgh, even under pressure from the Church's hierarchy, his presence at the Rally on Calton Hill and at the Award Ceremony in the City Chambers make him the obvious recipient of the gift.

Did St. Patrick's Church receive the gift from the artist himself or from his brother, James J. O'Kelly, who had shared imprisonment with Parnell? Aloysius O'Kelly was an established artist and the painting would have been very valuable even then. The first Irish painting to be shown at the *Paris Salon,* later exhibited abroad and in London it could be claimed to be Aloysius O'Kelly's most famous work. It is known that it disappeared at the end of the nineteenth century.

James J. O'Kelly stayed loyal to Parnell even after the Party split and he gave support to Kitty and the family on Charles Stewart Parnell's death. He lost his Parliamentary Seat as a result of his loyalty to Parnell to an anti-Parnellite but was re-elected at a subsequent election. Did he, and his brother Aloysius, give it to Canon Hannan because of St. Patrick's long time support for Charles Stewart Parnell?

Or could it be possible that '*Mass in a Connemara Cabin*', this political and highly valuable painting, had actually been a gift from Charles Stewart Parnell himself to thank the priest and the people of St. Patrick's Church in 'Little Ireland' for their campaigning work that resulted in him being granted the Freedom of Edinburgh? We will never know but given that the painting remained in St. Patrick's parish, even after the death of Canon Hannan, shows that the gift was meant for the people of the parish who had suffered so much in the Cause.

One thing I am sure of is that Luke Joseph Boylan, as President of the National Land League branch in 'Little Ireland', would have been there when it was gifted.

Many years later, it was to be another political activist, 'Little Ireland'-born James Connolly, who was to lead Ireland on the first steps to Independence.

While it was the land ownership question that first drew Charles Stewart Parnell into politics and the fight for Home Rule for Ireland, for James Connolly his motivation was first, last and always, the promotion of socialism. Though he was Scots born he always acknowledged his Irish heritage and his years in the British Army, in Ireland, engendered in him a hatred of that army. But socialism, with it's belief in the rights of the working man, was always his governing creed. It was in the promotion of that Cause that he was ultimately to give his life. He is credited with laying the foundation for Christian socialism in Ireland. On his deathbed he returned to his Catholic faith.

Though remembered now as a founder of Irish Republicanism, James Connolly was never in doubt that there was no guarantee that would secure Socialism. Writing in the *Workers Republic* in 1899, he stated -

"After Ireland is free, says the patriot who won't touch Socialism, we will protect all classes, and if you won't pay your rent you will be evicted same as now. But the evicting party, under command of the sheriff, will wear green uniforms and the Harp without the Crown, and the warrant turning you out on the roadside will be stamped with the arms of the Irish Republic."

After he moved with his family from Edinburgh to Dublin to work as Secretary for the Dublin Socialist Club he was instrumental in forming the Irish Socialist Republican Party (ISRP) in1896.

Connolly was frustrated at the slow progress of the ISRP and he and his family were struggling economically so, in September1903, they emigrated to the United States. There he threw himself into Socialist activities. He joined the Socialist Labor Party of America in 1906, the Socialist Party of America in 1909 and the Industrial Workers of the World organization. He founded the Irish Socialist Federation in New York in 1907. He also became the Editor of the *Free Press,* a weekly Socialist newspaper in Pennsylvania, in 1908.

In 1910 he published his book *Labour in Irish History*. He was obviously a very literate and able man. His education up to age eleven, in a Catholic Primary School in poor 'Little Ireland', seems to have stood him in good stead.

He returned to Ireland in 1910 and became involved in the Irish Transport and General Workers Union, and worked closely with it's leader James Larkin. In the 1911 Irish Census he gives his occupation as 'National Organiser Socialist Party'. He stood as a candidate for the Dublin Corporation elections but was unsuccessful.

In 1912, Connolly, along with James Larkin and William O'Brien, founded the Irish Labour Party as the political wing of the Irish Trades Union Congress and he served on its National Executive.

In 1913, in response to the Dublin Union lock-out he, James Larkin and Jack White, founded the Irish Citizen Army (ICA).

This was an armed, well-trained group of working men, whose purpose was to protect workers and strikers from the brutality of the Dublin Metropolitan police force.

James Connolly was Editor of *The Irish Worker* newspaper. It was closed down by the Defence of the Realm Act of 1914.

Throughout this period of his life you can see James Connolly's attempt to educate working people as to their rights, and to act to protect those rights against a brutal opposition.

World War I broke out in 1914. In Ireland, Connolly vehemently opposed the war - on Socialist principles - declaring -

"I know of no foreign enemy of this country except the British Government."

Back in 'Little Ireland', my grandfather, Patrick Delaney, signed up, taking the 'King's shilling' as a means of supporting his widowed mother. In later years he was to say to me - "Patricia, never volunteer for anything !"

Taking the opportunity of the British being distracted by the war, Connolly and the Irish Citizens Army made plans for an armed uprising. The Irish Republican Brotherhood had already been secretly laying plans for an insurrection that year. Believing that the Irish Volunteers were dithering, Connolly told them, if necessary, the Irish Citizen Army would go it alone against the British.

This alarmed the Irish Republican Brotherhood (IRB) and, trying to talk Connolly out of any action, its leaders, Tom Clarke and Patrick Pearse, met with James Connolly to see if an agreement could be reached. Instead, he convinced them that the time was now and they agreed to plan together the 'Easter Rising'.

The Rising began on 24 April 1916 and as James Connolly was Commandant of the Dublin Brigade, the dominant force, he was regarded as Commandant in Chief. His leadership was formidable. Later, Michael Collins, the future Irish Leader who returned from living in London as a young man to fight in the Easter Rising, said - "He would have followed Connolly into Hell."

There was fierce fighting, mainly around the General Post Office in Dublin, but ultimately the Rising failed. James Connolly had warned his volunteers that they would probably all die in the struggle.

James Connolly himself was badly wounded during the fighting and, when he was captured, he was taken to a room in the State Apartments at Dublin Castle, which had been converted to a First Aid Station for troops recovering from the conflict.

He was sentenced to death, by firing squad, for his part in the Easter Rising. While in Dublin Castle he was visited by his wife and daughter. He said to them - "The Socialists will not understand why I am here; they forget I am an Irishman."

James Connolly had given up the practice of his Catholic faith in the 1890s but returned to the Catholic Church before his execution. Three months after his execution, his wife, Lille Connolly, who had been a Protestant, converted and became a Roman Catholic.

Connolly had been so badly injured in the fighting that a doctor said he only had a day or two to live. Nevertheless, on 12 May 1916 he was taken by military ambulance to Royal Hospital Kilmainham and from there taken to the gaol for the execution. He was unable to walk so was carried by stretcher to his execution. Being unable to stand, due to his injuries, he was not marched to where the other leaders had been executed, but was tied to a chair and then executed by firing squad where he sat.

His body, along with the rest of the leaders, was thrown into a mass grave without a coffin.

The majority of the Irish population had shown no support for the rebels up to and during the Easter Rising but the manner of their deaths caused anger and widespread condemnation. It was the manner of James Connolly's execution, shooting an already dying man, in a chair, that caused the most controversy.

It caused outrage, even in Britain, and particularly in the USA with its large Irish Diaspora. It happened at a time when Britain was trying to encourage support from the Americans for their war with Germany. As a result of the outrage, H.H. Asquith, the British Prime Minister, ordered there be no more executions.

Ironically, as historians have pointed out, the manner of Connolly and the other rebels' executions, along with their actions, drew attention to the Cause for which they had given their lives, and raised awareness, and in time, support for Irish Independence. It would be be a long and bloody struggle but at last the Irish Free State would be founded.

After the failure to deliver Home Rule for Ireland, support for the Liberal Party in 'Little Ireland' began to decline. In time, support for the Labour Party grew among the working men of 'Little Ireland'.

I have no way of knowing if Luke Joseph Boylan continued to be involved in the Liberal Party after the highlight of Charles Stewart Parnell's triumphant visit to receive the Freedom of Edinburgh in 1889, which he had helped organize. I suspect that he did as my grandfather said that the family in 'Little Ireland' were Liberal voters, seeing the party as being committed to social change.

For Luke Joseph Boylan himself, like Parnell, the visit in 1889 was to be the high point in his life. In January 1890, his beloved mother, Helen Delaney Boylan, died. She had been suffering illness in her home on George IV Bridge and he decided to move her into the care of the nuns. The Order of the Little Sisters of the Poor ran a care home in Gilmore Place and, in January 1890, Helen was taken there. Her death certificate says she died there, and notes that her usual address was George IV Bridge. My sister, Frances Connolly (nee Delaney), made contact with the convent, which was still in existence until recently, to ask for further details. They searched their records but found that Helen had never actually been admitted to the Home. We can only assume that when she was taken in Helen died immediately on arrival.

We had assumed that she would have been buried beside her husband, Philip Boylan, in the large family plot in the Canongate Graveyard. However, she is not mentioned in the inscriptions on the large ornate Boylan Monument there. Many years later, my brother, Michael Delaney, discovered that our great-great-great grandmother, Helen Delaney (nee Collins), was buried by her son, Luke Joseph Boylan, in Morningside Cemetery in the city. Sadly, no gravestone survives from 1890 though we feel sure that Luke would have marked his beloved mother's grave. We later learned that buried in the same plot were her son, Philip Boylan and her grand-daughter, Jessie Boylan.

Eleanor Lennon (nee Boylan)

Eleanor, born 1828, was the daughter of Philip Boylan's first marriage to Dorothy Warrick. It was she who had erected the ornate Boylan Monument, on the large family plot, in the Canongate Graveyard. When her mother, Dorothy, died in 1850, her father, Philip Boylan, had her interred in the family plot in the Canongate Graveyard where Eleanor's four brothers had been buried. When Philip himself died in 1875 he also was buried there, beside his first wife.

Eleanor was devoted to her mother. When she bought her large mansion house in South Fort Street in Leith, she changed it's name to 'Warrick House' after her dead mother. Could it be that Eleanor disapproved of her elderly father marrying the much younger Helen Delaney just six months after her mother's death?

Could that be the reason that she refused to let her half-brother, Luke Joseph Boylan, bury his mother, Helen, beside Eleanor's parents in the Canongate Graveyard?

It was certainly not lack of space as Eleanor's son, John Lennon, was later buried there in 1881, as was Eleanor herself in 1891, as well as Luke Joseph's wife, Patricia Campsie, in 1892 and finally, Luke Joseph himself in 1913.

Eleanor Lennon (nee Boylan) sounds like a formidable woman. A worthy daughter of her entrepreneurial father, Philip Boylan. Unusually for a woman at that time, following in her father's footsteps she built up a large rental property business in Edinburgh and the Port of Leith.

She married John Lennon in 1845 and and they had a son, Philip Lennon, born in 1849, named after her father. He died as a baby and was buried in the Boylan plot in the Canongate. In 1851, the year after her father married Helen Delaney, they had a second son named John Lennon after his father. It was obviously Eleanor herself who was the brains behind the business. Later, her husband, John, left her and ran away to Australia!

Looking through the Valuation Rolls we discovered that Eleanor owned forty-nine properties, which she rented out. She also bought a mansion house, standing in its own walled grounds in South Fort Street in Leith. We discovered, from a census, that the house had seventeen rooms (with windows). It was in this substantial house, renamed Warrick House, that she lived with her son.

In a census, Eleanor, as Head of the household, states that her son, John Lennon, lives with her and she gives his occupation as 'gentleman'. We wondered how being a 'gentleman' could be regarded as an occupation and thought perhaps that it meant he did not have to work!

A later census reveals that John is in fact a surgeon. The honorary title 'gentleman' was always used for a surgeon. Quite amazing that the grandson of a poor Irish emigrant, Philip Boylan, was able to qualify for such a prestigious occupation in two generations. This census also reveals that Eleanor has a young grand-daughter, Ellen, living with them. This can only be John's illegitimate daughter.

Tragically, in spite of their wealth and John's prestigious job, John Lennon dies, aged thirty, of a drug overdose in 1881. After the death certificate was issued with that information, Eleanor obviously asked that a correction be made to the death certificate. The corrected certificate states that his death was 'accidental' as he had been taking the drug to help him get some sleep. It was important that Eleanor got this correction as otherwise a suicide victim would not be allowed to be buried in 'hallowed' ground. With the corrected certificate Eleanor was able to bury her son in the Boylan plot in the Canongate Graveyard and his name is inscribed on the ornate Boylan Memorial.

We do not know what became of Eleanor's grand-daughter, Ellen. We assume she too must have died young, but we can find no death certificate for an Ellen Lennon, so presumably she was not given the surname Lennon. She certainly did not benefit from Eleanor's Estate in1891.

Eleanor Lennon (nee Boylan) died the year after her step-mother, Helen, in 1891, and is buried in the Boylan plot in the Canongate

Graveyard, under the large ornate Monument that she designed and paid to have erected.

She left no Will but I found the Intestate entry and the Inventory in the 1891 register. It stated that –"Eleanor Lennon owned extensive properties in Edinburgh and Leith but on hearing of her death all her tenants absconded without paying the rent owed."

This was quite a common occurrence. In Edinburgh it was called –'doing a midnight flit'! These tenants would be very poor and it was usual for them to move from property to property, seeking cheaper rents. So, hearing of Eleanor's death they would simply up sticks and move to another slum property, leaving rent owing. The entry states that therefore the rents owing could not be recovered.

Since Eleanor Lennon died Intestate, with no heirs, Luke Joseph Boylan, her half-brother, claimed her Estate on behalf of himself and his surviving siblings, James Boylan and Mary McGill (nee Boylan). Luke Joseph himself, as oldest male, inherited all her properties, while her 'moveable' estate - cash, bank deposits and furniture was divided among her half-siblings. Eleanor was an extremely wealthy woman and the inheritance of her properties made Luke Joseph even wealthier. He sold Warrick House and some of the rented properties, retaining only twenty-nine of them.

Whether his good fortune made him happy is however another matter.

Three months after his mother, Helen, had died in January 1890, his younger brother, Philip Boylan, died. When we found details of the grave we discovered that Luke had buried his brother in the same plot as their mother in Morningside Cemetery.

Then on 27 July 1892, Luke Joseph's wife, Patricia Campsie, died. We had found it curious while researching his life why his wife is never mentioned. When Luke Joseph travelled to meet Charles Stewart Parnell at Carlisle Railway Station, he took his mother, Helen, not his young wife with him.

When we found Patricia Boylan's death certificate we realised why. Tragically, Patricia died in their home at 5 Thirlestane Road on 27 July 1892 of "Alcoholic poisoning, with paralysis of the upper and lower limbs". She was only twenty-eight years old.

Whatever had happened to the teenage bride over the eleven years of marriage to Luke Joseph, to have driven her to such a condition? It is true her father, James Campsie, was a publican, so she would be used to being around alcohol, but she was only seventeen when she married. Something had gone sadly wrong for this young woman. Her husband, Luke, buried her in the Boylan plot in the Canongate Graveyard, and her name is inscribed on the Monument. They had no children.

Within two years, Luke Joseph Boylan had lost his mother, Helen, his brother, Philip, his half-sister, Eleanor, and his young wife, Patricia.

His parish priest, Canon Edward Hannan, had died in June 1891, a year after his mother. They had shared so many hopes for Ireland and Luke had worked tirelessly to bring about Home Rule. Now those dreams of Home Rule lay in ruins.

His great political hero, Charles Stewart Parnell, had died on 27 September 1891, four months after Canon Hannan. Luke Joseph must have felt his world was falling down around him. Then the final blow, the loss of his young wife.

He continued as a pawnbroker in 'Little Ireland' but he moved from his married home in Thirlestane Road to a flat in a gracious stone block, in Hillside Crescent, not far from Hibernian's football ground at Easter Road. He never remarried.

Luke Joseph Boylan died in his final home, a lavishly furnished apartment – complete with grand piano - in a Georgian block - at 61 Elm Row, on Leith Walk in 1913.

He is buried in the family plot in the Canongate Graveyard and his name is inscribed on the grand Boylan Memorial. He was a man who never wanted for anything, who led a privileged life that his humble Irish heritage could never have predicted, he was involved in momentous times for Ireland and sought to bring about change in that country, but he also had great unhappiness in his life.

He died a very wealthy man but he made no Will – but that is a whole other story!

Fig.1 Arthur Delaney's tombstone

Fig.2 Emyvale village in 1910

Fig.3 Guards in Emyvale in 1923

Fig.4 Brown Square

184

Fig.5 St Mary's Wynd

Fig.6 St Mary's Wynd

Fig.7 St Mary's Wynd

Fig.8 The collapse of Paisley Close

Fig.9 The Boylan Monument

189

Fig.10 Tregilgas/Barry family group

Fig.11 Ellen Clarke Tregilgas

Fig.12 JOhn Sylvester Delaney

Fig.13 Elizabeth McAlpine

Fig.14 Luke Terence Delaney

Fig.15 Luke Terence Delaney starting the Paris to Madrid Road Race

Fig.16 Luke Terence Delaney at the Paris Motor Show

Fig.17 Luke Terence Delaney with Desmond and Dorothy

Fig.18 Luke Teerence Delaney driving his family Tourer

Fig.19 Luke Terence Delaney with his wife and family

Fig.20 Luke Terence Delaney setting off by plane for the Paris Motor Show

Fig.21 Luke Sylvestre Delaney

Fig.22 Arthur Philip Delaney

Fig.23 James Delaney and his family

Fig.24 Cecilia Clifford

CHAPTER THIRTEEN

LUKE TERENCE DELANEY

When John Sylvester Delaney, the actor, died in Oldham on 27 December 1884 and was buried under the wrong name, he left behind in London his wife Elizabeth McAlpine and his two sons, Luke Terence Delaney born 3 November 1879 and John William Delaney born 15 June 1884.

Elizabeth was living in a new block of upmarket flats, called 'The Palatinate,' on the New Kent Road. The news of her husband's death must have come as a terrible shock. She had only seen him off a few days before. John had been signed for the lead role of Mrs O'Sinbad in the Oldham Theatre's Christmas Panto, he was only 36, apparently in good health and at the top of his profession. He was a famous actor in Victorian Theatre well known for his portrayal of Irish comedy roles, who had performed in America and Canada as well as in theatres across Britain.

Elizabeth had stayed home because she had recently given birth to their second son, John William, on 15 June 1884. The couple tragically lost their young daughter, Kathleen, to tuberculosis, four months later on 13 October 1884. Since their marriage, Elizabeth had usually travelled with her husband and stayed in theatrical digs or rented houses while he performed in lengthy runs in theatres across the country. As their family increased they had settled into this new apartment in London.

I wonder how soon Elizabeth heard of John's death. He took ill in his digs when he had just arrived in the town to rehearse the Panto. He was admitted to the local Infirmary, in a town where only the Theatre Company would know him. From the records it is obvious there was complete chaos at the Infirmary, attached to the local workhouse, leading, we believe, to John being wrongly identified and confused with a workhouse resident who also died. It would have taken time for the Theatre Company to hear of his admittance and then death. No doubt they would send a telegram to his wife, miles away in London, alone with a baby and a toddler. What could Elizabeth do? I suspect from the dates that John was buried within three days, as was the custom then. Hence the mistaken identity that resulted in John Sylvester Delaney being buried under another man's name.

It is hard to imagine how desperate Elizabeth's situation was. Her own mother was dead and her father had remarried. How much help did she get? We just don't know.

The first evidence we have been able to uncover was when ten months later the widowed Elizabeth Delaney (nee McAlpine) appears in Edinburgh with her five-year-old son, Luke Terence, and her baby, John William. She had brought her children to see their grandmother, Helen Delaney, who had married Philip Boylan, but he was now dead. It appears that when they arrive, Helen, a devout Catholic, asks if the children are baptised. We know that Luke Terence was because the London Delaney family have traced his baptism record in St. Mary and St. Boniface Catholic Church in Plymouth in November 1879, where his father had been performing in the theatre. Obviously, the couple had not had their second son baptised before John died. Helen immediately arranged to have John William baptised in St. Patrick's Church, in 'Little Ireland', on 30 March 1885, where his godmother is recorded as being – Mrs McKenna.

It was through another of the cases of serendipity that occur in this story that we were able to place the baby's baptism in context.

Many years ago the London Delaney family, seeking information on John Sylvester Delaney's parents, put a post online which my brother, Michael Delaney, spotted. That contact has resulted in close friendships developing between the Edinburgh and London Delaney families!

The contact solved another mystery for us. In the collection of old photographs, belonging to my grandfather, Patrick Delaney, was one of an attractive woman, looking very prosperous, dressed in furs. We wondered if it was Helen Delaney, our great-great-great grandmother, but by then, my grand-father, Patrick, was dead and there was nobody left who knew. It was not until our cousin, Janet Croome (nee Delaney), one of the London family, sent me an identical photograph that we learned the lady was Elizabeth Delaney (nee McAlpine), wife of John Sylvester Delaney, the actor. Janet knew the lady's identity because her own father had told her the photograph was of her great-grandmother, Elizabeth. He added that she was 26 years old when it was taken. Knowing now that Elizabeth had visited 'Little Ireland' after her husband's death, we realise that is how the photograph ended up in my grandfather's possession. Looking at it with fresh knowledge we realised it showed Elizabeth in mourning clothes. Judging by the quality of her clothes it seems Elizabeth had not been left in poverty.

Piecing all this together we assumed that Elizabeth had paid a visit to John's grieving mother, to let her see her grandsons, had John William baptised, then returned to London. However, now we had made contact with our cousins Janet and Terry Delaney of the London family, snippets of information shared by them began to create a more intriguing scenario.

Janet and Terry's grandfather was Luke Terence Delaney, Elizabeth and John Sylvester's first-born son. Luke Terence had six children with his wife, Amy Farquhar, including a daughter, Constance Delaney. Auntie Connie was well remembered by both Janet and Terry and she told the family that her father, Luke Terence, had told her that - "He was brought up by the family in Edinburgh"!

Well this information changed the whole scenario for us - Luke Terence Delaney was brought up by our family in 'Little Ireland'!

Since it was unlikely that Luke Terence, a highly successful businessman in London, would make this up, we began to wonder how this came to happen. The conclusion we have reached is that when the widow Elizabeth brought her two sons to Edinburgh a family discussion took place. Though Elizabeth looks like she has not been left destitute (and how could she be as we know that her husband, John Sylvester Delaney, had been a well known actor) his death still left the little family with no breadwinner. Elizabeth, aged 26, was left to bring up her two young sons alone in London without family around. She had earned her living as a dress-maker prior to marrying John Sylvester, so perhaps she could return to that to supplement her income? But that would not be easy if she had two children, one just months old, to care for.

I believe she was persuaded by the Edinburgh family to leave five-year-old Luke Terence with his grandmother, uncles, aunts and young cousins, in Edinburgh. It must have been a heart-breaking decision for Elizabeth to leave her young son behind but she must have realised that here he would be surrounded by a large extended family, with cousins around his own age to play with. It would be easier for her if she only had a baby to cope with while she worked.

There was another consideration – the Edinburgh family were very comfortably off – Luke Terence would want for nothing. We know from Luke Terence Delaney's later life that he appeared to be very well educated and his time in Edinburgh covers the compulsory education years between age five and age twelve - he could also do Scottish Country dancing!

We assumed that the family story was true and that Luke Terence had been brought up in 'Little Ireland' but it was not until recently that our cousin, Janet Croome (nee Delaney), found written proof. She discovered an old publication – *'Grace's Guide'* – which gave a 'who's who' of prominent people in the car industry. It gave 'potted' histories of the Delaney family, featuring Luke Terence, Desmond (Luke's oldest son) and Cyril (known as Tom- Luke's second son). In the extract about Luke Terence Delaney it said he was educated in Edinburgh – great find!

Unfortunately, Luke's time in 'Little Ireland' fell between two censuses so we do not know which family members he lived with. The London Delaney family have, however, a collection of letters, known hereafter as -'The Edinburgh Letters', in which,when he is an adult, Luke Terence Delaney corresponds with the family back in the Old Town, letters which express mutual affection. He obviously knew these people well, and they knew him. In all of the letters, from different family members, Luke Terence is always addressed as Terry, and in the letters from Luke he always signs himself, Terry. This was obviously to avoid confusion with his uncle and namesake, Luke Boylan, so hereafter I will refer to him by his family name of Terry.

It is likely then, given these dates, that Terry Delaney would have attended one of the Catholic schools opened by Canon Edward Hannan, and that he would have received his First Holy Communion from the priest and been confirmed in St. Patrick's Church. The Delaney family in 'Little Ireland' were devout Catholics and prominent members of the congregation of St. Patrick's Church. Terry's father, John Sylvester Delaney, first learned his stage skills in Father Hannan's Catholic Young Men's Society Dramatic Group.

Terry would have been surrounded by people who had known his father.

In his adult life in England, Terry described himself as a 'lapsed Catholic' but he was reconciled to the Faith on his deathbed.

Luke Boylan was the boy's half uncle and his namesake and, given Luke's close political involvement with Canon Hannan in the fight for Home Rule for Ireland, Terry might well have been among the crowds who welcomed Charles Stewart Parnell to Edinburgh. It is even more likely that the boy would have been there to see Hibernian returning home to 'Little Ireland' after winning the Scottish Cup on 12 February 1887.

We know from the census records for England, that Terry, aged twelve, was back living with his mother Elizabeth and his young brother John William in London in 1891.

I believe he had not long returned and that he had lived for the preceding seven years in 'Little Ireland'. Many years later, once he had become a well-known, highly-successful businessman in London, an interviewer, in an article, described him as a Scotsman. This could only be because he spoke with a Scot's accent, acquired during his formative years in Edinburgh. Also, a humorous article, titled – 'Between Ourselves' in *The Auto Journal* dating from July 1921, written by 'Iolaus', refers to Luke - "I remember taking little Teddy Delaney for a ride in that old Panhard, round Regents Park, and he cried because he heard the lion's roaring in the Zoo! In a Highland costume with a kilt, young Delaney was about five I should guess. A nice child! They tell me *he* went into the motor trade." 'Teddy' was the name Terry was known as in the motor trade and the reference to the kilt makes it clear he was regarded as a Scotsman! It also makes it clear that by 1921, Terry was very well known in the motor trade, for the joke to work - a celebrity!

Of course, the writer made up the story. Terry Delaney wasn't in London when he was five years old as he was living in 'Little Ireland.'

So why did he leave? It might have been what had previously been agreed to between his mother and the family in Edinburgh - but why at age eleven?

I think the most likely reason was that in January 1890, Terry's grandmother, Helen Delaney (Boylan), died. I feel sure that it was she who had brought him up in Edinburgh, supported by her sons and daughter. Even then, he might have stayed but his uncle, Philip Boylan, died three months after his grandmother Helen. Philip and his wife, Catherine, had children near in age to Terry and going on the sentiments expressed by his Aunt Catherine later, in the 'Edinburgh Letters', it seems Terry was particularly close to that branch of the family. In the London Delaney family archive they have discovered a photograph of Terry and his family, on a beach in England, with his cousin Philip Boylan and his family. We already knew from our Edinburgh research that Philip had moved to England as a young man. So, Terry and his close cousin, Philip, must have re-united in adulthood. Back in Edinburgh in 1890, however, Catherine Boylan was a young widow and without the support of her recently deceased mother-in-law, Helen, would be struggling herself so likely unable to continue to support young Terry. The only one left who could help was his uncle, Luke Boylan, and as we have learned Luke himself had problems with an alcoholic wife.

It seems like the perfect storm and the likely reason why Terry returned to London to live with his mother. He must have missed his life with the family in 'Little Ireland' having been with them for all his childhood. He had probably assumed he would stay there and perhaps work in one of the family businesses. We don't know if Elizabeth visited Edinburgh regularly during those years, or if they barely knew each other. Certainly, his young brother, John William, would be a stranger to him.

Perhaps the experience of leaving 'Little Ireland' at such a young age, to live with a mother and brother he hardly knew, left it's mark on Terry because he became a strong, determined, resolute, independent man – and a practical one. We know that in his early adulthood he took out a Life Insurance policy on his mother and brother - presumably to cover any future funeral expenses!

He was also a multi-talented, resourceful, brave and successful one.

His first job seems to have been as a cub reporter for The Sun Newspaper. The London Delaneys have, in their family archive, a letter of reference from the newspaper. It confirms (for any future employer) that Terry has - "been in the employ of The Sun for about six months" - it is dated 25 April 1895. So he must have joined them about November 1894 when he had just turned fifteen years old. Could it be hearing of the emerging exciting developments in the new motor industry that fired his interest and made him realise that journalism was not for him?

In an article in the 'The Aeroplane Magazine' of 16 April 1919, the journalist who interviewed Terry, reports that as early as 1898 Terry had already been "tinkering with belt-driven Benz cars."

In 1900, Terry joined the International Benz Company, the original and only motor firm assembling and selling cars on Great Portland Street in London. In the 1901 census in London, when Terry is 22 years old, he gives his occupation as motor engineer.

We also learned in the 'who's who' entry that Terry continued his education in London at the Northampton Institute. Could that have been between the ages of twelve, when he was back living with his mother, and fifteen, when he joined The Sun newspaper as a trainee reporter? Or could it be after leaving The Sun newspaper in1895, aged sixteen, that he took a Course at the Institute? One of the courses the College offered was Engineering and Metal Work – seems tailor made for Terry's interests.

Or could it be that Terry got an apprenticeship with a car manufacturer?

Among the pioneers of the internal combustion engine car industry were two Germans, Gottlieb Daimler and Karl Benz. They set up the first two companies to go into serious car production in France.

By 1895, Bersey, a London based engineering business, had been building cars powered by electric motors but soon turned to manufacturing taxi cabs – presumably seeing them as a more lucrative business. In 1897 the taximeter had been introduced, a mechanical device for accurately measuring the fare payable by passengers according to distance travelled. In time these vehicles became known as taxi-cabs and by1900 75 Bersey taxi-cabs were operating in London.

In the late 1890s, the German Daimler's cars were being manufactured, under his name, by an English Company in Coventry who had bought the rights. The Wolseley car (originally Australian) was in production in Birmingham in 1889. Its director was Herbert Austin who, in time, left to found his own company manufacturing his own cars and going on to produce the iconic Austin Seven. In 1901 the New Orleans Car Company was manufacturing in its premises in Twickenham. There certainly seems to have been the opportunity for a motor apprenticeship.

We do know, for certain, that Terry went to France to obtain practical training in French motor car engineering because the London family have a copy of a document, complete with his photograph, dated 10 March 1899, when he was not yet twenty, which is a French Driving Licence. This is a little bit of history as France was the first country in the world to introduce driving licences. This was in 1893 when the Chief of Police in Paris, alarmed at the increasing number of cars on the streets of the city, decided regulation was needed for public safety reasons. All drivers needed to prove they were capable of controlling the vehicle and all cars required to display a number plate – another first! Driving licences were not introduced in Britain until 1903, ten years later.

I think we can safely claim that Terry was the first member of the Delaney family to hold a driving licence!

He would require it, of course, as he went to France to train with the famous De Dietrich and Delaunay-Bellville firms – the luxury end of car manufacturing. How did he manage that? It seems that he must have already been a fully-qualified motor engineer at just nineteen. Apart from anything else he must have been fluent in French to get such training. The French are not noted for pandering to English speakers! Such training wouldn't come cheap one would imagine.

We know that he joined the International Benz Company in 1900, in London, but his French Driving Licence is dated March 1899, at least nine months previously. His widowed mother, Elizabeth, would hardly have been in a position to help financially. Even if his father, John Sylvester, had left her comfortably off, it had been some fifteen years since he died and any money was probably long gone. Indeed, I would have thought the widow would have needed Terry's earnings to support her and Luke's young brother by this date.

It may have been that his wealthy, childless uncle, Luke Boylan, back in 'Little Ireland' helped fund his further education and training. Terry's late father, John Sylvester Delaney, had been Luke Boylan's closest older brother and young Terry had been close to his Uncle Luke while growing up in 'Little Ireland' – but we have no proof of this.

Having reached this point in his career, Terry's great drive, ambition, talent and sheer inventiveness would have taken him forward.

Recently, one of Terry's grandsons compared his grandfather's success to the original dot.com creators – Terry got in right at the start of the luxury car market, seized the moment and made a fortune.

Terry was highly intelligent and he must have been a quick learner because we know that having gone to France for practical training, the French car manufacturers later allowed him to test drive their vehicles in several races abroad – and we are talking high-end vehicles here!

He was still only twenty-four when the De Dietrich company, with whom he had trained, allowed him to drive a works 45 h.p. Dietrich Car - No 125, in the notorious Paris to Madrid Race. A rare honour for an amateur driver. The race obtained notoriety because of the speeds the route demanded over rough terrain. Terry later wrote that some of those early cars reached speeds of 80mph, or more, on undulating roads. Five competitors and three spectators died in the race and many others were injured.

Terry later told his son, Tom Delaney, that the organizers had hired professional racing cyclists to go ahead of the racing cars to stop them getting lost going through the villages. They went so fast and, of course, could go where cars could not, and set such a pace that drivers struggled to keep up with them.

The point of the race had been to display the reliability of cars to buyers and the safety of motor cars to a concerned public.

"The race was to be held over three stages amounting to 812 miles of racing through winding streets of villages and towns and out onto tortuous and unpaved tracks in the countryside." (Steve Lanham)

The race set off from the Palace of Versaille on 24 May 1903. 137 cars, as well as other vehicles, started that day. In Paris, uncontrolled crowds lined the route, causing obstacles and slowing the race. Some drivers sped on regardless. The first casualties were Marcel Renault and his mechanic. Going too fast their car left the road and crashed. The mechanic died instantly and Renault died later in hospital.

Leslie Porter, driving a Wolseley, crashed into a gate at a railway crossing. His car burst into flames, he escaped but his mechanic died in the resulting fire.

Later a soldier was hit and killed trying to rescue a child who had run into the road.

"The car, a Tourand, driven by Brunhot, then swerved out of control and piled into onlookers, killing one and injuring many others. While the front runners sped on, breakdowns and crashes accounted for over half of the rest of the field, and the death toll rose with the lives of another spectator and several more participants claimed during the course of the morning." (Steve Lanham)

When the French and Spanish Governments heard of this unfolding disaster they ordered the race to be ended immediately and the other two stages abandoned.

Terry himself crashed but walked away unhurt. The family archive holds photographs of Terry before the start, another of his overturned car and one of him standing looking at the wreckage - he was a very lucky young man!

He must have been a very brave young man as well as an ambitious one and his luck held.

The 1903 Paris to Madrid disaster called a halt to the sport of motor racing. Known as the 'Race of Death' it brought to an end European open road city to city racing - for the time being racing was confined to closed circuits – a sport that, in the future, Terry's son, Tom, was to excel in.

Though Terry's open-road racing came to an end he continued to make steady progress in the motor car industry. Through his time in France he knew many of the famous names such as Louis Renault, Emile Mathis and Ettore Bugatti, so had excellent contacts.

Two years after he had taken part in the Paris to Madrid race, Terry was importing Continental chassis and selling them from the showroom of the International Benz Company on Bond Street in London. The Proprietor of the company was a Mr. O. Syed. The other staff members were a well known cyclist, W. Williamson, and young Terry himself. In 1905 he brought over a very rare 45/60 h.p. PS - type Hermes-Bugatti and drove it in the Blackpool Speed Trials, finishing 5th in his class. This model did not sell well, however other better known continental cars were selling well including the De Dietrich badged Burlington. Terry later wrote that the firm required a 30% deposit, before importing a car for a customer and that they operated a hire purchase scheme for those buyers who required it!

The most popular car, and his best seller, was the Delauney-Bellville, regarded by many to be the best car in the world.

Terry Delaney married Amy Farquhar, a Scottish tailor's daughter, on 2 October 1905 in the St. Pancras Registry Office, London. On the marriage certificate Terry gives his name as Louis Delaney. The founder of the famous French car company – Delaunay - Bellville – which Terry was involved in selling - was Louis Delaunay. Terry, ever one for the main chance, would realise that introducing himself to customers as Louis Delaney - depending on how he pronounced it - while selling the car to rich customers - would make them think he was actually related to the owner!Later, within the English car industry he was known as Terry, or sometimes, Teddy. Back home, in 'Little Ireland,' he was always known as Terry.

When I was young, my grandfather, Patrick Delaney, showed me a business card for the Delauney car company. He said we were related. I thought at the time that he was trying to suggest our name Delaney and the Delauney name might be the same – a bit far-fetched I thought! Now, after our research, I realise that it was Terry's business card, kept by our 'Little Ireland' family for almost one hundred years!

Terry left the International Benz Company and went to work for Frank Wellington whose motor business was at Regents Park. His company was a famous Gas Engine manufacturer. Among the cars Terry handled there were the Hurta, Orient Express and Mors. After leaving Frank Wellington, Terry was asked by W. Williamson, with whom he had worked in the International Benz Company, to take over the London business for his company, Messrs Allard of Coventry. Arrangements were made with the Burlington Carriage Company of Oxford Street for the London Agency.

In 1902, Baron Turckheim brought over two of the new type French De Dietrich cars made at the Luneville factory in France and Terry secured the Agency for them to be taken up. In addition to the French De Dietrich Agency, Terry made an arrangement with E.C. Mathis to purchase a number of De Dietrich cars from Germany, which he thought were better made. These cars had been designed by Bugatti. Again, Terry was one of the first to spot the genius and potential of this Engineer and Inventor, and he was able to sell the cars easily.

Between 1902 and 1903, Terry was finding life very demanding and had to let go of his racing ambitions - the exception being participating in the 1903 Paris to Madrid Race. At that time the companies Terry worked with assisted with the building and testing of the racing cars they were selling and this meant him spending months working abroad.

Terry worked free-lance and as a consultant to the Burlington Carriage Company, importing a range of high-end cars. The number of sales quickly increased. He joined the Burlington Carriage Company to manage their motor car selection. For business policy Terry advised the Burlington Company to adopt a new Agency and visited the Paris Show of 1904 – the family archive holds a photograph of him posing beside these classy cars. While there he spotted the new Delaunay- Bellville car which he thought had the greatest possibilities. Terry arranged to represent the company in England.

Having secured the Delaunay-Bellville concession for what many considered, at the time, as the best car in the world, Terry was on his way! He opened his first factory at Carlton Vale, Maida Vale, London in 1910. It was specially built to supply the luxury Delauney-Bellville car to rich British buyers. The cars were in such demand that within two years the factory had to be extended.

Terry became co-Director of the Burlington Carriage Company. His fellow-Director was Sir Alfred Mays-Smith with whom he was later associated in the foundation of the Bureau des Moteurs Francaises. This company acted as liaison for the purpose of supplying material, to Continental contractors to the British Government, for the manufacture of aircraft engines. Terry's four companies, Delaney Gallay Ltd., L.T. Delaney and Sons, Gallay Ltd. and Gallay Radiator Company, specialised in light alloys and the manufacture of sheet metal components for the automobile and aircraft industries as well as radiators.

I think Terry must have learned his entrepreneurial skills from his family back in 'Little Ireland'!

Two years after extending his factory the First World War broke out. The Great War, the 'War to end all wars' and the Delaunay-Bellville chassis were turned into armoured cars. Terry was 35 years old when the war began. He spent the wars years driving between

Paris and the Royal Navy Air Base at Dunkirk, in France, delivering armoured cars! A brave man, providing a vital service.

Strange to think that during those years his Tregilgas cousins, Ellen and Sarah (Jane Delaney's grand-daughters), were also in France nursing wounded soldiers, his cousin, Patrick Delaney (Arthur Delaney's son), was fighting in the trenches, as were John and James Martin and, tragically, his cousin, William Ferguson Martin, was to die of his wounds in a field hospital in France. The three Martin boys were Jane Delaney's grandsons. Seven descendants of James and Mary Delaney, from County Monaghan, raised in 'Little Ireland', all serving in France at the same period.

In spite of his exploits during the war, and continuing to run his factory in Maida Vale, Terry found the time to get involved, along with the family back in 'Little Ireland, in trying to claim a legacy from a mysterious George Delaney.

A notice had appeared in an Edinburgh newspaper in October 1913, placed by a law firm, asking for possible heirs of a George Delaney, born in Edinburgh in 1856, to Scots born parents. He had died on 28 August 1913, in Greensboro, Hale, Alabama, USA, aged 57. He had been a mechanic (like Terry) and a Plantation owner, and had left a substantial estate, but no heirs.

Terry's aunt, Mary McGill (nee Boylan), who was his father John Sylvester Delaney's half-sister, spotted the advert first and cut it out and sent it with a letter to Terry in London. This newspaper advert sent the Delaney family into a frenzy, and none more so than Terry. However, by now, there was a war on and Terry was dividing himself between France and his London factory. The remaining Delaneys were still in 'Little Ireland' and any evidence must lie in Edinburgh. This resulted in a flurry of correspondence between the two which, amazingly, survive in a collection the London family call -'The Edinburgh Letters'.

Terry's first action was to write to the Edinburgh City Police to ask if the notice was genuine. The Chief Constable, no less, wrote back to him to say that it was. He then wrote to the lawyers handling the case stating he had a possible interest. They wrote back saying send us the proof. Terry then wrote to General Register House, in Edinburgh, sending money and asking them to send him documentation of his own family, as proof of his possible interest. Unfortunately, he did not know his grand-parents names so asked for proof of John Delaney, son of a James Delaney and a woman with the surname Collins. Obviously, he did not know his grandparent's Christian names. His grandfather was actually Arthur Delaney, not James, and his grandmother was Helen Collins.

This is strange since he spent his childhood in Edinburgh with Helen, but perhaps she was only ever Grandma to him, and it had been 23 years before, when Terry was just eleven. The Register General wrote back to say that no such records existed for that couple, he was charging him two shillings for the search and returning the rest of the money he had sent.

Terry then asked his mother, Elizabeth, to write to Thomas Delaney, who was her brother-in-law (John Sylvester's brother). Thomas replies with a warm letter beginning - 'Dear Lizzie' – so obviously they were on familiar terms – and he gives them the correct names of his parents. Unfortunately, poor Thomas has been ill and is now in the Craigleith Poorhouse hospital.

Armed with the correct names, Terry starts to bombard the Catholic priest at St. Mary's Cathedral in Edinburgh with requests to search the records for a George Delaney and his parents. He writes so many letters back and forward to the priest that, eventually, the poor man writes he is fed up hearing from him and suggests that if Luke Terence wants him to check any further entries he should send a donation for the Cathedral Funds, as one of their schools has just burned down!

It is obvious that the George Delaney does not appear in the Cathedral records.

Terry is working alongside his Delaney family to try to stake their claim to the fortune! Ellen Delaney, his cousin, and Thomas Delaney, his uncle, feature in the 'Edinburgh Letters'. He even writes to his cousin, Arthur Delaney, who he has never met, and who is serving in the King's Own Scottish Borderers now that World War One has begun! Arthur has no information but writes back to Terry to say he has been contacted by the lawyers and has sent a photograph of his grandmother (Helen Delaney Boylan) to the American lawyers. The only reason the lawyers would request such a thing is if they had a photograph of George Delaney's mother.

The 'Edinburgh Letters' begin in October 1913 and continue through the war years until August 1915, back and forward between

Terry and the family in 'Little Ireland', revealing all sorts of insights into their lives. Eventually, there is a letter from the American lawyers saying that they do not believe Terry has proven any right to George Delaney's Estate, though they agreed that no doubt the families were connected in some way.

Reading the letters, I feel so very sad for the remaining Delaneys in 'Little Ireland'. They had fallen on such hard times and were very poor. It was different for Terry. By this time he had already built his factory at Maida Vale in London and was on his way to making a fortune. Ellen Delaney was working as a maid in a hotel on Princes Street, but lost the job and her accommodation when the hotel was requisitioned by the army as a troop billet. Having lost her accommodation she went to lodge with her widowed sister-in-law, Cecilia Delaney, my great-grandmother, in St. James Street. By this time she has no family left, her mother, father and both her brothers are dead. In one letter Ellen Delaney asks Terry if he could send her a shilling and in another letter she thanks him for it.

We had spent years researching the Delaney family in Edinburgh, so when our cousins, Janet and Terry of the London family, first sent us copies of the letters and we learned of the search for a George Delaney, we were puzzled. We had identified every Delaney in the records, for that period, and only one George Delaney had come up. He was our great-grandfather, Arthur Delaney's, infant son, who died within hours of being born. George is not a Christian name that appears in any Delaney family, in Edinburgh, or in Ireland. The only reason my great-grandfather's son was so named is because it was the name of his first wife Mary Mowat's brother. I suspect he was only called that because he died before being registered. Our Delaney family stuck, obsessively, to traditional family names.

If we could not find George Delaney in the present times when we could physically go to Register House and search through the actual Registers or, later, trace the records online, how on earth could the family back in Edinburgh, and Terry in London, possibly find him in 1913? It has to be said from 'The Edinburgh Letters' that they had a pretty good try!

Our cousin, Janet Croome (nee Delaney), later found American Naturalisation papers for this George Delaney. They state that George Delaney was born on 17 June 1859 in Edinburgh, and left

Scotland on an unnamed ship on 15 September 1860 arriving in New York. These dates would make him just a baby when he emigrated. But the form has no place for details of his parents, though his Will states that they were both born in Scotland. This George seems very precise about his dates and facts so who was he? One curious fact is that he signs his name – De Laney – this is the way my great-great grandfather, James Delaney, the artist, signed his marriage certificate in 1859.

Further research revealed that nobody proved they were George Delaney's heirs and so his money was given to the local school in Greensborro, Alabama, where he had lived and died. His Estate, in 1913, was worth the equivalent today of over one million dollars!

Uncle Thomas Delaney died in the Poorhouse in Edinburgh.

After the war ended Terry's factory at Maida Vale continued selling the Delaunay-Belville, but sales were gradually run down as production changed to general engineering works. Even before the war Terry had diversified into making car radiators for many car models, including the Lancia and Peugeot, in a partnership with the Swiss Gallay Company, who held the patent. Terry later supplied radiators to Bentley, Lagonda, Lea Francis, Austin, Bean, Swift, Talbot, Rover, Frazer, Nash and Marendaz giving him many contacts in the Motor Industry. But, even into the 1920s, Terry was still producing the popular Delaunay-Belville. An old photograph of 1922 shows rows and rows of the car's chassis parked on the factory forecourt.

Terry's business continued to expand and he built another factory. The Delaney/Gallay company's radiator business was at the forefront of innovation and Terry himself patented many technological improvements in car manufacturing.

Towards the end of the war, Terry became more and more convinced that in any future conflict an efficient aircraft industry would be vital for the defence of the country. His connection with the radiator business showed him that the water-cooling of big aero engines was a problem which had to be seriously considered. He gave careful study to the radiators fitted to the German aeroplane engines. His firm was tasked with investigating the cooling properties, weights, etc. of the Mercedes radiator on German aeroplanes captured by the French He was convinced that the water-cooled engine was the motor of the future.

Before the war ended, Terry was able to design a radiator that, being lighter, beat the best German version in efficiency, strength and lightness. This gave the British air forces an advantage over German aircraft.

Later he designed the radiator for the Sopwith Dolphin engine, the cooling apparatus of which weighed only 21 lbs. and effectively cooled the 200 h.p. Hispano-Suiza motor.

As well as his many designs for radiators for aero and car engines Terry took out numerous patents on change-speed gears, trailers and other inventions.

The Royal Aircraft Establishment, at Farnborough, allowed the Gallay Company top secret access and assistance by carrying out exploratory tests the results of which were put at Terry's disposal, in order to guide him in the design of his aircraft radiators. He later carried out confidential work on the new designs for most of the leading aircraft companies. His work continued when the war ended – again he was ahead of his field.

He became very interested in the developments in the aircraft industry and experimented to make radiators lighter for aircraft – weight being a crucial factor in their performance.

Then in 1939 the Second World War broke out. The 'War to End All Wars' had been no such thing and Britain and France were again fighting against Germany and Italy in a world war. It was a war that was to come at great personal cost to Terry.

In January 1938, Terry and Amy's youngest son, eighteen-year old Luke Sylvestre Delaney, had joined the Royal Air Force. Luke shared his father Terry's passion for aircraft and was regarded by his family as - "the up and coming blue-eyed boy".

Luke Sylvestre (nicknamed Duke) Delaney began his RAF training as Acting Pilot Officer at 1 FTS Wittering, in England. By August 1938 he was under instruction at the School of Air Navigation, RAF Manston. In November 1938, training completed, he was posted to 108 Squadron at Bassingbourn.

On 22 November 1938 he was posted to 211 Squadron in England, which were now flying Blenheim Bombers and he trained as a Bomber pilot.

My husband, Brian, discovered an amazing website on No.211 RAF Squadron created by Don Clark whose father, Nobby Clark, had been a pilot in 211 Squadron at the same time as Luke Sylvestre Delaney. Don has amassed a wonderful collection of pilot's logs which, along with his late father's reminiscences, give a vivid picture of what life was like in the Squadron at that time. We are so very grateful for all the information he has provided on our Luke Sylvestre's RAF career and all the support he has given to the extended Delaney family. He has done a great service to the history of 211 squadron and we are sure his late father would be very proud of him.

On 28 December 1938, Luke was formally posted to the Squadron in El Daba, Egypt. On 29 December, navigational training was carried out by all Flights. On 30 and 31 December 1938, all crews were given New Year's Leave, meaning no flights took place – I can't imagine where they could have gone on such Leave!

On 3 September 1939 Britain declared war on Germany.

The next time we find Luke in 211 Squadron records is 27 and 28 February 1940. Flight Lieutenant JR Gordon-Finlayson and Pilot Officer Luke Sylvestre Delaney had been sent to Fuka for a Court of Enquiry. Apparently, part of an Officer's duty was to sit on such an Enquiry held in the event of accidents and the like. Over the whole of Luke Sylvestre's flying career JR Gordon-Finlayson is his Squadron Leader and, it appears, his mentor.

The 5th April 1940 finds Luke taking over the duties of an Adjutant during the temporary absence of Flying Officer P. Burnett. The same report talks of problems with flying and airports becoming unusable and flights cancelled due to strong winds, rising dust and flying sand. A reminder they are based in desert areas - it must have been a nightmare.

In May 1940, a Record in the 211 Squadron Archive notes that a signal arrived asking for volunteers for England and it is noted that Flight Lieutenant Gordon-Finlayson and Pilot Officer Luke Sylvestre Delaney were among eight men who volunteered. Why they were looking for volunteers is not stated and there is no follow up to say who was accepted, or whether they went.

This is just prior to the Battle of Britain so could that be relevant?

Strangely, and unfortunately, no official forms survive for the squadron from May until June but a reconstruction of June 1940 records was later created from pilot's and crew's logs. One of the logs was that of Flight-Lieutenant Gordon-Finlayson who volunteered, along with Luke Sylvestre, to return to England in May. Did either man go? If so, by 11 June 1940, they were both back in Libya and Pilot Officer Luke Delaney was involved in reconnaissance flights over specific areas of Libya. It is recorded that he landed at Maaten Bagush after these flights. Libya was an Italian colony so that is why they were bombing there.

The next day on 12 June 1940, Luke took part in a raid on Tobruch (Tobruk) and again the Report says that he landed back at Maaten Bagush. Then on 15 July 1940 he took part in a raid on Ain-el-Gazala and force landed at Sidi Barrani.

On 19 July 1940, nine aircraft were ordered to intercept an Italian Cruiser but the Cruiser was not seen and so the aircraft bombed Tobruch harbour as an alternative target. Pilot Officer Luke Sylvestre Delaney piloted one of the planes.

On 25 July 1940, a successful raid was carried out on LG South of Derna when most bombs were observed bursting on the target area. Luke took part in this raid. All of the aircraft landed at Sidi Barrani for refuelling.

On 9 August 1940, he took part in another bombing raid on the harbour at Tobruch and on 22 August 1940, he took part in a raid on Tobruch but had to return to base due to engine trouble.

On 27 August 1940, he took part in another raid, bombing shipping in the harbour in Derna then on 31 August 1940, Luke went out twice - once on a raid on Ain el Gazala in the morning then, in the afternoon, on a raid on LG west of Tobruch when he made a direct hit on one Italian aircraft.

On 4 September 1940, he took part in the bombing of Ain-el-Gazala landing ground and hit the camp at the South West corner. Then on 9 September 1940, Luke bombed Tobruch foreshore and across the centre of the town.

On 11 September 1940, he took part in a raid on a large transport concentration 15 miles west of Sidi Omar then on 13 September 1940, he took part in a raid on Bomba sea-plane base.

On 18 September 1940, Luke launched an attack on El Timini. He reports that he was about to jettison his bombs because his aircraft was becoming very unstable due to tail flutter, when an Italian seaplane Cant 25096B was flying underneath, so the bombs were aimed at that. Reports that the - end of stick fell short of Cant - which was doing evasive action. Luke also queries the unexpected effect of bomb doors removal. Could this be what caused the tail flutter?

On 21 September 1940, another attack took place on Sidi Barrani aerodrome, then on 23 September Luke took part in bombing Tobruk town and jetties with direct hits on five ships and jetties, and the south end of town was also hit.

By 25 September1940, he was back on a bombing raid on the north foreshore of Tobruk harbour. On the way back the plane of his Squadron Leader, Gordon-Finlayson, developed a fire in the Starboard Engine and he had to force land at Quasaba but the fire was brought under control and he landed safely.

On 9 October 1940, Luke bombed the foreshore at Tobruk and scored a direct hit on a large enemy ship - "Two and a half times as broad as the San Georgio and one and a half times as long, and on an oil tanker alongside. A fire was started on the latter - another tanker was hit but no fire observed".

On 14 October 1940, Luke bombed an Italian Military Camp at Bir Sofofi. Bombs were observed to burst among pom-pom units and along the western fringe of the camp.

On 17 October 1940, Luke returned to bomb the same camp but it was too dark to observe the results. This is the first flight on which he is described as Flying Officer Luke (Duke) Delaney - so a recent promotion?

On 24 November 1940, the squadron was sent to Midini in Greece, to support the country's defence against invasion from Italian Albania. Midini was really too far from Albania but the Greeks would not agree to any base nearer, at that time. They were afraid the RAF being stationed nearer would draw the attention of Germany. Flying Officer Delaney takes part in a raid on the port of Durazzo, in Italian Albania, from Midini and fires bomb salvoes along the harbour side of the jetty. One ship was destroyed in a direct hit by Luke's plane.

On 26 November 1940, Luke returned to Durazzo, which was one of the main sea ports used by the Italians in Albania, and bombed an enemy cruiser but missed by 200 yards. At this point in the war, the RAF is being used to harass the Italians, from the air, to allow the Greek army to defend itself from the land invasion.

By 4 December 1940, Luke was being named as 'B' Flight Commander, 211 Squadron, and in a raid on Tepelene his plane hit the northern side of the town with bomb salvoes. Then on 7 December 1940, he took part in a raid on shipping and docks at Valona, in Albania. This was the other important seaport in Italian Albania.

On 1 January 1941, the records on 211 Squadron announce - "His Majesty the King, on the recommendation of the Air-Officer Commanding-in-Chief, RAF Middle East, has been pleased to award the Distinguished Flying Cross (DFC) to Squadron Leader JR Gordon-Finlayson Officer commanding 211 Squadron." This was Luke's Squadron Leader and an incredibly brave Officer well deserving the medal.

Unfortunately, this New Year's Day of great celebration was marred when Flight Lieutenant Jones, Flying Officer Luke Sylvestre, Flying Officer Barrett and Pilot Officer Pearson, were involved in a motor transport accident. They were all admitted to hospital and Flying Officer Barrett was placed on the dangerously ill list. The others received only minor injuries but were kept in hospital. Luke was discharged from hospital the next day.

On 3 January 1941, Flying Officer Barrett died at 2/6 General Hospital, Kephissia, from injuries sustained in the accident. On 4 January 1941, Flying Officer DC Barrett's funeral took place at Kokkoaia cemetery near Athens, conducted by Rev. W.A. Grice. Luke Sylvestre was a pall-bearer at the funeral. What must Luke have thought having come through all he and Flying Officer Barrett had been through for his comrade to die as the result of a motor transport accident?

On that same day, nine aircraft took off on a bombing raid on Durazzo, refuelling on the outward flight at Larissa, over 300 miles north-west of Athens where Flying Officer Barrett's funeral was taking place. Luke would normally have been part of that raid. The sky over Durazzo was completely cloudless – too clear for the raid – and so the attack turned instead onto Italian military buildings at Elb.

On 6th January 1941, nine aircraft left from Menidi and bombed the foreshore at Valona, in Albania, from 4,000 feet. After hitting their target the bombers were intercepted by Italian fighters and cloud cover was sought. The Formation leader's aircraft landed back at base with a burst tyre and fuselage pierced by gun fire.

An AA shell which lodged itself in the tailplane of another aircraft, piloted by Sergeant Marshall, exploded 25 minutes after leaving the target but the aircraft was kept under control and returned to base. Flying Officer Campbell was last seen in cloud south-west of Valona. He and his crew ditched their aircraft in the sea, were rescued by an Italian vessel and became Prisoners of War.

Flying Officer Luke Sylvestre Delaney's aircraft was attacked by a pilot of an Italian CR42 aircraft. He and his crew were last seen near Kelcyre, losing height, with only their aircraft's starboard engine functioning. Luke was able to nurse his badly damaged aircraft, on starboard engine only, as far as the ancient Silver Castle, Argyrokastron (modern Gjirokaster), in Albania, about 15 miles from the Greek Border and some 60 miles short of Ionnina.

Tragically, in spite of all his heroic efforts, as he made a forced landing, young Luke Sylvestre Delaney's aircraft ran into boulders, overturned, and he and his crew, Sergeant Vynor Pollard and Sergeant Thomas Alexander McCord, were killed and the aircraft destroyed.

He was 21 years old.

Luke Sylvestre Delaney is commemorated on column 241, Alamein War Memorial, in Egypt.

Terry tried desperately to find his son Luke Sylvestre and his crew's last resting place- even writing to the King's son for help – all to no avail.

To understand why young Luke Sylvestre found himself in that particular theatre of war I had a look at the history around the Balkans at that time.

Britain and Germany went to war in 1939. Italy, under Mussolini, allied with Germany. On 10th June 1940, Italy declared war on France and Britain and invaded France. In September 1940 they invaded Egypt. Egypt was actually neutral during the war, until 1945 when they opposed the axis powers, but though technically an Independent country it had been a British Colony and then a British 'Protectorate' – Britain being anxious to protect the Suez Canal with its importance for British India.

On 22 October 1940, six days before the Italian invasion of Greece, despite the Italian invasion of Egypt, the RAF Air Officer

Commanding-in-Chief Middle East, in Cairo, was ordered to prepare squadrons for Greece.

Using the information based on Ultra decodes of orders to the Italian Air Force, and other sources, it was obvious that an Italian invasion of Greece (Britain's ally), from Albania, was imminent.

The RAF first sent 30 Squadron consisting of one flight of Blenheim IF night fighters and a flight of Blenheim I light bombers that were based at Athens-Eleusis airfield. Soon afterwards, six Vickers Wellington medium bombers were detached from 70 Squadron and a flight of Blenheims from 84 Squadron arrived. All RAF assets were placed under the command of Air Vice Marshall John D'Albiac.

After Adolf Hitler annexed Austria and moved against Czechoslovakia without informing his ally, Mussolini, the Italian dictator, feeling slighted, and afraid that Germany intended to take all the spoils of war, decided to annex Albania in early 1939.

He tried to bribe King Zog of Albania to agree to this annexation of his country but the King refused. When Italy invaded Albania on 7 April 1939, with an invasion force of 100,000 men and 600 aircraft, King Zog fled, first to Greece, then to London. Greece had allied itself with Britain. Fascist Italy then set up Albania as a puppet State. Mussolini did not tell his ally, Hitler, in a tit for tat gesture, that he intended invading Albania.

On 12 April 1939, the Albanian Parliament voted to unite with Italy, and occupied Albania withdrew from the League of Nations on 15 April 1939. The Albanian army merged with the Italian army in 1940 and Albania became a Fascist State under Italian control.

In October 1940, what became known as the 'Greco Italian War' began. Italy tried to invade Greece from Italian Albania. This local war began the Balkans Campaign of World War II.

Greece repelled the Italian Invasion with British Air and material support. It then made a counter-attack, on 14 November 1940, which the RAF aircraft participated in with 84 Squadron operating forward from Menidi. A few days later the Gloster Gladiator fighters of 80 Squadron moved forward to Trikaia, causing significant losses to the *Regia Aeronautica (The Italian Air Force)*.

Luke Sylvestre Delaney and his 211 Squadron, flying Blenheim Is, followed before the end of November 1940, joining 84 Squadron based at Menidi. No 80 Squadron moved to Ionnina, about 40 miles from the Albanian Border. In the first week of December 1940, fourteen British Gladiator planes were transferred from the RAF to the Greek Royal Hellenic Air Force.

From mid November to the end of December, the Blenheim and Wellington Bombers flew 235 sorties but almost one third failed due to the lack of all-weather airfields and the season, when flying was only possible for about 15 days per month.

The bombing raids were concentrated on Durazzo and Valona ports in Albania, but some close support operations were carried out and the British fighters near Athens helped to reduce the Italian raids.

By mid November 1940, Greece had stopped the Italian invasion into their territory just at the Albanian Greek Border. Aided by British Bombers and fighter aircraft it struck Italy's forces and bases. This was the action that Luke Sylvestre Delaney and his RAF comrades were involved in.

By the end of 1940, the Gladiator pilots had claimed 42 Italian aircraft shot down for the loss of six, which established their air superiority over the Pindus Mountains.

At the beginning of January 1941, 11 Squadron and 211 Squadron, Luke Delaney's squadron, were sent to Greece despite being at half strength. As a result of their air support, Greece was able to push the Italians back inside the Albanian border.

RAF losses in the whole of the Greek campaign amounted to 150 aircrew and 209 aircraft. Three of those losses were Flying Officer Luke (Duke) Sylvestre Delaney (aged 21), Sgt. Vynor Pollard (aged 22) and Sgt. Thomas (Jock) McCord (aged 19). Three young men, with all of their lives ahead of them, gave their lives for their country. What might they have achieved if they had lived? Tragically, in spite of their sacrifice, and in spite of Greece fighting bravely, the Greeks were forced to surrender and were invaded by the axis powers.

Back home in England, Terry, Amy and the family were devastated to hear that their adored son and brother had been lost. None of them ever really got over it and having no knowledge of his last resting place was a continuing hurt that never healed.

Janet Croome (nee Delaney) remembers, when she was a child, asking her Grandmother, Amy Delaney, when were they going to pull the giant Christmas Cracker that always hung on the wall of the hall of her grandparent's house. Her reply was - "When uncle Luke comes home, dear".

Soon after the loss of Luke Sylvestre, Terry and the company, paid to have an Appeal placed in a newspaper -

THE ROYAL AIR FORCE
BENEVOLENT FUND

This space is given by Messrs Delaney Gallay Ltd. To be used for the purpose of calling your attention to the urgent requirements of the above Fund, also in Loving Memory of the Sons of Members of our Organisation who have given their young lives in the great cause.

We, in our turn, cannot do less than help the dependents of others placed in necessitous circumstance by the loss of their beloved relatives.

We now know that Terry and the family personally donated the equivalent today of £65,000 to the Benevolent Fund to help the poor families of those who had been lost in the RAF war effort.

After the loss of Luke Sylvestre, Terry and Amy received many cards and letters of condolence which Auntie Connie kept carefully in a scrapbook.

Among them is one that recalls the link between Terry and his time in 'Little Ireland.' It is from his cousin, Philip Boylan, with whom he had spent many happy childhood days. It reads -

"Dear Terry and Amy

I am almost at a loss to express what we feel in the tragic loss that has entered into your lives. As parents and relatives we share your grief. We do know however that you will take this awful blow proudly in the full knowledge that you were the possessors of a very gallant and brave boy. Luke cannot die, his soul and spirit will live on for all eternity. May I repeat the Prime Minister's words, "Never was so much owed by so many to so few".

Knowing your stock as I do, you will bear up bravely and with pride, happy perhaps in the knowledge that his and your contribution will help cleanse the world from the vile beasts that have brought so much sorrow and destruction into the world. I take my hat off to Luke and our incomparable boys in the RAF.

This is not the moment to touch on other matters, so I will conclude by repeating that we are with you in your hour of sorrow.

Yours affectionately
Phil, Ida and the children"

Such beautifully expressed sentiments from a member of the extended family from Edinburgh.

No doubt, after the loss of Luke, Terry, his sons and the rest of the workforce, would indeed take Philip's words to heart and redouble their efforts on war work to defeat Nazi Germany.

By 1942, Terry and his companies were exclusively engaged on aircraft contracts for the war. As Chairman of the Sheet Metal Industries Association he was involved in bringing as many sheet metal working companies as possible into line on aircraft production to increase the national effort. At the peak of their wartime production Delaney Galley were employing around 2,000 workers. It must have been a constant reminder to Terry working on aircraft every day, after the loss of his son.

One of the innovations that Terry and the company made were flame suppressors for Merlin engines. One of the problems during the war was that the glow of the exhausts would give away the presence of British bombers on night raids. The flame suppressors protected the RAF planes from being spotted by the Germans thus making a crucial contribution to the war effort. The company also made heat exchangers for armoured fighting vehicles. They developed salt bath braising of heat exchangers which was far superior to normal soldering.

After the war Terry's companies continued to thrive though, immediately after the war, there were difficulties obtaining metal, which hampered some production.

Later Delaney Galley also expanded into improving and manufacturing accessories for cars. The company was always at the forefront of improvements. The most significant development was introducing heaters to the motor industry. Delaney Galley won a contract with Ford that led to them setting up a new factory in Barking. Later they were the first in the UK to fit seat seat-belts to their cars. They also won a contract with Rolls Royce cars to fit anti-vibration mountings for the bodywork mounted on the chassis. The basis of the design was the use of compressed stainless steel wool. They went into partnership with an American company to make jet pipe insulation blankets to protect the airframe structure from the heat from a jet engine. The blankets were a sandwich of stainless sheets containing rockwool, moulded to the shape of the jet pipe. These were fitted to Concorde and can still be seen on the plane in aircraft museums.

Delaney Galley components also flew on Spitfires, Lancasters, Typhoons and many modern civilian and military aircraft, including Concorde. They followed in their founding father's example always to be in at the beginning of every enterprise.

Terry Delaney was one of the few surviving members of the '19th Century Circle of Motorists' and a member of the Fellowship of the Motor Industry.

In a letter to a Motor Trade magazine on 31 January 1945, Terry wrote that - "Now my interests are chiefly confined to three family companies engaged in Aircraft and Automobile work, namely, L.T. Delaney & Sons Ltd., Delaney Galley Ltd. and Galley Ltd.".

Luke Terence Delaney – Terry – died in August 1949, aged 70, in hospital, in Kilburn in London.

His obituary, in The Kilburn Times, on 19 August 1949, stated - "In the two world wars Mr Delaney's genius for inventing came to the rescue of production needs in many ways."

He was a 'self-made' man whose intelligence, courage, audacity and inventiveness, brought him great success. He was a pioneer of the early motor trade in the United Kingdom, and a fearless racing car driver. He foresaw the importance of Britain developing an aircraft industry both for defence and commercial purposes and led the way in promoting it.

The fatherless wee boy who grew up in 'Little Ireland' made good! His Delaney family have every right to be immensely proud of his achievements.

Terry's surviving three sons, Desmond, 'Tom' and Eric took over the businesses when he died.

Terry and Amy also had two daughters, Constance and Dorothy (Dosh), both of whom worked as secretaries to their father in the business. Constance joined the Army Territorial Service (ATS) during the war. In later years Dorothy accompanied her father on the MCC Trials. Neither of them married.

Terry's first born child was Desmond Cecil Delaney, born 16 August 1906 in London. He was educated at Bishop Stortford College and trained with Delauney Bellville Motors Ltd., his father's company. In 1932, at Rhon - Rossitten Gesellschaft at Wasserkuppe in Germany, he went on a training Course in glider flying. He was also a fearless driver taking part in motor racing and trials, on Lea Francis cars, and he also trialled motorcycles in MCC events – he sounds like a real daredevil!

As well as being meticulous, and a trained motor mechanic, Desmond resembled his father, Terry, in his sense of adventure and sheer bravery. His family have an amazing scrapbook with photographs of Desmond participating in gliding back in Germany in 1932. German gliding was a forerunner in the renewal of the aircraft industry in the country before the Second World War.

The Wasserkuppe is a mountain in the German state of Hesse. At 3,120 ft it is the highest peak in the Rhon Mountain range with a large plateau ideal for gliding activities. Students from the University of Technology began flying gliders from there, as a sport, as early as 1911.

But it was as a result of the *Treaty of Versailles*, held after the allies had defeated Germany in World War I, among whose terms was that Germany was not permitted to produce, or use, powered aircraft in their country, that led to Germany being in the forefront of gliding.

From 1920 onwards, annual gliding competitions were held leading to records being continuously broken for unpowered flight. Arthur Martens founded the world's first glider pilot school, in the early 1920s, at Wasserkuppe. In 1924, Oscar Ursinus built a clubhouse on the plateau and organised competitions – which by 1930 were attracting pilots from all over Europe and the United States.

He also persuaded the German Secretary for Transport, Dr. Brandenburg, to turn the gliding school into a state-funded research and glider-building facility – The Rhon-Rossitten Gesellschaft. This was the facility that Desmond Delaney was later to attend. It had its own workshops for constructing gliders and its own research team to develop newer and better gliders. By 1925 the ban on powered aircraft in Germany was partially lifted and the Rhon Rossitten Gesellschaft began experimenting with motor gliders.

Nearly every famous German aeronautical engineer and test pilot of the period prior to the Second World War had trained, built, tested and flown gliders, at Wasserkuppe, and great advances in new technologies took place there.

Also, in the 1930s, a Hall of Honour was constructed at Wasserkuppe. In the centre lies an empty tomb atop which lies a large effigy of Otto Lilienthal - known as the Father of Flight - regarded as being the first human to fly, in 1891. He was a pioneer of aviation who died after his glider crashed. The monument is inscribed with his last words which translate as "Sacrifices must be made." It is a memorial to all pilots who have died in aviation accidents and, no doubt at the time, was meant to inspire the progress of aviation, but it has a more chilling sense with hindsight now that we know what followed.

In 1933, the Nazis came to power, eventually the Rhon-Rossitten Gesellachaft as an independent Society was no longer allowed to exist in an authoritarian Nazi Germany and it was broken up.

In Nazi Germany, gliding activities then became largely controlled by the state. For Hitler Youth, pilots' proficiency in gliding was viewed as a first step towards the *Luftwaffe*. Gliding was also nationalised under the German Research Institute for Sailplane Flight. The research facility was preserved under the new name of the German Research Society for Gliding. This continued to produce many successful gliders and they were at the forefront of aeronautical design up to the Second World War.

A Wikipedia article includes a quote from Thedore von Karman in which he comments on the prohibition on motor flight in Germany, in the *Treaty of Versailles*, as a big mistake.

"I have always thought that the allies were short-sighted when they banned motor flying in Germany. They stimulated the very development they wanted to stop: the growth of German aviation. Experiments with gliders in sport sharpened German thinking in aerodynamics, structural design, and meteorology. In aerodynamics, for instance, they took attention away from the limited double – and triple wing arrangement of World War I planes and showed how the single long span increases efficiency. In structural design gliders showed us in Germany how to distribute weight in a light structure and revealed new facts about vibration...... we uncovered the dangers of hidden turbulence in the air, and in general opened up the study of meteorological influences on aviation."

When Desmond Delaney returned from his Glider Training Course in Germany, in 1932, his family told me that he had gone to the Royal Aircraft Establishment (RAE) in England to warn them of the advances being made in aircraft production at Rhon-Rossitten and his belief that Germany was developing war planes for a future conflict. The RAE dismissed his fears as the product of an over-active imagination.

A cutting from Desmond's scrapbook mentions the death of a famous German glider flyer - Wolf Hirth. As a young man Hirth had joined the Wasserkuppe. He graduated in Engineering from the Technical University of Stuttgart and became involved in aircraft construction. He also toured the world in the early1930s promoting gliding and in 1933 he became the Head of the new Gliding School in Hornberg. Interestingly, that was the year that the Nazis came to power and shortly afterwards Wolf Hirth emigrated to the USA. But he returned to Germany in 1934 as the American Depression struck causing economic hardship. I wonder if Desmond kept the announcement about Wolf Hirth's death because he had known him in Germany before the Second World War.

Strange to think that a few years after these fearless young German and British men were training together at a gliding school in Germany, that many of them would be fighting each other, in the skies, in the Second World War, and that Desmond's youngest brother, Luke Sylvestre, would lose his life flying a Blenheim Bomber during that war. Desmond seems to have shared his father and youngest brother's fascination with aircraft - and their fearlessness.

Desmond married a Swiss lady, Mariette Kohler, in 1939. Tragically, their first born child, Louis Joseph, was stillborn in May 1941, five months after the family had lost Luke Sylvestre in the plane crash. It must have been a really dark year for the whole family after those losses, and the war was still raging.

Fortunately, in 1943 a daughter, Marie Therese, was born followed in 1946 by a son, Terry, named after his grandfather, Luke Terence. After his father, Terry, died, Desmond saw his role as to protect and support his mother Amy. She lived nearby and was regularly at their house eating Mariette's amazing meals!

Marie Therese describes their childhoods as idyllic, filled with an assortment of pets! Her parents liked nothing better than filling the house with friends and family from all over the world. Mariette had an amazing joie de vivre and loved to sing. Their parties were legendary! All the while Desmond looked on quietly smiling – the attraction of opposites! They also spent many happy holidays with Mariette's family up at La Reselle, the farm where their mother grew up. Somehow, Desmond managed to communicate with his French and Swiss-German speaking relations. Perhaps, his time training at the Gliding School in Germany as a young man helped.

After being an apprentice mechanic he kept his interest in cars all his life having at different times a Standard Vanguard – reg LMC (Little Man's Car) followed by an Austin A35; a Westminster A95; a Humber Super Snipe and, finally, a Rover 3500.

Desmond was also an adored uncle to all his Delaney nieces and nephews who remembered him as exceptionally kind. He and his wife, Mariette, were very hospitable and present members of the family remember many wonderful holidays with them and great family parties, especially those held on Mariette's birthday. Reading their reminiscences I got a strong sense that, in spite of his obviously exceptional courage, Desmond was an especially kind and gentle man. Marie Therese describes her father as - "kind, honest, considerate, loyal, caring, understanding, never critical, with a love of his fellow man/not forgetting a lover of the countryside and the air above us – he lived to see Concorde fly!"

It is Desmond Delaney that we have to thank for also being a careful custodian of the Delaney Family Archive. Without his care in preserving the material and all the family photographs it would have proved almost impossible to tell the story of Luke Terence Delaney and his family. Desmond seems to have kept everything! In this he reminds me of my grand-father, Patrick Delaney, who had the same trait. One of these treasures is his actual Apprenticeship Agreement invoice. It is headed up to 'Delaunay Belleville Motors Ltd.', Carlton Vale, Maida Vale, London stating – To fee per terms of Apprenticeship Agreement re Desmond Delaney, dated 28th February 1924 and the sum is £100. Desmond would be sixteen years old when he began his apprenticeship. His father obviously believed in his sons beginning at the bottom and working their way up – no fast-tracking for the boss's sons! Fortunately for us researchers, Desmond's son, Terry Delaney, has kept his father's archive safe. I am grateful for all he shared with me and my brother Michael over the past years – it has brought the story to life.

Luke Terence's second son, Cyril Terence Delaney, (always known as Tom) became Managing Director of the company on his father's death. He was born at Willesden, London, on 8th January 1911. He was educated at Bishop Stortford College and, like his father, at the Northhampton Institute in London, before joining his father's business. As a boy he had taught himself to drive on the Delaney family Tourer when his father was not around!

His father first took Tom to Brooklands Race Track during school holidays. His first visit to the track was in 1925, when he was fourteen years old. He thought, even then, his father was grooming him for future racing. Terry knew all the well-known drivers, having raced against people like Malcolm Campbell. He had become Managing Director of the Lea Francis Company after WWI. In 1928, the young Tom went to Brooklands with the company cars for testing and tuning them in preparation for the first ever Ards Tourist Trophy race in Ireland and he later accompanied the team to Ireland as a young pit mechanic.

Terry bought his son, Tom, his first car – a Lea Francis – in 1930 when he was nineteen years old. He won two trophies in 1930, his first year of competition, at the wheel of the Lea Francis Hyper and many more in the years that followed at all the top racing circuits including Brooklands, Brighton, Donnington, Goodwood, Silverstone and he drove in the Grand Prix. He was also one of the first men to gain his pilot's licence at Brooklands!

In the 1930s, Tom Delaney became more involved in the family business but he did manage to compete in the first race at the new Donnington circuit in 1932. For years the Lea Francis Hyper was his only car until he could finally afford the price of a second-hand Ford V8 to use on the road.

When the Second World War loomed, and there was no chance of racing, Tom sold his faithful Lea Francis to a Dr Bomford – but later realised he wanted it back. Dr Bomford had taken the car out to Aden but was so touched by Tom's appeal that he wrote to him to say he "couldn't sleep at nights and Tom must have the car back".

After the Second World War ended Tom Delaney went to France to check out a prototype of a car made by the French Chausson motor company. The company had secretly developed the car during the German occupation but had been unable to further promote the car because of a shortage of materials in France after the war. It was called the CHS and had been shown at the Paris Motor Salon of 1946. Tom went to France in 1947 and bought one of the the prototypes, with a view to putting it into production at Delaney Galley. However, because of the shortage of sheet metal in the UK it was impossible to proceed to production and also because the Bond Minicar would sell for less – an advantage in post-war Britain.

There are a few photographs that survive of Tom driving the CHS. Including one outside L.T. Delaney & Son's entrance, filling up with petrol. But when production did not proceed the car was left in Tom's garage until 2000, when Tom gave it to a friend. Unearthed in 2012, it was bought at auction by Christopher Chausson, the grandson of one of the company's French founders.

When he married, his wife put a stop to his motor racing activities which she considered too dangerous so Tom got more involved with aviation! Like his older brother, Desmond, and younger brother, Luke Sylvestre, flying was an activity that he loved. However, commitments at work and a growing family (the couple eventually had five sons) meant racing activities took a back seat for a time.

When the Delaney Galley company was sold in the 1960s Tom had the free time to return to racing in his beloved Lea Francis Hyper, which again he did with great success.

In 2004 Tom Delaney suffered a serious accident when he was thrown from his car while racing at Silverstone. The car then bounced off a barrier and ran over him! In hospital he was told that, amazingly, he had only injured his wrist. He promptly phoned his mechanic to ask if the car could be repaired in time for the next race!

In 2005 he received the Motor Sports Association's first ever "Lifetime Achievement Award" to mark his 75 years of motor racing! In the same year he won a race at Bentley DC Silverstone to become the oldest race winner ever recorded.

In 2006, Tom Delaney, at 95 years old, was the oldest licensed racing driver in the world.

He died on 31 August 2006 after a short illness. His funeral took place on 14 September at St. Paul's Church, Knightsbridge, London. His wife predeceased him in 1995. His five sons survive him.

Terry and Amy's third son was Eric Delaney. He also entered the family firm and, like his brother Tom, he also became involved in motor sports. His daughter, Janet Croome (nee Delaney), remembers navigating for her father during motor rallies, when she was a young woman. Though she thinks now that she was not so much there to navigate but to keep him awake on long-distance rallies!

Eric, like his father, Terry, was a skilled motor engineer and inventor as well as a Director in the company.

In the 1950s he decided to design and build his own car. He called it the 'Delaney Delta' and it is the only one of it's kind in the world.

Bringing together all he knew about design, construction and drive-ability he designed this unique car – a work of great creativity. Though it was an open car, he even designed a matching hardtop for inclement weather!

Using his skills, and supported by the mechanics at his firm, Delaney Galley, in their spare time, he designed the car around a supercharged Ford Engine. Eric got John Griffiths to build him a ladder frame chassis scaled down to fit the Ford 10 engine and, to keep the centre of gravity low, the fuel was carried in three small underfloor petrol tanks.

Writing in the *Autoweek* magazine of 4 March 1993, the journalist, John Matras, is filled with admiration for the car. He describes how Eric designed it so that the seats hinge up with the rear bodywork, while the spare wheel stays put.

Eric then took the completed chassis - "the parallel main tubes large enough for a Rolls Royce aircraft engine" - to the workshop. There, he designed and crafted a custom made aluminium body. Comparing it with a contemporary Lotus, Morgan or MG, Matras again waxes lyrical, stating - Delaney's Delta - "was a sophisticated complex shape" - far superior!

Apparently, the aluminium bracing underneath took hours to cut, shape, weld and finish and "instead of simple off the shelf stampings" – Eric - "covered the front wheels with magnificent aeroform spats".

With all his years of experience with cars, Eric seems to have thought of every improvement in maintaining his. "Both front and rear body sections pivot up to expose the mechanical parts underneath – and the rear bumpers pivot to clear the rear section." It made the car very accessible for servicing.

John Matras then goes on to say – (and this part of the book is purely for 'petrol heads' – I don't understand a word of it myself!).

"Under the bodywork, however, lurks the real wonder of the Delaney Delta. Double A-arms of undetermined origin along with coil spring, tube shocks and a custom upright comprise the front suspension. In the back there's torque tube rear axel with a transverse leaf spring and lever shocks. Brakes are big Ford hydraulic drums. Steering is a very direct Citroen rack and pinion and wheels are 16 inch Ford popular type with 5.60 X 13 Michelins (mud tyres at rear)."

"There are three interconnected fuel tanks under the floor with independent leads from two, each with it's own floor-mounted petcock, designed almost as if Delaney was into say 'custom fuels' for his competition outings."

"In addition to a straight pipe for racing, the Delta has a muffled road exhaust system. Full road equipment, by the way, was furnished: Headlights, parking lights, brake light, speedometer, windscreen, charging system and electric cooling fan with blades seemingly big enough only to cool it's own motor, much less draw air through the radiator. Oddly, there's no tach, perhaps because you could rev the little flathead 'til the valves float' without hurting anything. And that engine is perhaps the prize gem in this rolling Jewellery."

"The standard Ford crankshaft is balanced, the rods polished, the head modified, valve springs competition type and a race cam is installed. There's a Vetrex magneto and four branch Tubular Headers sweep back towards the rear. Twin vee-belts drive all the accessories, including a remote side mounted water pipe that supplements the normal thermo-siphoning of the Ford four banger."

Matras says that the car is not perfect – but obviously thinks it's as near to it as possible! - and bear in mind the Delaney Delta car was built in 1954.

Well, I might not understand the technical aspects of the car design but what comes over, loud and clear, is that the man was a genius! Eric Delaney seems to me to have been the son of Luke Terence Delaney that shared his father's exceptional gifts and talents in design, invention and innovation.

Eric raced the car primarily with the London Motor Club throughout the 1950s. It then sat unused for years before being sold in 1970. It changed hands again, in the late 1980s, before it was bought, and some restoration done, by Marc Evans, owner of New England Classics in Stratford, Connecticut, USA. It made it's American debut at the vintage racing Hunnewell Hill Climb in May 1992. It competed in a few historic car events in the USA then disappeared from view. An enthusiast, Frank Barnard, traced it there, swapped it for an old Formula Ford, and shipped it home.

I will leave the last words to John Matras - "Many dream of building their own cars. A few try. Fewer still complete the task. Only a handful build their own car as well as Eric Delaney's highly individual and wonderfully unconventional Delta."

Eric and Sheila Delaney had one daughter Janet (later Croome) and three sons, Michael, Patrick and Nick Delaney.

Janet Croome (nee Delaney) has long been interested in her Delaney family history – she is the 'tradition bearer' in the family – and has carried out years of research which she generously shared with myself and my brother Michael. I could not have told the story without her in-depth research into her family and in the process we have become great friends!

Eric's son, Nick Delaney, Janet's brother, had been fascinated by his uncle Luke Sylvestre Delaney's story since he was a boy when his father, Eric, gave him a copy of the book -'Wing's Over Olympus' by T.H. (Tommy) Wisdom. This told the story of the RAF in Libya and Greece in World War II. In adult life, knowing his uncle Luke had been lost in that campaign, and that the family did not know his exact burial place, Nick became interested in trying to trace Luke's grave. He knew that he had a grave because Tommy Wisdom had recounted visiting it in his book. The problem was that Albania had been a closed country for many years. More years went by and it was not until Nick retired in 2019 that he decided he would try and find where Luke had died. A breakthrough came when he learned that his cousin, Joe Delaney, grandson of Desmond and son of Terry Delaney, had also been seeking information. Joe led Nick to Brian Cull's book -'Blenheims over Greece and Crete.' In this book there was -'what appeared to be a first hand description by – 2/Lt Kaneuopoulos (sic), 34th Greek Regiment, of the crash of Luke's aircraft and the burial of Luke and his aircrew at the village of Topova in the Zagoria valley, east of Gjirokaster'. Lt Kaneuopoulos' description tells how he and a group of Greek soldiers actually witnessed Luke's plane crashing. His army commander ordered them to make their way to the site. He describes the wreckage of the plane and discovering the bodies of the three airman. He goes on to recount how, with some difficulty, they carried the men to the village. There Luke and his two comrades were buried in the churchyard at Topova with full military honours.

Nick had been researching using letters written, in 1942, to his grandfather, Luke Terence Delaney,giving information on Luke's crash, but the Greek names of places given could not be found – over the 80 odd years boundaries and names had changed causing confusion. But now Nick had a possible location – then the Covid pandemic struck!

During lock-down Nick's research continued. He and Terry Delaney (Joe's father) searched for possible churches, with graveyards, on the internet. They had found a 'Kisha e Shen Kolli, Topova' on the St. Nicholas Center website but it was not marked on Google Earth so Nick dismissed it as no longer in existence.

He also sought help to straighten out some inconsistencies in the evidence. Don Clark's 211 Squadron website (http:/211squadron. org/) proved invaluable in this. The village was in a very remote location and he knew he would need help once in the country. He sought assistance from Gillian Gloyer, author of the *Bradt Guide to Albania* who gave generous help and support. He also contacted the Commonwealth War Graves Commission who suggested he contact the British Embassy in Tirana. Gillian Gloyer was able to confirm that Luke and his crew had died near Topova and had been buried in the village churchyard. The British Embassy offered help with transport and interpreting support. Nick immediately booked flights for himself and his wife, Pauline, to Albania.

The day after their arrival in Tirana Nick and Pauline met with his British Embassy contact Major Imran Ahsam and his colleagues Richard Bone and Gerd Kaceli. Richard Bone had visited Topova the week before and confirmed that the church was indeed Kisha e Shen Kolli (Church of St. Nicholas). They later learned that the church had been destroyed during the dictator Hoxha's Atheist State period, but in recent years the bell tower had been rebuilt. On his visit Richard had met a villager, Vasil Dilo, who confirmed the graves were there.

On the 18th May 1923 Imran and Gerd drove Nick and Pauline 5 Km - 'on a very difficult mountain track down to the village from the end of the metalled road at Fusha e Cajupit.' There they met a group of villagers who led them to the churchyard and one of them, Vasil Dilo, pointed out 'with certainty' where the graves of Luke Sylvestre Delaney, Vynor Pollard and Thomas McCord were - though there was nothing to see after 80 years.

While they were standing quietly at the site another villager said he had a piece of the aircraft! They went to his house and from behind a shed he 'brought out a long narrow piece of metal with bracing on the long edges. From detail of the riveting, it was clearly highly engineered and a patch of colour suggested RAF origin to Imran'. The metal was later confirmed by a Blenheim Society expert to be a wing spar from a Bristol Blenheim. Ian Carter of the Blenheim Society provided much help with information on the squadron and the Blenheims.

Nick related how they returned to the churchyard and he laid a poppy wreath in the area where they had been told the graves were and he said a few words in remembrance of his uncle and his comrades. 'We all agreed it was a good resting place for the three men.'

It must have been an incredibly moving moment. After 82 years, Nick, the grandson of Luke Terence and Amy, representing all the Delaney family, was able to honour a much loved son, brother and uncle, and his crew. It seems fated that he, bearing the name Nicholas, should have found his uncle's remains in the graveyard of the Church of St. Nicholas!

Incredibly, next day, Nick and Pauline were able to meet up with a 91 year old man, Ksenofon Dilo, who, as a young boy, had witnessed Luke's plane crash-landing, and had attended the subsequent funeral! He was able to describe the exact location of the graves. That young boy was later to become a well known artist in Albania, and later, Director of the Museum of Fine Arts, in Tirana. He was able to indicate, on one of his drawings, of the original church, where exactly Luke and his crew were buried, as the graveyard had been destroyed. He told Nick that originally each grave had borne a small white cross with the name if each airman but over the years the crosses had rotted away.- and now Nick had laid a poppy wreath at just that location!

The Delaney family archive had revealed that Luke Terence and the family had donated the equivalent of £65,000 to the RAF Benevolent Fund, in 1941, after Luke Sylvestre's death. A substantial sum at that time. Nick's recent research found a letter, in the archive, from RAFBF, thanking Luke Terence for a later donation of the equivalent of £6,000. Nick writes -

'Clearly, despite the tragic loss, Luke Terence Delaney wanted to contribute to ease the suffering of others serving in the RAF, or their dependants.'

Nick contacted the RAFBF for any information on these donations and to his surprise discovered that the Flying Officer Luke Sylvestre Delaney Trust is still in existence – 82 years after his death!

'The Trust Fund is unrestricted, meaning it can be used for any eligible veteran or dependant who is in financial hardship or struggling to live independently'. Nick writes -

'That the F/O Luke Sylvestre Delaney Trust Fund is still active is I think, above all, an enduring legacy to all those young men of 211 Squadron who fought in support of Greece in 1940/41.'

I am so grateful to Nick for sharing his account of finding our lost boy, and his comrades, and permitting me to recount his telling of part of the story in this book. His painstaking detective work has uncovered the whole story, and explained some of the mysteries, in fascinating detail, of his uncle Luke's last months and tragic death and an account of RAF 211 Squadron's heroic efforts in the Italian / Greco war. It is a heart-rending read.

'Their Names Liveth For Evermore'

JOHN WILLIAM DELANEY

Luke Terence Delaney's younger sibling was John William Delaney. Known as Jack, his life took a very different path from his brother. Born in London on 15 June 1884, he was named after his maternal grand-father, John William McAlpine, who was a carriage painter. John was only six months old when his father, the actor, John Sylvester Delaney died. In March 1884, his mother, Elizabeth McAlpine, took him to Edinburgh with his older brother to meet their paternal grand-mother, Helen Delaney (later Boylan). I believe it was at Helen's insistence that John William was baptised in St. Patrick's Church on 30th March 1885. Elizabeth McAlpine was not herself a Catholic. She was baptised in an Anglican church in London. Her parents John William McAlpine and Catherine McCarthy were obviously Anglicans. But John Sylvester Delaney was a Catholic and Elizabeth and her husband had their first born son, Luke Terence, baptised in a Catholic Church in Plymouth so Elizabeth might have thought John would have wanted his second son baptised as a Catholic. It was on this visit that I believe Elizabeth left her older son, Luke Terence, in 'Little Ireland', to be brought up by his father's family.

The next record we have of John William Delaney is the 1891 English census when he is living at home with his mother Elizabeth (a Dressmaker) and his brother, Luke Terence (newly returned from Edinburgh). John William is age seven and Luke Terence age twelve and they are both listed as scholars.

By the 1901 census, John William is aged seventeen, and a grocer's assistant, and Luke Terence is aged 22, and a motor mechanic.

By 1910, his brother, Terry, had opened his first factory in London. In the same year, John William, aged 26, married a woman who called herself Ada Weeks. A wedding photograph in the Delaney family archive has now been identified as John William and Ada. It is a lovely photograph and they look very prosperous. I think John William looks very like his father, John Sylvester, when he was a young actor. Ada stated that her father was Eldred Weeks, an Engine Driver, from Battersea. Ada's occupation was Furrier Finisher and the witnesses at the wedding were George Startin and Elizabeth Delaney – her mother-in-law.

Our cousin, Janet Croome (nee Delaney), researched the couple some years ago. Janet's Auntie Connie (Terry's daughter) had told her that John William and Ada had a daughter but, because her father and his brother had fallen out, she never met the child.

It was many years later, when a family member mentioned that John William's daughter was named Eileen, that Janet decided to investigate. Until then she had no particular interest in that branch of the family. Her research uncovered an Eileen Madora Delaney, born in 1915. She sent off for the Birth Certificate and discovered, to her surprise, that, though the father is recorded as our John William Delaney, the mother's name is Alice Delaney (nee Neale) and the couple are living at 89 Chesterton Road, North Kensington.

So, Janet wondered, what had happened to Ada Weeks?

Search as she might, Janet, could find no trace of Ada Weeks – she had vanished off the face of the earth as if she had never existed – but she had – she had married John William Delaney in 1910.

In desperation, Janet put Eldred – Engine Driver – Battersea- into an *Ancestry search* and up popped an Eldred WIGG who was an Engine Driver, lived in Battersea, and had a large extensive family including our Ada! So, Janet thought, here we have it- a mystery lady who married John William! Well yes, but not under her own name, so who was she really? Janet then searched for months, trying to unravel the story, using Ada's own name. She discovered that Ada, and her sisters, seemed to use false names even when being witnesses at various weddings – just what were they playing at? Were they a family of con artists?

Janet decided to try the 'Genes Reunited' Genealogical site seeking further information. Almost immediately she struck gold! A lady named Josie made contact. She said that she also had been searching the Delaney family. Janet was flabbergasted! Josie told her that the name Wiggs came from her mother's line, that Ada had remarried a man named Richter, had two children but died rather young.

Ada had married a Harry Richter in 1914. His father had a Furrier's firm and Ada's occupation, on marriage to John William, was a Furrier's Finisher. So did she marry the boss's son? Harry's father was German so it couldn't have been easy, in 1914, when war broke out.

There is no evidence that John William and Ada divorced. It was unusual to do so, at that time, and expensive.

On her marriage certificate to Richter, Ada marries under her own name (so it would appear to be a different person from the Ada Weeks who had married John William) and she gives her father a different name and occupation.

Was Ada up to her old tricks? Could she have committed bigamy? It seems a possibility.

So, it appears that John William's wife had walked out on him. However, by 23 November 1915, John William has a daughter, Eileen Madora, to an Alice Maud Delaney (formerly Neal). Janet found, in the 1911 census, that Alice and her sister, Edith, came to London from Letheringsett, and were both employed as parlour maids in the house of a solicitor and his family in London. Alice must have been fond of this family because she gave her daughter Eileen the middle name of Madora, after the solicitor's wife. On the child's Birth Certificate, John William states he is a Grocer's Assistant. In 1919 another daughter, Phyllis Joan, is born to the couple and John's occupation is now Master Grocer and they are now living at Paradise Road, Richmond.

In the 1939 census the family was still together. John William was at the weddings of both his daughters. Neither of these Delaney girls had children so the family genes were not passed on. Phyllis Joan died before her father but Eileen was with him at his deathbed.

Janet Croome has a photograph showing Terry and John William together with a family group, on a beach. Luke Terence and John William are wearing formal dark suits, so Janet speculates that it may have been at the unveiling of their mother Elizabeth's gravestone in Margate. This would make it about 1920/21. The rest of the group are wearing casual beach clothes. As well as Luke Terence and John William, Janet can identify her grand-mother, Amy Delaney, and she and Terry's children, Desmond, Dosh, Tom, Eric, a very young Luke Sylvester and Connie.

She cannot identify the other adults, or the child, but sitting beside Connie is a girl about the same age, and they could be twins!

From Janet's research we know that John William had a daughter, Eileen, born the same year as Connie – could this be her? The girl is sitting at the feet of a lady, who is seated beneath John William in the photograph. Could this be Alice, mother of Eileen? We know John William and Alice also had another daughter, Phyllis Joan, but if the date is right she would be a one year old baby, perhaps too young to make the trip?

Though, on their daughters' Birth Certificates and in the census return, Alice's surname is given as Delaney and on her Death Certificate she is described as -'widow of John Delaney' - Janet has been unable to find a Marriage Certificate for the couple. One wonders why, since Ada died young, John William could not then have married Alice. Strangely, in John William's Will, he leaves over £2000, a fair amount at that time, to his son-in-law, Albert Pilcher, even though his daughter, Eileen Pilcher, was still alive - as was Alice.

Janet's Grandma, Amy Delaney, did keep in touch with John William, according to Auntie Connie, and in Amy's diary, which Janet owns, Amy notes 'Jack's 75th Birthday' so perhaps John William and his brother Terry did, eventually, reconcile.

In 2023 Janet made a surprising discovery. She discovered the existence of a Leslie Delaney, apparently John William's son. After discovering the 1921 census entry, listing Leslie as John William's son, born in 1909, Janet traced back but could discover no further information on a Leslie Delaney. In the census in which Leslie is listed as John William's son he is living with him, Alice and their two daughters. Leslie is twelve years old, so born in 1909. Further research by Janet uncovered the fact that Leslie Albert was an illegitimate son of Alice (father's name unknown), born before she met John William, and whom he was bringing up as his own. Janet can find no further record of him.

John William Delaney, son of the actor, John Sylvester Delaney and Elizabeth McAlpine, died aged 78, on 25 May 1963, at his home at 104 Minet Avenue, Willesden, London.

John William was not the shining star that his father John Sylvester Delaney was, nor did he reach the heights of success that his brother Luke Terence did. One wonders if he felt constantly in their shadows. He did not have his sorrows to seek in life, his father dying so young, but at least he had the undivided attention of his mother, Elizabeth, as he grew up, unlike his brother Terry. John William and his mother must have been very close because she was a witness at his wedding. Though his wife appears to have left him for a richer man, he did seem to have a happy family life eventually, with Alice and their two daughters. His daughter Eileen was with him at the end. He became a Master Grocer and owned his own business, so he does appear to have inherited the business acumen of his Delaney family back in 'Little Ireland.'

CHAPTER FOURTEEN

THE LOST CHILDREN

When my grandfather, Patrick Delaney, died he left behind a bureau full of paperwork. But it was not until his daughters, my aunts, Margaret and Frances Delaney, were moving house that they got round to clearing it out. To their amazement, they discovered a few pages of a nineteenth century document relating to a case in the Court of Session, in Edinburgh. The document was a legal Petition to the court in a Custody Case demanding the return of Arthur Delaney's children. Reading the documents they discovered that their grandfather, Arthur Delaney, had been married before his marriage to their grandmother, Cecilia Clifford. And what's more he had three children, James, Annie and Robina Delaney. Their father Patrick's half-siblings! He had never told any member of the family these facts, indeed, my aunts did not believe that even their mother Margaret knew. Knowing that we would be interested, my aunts shared this information and gave us copies of the Court document. The Edinburgh Delaneys are a very close family – all our father's aunts, uncles and cousins were well known to us. So what, we wondered, had happened to the James, Annie and Robina Delaney that nobody knew anything about? And so we set off to try and find 'The Lost Children', searching birth, death and marriage registers, records from St. Patrick's Church in 'Little Ireland,' census records and, gradually, we acquired the complete documents of the Court of Session case.

This is the story of what we discovered.

My great-great-grandparents were James Delaney and Anne Maloney. James was the son of Arthur Delaney and Helen Collins. He was born in 'Little Ireland' in 1840. Anne was the daughter of Patrick Maloney and Catrin Gorman. By the time of their marriage, James' father and Anne's mother were both deceased. James and Anne married in the Catholic priest's house, in Viewfield Terrace in Dunfermline, in Fife, on 9 August 1859. Their witnesses were

Margaret Hughes Wilnip and Edward (name indistinct). By another of these coincidences that occur in this story, we later discovered that another descendent of the Delaney family of County Monaghan, whose parents settled in 'Little Ireland', became a priest, Fr Richard Delaney, who built the Chapel of Ease in Dunfermline. I heard about him from an old lady I met at a church meeting in Edinburgh. She had been baptised by him in St. Margaret's Church in Dunfermline. We later obtained a copy of Monsignor Delaney's obituary and he seems to have been a well-respected priest.

On his marriage certificate, my great-great grandfather, James Delaney, states that he is 'an artist of Dunfermline' and is aged twenty-one. He lied about his age as he was only nineteen. Anne is a spinster, of Dunfermline, age nineteen. We have no idea why the couple married in Dunfermline as James' family home was in Edinburgh at 17 St. Mary's Wynd (the home of his step-father, Philip Boylan). His mother had married Philip after her husband, Arthur Delaney, died in 1850. There is no trace of Anne's father in the Scottish records. Anne states she was born in Ireland so perhaps her father, Patrick, was still back in Ireland. She gives no occupation on her marriage certificate (none was requested) but Dunfermline was at the heart of the damask industry so perhaps she was a spinner or weaver. Later in life, Anne gives her occupation on an Edinburgh census form as 'machinist'. James might have been a painter, he was obviously artistic, but we can find no evidence of him in the Art College's records.

We wondered if, perhaps, James was employed in the damask trade as a designer. Certainly, that was the occupation of Joseph Paton, the founding father of the famous Paton family of artists in Dunfermline.

We also wondered if the couple might have eloped to Dunfermline, given that James Delaney lied about his age. You could get married in Scotland younger than twenty-one, but only with your parent's permission. But even if they did elope, by 20 April 1860 the couple are living with James' mother, Helen, and his stepfather, Philip Boylan, at their home at 17 St. Mary's Wynd, in 'Little Ireland', and that is where their first child was born. He was given the name of Arthur, after his paternal grandfather, and Philip, after his step-grandfather, Philip Boylan, who stood as his god-father at his baptism in St. Patrick's Church.

Arthur Philip Delaney, was my great-grandfather, and he was to live a very unfortunate life.

When Arthur Philip was born, his father, James, states on the birth certificate that he is now a photographer. Photography had become the latest rage. People who had previously had their portrait painted now preferred to have their image captured in this new art form. If James had been a painter he might have found his commissions were drying up. Certainly, photography was within the reach of people on more modest incomes who wanted their image captured, making it a more lucrative occupation for James Delaney. He would certainly have a good eye. We only have one old photograph in the Delaney archive that we think may have been taken by James Delaney. It bears no studio name and the setting looks like a room in a house rather than a studio. It is a beautiful photograph of his wife Anne Maloney.

The pioneers of photography in Edinburgh were David Octavius Hill and James Adam, who turned their craft into an art form. Their work is much sought after by collectors today. Coincidently, David Octavius Hill married Amelia Paton, a sculptress, who was part of the famous Dunfermline family of artists! Her statue of the Explorer and Missionary, David Livingstone, stands in Princes Street Gardens beside the Scott Monument.

Though photography was the coming thing it was an expensive business to set up, needing camera equipment, glass plates, paper, chemicals and, of course, a studio for sitters and a place to develop the film. We suspect that his wealthy stepfather, Philip Boylan, funded James in this enterprise. From our research he appears to have been an indulgent father and stepfather.

James and Anne went on to have another three children. A daughter, Ellen, was born in 1861 at 43 High Street, in the Old Town of Edinburgh. This building is now known as 'John Knox House'. This is, allegedly, the house in which the Protestant Reformer lived in the sixteenth century. By the nineteenth century it was one of the many ancient historic buildings sub-divided into flats.

The couple's third child was Anne named after her mother, born in 1863 at 327 Canongate. She was baptised in St. Patrick's Church by Fr Edward Hannan and her godparents were Robert and Rachel Baigley. Tragically, wee Ann died of croup, aged three, at the Royal Infirmary, Edinburgh. Their final child James, named after his artist father, was born in 1865 at 8 St. Mary's Wynd. His godparents, in St. Patrick's Church, were his father's brother, John Sylvester Delaney, the actor, and Jane Gillon.

It seems that James and Anne's marriage was not a happy one.

James is not present in the house when the 1871 census was taken. My brother, Michael Delaney, later found him recorded in Anstruther, in Fife, at that census. Had the couple separated?

Perhaps, but it appears that James Delaney may have become a travelling photographer. To enable them to reach customers outwith the big cities many photographers created a photographic studio in a horse-drawn wagon. This acted as a portable studio and dark room, as they travelled around more rural areas. We think that is why James was in Anstruther. Anne, her son James and her daughter Ellen, were living together in the Old Town, but Arthur Philip, my great-grandfather, was missing. My sister, Frances Connolly (nee Delaney), later found him in the 1871 census, in what appears to be workers' accommodation located beside the famous Edinburgh Crystal works near Easter Road. Arthur is training as a glass-cutter and he is only eleven years old. This was the normal age for apprenticeships then but it seems so young to be away from his mother. However, the trade stood him in good stead and that is how he earned his living for most of his life. It was a skilled job and reasonably well paid.

By the 1881 census it is obvious that James and Anne Delaney have separated. This was very unusual in Catholic families and his mother and stepfather must have been shocked. James is living in an up-market boarding house, in the High Street, in 'Little Ireland', which obviously caters for professional men. Anne and her daughter Ellen are together, lodging in a single room in a house in the Cowgate, but Arthur and his young brother James are missing. We later discovered that young James had joined the army, as a boy soldier, aged just fifteen. He trained as a musician in the army, became a professional soldier and a crack-shot with a rifle, winning competitions. When he left the army he returned to Edinburgh and became an orchestral musician. He never married.

After the 1881 census we lose track of James Delaney the photographer. I later discovered he finally settled in Wigan, an English industrial town, where he continued to ply his trade. I phoned the Registrar in Wigan for information on James Delaney's death. When he heard the name Delaney he started to laugh. Wigan was an Irish emigrant heartland in the nineteenth century and Delaney was a common name. "It will be like looking for a needle in a haystack," he said. In an attempt to narrow it down, he asked James Delaney's occupation. When I said 'photographer' there was a pause - "Ah well, that's different," he said. There was only one James Delaney who was a photographer in Wigan! He gave me the details of his death. My great-great grandfather was still working at his profession in Wigan when he took ill. In 1888, he was admitted to the local Infirmary, the only public hospital before the NHS was founded, which was attached to the Union Workhouse. He died there of heart disease, age forty-eight.

So where was my great-grandfather, Arthur Philip Delaney, at the time of the 1881 census?

He was now a qualified glass cutter in a Glassworks on Holyrood Road. He had a relationship with a girl named Mary Mowat. She became pregnant but it seems her father, Robert Mowat, a Protestant Presbyterian, refused to allow her to marry a Catholic. Mary gave birth to a son in 1877, at 2 Morrison's Close (her sister Betsy's home in 'Little Ireland'). He is registered as James Mowat, but Arthur's name is on the birth certificate. Obviously, the relationship continued because, in 1878, Mary became pregnant again. This time her father allowed them to marry which they did, in St. Patrick's Church, their witnesses being Mary's sister, Robina Mowat and a Mr Robertson. Mary was nineteen years old, Arthur was only eighteen.

Mary gave birth to her second child, a daughter, Annie, on 27 July 1878 at 2 Morrison's Close. Mary's father, while agreeing to the couple marrying in St. Patrick's Church, obviously refused to agree to the children being baptised as Catholics. But he died in the middle of April 1880. One week later, on 22 April, James and Annie were both baptised in St. Patrick's Church. Two months later, on 15 June 1880, Mary gave birth to another daughter. They named her Robina after Mary's sister Robina Mowat.

Robina was born at 17 St. Mary's Street, Arthur's grandmother Helen's home, where Arthur Philip himself had been born twenty years previously. That house had seen it's share of births, marriages and deaths, including that of old Philip Boylan himself in 1875.

By the time of the 1881 census, Arthur Philip was a married man with three children, living at 2 Morrison's Close. Given that his father, James Delaney the photographer, was living nearby on the High Street then, I wonder if he ever had contact with his three grandchildren. Did he perhaps photograph them – if so none of those photographs survive.

Mary gave birth to their fourth child, a son, George Delaney, on 17 June 1882 at 2 Morrison's Close. Baby George died five hours later of prematurity.

On 24 June, five days after the death of baby George, Mary Mowat Delaney died of septicaemia, at 2 Morrison's Close, aged twenty-three. Yet another victim of the child bed fever that killed so many women in 'Little Ireland'.

Arthur must have been absolutely heartbroken. Mary had provided the loving home he had not had since he was eleven years old. Their three children had lost their mother, their world must have fallen apart. James was five, Annie four and Robina only two years old. The little family's lives were about to go into a downward spiral from which none of them would ever recover.

Arthur looked after his three children on his own for six months, paying neighbours to care for them while he was at work. It must have been a sad and difficult time for him and the children.

But fate was to deal Arthur a further blow. He had been employed as a glass-cutter for many years, by a Glassworks on Holyrood Road, in 'Little Ireland'. One day in November 1882, the company made three hundred workers redundant. A new sand-blasting machine had been invented which meant that the men's skilled work was now obsolete. Three hundred men lost their livelihoods overnight, in a time when unemployment was already high. One of those men was Arthur Delaney. There were no redundancy payments or unemployment benefits in those days. Their only recourse was to the Poor Law. Any small savings Arthur might have had would have been already depleted from paying the neighbours to care for the children.

Arthur was back to looking after his children on his own and could find no work. One day a lady 'Missionary' called at his door. These were women belonging to an Evangelical Protestant Church, who went round the doors in the Old Town handing out religious tracts. Learning of the situation Arthur was in she suggested he have the children admitted to Emma Stirling's Children's Home. She made the appointment for Arthur to admit the three children.

He explained later that he was desperate, that he needed to find work and it would give him a temporary solution to his problems.

He took his children to the home at 11 McKenzie Place, in Edinburgh's Stockbridge district. The house still stands to this day, though much altered. There he was interviewed and his children had a medical examination. A copy of the actual admission form was among the law case documents we later uncovered. In answer to the question - "Why do you need your children admitted?" - he wrote - "I have no one to look after them." It is absolutely heartbreaking. To make matters worse, 11 McKenzie Place was only for very young children and girls. Since his son, James, was five years old, Arthur had to leave his daughters behind and walk to Bayton Terrace in Granton, to the Boys Home, and leave him there without even his sisters to keep him company. James must have been absolutely terrified, alone in this strange place, and Arthur must never have recovered from the trauma – it must have haunted him until the day he died.

Arthur was not to know then that worse, much worse, was to come.

In the Homes, the parent was only allowed to visit once a week, on a Saturday. The three children must have thought their father had disappeared as their dead mother had done so recently. Later, in the case in the Court of Session, Arthur testified he visited his children weekly or, if he could not go, he sent his mother Anne Delaney and his sister Ellen, in his place. His mother Anne Delaney also testified, at the Court of Session, that she and her daughter Ellen visited the three children regularly of their own volition, during their time in the Homes, when they were permitted to do so.

Emma Stirling's Homes were not free. She charged the parent 2/6d per child per week. Arthur managed to get a part-time job which paid him 15/- per week. He testified that he made the payments when he could but when he again fell out of work his payments went into arrears.

Though Emma Stirling was a very wealthy woman and used her own money to establish the Homes, she writes in her book – 'Our Children in Old Scotland and Nova Scotia' - that, as well as the parent's contributions, Edinburgh City Council made an annual contribution. This would be to cover the cost of otherwise having to house such children in the Poorhouse. She also received charitable donations from the public, in money - and in kind - in the way of clothing for the Home children.

Because Arthur could not afford to pay his rent he had to give up his flat in Morrison's Close and go and live with his mother and sister in one room in the Cowgate, during periods of unemployment.

Emma Stirling lived in a large mansion house in the Trinity district of Edinburgh with a staff of servants. She also had two large houses in Craigholme Crescent in the seaside town of Burntisland, across the Firth of Forth. One of these she used for holidays for the children, from her Edinburgh Homes, and one she lived in herself for the whole of the summer season. Apart from a volunteer benevolent lady, who did not live in the house, but bought food and paid bills, her Homes were staffed by older Home children, mainly teenage girls. They also supervised the children overnight when Emma herself went home to her private houses in Edinburgh or Burntisland.

So, who was Emma Maitland Stirling? We know a great deal about her because she wrote a book about herself, and she was a great self-publicist! The book is called – 'Our Children in Old Scotland and Nova Scotia'. Who wouldn't – if we could afford it - want to leave an image of oneself, for posterity, completely created by ourselves – with no one to contradict!

In her book, Emma Stirling relates that, though born in Edinburgh in 1838 - oddly enough the year that Arthur Delaney, the children's great-grandfather, arrived in Edinburgh from Ireland - her family later moved to St. Andrews, in Fife, where she grew up. Her father was very wealthy and she lived in a large mansion house beside the Cathedral, overlooking a row of fishermen's cottages. She describes the fishermen's children as - "our troublesome neighbours". Her father could trace his lineage back to the Stirlings of Cadden who could trace their origins back to the 12th Century. Her paternal great-grandfather had been a linen manufacturer in Glasgow who exported linen to the United States and imported tobacco on the return voyage - one of Glasgow's 'Tobacco Lords'. Later, he expanded the business, importing raw cotton from the USA and set up cotton-spinning mills in Manchester. Many of those Glasgow merchants, we have now learned, made their fortune through slavery. When slavery was, at last, abolished, these families received large amounts of compensation from the government and became even richer. Later, some of those profits were used by Stirling family members to enter banking.

Her father, John Stirling, had his country Estate at Eldershaw when he married her mother, Elizabeth Willing of Philadelphia. She was the granddaughter of Thomas Mayne Willing, who served as Mayor of Philadelphia and was president of the first chartered bank of America. Emma states he was a man of high principles - "being one of only two delegates of the Continental Congress who refused to sign the Declaration of Independence which would have meant him breaking the oath of loyalty he had sworn to George III". I think she gives us a clear description of her antecedents and perhaps that was why people were afraid to oppose her – as was stated in the later law case.

Her mother and father had eleven children and she was the youngest. They were brought up to be devout Protestants and she describes how her father's factotum told her and her brother gruesome stories of the Protestant Martyrs and John Knox. Her parents were equally firm on these religious matters and she writes - "Who can wonder I grew up a staunch Protestant". Her Protestant beliefs were to have a profound impact on her treatment of Catholic Arthur Delaney and his children.

She goes on to write - "We children had been brought up strictly in the Protestant faith and impressed from our earliest years with a perfect horror not only of the Romish Church but of that portion of the Episcopal Church....commonly called High Church.".

The Stirling family attended the Episcopal Church, but what we would now understand as the Low Church. Her father was the vestry man in that church and she writes - "it seemed to me as a child that his whole efforts in connection with the church was in resisting all the various forms and ceremonies – innovations they are called....". She goes on - "my mother also held these views quite as strongly, we therefore were never allowed to make any Roman Catholic acquaintances or to mix much with those who were known to be High Church. No doubt our parents were considered very narrow minded. I have often since been glad that it was so." This then is the foundation of Emma's later behaviour when she established her children's Homes. She was to bring up all the children in her Homes as staunch Protestants regardless of what faith they had previously held. Later, in Nova Scotia, she relates that she had been congratulated for bringing a colony of Protestant children into the Province. She saw her work in terms of a Protestant Mission.

In her defence she states that she never refused to admit Roman Catholic children into her Homes, writing that - "I received all alike, contenting myself with the stipulation that no popish practice or idolatrous prayers should be permitted in my houses and that no priests or sisters should, on any pretence whatever, be allowed to visit the Day Nursery. If I shut the door to keep the priests out; while I let the children in, it was only because I instinctively dreaded the fascination of the Old Enemy ROME!" When we read her views in her book most people's reactions would be – this woman should not have been allowed within a mile of children – but that is now – it was different then.

Her father, John Stirling, died in 1853 and Emma nursed her mother through ill health until she also died. She was the last remaining family member left in the house in St. Andrews and, it being too big for her, it was sold and Emma moved back to her birthplace, Edinburgh, and bought the large house 'Merleton' in Trinity. The house still stands but has long ago been converted into four separate houses. Her eldest brother managed the family concerns. He lived in the New Town and he and his wife had thirteen children. Her older sisters also lived in the New Town, one was married to a stockbroker and another to an advocate. However, it appears that her remaining family had little to do with her because Emma writes - "I was a great deal alone in the world." Later, after the scandal of the court case, it appears they more or less disowned her. In a later history of the Stirling family, against the biographical entry for Emma Maitland Stirling it only states - "Died unmarried."

Emma seemed to have always had philanthropic tendencies. Even back in St. Andrews she sewed garments for her 'troublesome neighbours', the fisher children, and became a 'visitor' at the local school. Now, alone in Edinburgh and feeling useless she heard of a possible outlet to remedy her isolation. She writes - "After residing in Edinburgh for some months a friend told me she had been shocked by the fearful stories she had heard of the ill usage of young children in the Old Town."

Using an inheritance from her mother, Emma opened a Day Nursery at 10 McKenzie Place in Stockbridge. She writes - "I opened a Day Nursery in 1877 where mothers who worked during the day could bring their babies and little children before seven years of age, and by paying a small sum, could leave them to be well taken care of until night. The offer I made in return for two pennies a day was a warm house, three meals a day ......for the bottle babies I obtained the best milk I could get and crusts for the teething babies." The reference to the quality of the milk is historically significant because in those days cattle were not tested for TB and much milk was contaminated and often diluted.

So Emma's initiative was not strictly a charity because the mothers had to pay a daily fee, but it was obviously subsidized by Emma's contribution. The importance lies in the whole concept itself. Emma Stirling was a trailblazer in providing child-care for poor working mothers. No such care was provided by the State at any level.

No one could doubt her sincerity in providing for poor children – and in such an innovative way. She must be admired, regardless of what came later, for the work she did in Edinburgh for poor children over many years.

Later, in her book she writes - "A few months after I began the Day Nursery work I felt constrained to open a (residential) Home in the autumn of 1877, as I found so many children who had no home to go to at night, unless the common lodging house could be called so". She continues - "and so many others brought in by fathers, the mother having died and the poor things left to the care of the even more to be pitied man who now had to be father and mother and all."

She later writes - "...it is true to say that at that time of general depression, and want of work, consequent on the commercial crisis, many (children) became destitute whose parents had been respectable and well to do people."

That is exactly the circumstances of Arthur Delaney when he placed his children in Emma Stirling's Home in December 1882. She could have used him as an example, he ticked all the boxes. Since she was aware of Arthur and the three Delaney children's circumstances, it makes one wonder, was what she wrote, as quoted above, just pious lies to show herself in a good light?

Because if it was true, how could she later inflict such cruelty on three young, innocent children? How could she lie and perjure herself in the Courts of Law? How could she refuse to return the children to their father when it was obvious he was desperate to have them back and had a safe home and a new wife to care for them? From later evidence, it appears that she was determined not to return the children to a Catholic father and a Catholic upbringing. So filled with hatred was she for - "the Old Enemy ROME" - that she was prepared to sacrifice them and expose three very young children to a risk of abuse and offer them no protection. By these actions she was to ruin the lives of Arthur Delaney and his three children, James, Annie and Robina Delaney.

So how did the children come to be at such risk?

Most of the evidence in what follows comes from two sources.

The first is the book that Emma Maitland Stirling herself wrote and published titled - "*Our Children in Old Scotland and Nova Scotia.*".

There have been many strange coincidences that have occurred during the researching of '*Little Ireland*' and this incident is among the strangest. After the discovery of the document in my grandfather Patrick Delaney's bureau, my mother Liz Delaney, my brother Michael Delaney and myself became obsessed by finding out more. Edinburgh has the most amazing free Public Library, known as the Central Library, located on George IV Bridge in the city. It was founded on funds provided by Andrew Carnegie, one of many founded around the world, by the man who, in his time, was the richest man in the world. He was born in Scotland in 1835, in the little town of Dunfermline, the same town where James Delaney was to marry Anne Maloney. His father was a weaver, and Carnegie's cottage birthplace still stands. The family battled poverty and so in 1848 they emigrated to the USA and settled in Pittsburgh. Andrew Carnegie grew up to be a multi-millionaire but by the time he died in 1918 he had given more that half his fortune away for philanthropic purposes.

Within Carnegie's Library, high up in the building, was The Edinburgh Room, a treasure trove of items donated and collected over a hundred years, of material pertaining to the history of the city. I began to haunt the place seeking further information on

Arthur Delaney and his lost children. The only thing I knew about Emma Maitland Stirling came from the nineteenth century Court of Session documents we had uncovered. Who was this woman? The ever patient librarian had gone off to search out a book for me and I was leaning, waiting, beside the card-index. No digitized records in those days! Suddenly, it came to me – could Emma Stirling have written a book? I opened the drawer and before I could begin to search through the cards they fell open. I lifted out the exposed card- *'Our Children in Old Scotland and Nova Scotia' by Emma Maitland Stirling*'!

I could not believe it! When Andrew, the librarian, returned I handed him the card with shaking fingers - "Do you have a copy of this book?" I asked. Off he went and back he came and laid the book down on my desk. I had to sit down because my knees were trembling. Over the years some people have asked why the lost children mattered so much to us, it was tragic certainly but it was a very long time ago. The Delaneys have always been a very close family – for us these children were blood of our blood – and they had been lost. The strength of those feelings has never waned, for any of us, over the many years of research that followed. The greatest blessing that has been bestowed on us is that, over those years, many, many, people, family, friends and even perfect strangers have understood and have done all in their power to help us find our lost children.

When I read Emma Maitland Stirling's book for that first time my feelings were quite different from when I read it after tracing all the relevant law documents on the case from the Court of Session in Edinburgh and the Supreme Court of Nova Scotia in Canada, because, by then, I knew that Emma Stirling was a convicted child abductor, a liar and a perjurer.

The second source are those court papers and through them we learned the true story, not Emma Stirling's made up version. Even in dry legal language the story they reveal would break your heart.

After Arthur Delaney had admitted his children to the Home in Stockbridge and the Home in Granton, Emma Stirling continued to run these Homes and also her holiday Home in Burntisland.

From Emma's book we learned the address of her Day Nursery and Home in McKenzie Place. We knew that all the tenement houses in the street had been demolished some years previously and the site turned into Community Allotments – small gardens where local people, in the Stockbridge area of the city, could cultivate vegetables. We were disappointed that we would not be able to see the Home where Annie and Robina had lived but, one day when we were driving past, I asked my husband to drive up to Mackenzie Place to have a look. We got out of the car and walked past the Allotments. At the end of the street I could see a rather ornate entrance and behind it was what was obviously a nineteenth century house. I could not believe my eyes! It was Emma Stirling's Home where the two Delaney girls had lived! Beside it was No.10, now the house's garage, but originally Emma's Day Nursery. They were the only surviving buildings in the whole street. Time and again in researching this story we have felt like an unseen hand was guiding us.

When we first researched the two Homes in Edinburgh we were surprised at how small they were. A previous owner of the Stockbridge house wrote to me that he found it hard to believe it could have functioned as a Children's Home as it was relatively small. We had the great good fortune, when we contacted the house's then owner, Collette Grant, that when she heard our story, she kindly invited my brother Michael and myself to visit. Another instance where a complete stranger showed us great kindness in our search for the lost children. It is a lovely house but not large. We also know, from Emma's book, that the Boys Home in Bayton Terrace housed only eight boys at a time. Emma states that this was done on purpose as she did not want her Homes to become -'Institutions'.

In her book she relates that later she was forced to open another house. This was -' The Shelter from Cruelty' at 150 High Street, in the Old Town, which she opened in December 1884. She explains - "The reason for this was that I was finding it necessary to receive so many children requiring special protection from cruelty at my own home at Merleton, and as this was extremely inconvenient for myself and my household I thought it better to incur the expense of another house somewhere near the Police Office. Besides, it was extremely desirable to have a kind of test house through which doubtful children could pass on the way to the Homes.". It is obvious from this that Emma Stirling is now embarking on a quite different Cause than the two Homes where the children's parents were continuing to contribute towards their own children's care.

Again, we can see Emma Stirling as a trail-blazer embarking on work that civil society made no provision for - rescuing children from abuse and neglect. The local authorities made no provision, at that time, for rescuing such children and there were no laws to protect them. Emma Stirling became involved in the Child Protection Movement and the Children's Shelter was the first step in her campaign. Some people claim that she was the founder of The Royal Scottish Society for the Prevention of Cruelty to Children (RSSPCC), in Scotland (now Children First) but this is untrue. When Emma opened her Children's Shelter in Edinburgh there was a group in Glasgow engaged in the same work. In her book she states - "At this time there was an idea of some other friends beginning a new Society for the same ends but finding how fully the Edinburgh and Leith Children's Aid and Refuge Society (ELCARS) occupied this ground, these friends thought it better to join us and all work together."

The RSSPCC's history states that the Edinburgh and Glasgow groups did join in 1889 but makes no mention of Emma Stirling. Hardly surprising given that she was living and running her Child Migrant Scheme in Nova Scotia by then. Perhaps the founders of the RSSPCC chose to distance themselves from any connection with Emma Stirling after the notoriety she had gained when my great-grandfather successfully brought the Court Case against her for child abduction. The RSSPCC were involved in protecting children in Scotland from abuse and neglect not exporting them as migrant workers to Canada and putting them at risk of abuse and neglect.

By 1882, seven years before the RSSPCC was founded, Emma Stirling had begun to explore the possibility of sending children to Canada as migrant workers. Canada was a vast country with great resources but with a very small population. The government was anxious to exploit its rich resources and made generous land grants to emigrants prepared to settle and farm and many pioneering people did just that but not in large enough numbers. It was not easy to recruit. The rewards could be great, but large tracts of the vast country were still wilderness and the climate, in winter, could be lethal. Many more workers were required and the pioneers could not 'grow' children fast enough to fill the need.

The Canadian government hit on the idea of paying a 'bounty' to any individual, or group, prepared to send out children to work as domestic servants and labourers to develop their vast wilderness. Surely, we would think today, not many would respond, take the 'bounty' and send such very young children to what could be a frozen wilderness to labour.

But people did, in large numbers. Town Councils all over Britain saw a golden opportunity to get destitute children off their Poor Lists and save taxpayers' money. Also, charitable organizations and churches, struggling to cope with the demands on them, hoped to move children on to make room for those still in need.

And Emma Maitland Stirling.

Emma opened the Children's Shelter in Edinburgh in December 1884 and in the summer of 1885 she travelled to Nova Scotia to explore the possibility of taking up the Canadian Government's generous offer to pay her for each child she brought out. Today we would call it 'child trafficking'.

While on that visit to Nova Scotia, Emma Stirling purchased Hillfoot Farm in Aylesford, Nova Scotia. This she planned to use as a sort of 'transit' place from which to send out the children as labourers and domestic servants. That is what the Canadian Government was paying her for after all. It was never intended as a Children's Home, as such, and only babies and very young children, in the first shipment, lived there for any length of time. It was that first shipment that Robina Delaney travelled out with in May 1886. She was only six and so would be living at Hillfoot Farm. Another young girl, Grace Fegan, around the same age as Robina, also travelled out on that first shipment. Her story is another of the tragedies that can be laid at Emma Stirling's door.

In her book, Emma said it was her policy not to send children out as migrant workers until they were eight or nine years old and - "could be of use". As a result, she said her children were known to give satisfaction and were much in demand. As a result of this policy, she explained, she very quickly emptied the farm and was able to bring another group of the Edinburgh children out. It was this second group that James Delaney travelled out with in September 1886 and since he was ten years old he would have been immediately farmed out to a local farmer, Rufus de Wolfe.

Having put everything in place, Emma Stirling returned to Edinburgh and informed the Directors of the Edinburgh and Leith

Children's Aid and Refuge Society (ELCARS) that she could no longer afford to provide for the children in her Homes. It was becoming too much of a financial burden. She was therefore taking the children to Nova Scotia to work under the Canadian Government's Child Migrant Scheme.

None of the Directors of ELCARS raised any objections. That was the reason the force of the law fell so heavily on them later.

In their defence case, in the Court of Session, the Directors pleaded that since ELCARS was founded, and mainly funded, by Emma Maitland Stirling, they were powerless to control her actions.

On her return from Nova Scotia, Emma Stirling took a short lease on a farm at Leadburn Park in the Scottish Borders in the summer of 1885. Her intention was to use it to train the boys she was taking to Nova Scotia to work as farm labourers.

Many of the girls in her care were 'boarded out', in groups of four or six, in private homes, mainly farms, in the Borders area where the farmers' wives looked after the children. Initially, Emma considered this a cheaper option than buying and setting up more Homes in Edinburgh. So her later claims that she had eight houses full of children prior to migrating the children to Nova Scotia are misleading as they refer to these farm lodgings. Only the two very small Homes in Stockbridge and Granton and the Children's Shelter were actually run by her. Later, she wrote that eventually the system of 'Boarding Out' became too expensive and had to be stopped but she does not say what happened to those children – she was always very selective when it came to actual facts.

Annie and Robina Delaney were among the girls 'boarded out' at farms in the Borders and James Delaney was sent to the farm at Leadburn to train him for farm labouring in Nova Scotia in 1885. It does not seem that parents were able to visit their children who were 'boarded out' as they were in private homes.

In the Court of Session case, Arthur's mother Anne testified, under oath, that she and Arthur's sister, Ellen, visited the children, even when they were staying for the summer in Emma's Home in Burntisland. Arthur himself testified that he also visited his children when they were staying in other summer accommodation in Joppa, a seaside resort on the outskirts of Edinburgh, as well as at Stockbridge and Granton. But there is no mention of visits to the children 'boarded out' in the Borders which suggests visits were not permitted there. Arthur, his mother and sister, also testified that on occasions they had visited little Annie when she was ill in Merleton, Emma's own home. Annie was always delicate which makes Emma's later decision to farm her out, alone, aged ten, as a domestic servant on a remote farm in Quebec, inexplicable. It was like signing her death warrant.

Arthur's life, after putting his children into Emma Stirling's Home, had been miserable. It was a period of high unemployment and he had to take any work he could find. He worked when he could as a painter and decorator but the work was erratic and, during periods of unemployment, he had to return and lodge with his mother and sister in the Old Town. But then his life took a turn for the better. He met Cecilia Clifford, who lived with her parents and siblings in Scott's Close in the Cowgate. Her father, Bernard Clifford, had been born in Ireland, and he was a stone mason. Her mother, Mary Anne Clarke, was from an Irish emigrant family but had been born in Scotland. We do not know how Arthur and Cecilia met but we know from one of her granddaughters that Cecilia was an extremely devout Catholic, all her life, and her family were well known in St. Patrick's Church in 'Little Ireland', so perhaps they met through that community.

Arthur eventually managed to get steady work back in his old trade, as a glass-cutter, and on 30 July 1886, the couple married in St. Patrick's Church. We do not know if Cecilia had met Arthur's children before their marriage but, from later testimony, it seemed that the couple had always intended to have Arthur's children back to live with them. Certainly, the judges in the Court of Session accepted that Arthur had a wife and home for the children to be returned to.

It was not until September 1886, some four weeks after Arthur's marriage, that he learned that his son, James Delaney, was not, in fact, living on the farm in Leadburn but had been taken by Emma Stirling to Nova Scotia to work as a farm labourer. He was nine years old.

Arthur's brief period of happiness came to an abrupt end.

When Arthur heard his son had been taken away he went immediately to the office of Mr MacDonald, the Secretary of

ELCARS, and confronted him about the loss of his son. The Secretary claimed to know nothing about James' migration but told him to come back the next day and he would try and give him information.

A distraught Arthur returned the next day to be told that James was indeed in Nova Scotia and, to add to his grief, Arthur was informed that his youngest child, Robina Delaney, had sailed previously, in May 1886, and was already in Nova Scotia! She was six years old.

The Secretary claimed not to know where Arthur's daughter Annie was. Arthur had assumed she also had gone out with Robina to Nova Scotia. In fact, eight-year-old Annie was still 'boarded out' on one of the farms in the Scottish Borders. Arthur could have saved at least one of his children but that information was deliberately withheld from him by Emma Stirling and the Directors of ELCARS. Arthur threatened the Secretary that he would go to the law to have his children returned, but the Secretary merely mocked him - "Tut, tut, what would you go to the law about?"

Arthur must have been out of his mind with grief and worry when he returned to Cecilia waiting at home in the Old Town. Cecilia's response was, as always, to turn to the Church. They both went to see Canon Hannan in St. Patrick's Church and told him everything. That good priest realised the seriousness of the situation. How, indeed, could a working-class man in 'Little Ireland' challenge a wealthy woman, like Emma Stirling, through the law? The scales were always going to be weighted in favour of the rich and powerful. But he was determined to help in any way he could. He wrote a letter to one of the few Catholic lawyers in the city, William Considine, and gave it to Arthur to take to the man and explain the situation. Arthur and Cecilia were aware that the law cost money and they had little to spare. Canon Hannan reassured them that he would fund this initial consultation and then, if further action in law was needed, he would try and raise more from donations by some of the wealthier members of his congregation. The priest did raise some money in this way but it was never going to be enough if Emma Stirling refused to return the children.

Mr Considine prepared the initial case and approached the Directors of ELCARS saying they also were responsible for the children being taken, illegally, without their father's permission. The Directors took fright when they realised that Arthur did indeed intend to go to the law to have his children returned. They wrote a series of letters to Emma in Nova Scotia politely requesting her to bring the Delaney children back to Edinburgh. These letters were later read out in the Court of Session case and we have copies of them all. Emma Stirling's arrogance and complete contempt for Arthur daring to demand his children back shows through them all. She refused.

However, with the Directors persisting and trying to avoid the weight of the law descending on them in the absence of Emma, she finally agreed to bring James and Robina Delaney back to Edinburgh. They sailed from Nova Scotia, on the S.S. *Carthaginian,* on 8 November and arrived back in Edinburgh on 20 November 1886. The Secretary of ELCARS met Emma and the two Delaney children on their arrival. But Emma flatly refused to return the children to their father, claiming they 'belonged' to her now and she wouldn't give them up without a fight. She was a determined woman but arrogant and totally lacking in compassion. After all, she did not intend to keep James and Robina Delaney with her in Nova Scotia. They were to be farmed out as migrant labour in Canada like the other children. She was motivated by religious hatred, determined not to return his children to this papist who had dared to challenge her, even though he now had a wife and home for the children to go to. Any sane woman would not have behaved in this way, especially one who claimed to be a devout Christian.

So arrogant was she that, when the Secretary arrived with her at the Caledonian train station in Edinburgh, Emma put the two Delaney children in a cab with her and refused to tell the Secretary where she was taking them – and he didn't challenge her! This action was to cause the Secretary and ELCARS a great deal of worry, stress and expense in the years of legal action that followed.

But for me the hardest part to take was, what were James and Robina thinking while all this was happening? They had been taken to Nova Scotia and now they had sailed back and they had arrived in Edinburgh. James, at least, was old enough to know that they were home and no doubt he would tell his sister. They must have thought they were to be reunited with their father. How must it have felt when they realised this was not what was going to happen? So near yet so far.

One wonders how Emma Stirling could have been so cruel as to inflict such extreme trauma on two innocent children while claiming to be a 'child saver'. But there are still people in Canada today who describe Emma Maitland Stirling as - a 'benevolent abductor' – arguing that she meant well! These admirers of Emma Stirling blame the Canadian Government instead for the Child Migrant Schemes and campaign for an apology from the present Canadian Government.

We have been unable to find out where Emma Stirling hid James and Robina Delaney after her return to Edinburgh. It would not have been in her own home, Merleton in Trinity, or in either of her properties in Burntisland, as she had closed them up when she left for Nova Scotia. In her book – '*Our children in Old Scotland and Nova Scotia*' - she revealed that later, when Arthur's case was taken up by the Court of Session, she took measures to dispose of them and all her assets in Scotland in case the Court tried to sequester her properties.

It must have been agony for Arthur knowing his children were back home but being unable to find them. We know, from later testimony, that he began to haunt the Homes in case his children were there. He also continued to visit the offices of the Secretary, Mr MacDonald, until barred and threatened with the police being called. Whereupon he took to waiting outside in the street and approaching the Secretary for information there. Eventually, the Secretary said if he would leave him alone he would try and persuade Emma Stirling to return his children to him.

CHAPTER FIFTEEN

THE FIGHT FOR THE DELANEY CHILDREN

In April 1887, Arthur finally received a letter from his lawyer, Mr Considine, asking him to visit him in his office. There he explained that Emma Stirling would not give up his children without a legal fight. The lawyer explained that he had all the legal papers prepared to present Arthur's Petition for the return of his children to the Court of Session, but it would cost 25 pounds in legal fees to lodge it with the Court. It was a fortune to someone in Arthur's position. Mr Considine advised Arthur to consult with Canon Hannan at St. Patrick's Church to see if such a sum could be raised.

When Arthur approached Canon Hannan the priest explained that he had only received enough in donations to support Mr Considine's initial work. There was no more money available to proceed with the case. It was a devastating blow.

When the lawyer realised that no more money was available he suggested Arthur have himself admitted to the Poor Roll. They had lawyers available to assist those too poor to take legal action themselves. These Poor Roll lawyers operated on a no win, no fee basis. Meanwhile he would keep the case open.

Arthur had to wait to see if he qualified for Poor Law legal help – he was in work so not on Poor Relief - and he had to see if he was eligible. After many months the judgement was given – Arthur's earnings were so low he was entitled to use the Poor Roll lawyers.

But it was too late.

After spending the winter in Scotland and waiting to see if Arthur's case proceeded, Emma Stirling had sailed back to Nova Scotia taking James and Robina Delaney with her. In a further act of vindictive cruelty Emma Stirling had picked up Arthur's daughter, Annie, from a farm in the Scottish Borders, where she had been 'boarded out' all that time and took her, with her siblings, to Nova Scotia. She farmed them out as child labour, on three different

271

farms, hundreds of miles apart in Canada. Three children who could have been kept safe at home with their father in the Old Town.

Before they sailed from England, Emma Stirling changed the surname of the three children to make sure that they would never be found should the law come looking for them. On the ship's Manifest they are listed as James Whitehead (10), Annie Whitehead (9) and Bessie (Robina) Whitehead (7).

We cannot bear to imagine what the Delaney children felt like as they boarded that ship. None of them would ever know of their father's desperate fight to get them back.

Once we had obtained the full set of the Court documents it became obvious that the mills of justice ground exceedingly slowly.

It was not until 15 November 1888 that Arthur's Poor Roll lawyer, Ross Stewart, presented his Petition to the Court of Session in Edinburgh. On 23 November 1888 the judge approved Arthur's Petition stating there was a case to answer. In the absence of Emma Stirling the Directors of The Edinburgh and Leith Children's Aid and Refuge Society (ELCARS) were ordered to appear before the Court to explain why they had not returned his children to him. The trial date was set for 1 February 1889.

The ELCARS's Directors' lawyer presented their case to the Court arguing that they had not been responsible for Emma Stirling removing the children to Nova Scotia. She was the founder and main funder of the Society and they had no power over her. They stated that on departing for Nova Scotia in September 1886, Emma Stirling had cut all ties with The Edinburgh and Leith Children's Aid and Refuge Society. The Society was now funded completely from public donations and only the Home at McKenzie Place and the Shelter from Cruelty were now run by the Society.

The Directors declared that they had no objection to Arthur Delaney having his children returned to him. They had been in correspondence with Miss Stirling to that effect but she was refusing to return the children. Her argument was that after placing his children in the Homes he had abandoned them, that he was in arrears of payment and that when she had brought the children back he had made no attempt to recover them.

The correspondence between the Directors and Emma Stirling was read out in Court. In a letter dated 28 November1888 from

Hillfoot Farm, Aylesford, Nova Scotia to ELCARS's lawyer, Mr Gray, Emma Stirling wrote -

Dear Mr Gray

As to the view of the judges that the directors should have had the Delaney children restored to the homes in November 1888, or have looked after them in some way or other, I frankly say that the directors did all that they could in that direction, and are entirely free from any blame.

They also did have them looked after most efficiently, as I gave them personal and repeated assurances to that effect.

As to where they now are, they were a considerable time ago located in excellent homes in Canada, and therefore having been away from my Home, and beyond my control entirely, I can hold out no prospect of restoring them to the old country.

Emma M. Stirling

The three children who were - "beyond (her) control entirely" were eleven-year-old James, ten-year-old Annie and eight-year-old Robina. Emma Stirling had lost no time on returning to Canada with the Delaney children if the children had been "a considerable time ago" farmed out as migrant labour.

It shows very clearly that Emma Stirling did not care, in any way, about the three Delaney children. She only wanted to spite their father and was quite prepared to abandon them to their fate.

We learned from later investigation that on her return to Hillfoot Farm she split up the siblings. James was placed with a farmer nearby in Aylesford, but seven-year-old Robina was sent many hundreds of miles away to New Brunswick and nine-year-old Annie even further to a farm in Quebec.

The Court took a dim view of Emma Stirling's response and on 19 January 1889 ELCARS's lawyer, Mr Gray, again wrote to Emma in Nova Scotia. -

Dear Miss Stirling

Since Mr Macdonald received your letter of 24 December, 1888, the court have settled that the evidence in the Delaney case is to be taken soon before Lord Adam.

With reference to what you now say as to the children being in Nova Scotia, but out of your hands, our counsel, Mr Guthrie, thinks it would be necessary for us to know the exact addresses of the children as there is no doubt we will be questioned on this point.

I am sure you understand that the Directors are not wishing to give you any trouble in this matter, but of course they have to answer to the Court, and it would only be right that they should not be put in the position of seeming to refuse information.

Would you kindly let me hear from you at your earliest convenience.

Robert C. Gray.

After the letters had been read out, the Court called another Director of ELCARS, Mr Colston, to give evidence.

He testified that - "Miss Stirling was the foundress and she was also the largest contributor to the funds. I think the Directors felt a diffidence in interfering owing to that fact."

He was asked when he first heard about the case.

He replied - "I first heard about Delaney when Mr Considene threatened us with an action towards the end of 1886."

He continued - "I had an interview with Mr Considine and Mr Gray and I stated I had not the slightest objection to giving the children back."

He went on to say that, in November of that year he had heard from the Secretary that the children had been brought back but Miss Stirling refused to give them up. She thought they were her property.

Mr Colston was then asked why, when he knew the children were in this country, he had not obtained from Miss Stirling the information as to where they were.

He replied - "One man can take a horse to water but he cannot make him drink."

Mr Colston concluded his evidence by stating - "We have all along and are now quite willing that the children be restored to their father; we have no desire to have litigation on the subject."

He stood down and Mr William Considine took the stand. He identified himself as Arthur's original lawyer and gave evidence of the legal action he had taken on Arthur's behalf.

He stated - "I had a meeting with Mr Gray and he told me that Miss Stirling had declined to give up the custody of the children.

He could give me no information about them other than that they had returned; he did not know where they were."

Mr Considine stated that he had written to his client that same day 3 December 1886, and he read the letter out in Court.

"Dear Mr Delaney,

I saw Miss Stirling's agent today. I gather that the children have been brought back but she refuses point blank to part with them, unless compelled by the law to do so. It is plain there will be heavy fighting before the children can be recovered. Before taking any steps, I would like to have a meeting with the very Rev. Canon Hannan.

Mr Considine"

He stated - "The sole reason I was unable to press the Petition was because I had no funds.".

He was asked if Arthur Delaney had ever instructed him to abandon the claim.

He replied - "Mr Delaney never authorized me to abandoned the claim."

After Mr Considine's evidence the judge adjourned the case and ordered that the Court be resumed on the 8 February 1889.

These Court documents give the lie to Emma Stirling's claim that, when she brought the children back, Arthur made no attempt to recover his children.

It must have been agony for Arthur, sitting in the Court hearing this evidence – reliving all he had been through more than two years before - with his children still missing.

When the Court reconvened on 8 February 1889 Mr MacDonald, Secretary of ELCARS, was recalled to the stand. He declared they had received a reply from Miss Stirling from Nova Scotia in response to the Director's request for the addresses of the Delaney children in Canada.

"Dear Mr Gray

I regret I cannot comply with the request of the Directors, in giving the addresses desired, I fail to see how the Court can hold them as refusing, or appearing to refuse, information which they do not possess and have no means of obtaining.

Emma M. Stirling."

It is obvious from this response why Emma Stirling was later held in contempt of Court.

Again, the Court of Session took a dim view of her response and the judge adjourned the case and ordered the Court to reconvene on 8 March 1889.

This date was the beginning of his lawyers putting Arthur's case and he must have been full of trepidation giving his evidence when so much depended on it. He had to convince the judge that his children should be returned to him. He told the Court how he had been forced, by circumstances, to put his three children into Miss Stirling's Home. He declared that he had never abandoned his children but had visited them regularly, when permitted to do so. He stated he paid the fee for his children when he was able but admitted he fell into arrears during periods of unemployment. He told of hearing of his children, James and Robina, being taken to Nova Scotia by Emma Stirling and his attempts ever since to have his children restored to him.

He described seeing Emma Stirling's carriage on the High Street after his children had been taken back to Canada. He had followed the carriage to The Cruelty Shelter and, on gaining admittance, he had tackled Miss Stirling demanding the return of his children. She refused.

After Arthur's testimony the Court called Detective Officer John MacPherson to give evidence. This policeman had been present when Arthur had tackled Emma Stirling at the Cruelty Shelter. He was now appearing as a witness on behalf of Arthur.

He stated - "I recollect, one day in January 1888, being in a room in the High Street with the Petitioner Arthur Delaney and Miss Stirling when he demanded his children from Miss Stirling, or to know where they were, and he got no information. She refused to tell him where they were."

Arthur's lawyer, Ross Stewart, asked the Detective - "Would you say the Petitioner was very anxious to have his children returned to him?"

Detective John McPherson replied - "I understood from her remarks that the Petitioner had been bothering her very much to get the children."

After the policeman stood down the Court called Arthur's mother, Anne Delaney, to the witness box. Anne testified to the circumstances that Arthur found himself in and said he had lived with her on and off after putting his children into the Home. She went on to give evidence in support of Arthur's claim that he never abandoned his children after he put them in the Home but visited them regularly. She also gave details of visiting the children over the years, both in Edinburgh and Burntisland, along with her daughter, Ellen Delaney.

The next person called to the stand was Arthur's uncle, Thomas Delaney. He testified that his nephew, Arthur, had gone frequently, over the years, to the offices of Mr MacDonald, the Secretary, demanding information about his children. He had accompanied him on many of these visits. On his first occasion he went into the office with his nephew. He testified - "My nephew asked about his children and said he had heard they had been taken away to Nova Scotia. Mr MacDonald asked him where he had heard that. My nephew made no reply but asked again where the children were and Mr MacDonald said he did not know." When my nephew pressed him he said - "Well Delaney my instructions are to give you no information about them." My nephew said he would compel him by going to law to which Mr Macdonald replied - "Tut, tut, there's no use going to law. How could you go to law about it?"

And here they were in the Court of Session.

Thomas Delaney stood down and Ross Stewart declared the Petitioner Arthur Delaney's proof closed.

The judge declared the Court would reconvene on the 7 June to hear his verdict.

Arthur was in Court that day to await the verdict.

The verdict went in Arthur's favour!

The judge ruled that Arthur Delaney was a fit and proper person to have possession of his children, that he was married to a respectable woman and that he had a home to take them to. The judge ruled that the children had been taken from him illegally. The Directors were ordered to take steps immediately to have his children returned.

One of the Court documents we uncovered was a copy of a submission to the Court presented by the Edinburgh and Leith Children's Aid and Refuge Society's lawyer, Mr Lorimer. It read -

THE COURT OF SESSION

EDINBURGH
17TH JUNE 1889.

Mr Lorimer - 'In consequence of the expression of the opinion by the Court that the prayer of the petition could not be refused, the respondents undertake to apply forthwith to Miss Stirling for the return of the children to them, and, if necessary, to take proceedings in the Canadian Courts for that purpose; and they crave that in the meantime any judgement pronounced by the court should be limited to the first finding of the prayer of the petition, namely, that the petitioner is entitled to the custody of his children.'

The Lord President - 'When Arthur Delaney applied to have his children admitted to the Refuge, they had been received by Miss Stirling and it did not appear that anyone else was responsible for the custody of the children, at that time, except her.'

'But it must be quite clear, I think, that when the respondents became Directors of the Institution in the year 1884 they assumed a responsibility for the safe custody of all the children that were in these Homes, or in other places, belonging to the Institution. And among other obligations and responsibilities that they thus incurred by becoming Directors was the obligation to redeliver the children to their parents when they were demanded.

Now in point of fact, these children were taken out of the jurisdiction of this Court and out of the United Kingdom in 1886 and that was certainly a most indefensible proceeding. Nothing could justify that without the consent of the parents.

The respondents, the Directors of the Institution, seem to have been sensible of that very fact after it took place, and they remonstrated with Miss Stirling, who had carried the children to Nova Scotia, and desired her to bring them back. In that I think they acted quite rightly.

But, then, I think, they acted very far short of their duty after the children were brought back to this country, because they allowed Miss Stirling, after she had brought the children to the neighbourhood of Edinburgh, to conceal them from their parent, and also from the respondents themselves.

Indeed there is an appearance on the part of the respondents of an indisposition to acquire any knowledge of where the children were, and to all applications on the part of the Petitioner for access to his children there could be no satisfactory answer made.

The consequence was again that the children were carried out of the country. Now for that I think the respondents must be answerable, because they were thus violating the obligation which they had undertaken to be responsible for the safe custody of the children while they were in the Institution, and to deliver them when the parents required them.

It is therefore, I think, impossible not to say that the respondents are under an obligation to deliver these children now to the petitioner; and the only question of course which perplexes one in dealing with the case is, as the children are not here, it may require the lapse of some considerable time, perhaps proceedings in another country, in order to accomplish the object for which this petition was presented.'

It was agreed in Court that Mr Lorimer should consult with the Directors of The Edinburgh and Leith Children's Aid and Refuge Society as to how they intended to rectify the situation and return to Court with their response. When Mr Lorimer returned to the Court he presented a Minute from a meeting of the Directors of ELCARS.

THE EDINBURGH AND LEITH CHILDREN'S AID AND REFUGE SOCIETY.

MINUTES of a special meeting of the Directors of the Edinburgh and Leith Children's Aid and Refuge Society on the 11th June 1889.

'With a view of carrying out in the most stringent form the injunctions of the Court of Session as given in their order of 7th June 1889, a solicitor be employed at Halifax, Nova Scotia, to wait on Miss Stirling and ask her in a kind, but resolute manner to produce or give needful information toward the production of the Delaney children and send them home, or if she refuses, to take legal steps, to enforce the requirements, telegraphing her that in furtherance of this procedure a statement of the whole case should be sent to the solicitor with a copy of the detailed judgements of the judges, and that the Directors while wishing every consideration and kindness to Miss Stirling are obliged unavoidably to protect their own position by taking decided measures.

Mr Young strongly deprecated employing a solicitor without first communicating with Miss Stirling, as he felt sure when the matter was fully put before her she would at once give up the children, in his opinion, the Director's object would be more likely to be obtained by such a course as that proposed by Dr Bell.

Dr Bell objected to writing to Miss Stirling first as in the event of Miss Stirling hiding the children away, the court might look on such action as being in collusion with Miss Stirling on the part of the Directors. To meet Mr Young, Dr Bell amended his motion by suggesting that a messenger be sent to Nova Scotia with full powers to act. On this motion being tabled, the Secretary being referred to and asked whether he could conveniently go to Halifax stated his readiness, if armed with full powers to proceed at once to Nova Scotia and act if need be officially on behalf of the Directors and to take such measures as might be judicious and necessary to bring the children back to this country with a view of carrying out the Court's decision. It was resolved accordingly.

When this Minute from ELCARS was presented to the Court the Lord President responded -

'I approve entirely of the spirit in which the Minute is expressed, which Mr Lorimer has just read, and I am very glad to find from that that the respondents are now fully alive as to what their responsibilities are.

But I think it would be hardly consistent with the duty of the Court to abstain now from pronouncing an order against the respondents *for the redelivery of the children. Of course that must be qualified to this extent, that they must have time.*

The order which I would propose, with your Lordships concurrence, to pronounce, is to ordain the whole parties called as respondents in the petition to deliver the petitioner his children, James, Annie and Robina Delaney, named in the petition, and that on or before the first sederunt-day in October next; and further, appoint the respondents to report to the court on Thursday 18th July next, what steps have been taken in pursuance of this order.'

It is obvious that the judges in the Court of Session have no intention of allowing the case to lapse.

I think Arthur and Cecilia must have felt the Court's resolve and were full of hope because we know, from the records, that they moved into a bigger house at 153 High Street, in the Old Town, to be able to accommodate the three children on their return.

The move was in vain.

The Secretary returned without the children.

In the Court documents we discovered a copy of another Minute from 'The Edinburgh and Leith Children's Aid and Refuge Society' dated 16 August 1889. It reads -

THE EDINBURGH & LEITH CHILDREN'S AID & REFUGE SOCIETY

MINUTES of a special meeting of the Directors of the Edinburgh & Leith Children's Aid & Refuge Society held on 16 August 1889.

Report from the Secretary Mr MacDonald on his visit to Canada in search of the Delaney children.

The Secretary reported that acting on the instructions he received at the last meeting, he had proceeded to Nova Scotia by the first available ship, viz, The Pavonia to Boston and that on landing he had without any delay travelled to Aylesford in Nova Scotia. After six visits he had succeeded in getting an interview with Miss Stirling when she had not only declined to give the Delaney children up, or any information regarding them but positively declined to discuss the matter with him. He then proceeded to Halifax the capital of the county and made application to the Supreme Court of Nova Scotia there for an order on Miss Stirling to deliver up the children. This the Court refused to do, that the Directors had no legal right to the children and that the only person entitled to ask for an order was the father. He laid on the table certified copies of all the proceedings. The meeting approved of Mr Donald's actions. ELCARS's lawyer, Mr Gray, reported that he had submitted the whole papers connected with the proceedings in Nova Scotia to counsel who strongly recommended that a mandate should be obtained from Delaney in order that the Directors might take proceedings in his name for the recovery of the children. The meeting moved and instructed Mr Gray accordingly and authorised him to assure Delaney's agents that although the proceedings are to be taken in Delaney's name, they are to be at the Director's expense.

Two months later, Arthur's lawyer, Ross Stewart, was informed that a writ of *Habeas Corpus* against Emma Stirling had been issued in Nova Scotia on 14 October 1889. This meant that she would have to explain to the Supreme Court of Nova Scotia why she had failed to return the Delaney children after being ordered to do so by the Court of Session in Edinburgh.

If Emma Stirling failed to respond she would be held to be in contempt of the Supreme Court and a warrant would be issued for her arrest.

Our aunt, Ella Lajoie (nee Delaney), had emigrated to Canada many years ago and, when she heard that our Delaney children had been lost in Canada and that a case had been brought in the Supreme Court of Nova Scotia, she contacted the Archivist for copies of the Court proceedings. Though the documents were very frail, being almost 100 years old, they had survived and my aunt was able to obtain copies for us. This is the earliest -

SUPREME COURT OF NOVA SCOTIA
HALIFAX
THE QUEEN *at the instance of Plaintiff*
ARTHUR DELANEY

against

EMMA M. STIRLING, *Defendant*

13th *August 1890*

On hearing read the rule nisi granted by Mr Justice Ritchie dated the 19th June 1890 and the papers therein referred to the two affidavits of Emma M. Stirling and the affidavit of John Peggie, all filed herein the 5th day of July 1890, and the printed case herein, and after hearing arguments of counsels on both sides -

This court does order and adjudge that the said rule nisi be, and the same is hereby made absolute, and that said return of the defendant, Emma M. Stirling be, and the same is hereby set aside and quashed, and that a writ of attachment for CONTEMPT OF COURT do issue against the said Emma M. Stirling, commanding the sheriff of the County of Kings, or any other of our sheriffs, to arrest the said Emma M. Stirling, so that he may have her before us in our Supreme Court at Halifax on Tuesday 9th day of December 1890 to answer to us for certain trespasses and contempts brought against her in our said court.

And it is further ordered that the said writ remain in the office of the Prothonotary for the period of thirty days, and be not delivered to the sheriff to be executed if within that period the said Emma M. Stirling shall make a satisfactory return and produce the said children or show that it is impossible for her to do so.

If the children are not produced, any amended return shall give full particulars of how, when and where, she disposed of each of said children, when she last saw or heard of them, and in whose custody she believed them to be at the date of the return, and the circumstances to show that she has made every effort and is unable to obtain any of the children in order to produce them in obedience to the writ.

MR JUSTICE RITCHIE

The second document obtained by our Aunt Ella read -

SUPREME COURT OF NOVA SCOTIA
HALIFAX

An amended return to the writ of habeas corpus was submitted by Emma M. Stirling to the Supreme Court of Nova Scotia on the 2nd September 1890. This contained no new information so the court ruled -

An application is now made to this Court for leave to put in force previously allowed on the ground that the conditions contained in the order of 13th August have not been complied with inasmuch that the children have not been produced, and the new return does not state circumstances to show that Miss Stirling had made every effort and was unable to obtain any of the children in order to produce them in accordance with the writ.

In the case before us this court has already decided that Miss Stirling has illegally parted with the custody of the children. She *has not produced them in obedience to the writ, and we are now called upon to decide, whether or not the facts and circumstances she has disclosed show she has made every effort, and is unable to obtain any of the children, in order to produce them in obedience to the writ of habeas corpus.*

The last return to the writ is clearly insufficient on this point. It merely states that she has instructed her solicitor on her behalf to endeavour to obtain the children, and furnished him with all the information to get possession for his assistance.

If we turn to her affidavit we find that the only thing she did in relation to this matter was to write to her solicitor, Messrs Gray and MacDonald, solicitors of this Court on 5th September, 1890, two days after the date of the return she submitted to this court.

If we look at the affidavit of Mr Wallace MacDonald to see what his firm did, we find that they wrote a letter to each of the persons mentioned in the return of Miss Stirling, asking where the children were, but obtained no information except that the boy had run away. They then instructed a Mr Cogswell to proceed to the places of the abode of the persons to whom they had written and make all necessary enquiries as to the whereabouts of the children, and use all legitimate means and his best endeavours to bring them to Halifax.

Mr Cogswell stated that he went to Middleton, Nova Scotia, and saw Mr Rufus de Wolfe who told him that James Delaney had run away from him, and that he did not know where he was and on making enquiries in Middleton he could not find anything as to the whereabouts of James Delaney.

He then saw Mrs Jones at Grand Metis, who told him that she had Anne Delaney, but did not have her then, and did not know where she was, and on making enquirers there outside of Mrs Jones, he could get no information.

The next paragraph of his affidavit referring to Robina Delaney is similar substituting a Mrs Smith of Blackrock for Mrs Jones of Shemogue for Grand Metis.

It does not appear that Mr Cogswell had written authority or credentials from Miss Stirling authorising him to enquire after the children, or requesting the persons with whom they had been placed to give him all the information they possessed, in respect if them, and I think it is evident that such information was withheld from the persons best able to afford it without questioning the bona fides either of Messrs Gray and McDonald or Mr Cogswell their messenger.

It seems to me that sending an utter stranger to enquire for the children was not calculated to obtain information to bring about their restitution but that Miss Stirling should have gone herself, or if that was impossible sent one of her confidential employees with proper authority in writing from herself, to make necessary enquiries.

Besides this, the Court has by this order required Miss Stirling to disclose the facts and circumstances which transpired so that the Court may judge whether it is impossible or not for Miss Stirling to produce the children.

It would be sufficient in order to comply with the statement in Mr Cogwell's affidavit, to go to the house, ask for the child, and if his informant did not know where she was, to make enquiries of two or more persons he met in the street. Did he do this? Or were his enquiries bona-fide and made to persons calculated to give him the information he sought? If they were the full particulars and the names and occupations of his informants should have been given to the Court, so that we might judge whether or not they were thorough and calculated to obtain the desired end.

I can come to no other conclusion but that the action taken by Miss Stirling in this matter subsequent to the order of 13th August falls far short of of the requirements in the Appeal Court in England in similar cases (The Queen v Mr Barnardo) and what should be required by this Court.

In the Barnardo case the Court stated - As a matter of law it is no valid excuse for not producing a child in obedience of a writ habeas corpus to state inability to obey, if such inability is the result of previous illegal conduct of the person to whom the writ is addressed. In this case the defendant's inability arises from him having illegally sent the child abroad against the will of the lawful guardian, and he did this before any legal action commenced is immaterial. Persons who illegally put a child out of their power do so at their peril, and if they are ordered to produce the child no excuse founded on their own ability to comply with the order will be held sufficient answer to the writ.

The English Court was of the opinion it was not sufficient to write letters, the person to whom the writ was directed must use every possible effort to get the child, must go abroad, if necessary, and use every personal influence for the purpose; and if he cannot get the child back in any other way, he must go after it himself and assist the parent, if necessary, by the legal processes of the country where it is, he must also advertise and do everything that mortal man could do in this matter.

In the English cases too, it must be remembered, Mr Barnardo did not know where the persons to whom he had given the child were, or their address, while in this case, the addresses of the persons who had the girls at the time the writ was issued or a very short time before, are well known to Miss Stirling and their residence are not very far away.

Now contrast the requirements of the English Court with what was done in this case.

Miss Stirling did nothing but write a letter to her solicitors. They wrote a few more letters and then sent a messenger who was a stranger to the persons supposed to have the children, not accredited in any way as coming from Miss Stirling. He makes some enquiries, but with the exception of the persons with whom the children were, and who under the circumstances would be expected to withhold the information, we do not know to whom they were directed. Having obtained no information he returns home.

Nothing further is done, and Miss Stirling and her solicitors appear satisfied that everything had been done necessary to show that it is impossible for her to produce the children.

If this is a sufficient answer to justify the non production of a child in obedience to a writ of habeas corpus, such a writ for that purpose is practically worthless, for I can hardly imagine a case in which judicious shuffling of a child from one party to another would not enable such a return to be made.

There is another point to which I have not averted, but which has somewhat impressed itself on me. Miss Stirling, greatly to her credit, has taken for years an interest in destitute children and spent a great deal of time and money in their maintenance and education, and according to her own statement they are under her charge until they become of age.

I cannot believe, if this is the case, that it is her usual practice to allow little girls of such a tender age, as these children were, and in whose welfare she claims to take a great interest, to be transferred at will from one person to another without her knowing where they are, and that they are being brought up in a respectable manner, and it seems to me very strange, that she should take so little interest in the boys she has brought to this country to allow one who was only twelve years of age to run away from the person with whom he was placed without making any inquiries about him, and endeavouring to trace him in any way, particularly when such a thing happened within a few miles of her residence in this Province.

I think it is due to Miss Stirling herself, and the benevolent persons who assist her, as well as the parents and friends of the children brought into this Province that a full explanation should be given of the course pursued in this respect with reference to these children.

For in the face of Miss Stirling's affidavit, I cannot but assume that the particular course followed in this case was for the purpose of removing the children from the jurisdiction of this Court, and enabling Miss Stirling to state in her return that she does not know where they are.

After the Justice's summing up the three judges retired to consider their verdicts and on the Court being reconvened Lord Justice Ritchie made the following statement -

Following the decision in the English Court (the Barnardo case) I am of the opinion Miss Stirling has not shown sufficient reason for not producing the children, and that the writ of arrest should be put in force, and she must answer the intterogatories, which may be submitted, and this Court can then ascertain whether she has purged herself of the contempt, or is liable to punishment therefore.

Mr Justice Townshend concurred in this judgement while the Chief Justice was of the opinion she had done everything that was required to get possession of the children.

The verdict of Lord Justice Ritchie and Mr Justice Townshend therefore, carried the majority decision and Miss Stirling was ordered to be arrested.

Emma Stirling later gave her version of the Supreme Court of Nova Scotia's proceedings in her book *Our Children in Old Scotland and Nova Scotia*. She claimed that in August 1890 the Court demanded that she give them the addresses of the children or where she had last heard of them and stated she did so at once.

She continues that the Court also ordered her to instruct a solicitor to find them. She claims she did this but the solicitor failed to find the children at the addresses she had given. She continues - "he did not tell me so until 23 December 1890" - five months after the Supreme Court ruling!

On hearing this, her own lawyer wrote to her saying that the Court required her to send a man to look for the children within twenty-four hours. She explains in her book - "Two men were suggested - one was my farmer - the other was a detective. To both of these I objected. The first because, having a large stock of cattle in the barn I could not do without his work, and also because that, being my servant I could not expect the Court to be really satisfied with any effort he might make. To the second I objected because he was a Roman Catholic so I could not employ him."

She stated she was asked by the Court's counsel, in January 1891, if she would advertise (presumably through the newspapers) for the children. She explains in her book that she refused, claiming that she had already done all she could to find them.

On reading that account, our family felt it was obvious that Emma Stirling had hidden the children away and she had lied and perjured herself in her responses to the Supreme Court of Nova Scotia. If the appeal had gone out to the public there was a chance that, in spite of their name changes, someone might recognize the Delaney children.

When we obtained the Supreme Court of Nova Scotia judgement we could see that the court believed Emma Stirling was lying. In fact, in time, that first examination of the case in the Supreme Court of Canada, and it's majority conclusions, were later borne out by the facts. Emma Stirling had indeed hidden the three Delaney children to make sure no one would ever find them.

The judge was scathing about the fact that Emma Stirling had brought very young children to Nova Scotia and then had appeared to have lost track of them and had left underage children to their fate, offering no protection.

Some years ago the University of Edinburgh carried out a Study on the Child Migrant Schemes operated in the nineteenth century by people like Dr Barnardo, Emma Stirling and other, so called, 'child savers'.

Their conclusions were truly shocking. They particularly criticised Emma Stirling for failing to look after the interests of her children after she sent them away all over Canada. Some of the other organizations had in place a fairly regular inspection regime to check up on the well-being of the children placed. Emma Stirling had none. The University's study concluded that Emma Stirling had completely underestimated the size of the country and had no system of checking up on the many children she placed outwith Nova Scotia itself. Emma, herself, claimed that she was very careful to check up on the respectability of the people with whom the children were placed. This 'system' involved asking a farmer to get a reference from a Minister of Religion of the farmer's good character. There were no follow up checks thereafter and, indeed, the children could be passed on to other people without her being informed.

In her book, *Our children in Old Scotland and Nova Scotia,* Emma wrote about her decision to take part in the Canadian Government's Child Migrant Scheme. She claims -

"As I could not make up my mind to resign them to the hands of strangers for the selection of their future homes, I preferred going with them and buying a farm where I could make a home for the little ones, and a headquarters for those who had already been placed, for it would obviously be worse than useless, to send boys and girls across the sea, without a home within reach of them, with their own people there to look after their interests and to hear constantly how they are getting on."

Of course, it was all lies.

Emma had taken the Canadian government's 'bounty' per child and so she had to place the children wherever there was a request. That could be hundreds of miles away from Aylesford, as in the case of both Annie and Robina Delaney and, no doubt, many, many other Edinburgh children, whose names we will never know. Whose stories will never be told. The children were very young and they received no wages - they were in effect slave labour - so how these children were meant to travel back to Hillfoot Farm she does not explain. Even children who were placed nearer, like James Delaney, did not appear to feel able to go back to Hillfoot Farm. He must have been very unhappy because the farmer said he kept running away but he certainly didn't run back to the bosom of Emma Stirling - who was within walking distance - he must have realised he would get short shift there. The same was true of another tragic girl, Grace Fegan, who Emma had taken to Nova Scotia as a six year old child in the first migrant children shipment along with Robina Delaney. When great harm was being done to her she obviously did not feel she could report the sexual abuse to Emma Stirling.

When we read the Supreme Court's assessment of Emma's explanation about our lost children we knew that, like all the other children, they could have been sent anywhere, passed from hand to hand and their whereabouts lost. Perhaps James Delaney had indeed run away. But, in spite of this possibility, we remained convinced that Emma Stirling had deliberately hidden the Delaney children somewhere. By this time, through our research, we felt we knew her character very well. We knew the harm she had done to the three Delaney children, we knew she had been found guilty by the Court of Session in Edinburgh of abducting the children from Scotland, we knew she was a consummate liar and we believed she would not flinch from committing perjury.

In time our instincts were to be proved correct.

The Supreme Court of Nova Scotia re-convened on 10th July 1891 to consider whether the charge of contempt of court by Emma Stirling stood, or whether she should be purged of the contempt on the basis that she had done all she could to find the three Delaney children but it was impossible to do so.

SUPREME COURT OF NOVA SCOTIA
HALIFAX

JUDGEMENT of Lord Chief Justice McDonald, Justice Wetherbe and Justice Ritchie dated 10th July 1891.

On 13th August 1891, an order was made directing a writ of arrest to issue against Miss Stirling, for contempt of this court, the contempt being the non production of the Delaney children. In pursuance of a previous Order of the Court. It was however, that the writ should *remain in the office of the court for thirty days and that the same be not delivered to the Sheriff to be executed 'If within that time Miss Stirling should make satisfactory return and produce the said children, or show that it is impossible for her to do so.' Subsequent to this order on the 2ⁿᵈ September 1890 Miss Stirling made an amended return made by her on 24ᵗʰ October 1889 explanatory of her dealings with the said children and showing how it was impossible to comply with the Order to produce them, she also filed an affidavit, setting forth the efforts made by her to comply with the Order of the Court – 'I have not done, so far as I know, anything in contempt of this Honourable Court, and I have used my best endeavours to comply with the Order of the Honourable Court, made herein on the 13ᵗʰ August last'.*

With this amendment were filed the affidavits of William A.B. Ritchie, Robert L. Borden, Wallace MacDonald and Edward E. Cogswell setting out the information received from Miss Stirling by her solicitors the employment by them of Mr Cogswell, a Barrister of this Court, in consequence of these instructions to make search for, and if possible, find these children that she might be able to produce them as commanded by this Court, and the efforts made by Mr Cogswell in pursuance of his instructions to find them. The efforts of Miss Stirling, as detailed in these affidavits and returns, were not, I believe satisfactory to the majority of the Court and, under a practice that appears to prevail in England, but not familiar here, it was directed that Miss Stirling should should be examined by a Master of the Court on a series of questions prepared by the solicitor for the Prosecutor and which she was directed to answer without any opportunity of consulting with or being advised by her own solicitors.

Under this order between ninety and one hundred questions carefully and skilfully framed, covering the whole ground of the Inquiry, have been answered.

These answers have been returned to this Court by the Master with his report that Miss Stirling has failed to purge her contempt of Court pronounced against her that the Court is now to determine whether the report be sustained.

The English practice does not, I believe, require the Master in such cases to give reasons for the conclusion he reports to the Court.

He has not done so in this case and so I am less reluctant in declaring my own inability to concur with the conclusion he has reported.

It will be kept in mind by the testimony produced by and on behalf of Miss Stirling has not been contradicted. No one has ventured to say that a single statement she has made was untrue.

It is not suggested that Miss Stirling or Mr Cogswell perjured themselves, and yet it is difficult to conceive how any other hypothesis the conclusion (of the Master) has been arrived at.

It would be an insult to Miss Stirling and those who have aided and assisted her, to discuss such a supposition.

Of course, we now know that Emma Stirling did indeed perjure herself. The Master who subjected her to such intensive cross-examination obviously came to the conclusion that Emma Stirling was lying throughout.

There is, however, no suggestion that Mr Cogswell perjured himself. He went to all the addresses that Emma Stirling gave him as being where the three Delaney children were living. He went in good faith. He had no way of knowing that Emma Stirling had removed the children from those addresses before giving the information to the Court.

Why Lord Chief Justice MacDonald chose to disregard the findings of the Master's cross-examination we have no way of knowing. It does appear that he disapproved of this 'English' custom being used in a Canadian law system. In actual fact it was not an 'English' custom at all, it was Scottish law - from the Court of Session in Edinburgh. It is hard, even now, reading his judgement because at that time there was still a chance that the Delaney children could have been saved. We will never know why the Justice made that judgment but he certainly bears responsibility for failing three innocent children.

Lord Justice MacDonald concluded -

I have not the slightest hesitation in holding that Miss Stirling should be purged of the contempt declared against her, and that she has not produced the Delaney children because – ' IT WAS IMPOSSIBLE FOR HER TO DO SO'.

I come to this conclusion because I believe the statements on which the Court has now to pass to be true, and being true, to be conclusive against ANY INTENTION ON THE PART OF MISS STIRLING TO DECEIVE OR MISLEAD THE COURT.

It is my opinion that Miss Stirling has purged the contempt declared against her and that she should be discharged from custody.

Unfortunately, the second judge, Mr Justice Weatherbe, concurred with this verdict.

But the third judge was Mr Justice Ritchie who had presided in the first Supreme Court proceedings and therefore knew the case very well. He had stated in that sitting that he believed Emma Stirling had shown contempt of Court in not returning the Delaney children. He had pointed out that allowing Emma's Stirling's defence would make a complete mockery of the terms of the writ of *Habeas Corpus* as anyone could plead that they did not know where the children were and thus get away with hiding them.

It seems obvious to us now that Mr Justice Ritchie was not taken in and knew that Emma Stirling was lying. His reading of her character was spot on. He knew she was a perjurer and seems to have instinctively known she had deliberately put the children out of the reach of the Court.

His summing up of the case read -

In this case the Court has already decided Miss Emma Stirling is in contempt of disobedience to the writ of habeas corpus directing her to produce three children named Delaney before one of the judges of this Court. Three children who she brought illegally to this province, without the permission of their father and who she claimed to be responsible for until they were of age.

She now states that she does not know where these children are.

This Court has already decided that the different returns made by her to the writ were bad.

These returns have not altered.

It is the opinion of the Master who examined her, in detail, that she had not obeyed the injunction.

It does not appear from her responses to the interrogatories that she has taken any further steps to obtain the children beyond those mentioned in the returns to the writ which this Court has already declared bad.

She has done nothing to purge her contempt.

In my opinion she should be punished for the contempt of which this Court has already found her guilty.

Perhaps, if Mr Justice Ritchie's opinion had carried the majority, the three Delaney children would not have suffered as they did. As it was the two other judge's decisions put him in the minority. He seems to us an honest insightful man who tried his very best to ensure the children would be found and history has vindicated his judgement.

With Emma Stirling being absolved of contempt of Court, by two of the judges in Nova Scotia, the attempts by Arthur to have custody of his children returned to the Court of Session in Edinburgh.

The Custody case resumed on 15 July 1891 in Edinburgh.

Arthur's lawyer, Ross Stewart, reflected on the fact that all the proceedingas taken by the Directors of ELCARS to obtain the children had proved futile. He stated that in these circumstances -

'The Petitioner Arthur Delaney had suggested to the Directors that either they employ a detective agency to find the children, or to offer a reward for them, or to advertise for them. None of these suggestions were taken up by the Directors. They had also refused to provide the Petitioner, Arthur Delaney, with funds in order that he and his agent might proceed to Nova Scotia to find the children'.

The judges did not think Arthur and his lawyer travelling to Nova Scotia to find the children was feasible, pointing out that the problem was that nobody seemed to know where the children were.

The Directors of ELCARS pleaded that they had done everything they could to find the children and should be absolved of responsibility.

The judges disagreed with this plea. The Lord President of the Court of Session stated -

'The position of your clients, Mr Lorimer, is not satisfactory and I think the Court is entitled to look to them for further aid in this

matter. It may be a very extravagent proposal on the part of the Petitioner that he should go to Canada to hunt up his children among several millions of a population; but we cannot let the matter stand as it is.'

The other judge, Lord McLaren stated -

'I would like the Directors carefully to consider whether they can suggest any practical measures to deal with the case as it now stands and whether they will provide the means for taking such a measure. It may be that using their best endeavours to solve the question, they may not be able to propose anything and in that case we will have to consider whether they are to be held in contempt, or whether Mr Delaney is to be left to his remedy of damages.

Before these proceedings can be allowed to come to an end, the Directors must be in a position to satisfy the Court that all practical means of tracing the children have been exhausted.'

When the lawyer for ELCARS returned to the Court of Session a few days later he stated that the Directors had agreed to employ a detective in Nova Scotia to search for the children at their expense.

I cannot begin to imagine what effect all of this was having on my great-grandfather Arthur and his wife Cecilia. He had been fighting through the courts for the return of his children for five years! He and Cecilia now had three children of their own but his resolve to have James, Annie and Robina returned to him never wavered.

We discovered in the Court of Session documents the subsequent Detective's Report.

REPORT

MR H.MELLISH, Detective Officer, Halifax, Nova Scotia of SEARCH FOR THE CHILDREN OF THE PETITIONER

ARTHUR DELANEY SEPTEMBER 9TH 1891

After receiving your instructions and perusing carefully Miss Stirling's answers and disclosures in connection with these children, I set about the task of endeavouring to locate the Delaney children.

About the 1ˢᵗ August 1891, I went to Little Shemogue, in the county of Westmorland, in the province of New Brunswick, a farming district about three miles from the nearest railway station on the N.B. & P.E. Island Railway, and found that Robina Delaney had been living there at the house of Smith Blacklock, under the name of Bessie Whitehead up to about the month of April, in the spring of 1890 when she was taken away by a man who came for her in the company of her brother (James Delaney, I suppose). I could find no clue as to the name of the party who came for her, nor of the place he went, or even the direction he took when going away with the child and from the best opinion I can form, it does not seem likely that the Blacklocks knew where the child was taken.

Up to within a few days, not more than a week previous to her being taken away, the child had been staying for some six months at the home of Fred Raworth, a farmer, residing in West Moreland county about eight miles from the Blacklock's where she had formerly stayed.

She was known in the neighbourhood as a bright child and a good singer.

I then went to Grand Metis, a French settlement on the River St. Lawrence, in the province of Quebec, about three miles from St. Octave, the nearest railway station, and found that a child who gave her name as Whitehead (presumably Annie Delaney) had been living with Joseph Jones, a married man with no family, up to the end of September 1890, when she was taken away by a man' d'une moyenne grandeur' whom the child recognized when he came for her. Mr and Mrs Jones who were much attached to the child at first refused to give her up and the child herself was very unwilling to go but the man who came for her is said to have represented himself as the child's uncle (not true, of course) and threatened to compel Mr Jones to give her up, and so the latter was forced to give way. She was then taken hurriedly to the railway station and put on board the train bound north but I could find no information which could make further search in that direction anything more than mere speculation.

This child used to speak of a sister who was better looking than she. She promised to write to Mrs Jones but does not seem to have done so yet.

I then proceeded to Black Point, in the county of Gloucester, one of the places named by Miss Stirling as the residence of Mrs Raworth, and found no person named Raworth resided there, or even in that county. But I heard of two of Miss Stirling's children there, one a girl named\Maggie Cowan, age fourteen, living with Ebenezer McMillan, and another, a boy named John English, age sixteen, living with Robert Harvey at that place.

I also visited Black Rock another of the places mentioned by Miss Stirling as the residence of Mrs Raworth. It is a small country district near the Caraquet Railway about thirty miles from Bathurst, in the province of New Brunswick, but found no person named Raworth residing there and no trace of any children not residing with their parents.

A fortnight later I visited Pugwash in the province and Wallace Bay, about four miles from Pugwash, in search of the children.

John Tuttle from whom Robina Delaney was sent to the Blacklocks resides at Wallace Bay but I could get no information of any value at that place.

I found, however, that a child whom I believe to be Annie Delaney had been living a mile from Pugwash with a married sister of John Tuttle about the month of September 1890, but found no trace of her after that date.

Lastly I visited Middleton in this province (Nova Scotia) in search of James Delaney. I found that he attended a little school about three miles from Middleton Railway Station for some time previous to January 14th 1890, at which date his attendance, according to the Register, ceases. He is registered as James Delaney, age twelve years.

At that time he was living at Rufus de Wolfe's, two miles from Middleton Station.

In March, 1890, he ran away from De Wolfe's but was back there again in September of the same year when he again ran away when Mr De Wolfe was not at home and since that date his whereabouts are unknown in that community.

Mr De Wolfe made no enquiry or search for him and never sent any people to look for him nor did he ever search for him himself after that date as he himself admitted. Mr De Wolfe also stated that he had seen nothing of the boy since that date, that the boy was not much use on the farm and was constantly running away.

He was said to be a bright smart boy with red hair and round features.

Mr De Wolfe also stated that the boy was not then in the county of Annapolis (Middleton is in that county).

I have no idea whatever, from any information I have been able to obtain from the most careful enquiry, in what way one should proceed in further prosecution of the search for any of these children.

I have no reason to believe in any case, except that of the boy, any of the parties interested knew of a search being made for the children, and I also believe that the parties with whom the children were living were not put in possession of any information which would enable their whereabouts to be traced.

I made the enquiries in the most cautious manner, staying for days in the different neighbourhoods where it was thought information could have been obtained, and working under assumed names, endeavoured in every way known to me to get trace of the present whereabouts of the children, but failed.

I am convinced that the changes in the girl's names and several changes effected in their various residences of late were made with the deliberate intention of avoiding location in case of enquiry and I know of nothing further I can do except to grope around somewhat aimlessly without anything to work upon.

H. MELLISH
Messrs Drysdale, Newcombe and McInnes
Barristers
Halifax
Nova Scotia.

Mr Mellish had come to the same conclusion as Justice Ritchie of the Supreme Court of Nova Scotia - Emma Stirling had deliberately hidden the children away when the Court had ordered her to return them. She had abducted the three Delaney children, lied and perjured herself in both Courts of Law.

I cannot begin to imagine the depths of despair of my great-grandfather Arthur when he read the report of the Detective Officer,

Mr Mellish. He must have known that the detective was an experienced and skilful officer of the law - indeed we discovered that, later in his life, Mr Mellish rose to the top of the legal profession in Nova Scotia - yet he had failed to find the children. What's more he had confirmed Arthur's belief that Emma Stirling had deliberately hidden his children to avoid them ever being found.

After receiving Mr Mellish's Report the judges reconvened the case in the Court of Session.

THE COURT OF SESSION
EDINBURGH.
20 OCTOBER 1891

Petition presented to the court of behalf of the Respondents, The Edinburgh and Leith Children's Aid and Refuge Society.

PETITION

The directors contend that they have done everything in their power to recover the children of Arthur Delaney. They beg the court to overturn the order of June 7ᵗʰ 1889.

DECISION

Lord Adam stated - This petition is before us upon a report by a detective officer who was sent out by the Directors to search for the children under an order of the court.

I cannot say that the report is satisfactory, but so far as I can gather from it's terms the detective officer has done all he could, and he tells us that he does not see any other means of following up his search.

As far, then, as that report goes, I cannot see any practical course which can be adopted to make further search successful.

It has been suggested to us by counsel for Arthur Delaney that in view of the fact that the judgement of the Supreme Court of Nova Scotia was not unanimous we ought to order the Directors to appeal it to the Judicial Committee of the Privy Council. The judgement of the Court Of Nova Scotia has however, by a majority of two judges to one, declared that Miss Stirling has satisfactorily answered the interrogatories put to her by the court, and has purged herself of the contempt of Court of which she was formerly found guilty. I do not then see how we could take further any further proceedings as regards the judgement which could be effectual. It is not suggested from the bar that any other effectual course could be taken.

For my own part I would be very willing to give fullest assistance to the father in his search for these children. It seems very remarkable that this lady who may be actuated by benevolent motives, should take the children outwith the jurisdiction of this Court, and allow them to disappear in the wilds of Nova Scotia without also being able to say where they are to be found.

I think, however, that the Directors have, bona fide done all that they can be expected to do.

In my opinion this Petition ought not to be sent out of court, for it may be that further information will come to the father or the Directors which may make it competent and proper.

We ought then, I think, to pronounce no further order in the meantime.

With this ruling it seemed that Arthur had come to the end of his long struggle to have his children returned to him but there was to be one last throw of the dice.

The judges in the Court of Session suggested to Arthur's lawyer that his client should make a claim to the Court for damages for the loss of his children. His lawyer advised Arthur that they should claim damages of £1000. He said that they were unlikely to be granted that amount because the Directors of the Edinburgh and Leith Children's Aid and Refuge Society had already incurred considerable expenditure in the case. They had to pay legal fees in both the Court of Session to defend their actions and in the Supreme Court of Nova Scotia in pursuit of the case against Emma Stirling, they had paid to send their Secretary to Nova Scotia to search for the children and then had the expense of hiring the Detective Officer, Mr Mellish, to search for the children. All this expense had fallen on the Society. Emma Stirling had escaped any contribution towards their costs.

COURT OF SESSION
EDINBURGH

24ᵗʰ February 1892

Case for compensation for the loss of children called by Arthur Delaney against the Directors of the Edinburgh and Leith Children's Aid and Refuge Society.
   The Court orders that compensation of £100, as agreed, should be paid by the Directors of the Edinburgh and Leith Children's Aid and Refuge Society to Arthur Delaney in settlement of his claim.

So in the event, Arthur received only £100 from the Directors for the loss of his children.

I wonder if the Directors had to pay these damages from their own personal funds. The Edinburgh and Leith Children's Aid and Refuge Society was a charity, now relying completely on public donations for the upkeep of the Children's Shelter in the High Street and the Home at MacKenzie Place. It is unlikely that the Directors would have been allowed to use these charitable funds, given for the protection of children in need, to be used to fight the case in the Courts.

Emma Stirling made no contribution to the damages awarded. The Directors must have rued the day they agreed to support her work! The case was reported widely in the newspapers so they must have also suffered damage to their reputations. Also, it must have been a source of shame to Emma's respectable family in Edinburgh with the case being continually reported in the press.

Among the Court documents our research uncovered was a copy of a Settlement of Damages form. It read -

COURT OF SESSION
EDINBURGH
8ᵗʰ April 1902

Final settlement of case for compensation for the loss of the children of Arthur Delaney.
   I, Arthur Delaney, glass cutter, presently residing at No.4 Niddry Street, Edinburgh, acknowledge to have received from James Colston and others, Directors of the Edinburgh and Leith Children's

Aid and Refuge Society, the sum of £100 in full of all claims of damages competent to me under the summons signeted on 24ᵗʰ February last, or otherwise against them or the Society past or present, represented by them for or in connection with the loss of my three children, James, Annie and Robina who were sometimes inmates of the said Refuge and are now believed to be in America or elsewhere out of Scotland; and my whole claims of every kind for damages in effect of the loss of the said children are hereby discharged, as is also the said summons, and all that has followed therein.

Signed – Arthur Delaney

It might have been better if Arthur's lawyers had advised against the wording of this statement as, when Arthur later brought a case for damages against Emma Stirling herself, the Court ruled that the wording of the above statement meant that Arthur had also absolved Emma along with the Directors of any further claim. So, the Directors paid the £100 and Emma Stirling got off 'Scot Free'!

As soon as Arthur received the sum of one hundred pounds he took the decision to use the money to go to Nova Scotia, with his lawyer, to look for his children himself! We can see in this action just how desperate Arthur was to find James, Annie and Robina. In later court documents, Arthur's lawyer told the judges that the long struggle to find his children, over many years of legal action, and even sailing to Canada and travelling across the vast country to search for them himself, ruined Arthur's health. This was undoubtedly true.

Our research enabled us to discover Arthur on shipping passenger lists to and from Canada. He sailed from Liverpool on 24 May 1892, aboard the *Nova Scotia,* to Halifax. The return journey was four weeks later.

We can only assume that Arthur and his lawyer followed the same route that Detective Mellish had described in his Report, visiting the same addresses. We know that Emma Stirling was not living at Hillfoot Farm at that time. She had spent the winter in the South of France, as she always did, to avoid the atrocious winter weather in Nova Scotia and had not yet returned. So she would be absent when Arthur visited the Home. As he and his lawyer travelled across Canada by horse and cart, train and riverboats his heart must have broken as the farmers and their wives told him about his children and repeated the facts they had told Mr Mellish.

It would have been obvious they did not know where the children had been taken. We now know that only Rufus de Wolfe, the farmer who had had young James, lied. The farm was very near to Hillfoot and the farmer would know Emma Stirling very well. He obviously lied on Emma's instructions in claiming that James had run away. We now realise, from my grandfather's comment to our mother, that Arthur had believed Emma Stirling's lie that James had run away. That is what he told my grandfather, that is the belief he took to his grave. It was so very cruel. But with the knowledge we now had we were not convinced. It beggars belief that the farmer or Emma would have allowed young James to disappear without searching for him - and he told Mr Mellish that he knew James was no longer in the Province.

The voyage back to Liverpool must have seen Arthur at his lowest ebb - all hope gone. He had seen the vastness of Canada, he now knew how impossible it was trying to find his three children in such a sparsely populated country with large areas uninhabited. He must have known he would never see James, Annie and Robina again. He was only thirty-one years old but the stress of the court cases, the unsuccessful journey to Canada and the loss of the children took a toll on his health from which he never fully recovered.

He took Emma Stirling to Court for a second time claiming damages for the loss of James, Annie and Robina but the case was unsuccessful, as I have explained. Emma Stirling later defamed Arthur in an article she wrote for a magazine -*The Christian* - and Arthur sued her for libel through the Court in Edinburgh. It wasn't enough for her that she had taken his children from him and deprived the children of a family home together, by hiding them from the Courts. So great was her hatred of this 'papist' that she wanted to destroy his name. Emma began by defending herself against the charge in the Court but in the middle of the trial she suddenly abandoned the case. Possibly, her lawyers had advised her that her allegations were unsound. Given the bad publicity Arthur's Custody Case had generated against her, and the fact that the lost children had never been found, she was unlikely to get a sympathetic hearing in the city. In the event she had to pay all costs and was also ordered to pay Arthur Delaney £500 in damages.

So, in the long run, Arthur's persistence in pursuing her for the return of his children had cost Emma Stirling dearly in monetary terms. She had the legal expense of responding to the charge of contempt of court in the Supreme Court of Nova Scotia, the action for damages in the Court of Session in Edinburgh over the loss of Arthur's children and finally the cost of defending herself in the libel action in Edinburgh. She then had to pay £500 damages to Arthur when she withdrew her defence. She was extremely rich so no doubt the money made little impact on her fortune but there is no doubt that she would be furious at being challenged by a follower of the - "old enemy ROME". Perhaps the greatest damage of all was done to her reputation - in spite of the glowing testimony she wrote for herself in her book - *Our Children in Old Scotland and Nova Scotia*. History has revealed the true extent of her wickedness through the sheer persistence of one man, Arthur Delaney, who pursued her through the law courts leaving behind legal documents that prove her perfidy. She dragged the ancient Maitland Stirling name through the mud - no wonder her family disowned her.

Emma Stirling was forced to flee Nova Scotia after an arson attack destroyed Hillfoot Farm.

Three years after Arthur Delaney returned from Canada, without his lost children, another child that Emma Stirling had taken to Nova Scotia from Edinburgh nearly died as a result of sexual abuse she suffered at the hands of a farmer for whom she worked as a domestic servant.

Her name was Grace Fegan and Emma Stirling had taken her out as a young girl in the first shipment of Migrant Children, along with six-year-old Robina Delaney in April 1886. Grace and Robina had lived together in the Home in McKenzie Place and were around the same age, so we were sure they must have been friends. I think that is why we were especially distressed to learn what had happened to her. It could just have easily happened to our Robina.

On 25 March 1895, Emma Stirling received a letter from a well respected doctor telling her about one of her girls, Grace Fegan, who had been living on a farm in the county of Annapolis, about thirty miles from Emma's home at Hillfoot Farm. The doctor told Emma that Grace was in great distress and he felt a serious investigation should take place as the girl had received most improper treatment.

That same evening Emma received a telephone call to say that the girl was getting worse and begged her to go and see her immediately. To Emma Stirling's credit she set off at once to travel the thirty miles to where Grace lay near to death. When she arrived a magistrate was present and had just taken the girl's dying Declaration. She had been the victim of a clandestine abortion.

In her book Emma Stirling says that the farmer had subjected Grace to the most revolting cruelty - "the marks of which were still visible on her". Emma writes - "When I was listening to her tell of the abuse and degradation she had suffered the doctor returned to the room and said that they would need a legal opinion on the matter.".

Emma Stirling travelled immediately to Halifax to consult her own solicitor. He advised her that if the allegations were true that the doctor who performed the abortion and the farmer responsible for Grace being in that condition would have to be arrested. After seeing Grace for himself the solicitor, Wallace McDonald, went with Emma to consult with a Queen's Counsel JJ Ritchie.

Emma then made an accusation against the alleged culprits, Dr Samuel Nelson Miller and the farmer, Robert Parker, and they were thrown into jail in Annapolis on 30 March. In her book, Emma relates that they had to send police from Annapolis to Nictaux Falls, where Parker lived, and where Grace had been his maid, because the constables there were said to be unreliable.

Emma writes that she was advised not to leave Annapolis until the men were in jail as they were said to be desperate characters. When it was safe she travelled, by train, accompanied by her solicitor. She said she told her solicitor that knowing the habits of that part of the country, which was that if you offended anyone of bad character your barn was likely to be burnt down, she had better look after her buildings at Hillfoot Farm. In this account she paints a completely different picture of life in Aylesford than that previously when she describes it as an idyllic paradise and her neighbours as being delighted that she had brought a colony of Protestant children to the Province.

She must have had a premonition as, three nights after arriving home, she heard voices outside the farm in the darkness but relates that going out with a lantern she could see nothing suspicious.

However, in the early hours of the morning, she tells how she was awakened by screaming and shouting and on going to investigate she discovered the house was on fire. There were twenty-six people inside. Herself, six servants and nineteen children, eighteen of whom were below twelve years old. She describes the horror of the situation as the house filled up with smoke and the small children were too scared to get out of bed. Eventually, with the help of the women and some older girls, they managed to escape. One of the boys, twelve-year-old Willie Fraser, had managed to rescue thirteen of the children from another wing of the house so all the occupants were saved.

She describes standing outside in her bare feet watching while the back of the house collapsed. The children were led barefoot, through the ice and snow, to the separate Boys Home which was at a distance. She watched as the Big House, which was made of wood, began to blaze and by 6.30am it had been reduced to a pile of ashes. It was no accident. The woodshed, which was nowhere near the house, had also been burned to the ground and there was a strong smell of paraffin around the Big House. Everything was lost. Clothes, books and personal possessions. It seems unbelievable that anyone could be so wicked as to try and burn the women and children to death in their beds.

In her book, Emma relates how the next day she packed up the whole household, including the contents of the Boys Home, and set off by train to Halifax, where she found temporary accommodation for them all. Once there she tells how she speeded up the process of placing some children with employers previously arranged for them and advertised for farmers to take the other children. Once she had disposed of most of the children she devoted her time to nursing young Grace Fegan back to health and fortunately the girl survived.

However, she describes how she had to move Grace from her sickbed to another house - "in spite of her perilous condition, as a bounty of $2,000 was placed on her head to prevent her testifying against the culprits" - and two policemen had to be constantly outside her door to prevent her being abducted.

When the case eventually came before the Grand Jury on 18 June the judge instructed the jury that they should find the prisoners not guilty, except for one charge against Miller for attempting to have the abortion done. Emma claimed that the trial was a miscarriage of justice and that the jury was 'packed'. She states that in order to pretend he was acting impartially the judge fined the sheriff $100 for contempt of court. Emma claimed that the judge had privately admitted to her afterwards that he knew the jury was rigged but that "no one can be convicted in this county unless some people please."

Emma was now thoroughly disillusioned with Nova Scotia. She went on to relate that she had since learned that forced abortions were frequent in Annapolis stating - "I was told by various respectable persons, among others an official of the crown, that one woman had been simply murdered from this cause at Middleton in the fall of 1894, and that between the months of January and May,1895, no less than three graves have been made in Middleton churchyard and filled with three young women from this cause alone". Middleton was where young James Delaney had lived.

In her book, Emma Stirling states that she never thought that any man could have used a young girl, like Grace, in such a way. One wonders how she could have been so naïve. Placing very young girls with farmers, often single men, in remote parts of Canada, with nobody to check on their wellbeing, hardly seems a responsible thing to do but that is what she did time and time again. She goes on to declare - "I am now aware that gross immorality is rampant in portions of this county."

We will never know if any of Emma Stirling's other migrant children, boys as well as girls, suffered abuse in silence, because their stories, unlike Grace Fegan and the Delaney children, will never be told.

Unbelievably, in spite of what had happened to Grace Fegan and in spite of her Home being burned to the ground, Emma Stirling writes that she had still hoped to be able to return to Aylesford and rebuild the Home! However, she was warned that - "the gang, or some of them, had sworn in the most horrible manner that they would not have me round that county. That it would be useless of me to think of rebuilding, for, as fast as my houses were built, they would be burned AS THEY HAD BEFORE!"

Emma at last took the hint. She writes - "I despair of this country now and intend to seek refuge among the Quakers in the United States of America."

She settled in Philadelphia, taking with her only one of the migrant children - Willie Fraser, - the boy who had rescued the children from the fire at Hillfoot Farm. She bought a big old house and intended starting her child migrant work there but seems to have had a change of heart and involved herself instead in the Prevention of Cruelty to Animals Movement. She also bought an Orange Grove Plantation in Florida, where she spent the bitterly cold winters, while Willie and two girls look after the animals in Philadelphia.

Meanwhile, back in Edinburgh, my great-grandfather, Arthur Delaney, continued to grieve for his lost children. His heart must have been broken. He never saw James, Annie or Robina again. Having been to Canada to search for his lost children he must have lain awake at night wondering what was happening to them lost in that vast country. His health deteriorated and he died of kidney disease, aged just forty-six, on 24 February 1907 at his home in 'Little Ireland'.

His son, my grandfather, Patrick Delaney, was only thirteen years old.

Six months later, Emma Maitland Stirling died at her home in Philadelphia, USA, aged sixty-nine, on the 2nd September 1907.

In 2019, when I gave evidence against Emma Stirling at the Scottish Child Abuse Inquiry, in Edinburgh, into the Child Migrant scandal, I said I was testifying, not just in the names of James, Annie and Robina Delaney, but on behalf of all the Edinburgh children whose names will never be known, whose voices will never be heard.

CHAPTER SIXTEEN

SEARCHING FOR THE DELANEY CHILDREN

In November 2017 I was contacted by a journalist, Alison Campsie, of The Scotsman newspaper in Edinburgh. Because of the Scottish Child Abuse Enquiry there had been a lot of press interest in the topic of the British Home Children Scheme. This was the scandal of the poor British children being sent to Canada, the USA and Australia to work as farm labourers and domestic servants. The Child Migrant scheme had begun in the middle of the 19th cent. and continued, in Australia, until the 1960s.

The aim was to empty the Poorhouses and Children's Homes of orphans and 'street arabs' - as they were often called. This would save the government and local councils the burden of poor relief. Not all of the children were orphans. Many had parents who, because of illness or poverty, were unable to look after their children. Many of the children who were sent away were told that their parent had died, even if they had not.

The individuals and organizations who took part in this programme of forced emigration called themselves 'child savers' but the tragic fact was that many thousands of these children suffered mental, physical or sexual abuse at the hands of those they were sent to work for. The largest of these organizations were charities, like Barnardo's and Quarriers, but many churches also sent out children.

The woman responsible for taking our Delaney children to Nova Scotia, under the Child Migrant scheme,was Emma Maitland Stirling. From the Homes she had founded in Edinburgh, in Scotland, we know she took out children to work as farm labourers and domestic servants. She established a Home at Hillfoot Farm, Aylesford, Nova Scotia, after receiving generous grants from the Canadian government. When she had disposed of all the children she took out she began receiving children from other 'child savers' back in Scotland. In the book she wrote about her time in Nova

Scotia she states that she did not send children to the farms until they were 8 or 9 years old and "could be of use".

My sister, Frances Connolly, had made contact with the British Home Children's Canadian website in an attempt to find out what had happened to the three Delaney children. So, when Alison Campsie contacted BHC to enquire if any of the families of the Scottish children were still alive they were able to give her my name.

Alison Campsie interviewed me about the Delaney case and as a result her article appeared in The Scotsman newspaper in November 2017. She told me that more than 50% of the newspaper's online subscriptions came from the USA and Canada. We both hoped that the article might result in someone in Canada knowing what had happened to our three Delaney children - James, Annie and Robina.

Two readers in Nova Scotia did respond.

Fletcher Wade did not have information on the children but he lived a short drive away from Hillfoot Farm, in Aylesford, where Emma Stirling's Home was based. That Home had burned to the ground in the arson attack against Emma Stirling but the farm still exists. Mr Wade, who himself has Scottish roots, very kindly searched the Canadian records for me and passed on links, but was unable to find any evidence of the children in Canada. We now know, of course, that the the reason he could not find them was that Emma Stirling had hidden them in a Home in the USA.

Joanne Galley, in Nova Scotia, also responded. While researching her own family ancestry she had come across Arthur Delaney's court case. She didn't know anything about the whereabouts of the Delaney children but, amazingly, her ancestors, Lizzie and Hugh McIver, were also part of the first group of children that Emma Stirling had taken to Nova Scotia! So they were on the same ship as our Robina Delaney. Another child in that group was little Grace Fegan who was later to be sexually assaulted by the farmer that she worked for. When she became pregnant he arranged for a clandestine abortion from which Grace almost died.

Lizzie McIver had been in the Home for Girls at 11 McKenzie Place in Edinburgh at the same time as Robina and Annie Delaney.

Lizzie and Hugh McIver were older than our children. Our James was 10 years old, Annie 8 and Robina only 6, when they arrived. Their experience would have been quite different. Indeed, Hugh

McIver continued to work for Emma Stirling, at Hillfoot Farm, until he was 18 years old.

Another coincidence, in a story full of coincidences, was that Joanne Galley's great grandmother, Mary McLuskie, was living in the building that collapsed in Paisley Close in the Old Town of Edinburgh in November 1861. She was living with her son, William McLuskie, and her daughter-in-law, Hannah. Also living in the same apartment was a 12 year-old boy, Joseph McIver, referred to in the 1861 census as a boarder. The other side of Joanne Galleys family are McIvers!

When the building collapsed William and Hannah McLuskie were killed, Mary McLuskie suffered injuries but survived and Joseph McIver was the boy pulled from the rubble alive! A stone carving of his head now stands above the rebuilt entrance to Paisley Close with his famous words -"Heave awa chaps a'm no deid yet" inscribed around it. Thirty-seven people died as a result of the collapse of the building with many more injured.

And the coincidence? William McLuskie was a shoe manufacturer. Obviously successful as he had £25 (a considerable sum in 1861) in his wallet. His shop and home were next door to that of Sarah Delaney and her husband, John Skiffington's home and business. They were both close neighbours and fellow shopkeepers. In my book- *The Delaneys of Edinburgh* - I describe how as the building collapsed it narrowly missed John Skiffington's building fracturing a gas pipe as it fell.

I also told of how a little dog was rescued from the rubble by John Skiffington and later auctioned for the disaster fund. Well, that little dog had belonged to William McLuskie!

Truth really is stranger than fiction!

On the 8 January 2018 I met two of my oldest friends for lunch. Rosalind Newlands, Isabel Lennie and I had met thirty-six years earlier when we had joined a training course for Scottish Tourist guides at Edinburgh University. We had remained friends after qualifying and had worked together in tourism, training and lecturing ever since.

They had been with me through all the years of researching my family history. They had listened patiently to my theories and encouraged me to write my novel - *The Delaneys of Edinburgh*.

They also suggested who would play the parts in the movie that would surely follow! As I recall, Maggie Smith, even then, was the favourite to play Emma Stirling!

However, neither of them had seen the recent article in The Scotsman. So, after lunch, Rosalind Newlands went home to look it up online.

And that's how it all began!

After Rosalind had read Alison Campsie's article it re-awakened her interest in the story. It had been five years since I had published my book and so much more was now online.

She says she doesn't know what made her do it but she decided to go online and see what she could find.

Almost immediately, she picked up a possible census entry for James Delaney.

But not in Canada. In the USA.

According to Emma Stirling's evidence to the court she stated that she had placed James Delaney with a farmer, Rufus de Wolfe, in Middleton, quite near her Home at Hillfoot farm in Aylesford, Nova Scotia. She claimed that the farmer said that James was a bright boy, but not suitable for farm work and he kept running away. One wonders why?

She told the court that he had finally run away in September 1890 when the farmer was away from home. He was 12 years old. The farmer told the detective, sent by the court later, that it was his opinion that James was no longer in the Province.

The James Delaney that Rosalind found appeared in a 1900 census. He was twenty years old and had been born in Scotland. He was a farm labourer working on a farm in Conquest Township, Cayuga, New York State, USA for a farmer Wes Van Nostraud.

Rosalind then brought up the 1910 census and found James Delaney again. He was now married and was a section hand on the railroad, living in a rented farm in Skippio, Cayuga, New York State. He is thirty two years old. His wife Frances is thirty years old. They had been married 4 years. Their children are Allan J. and Anna R. aged 3 years, Agnes, aged 2 and Alma one month. He stated that he, his father and mother had all been born in Scotland. This was useful information. Trying to find a James Delaney with Irish parents would have been almost impossible. There are hundreds of them!

But the census that caught Rosalind's attention was that of 1920. The family were now living in Tonawanda, Erie, NY. James is now a welder. Their daughter, Alma, appears to have died but they now have three other children. A daughter, Marie aged 9, a son, Arthur aged 7, and a daughter, June aged 4. It was the name of his son, Arthur, that claimed Rosalind's attention. The name of James' own father. He had also called one of his daughters Annie, his sister's name. He had married a woman named Frances, who was born in Vienna, Austria, but her surname was not given.

Rosalind found that by the 1930 census the family are living at Auburn, Cayuga. James is a labourer in a shoe factory, his wife, Frances, is a laundress, his son, Allen, is a labourer in a forge, his daughter, Anna, is a machinist in a shoe factory, his son, Arthur, is a radio repairer and his daughter, June, was just 14 years old. His daughters, Agnes and Marie, were no longer at home.

Rosalind now enlisted her cousin, Lorna Wallace, to help with the search. Lorna is the most amazing family history buff. She and Rosalind had been researching their joint family histories and Rosalind had told me previously how great Lorna was at drawing up their various family trees. So, I knew I was in expert hands.

They went to work using a free search site called *Family Search* and made great progress. But then they couldn't take it any further to prove they had indeed got the correct James Delaney.

Rosalind phoned our other lunch companion, Isabella Lennie, to pass on the exciting information she had found so far. Isabella wasn't home but Rosalind spoke to her daughter, Sarah Ryan-Frost, and told her the story. In a case of serendipity, Sarah was an enthusiastic family researcher herself having been engaged, for some time, in tracing her own Ryan ancestors.

Sarah had an account with the family history site *Ancestry* and she enthusiastically offered to join the search.

I named them Team Delaney and they were off and running!

It was Sarah who discovered that James Delaney's wife Frances's surname was Metosh.

Team Delaney kept coming up with bits of information on a daily basis – just like fitting all the pieces together on a giant jigsaw.

Sarah then decided to put a post on the *Ancestry* site seeking information on a James Delaney from Scotland.

Almost immediately she got a response and it was a bombshell!

Ancestry had linked her post with one placed four years earlier, in 2014, also seeking information on a James Delaney.

Sarah contacted the Michael Delaney in the USA who had posted. To say he was surprised was an understatement!

Michael Delaney had taken a 2-week trial on *Ancestry* in 2014 but had had no response so he no longer subscribed to the site.

But four years later *Ancestry* linked him with Sarah!

She immediately contacted him while the rest of Team Delaney held their breath. They felt they had got their man but there was no way of proving this was the right James Delaney.

Michael's family story was amazing. He was the great grandson of James Delaney from Auburn, New York State, that Team Delaney had found in the census.

His great grandfather had told his family that he had been kidnapped from Scotland by an 'aunt' who had grown tired of him and had put him in the Cayuga Asylum for Destitute Children, in Auburn, New York State.

It seemed to fit but further proof was needed. It came in Michael's final paragraph. The 'aunt' had changed his name to Whitehead !

Rosalind tried to phone me to give me the exciting news but I was out for lunch with a group of friends in Edinburgh and, of course, I had forgotten to switch on my mobile phone.

She took a chance that I might be lunching with another mutual friend and phoned her mobile – this was news that could not wait!

And so it happened that my puzzled friend, Karen, (who just happens to be American) passed me her phone saying - "It's for you".

Rosalind was in bits and I was so emotional as she told me the news.

So there I was in the middle of a busy restaurant, stuttering and stammering, while Rosalind gave me all the details and three friends looked on in astonishment. The rest of the meal passed in a daze and I only vaguely remember travelling home.

When I arrived my husband, Brian, who had been with me on the long journey to find the lost children had got the e-mail that Sarah had sent. He said when he saw it his eyes just filled with tears – he knew how important it was to me.

It may seem strange to some people that the loss of three children, one hundred and thirty years ago, should matter so much to our family. But from the moment we read of the loss, over thirty years ago, we were all devastated. They were blood of our blood and they were such little children lost in a vast country. The thought of what might have befallen them filled us with horror.

My great good fortune was that I had friends who understood our sorrow and were prepared to go to a great deal of effort to help.

Michael Delaney had given Sarah his e-mail and telephone number in Florida and, of course, I couldn't wait. I had to phone him.

When he answered I said "Hello Michael, it's Patricia Delaney from Scotland."

We were both completely overcome.

Michael had, at last, solved the mystery of his great grandfather James's story and we had found one of our lost children.

Michael told me there had been some mention of a sister of James but none of the family knew anything about her.

We, of course, were looking for two sisters but it seemed hardly likely that they had been together given Emma Stirling had sent them to farms hundreds of miles apart, in Canada, and here was our James in the USA.

Sarah e-mailed Cayuga Centers, which was the name that the Destitute Childrens Asylum was now known as. They were still in the business of caring for children in difficult circumstances.

Cayuga Home had been founded in 1852. Three women, Eliza Wright Osbourne, Caroline Flint Metcalf and Frances Flint Seward, all wives of prominent citizens in Auburn, had been horrified at the treatment of poor children and had demanded a Home be set up to improve their lives. The Home's first Superintendent was Jane Rodgers and she was to serve for 32 years, until her death.

The Cayuga Asylum for Destitute Children was considered 'cutting edge' at the time. It was the first Orphanage to be established in New York State. It was also one of the first to care for children in an Institution instead of placing vulnerable children in private homes, where they were often abused and taken advantage of by the adults who were supposed to be caring for them.

Initially, the children were taken from the County's Poor Houses to give them a more wholesome atmosphere and prevent abuse by adults in the Poor House. In the beginning it seems that children were often placed by a family member and a weekly board fee paid. This happened when one parent died and the other had to work. In other cases a Poor Home Master, from one of the county townships, ordered the children to be placed at the Home and that Township paid the fee.

Previously, it had been considered in the public interest, economically, to remove them from the county rolls quickly and this led to children being 'placed out' – a kind of fostering system. Often, the records show, such children were repeatedly taken 'on trial' by numerous families and then returned.

When Sarah's e-mail arrived it was received by Kim Dungey of Cayuga Centers. Kim was the first of the many people in the USA who responded to us with great kindness on hearing the story of our lost children and went out of their way to help us.

She said she would search the historic records but it might take a while as they were very old and the writing was sometimes difficult to read. However, within a few days she got back to us. The ledger for 1890 had survived and she had found information on a James Whitehead. A later entry stated that James Whitehead's real name was James Delaney!

Kim had also found his two sisters!

The impossible had happened. All the children were together in the Cayuga Home in the USA, in 1890.

Kim forwarded the details. James and Bessie (Robina) Whitehead had been admitted to the Cayuga Home in Auburn on 10 September 1890. Annie Whitehead had been admitted on 25 September 1890.

The person who had admitted the children on both dates was a Mr James Sutherland.

We later found information on this James Sutherland. He had been born in Scotland in 1839, making him around the same age as Emma Stirling. He had married and he and his wife, Sarah, had two children. In the 1879 census he was living in Maine, USA. By the 1880 census the family had moved to Weedsport, Brutus, Cayuga and he was now a Freight Agent on the railways with four children. Could there be a connection between him and Emma Stirling we wondered? But, apart from the fact they were both Scots there didn't seem to be one. James Sutherland had been living in the USA many years before Emma arrived in Nova Scotia in 1886. Perhaps the fact that he was familiar with the railways and lived near to Cayuga Home was made known to Emma Stirling.

For it was instantly obvious to us all that Emma Stirling was behind it.

Only Emma Stirling had any reason to quickly remove the Delaney children from the three different farms, hundreds of miles apart, where they had been living.

She had learned that the Court of Session in Edinburgh had ordered that a Canadian detective was to be sent to find the children.

As we had always believed, Emma Stirling had known all the time where the children were. She had lied and perjured herself in the Court of Session in Scotland and the Supreme Court of Nova Scotia.

The court in Nova Scotia had already threatened her with a charge of contempt of court for failing to return the children. She was faced with going to jail. If the children were found it would have been disastrous for her since she testified that she did not know where the children were. The two judges who believed the lies she told and cleared her of contempt of Court would have been made to look very foolish – as indeed they were. Justice Ritchie's findings that she was guilty would have been vindicated. Imprisonment would have surely followed and justice done to Arthur and his children.

No random person could have had any reason to travel across Canada to three different destinations, hundreds of miles apart, and take three related children to a Children's Home over the border in the USA.

Mr Sutherland, as a Freight Agent, familiar with the railway system would be an obvious choice to pick up the children and take them to a Home near where he lived. We knew from Detective Mellish's Report that, in the case of Annie and Robina, both girls had been hurried away by train.

Emma Stirling's name could never be mentioned - it would have been fatal for her.

Did Emma Stirling pay to have the children admitted?

We will never know but it seems likely. She was very rich and it was worth a few dollars to hide James, Annie and Robina and save herself from jail. By this time I believe she had grown to hate the Delaney children and she had already proved how vindictive she could be.

Cayuga Asylum was not a receiving Home for migrant children. It's purpose was to care for local children in distressed circumstances.

What story could Mr Sutherland tell when he admitted the children? Again we will never know.

But he could hardly claim to have just happened upon three related abandoned children, in three different locations in Canada. Especially not since he had admitted James and Bessie (Robina) first and then gone to pick up Annie and had her admitted two weeks later. He was complicit in Emma Stirling's crime and should have been jailed for kidnapping the children. He quite literally kidnapped James, Annie and Robina and put them beyond the protection of the law. I wonder if his conscience ever troubled him or, like Emma Stirling, he didn't have one.

We know from Detective Mellish's report to the Court of Session that it was his opinion that Emma Stirling had deliberately changed the children's names to Whitehead to avoid them being traced. Also, that some of the last addresses that Emma had given to the Courts, in the case of Annie and Robina, were unknown and that the people Emma said she placed them with did not exist.

sDetective Mellish was obviously a very skilled and astute detective. Indeed, in later life he went on to be a prominent member of the legal profession in Canada. Humphrey Mellish was called to the Bar in 1890 and was appointed a Justice of the Supreme Court in 1918. I wonder if he ever thought back on the children he had tried to save.

The statements he took from the farmers who had the girls, under the name of Whitehead, told the same story. Both girls were picked up by a man claiming to be related to them and despite the farmers' and the girls' reluctance had been hurried away to the train. We now know that is how they entered the USA, by train across the border – did James Sutherland forge passports for them?

I now believe he picked up James Delaney first and took him with him when he went to pick up Robina in New Brunswick. Emma Stirling and Rufus de Wolfe lied, James had not run away. The farmer who had Robina stated that one of the men was her brother.

This would explain the records showing that James and Robina (Bessie) both arrived at Cayuga Home on the same day.

Our children were the victims of three corrupt people masquerading as respectable citizens, as upstanding members of society. They did not stand a chance. There was no pity shown.

Kim Dungey, at Cayuga Centers, also sent us details of where the Delaney children had been placed. Though the Cayuga Home was not for migrant children their children were also 'placed out' with local farmers as agricultural workers, or domestic servants, from a young age.

The Home had a system of "Trial and Indenture". Children were sent out on "trial" and could be returned to the Home if not suitable or no longer needed. If a child was "Indentured" this seemed to mean that the farmer who took them made a legal pledge to care for them and teach them skills until the child "came of age" (which seems to have been 15 years old) but did not pay them. After that the child was free to seek their own paid employment.

The Cayuga Home does not seem to have received payment for the child 'placed out' but, of course, the cost of caring for them in the Home was reduced.

James Delaney arrived at Cayuga on 10 September 1890 when he was 13 years old. He was in the Home for10 months before being 'placed out' to Mr Charles Rogers in June 1891. He was returned by him on 14 September 1891. Perhaps James had been helping with the harvest. He was taken again by Charles Rogers on 14 November 1891 and returned by him on 17 January 1892. He stayed in the Home until 2 February 1892 when he was taken by Mr Martin Brinkerhoff of Owasco. The Brinkerhoffs were an original settler family in the area. He was "Indentured" by Mr Brinkerhoff on 30 June 1892. He was returned to to the Home by Mr Brinkerhoff on 18 October 1892.

Thereafter, the Home's records state that James Delaney had gone to Mr Thomas Kerr of Victory, New York State to "work for wages". He was now 15 years old and he was on his own. The next mention of him is in the 1900 census where he is a farm labourer working for Wes Van Nostraud in Conquest Township, NY. He is a farm labourer and said to be twenty years old. He is, in fact, twenty three years old. We have no knowledge of where he was between these two work situations.

Annie Whitehead (Delaney) arrived at Cayuga on 25 September 1890. She was 11 years old. She remained as a boarder in the Home for one year and ten months. A note in the records states she had never been "Indentured" because of poor health. She was 'placed out' with Mrs Rosa McKinney of Dansville, New York State on 13 July 1892. She stayed with her for three years and three months before being returned on 22 October 1895. On returning Annie, Mrs McKinney had stated she was returning her "because she did not wish the care of an invalid". We have to pray that, until she became ill, Annie was doing well since she had stayed so long.

Kim Dungey, of Cayuga Centers, sent me a copy of a report from the Annual Meeting of the Cayuga Asylum for Destitute Children's Board of Managers on 14 October 1896. Included in it is a reference to Annie being returned to the Home. It states - "A young girl of sixteen, a former resident of the asylum, who had been away for three years, returned in October, saying she had come home to die. Although too old for admission to the asylum she was given a home here, with light work to do, but that dread disease, consumption, had already undermined her health and she passed away on the 30 April 1896."

She had been back in the Home for six months before she died. Our poor Annie died among strangers, far from home. It is tragic that she considered an Institution, caring for 80 children, home. At least we know they must have cared for her with kindness. She is buried in the county cemetery, in an area called 'Childrens Hill' set aside for the 60 children who died in the Cayuga Home from it's founding.

Kim Dungey kindly sent me a photograph of the cemetery and later went out, when the snow had cleared, to take a photograph of Annie's grave. She lies beneath a grave slab inscribed 'Anna Whitehead'. Emma Stirling even stole her identity from her. She has such a lot to answer for.

Robina (Bessie Whitehead) Delaney was admitted to the Cayuga Home, along with her brother, James, on 10 September 1890. She was ten years old. She was reunited with him for 20 days and with her sister, Annie, for 5 days, before being taken 'on trial' by Mrs Sarah Tisdale of Homer, Cortland, New York State on 30 September 1890.

Robina (Bessie) was never returned to the Cayuga Home.

When Rosalind and Lorna heard about Bessie's placement they went into overdrive to try and find out all they could about the Tisdales of Homer!

They found that in the 1892 Census the Tisdale household is given as -

J. Tisdale, age 56, a miller born in the USA
S. Tisdale, age 55, born in the USA
A. Tisdale age 36 born in the USA
B. Tisdale, age 11, born in the USA

This created a bit of a mystery for Team Delaney. We knew that Bessie Whitehead (Delaney) had been placed with them in 1890. So could this B. Tisdale be her? The age was about right. But why did she have the surname Tisdale We began to wonder if the Tisdales had adopted her!

We knew from previous reports that Bessie (Robina) was a very good looking child, very smart and with a lovely singing voice. A prime candidate for adoption. We knew from the Cayuga Home records that prospective employers were invited to call at the Home to express an interest in any child.

Team Delaney' later discovered that James Tisdale and his wife, Sarah, had lost their daughter, Florence, from scarlet fever, when she was Bessie's age, the year before taking Bessie in.

So, was Bessie intended, from the beginning, to be an adoptive daughter and not a domestic servant?

Team Delaney later discovered that the A.Tisdale on the census was an Abbie Card. She was Sarah Tisdale's niece and it looked as if the Tisdales had also adopted her, when she was young, as she was also called Tisdale in the census above. Abbie is listed as a teacher, aged 21, on the previous census.

Rosalind and Lorna discovered that there was a Historical Society in Cortland (where Homer was located) so they contacted them. Again, they met with a positive response and the Society very kindly sent information.

This revealed that the Tisdales were a prominent Baptist family in Homer. James Adrian Tisdale was a successful businessman in the town. He owned a flour mill and had built a large residence opposite his mill on Union Street, Homer.

The Society also sent Rosalind a number of mentions of Bessie from the newspapers in which she is referred to as singing in the Baptist choir and at various social events. We knew, from Detective Mellish's Report, that Bessie had been described by the farmer in Canada as "a bright child, well known in the area for her lovely singing voice". It was looking more and more as if Bessie Tisdale was indeed Robina Delaney.

Bessie had been with the family for four years when James Tisdale took ill of Brights Disease and died, aged 57, on 12 April 1894. He was buried in Cortland Rural Cemetery.

One of the cuttings Rosalind was sent was a newspaper notice that the probate of his will was to be read out on a certain day and several named people were requested to attend as having an interest. One of the names was Bessie Tisdale. It looked as if Bessie was to receive a bequest in his will!

My friend, Sarah Ryan-Frost, then found the whole of James Adrian Tisdale's will and, quite apart from the bequest she received, it also stated that Bessie Tisdale had previously been Bessie Whitehead!

So, at last, we had confirmation. Arthur Delaney's daughter, Robina Delaney, later known as Bessie Whitehead was now Bessie L. Tisdale, adopted daughter of James Adrian Tisdale and his wife, Sarah Tisdale, of Homer, Cortland, New York State. Team Delaney had found the last of the lost children!

James Adrian Tisdale's will, of 1894, was a long handwritten document so Rosalind Newlands transcribed the relevant parts.

"This bequest to my wife is on the express condition that she shall properly support, clothe, maintain and educate Bessie Lauraine Tisdale (formerly Whitehead) as long as she is a good girl and remains with my said wife, obeys her and until the said Bessie shall arrive at the age of eighteen years at which time my wife shall purchase for said Bessie one hundred dollars worth of wearing apparel for her and give her one hundred dollars in cash, and my said wife shall not be bound to support said Bessie after she arrives at eighteen years. If said Bessie should at any time before arriving at the age of eighteen years voluntarily leave my said wife and her abode against her wishes or should she turn wayward and refuse to obey her the obligation imposed upon my wife as herein to support, pay amount of money and purchase of clothing shall cease and the legacy to said Bessie shall thereafter be revoked. The bequest to my said wife as herein on the express condition that she shall properly support, clothe and maintain Abbie Amelia Card for and during the rest of her natural life, if she shall remain and live with my said wife at all times.......Abbie one thousand dollars in cash. I hereby expressively charge the foregoing legacy to my wife with the execution of the care and maintenance of said Bessie Lauraine Tisdale and of said Abbie Amelia Card and with payment of the sums of money to them respectively as herein provided. I further will that in case my wife shall die before Bessie Lauraine Tisdale arrives at the age of eighteen years in that event I direct my executors hereinafter named, out of my estate to properly support, clothe, maintain and educate said Bessie until she reach the age of eighteen years at which time give to her the sum of two hundred dollars in money."

Rosalind found various items of news about Bessie in some old newspapers. It seems she was always attending friends' parties and picnics and one report states that she was helping Sarah and Abbie clean out their summer cottage ready for occupation. There are also reports of her singing at various events, including singing a solo – *Hear me in my* prayer -at the Keator Opera House, Cortland, in 1894 – the only solo on the programme so she must have been good. The evening ended with a duet - *"Goodnight"* by Miss Bessie Tisdale and Mr James Fowler - the guests then marched to the dining rooms where they partook of an elegant oyster supper".

Sounds like Bessie (Robina Delaney) is living the high life and she is only fourteen years old!

Sadly, 1894 was also the year that her 'adoptive' father, Adrian Tisdale, died.

The next information Team Delaney found was that Bessie had been sent to an exclusive Boarding School called Elmira. Sarah had followed her husband's bequest to have Bessie educated. She must have been a bright girl. We also know that Abbie Card had been a teacher so presumably she would tutor Bessie at home when she was a child.

There is a report in the *Elmira Gazette and Free Press*, dated 14 September 1898, that – "Miss Bessie L. Tisdale of Elmira, who for three years has been attending the Elmira Boarding School, has been spending a few days in Cortland, the guest of her aunt, Mrs Emily Loucks, 34 Union Street, Cortland"

Curiously, in the 1905 Census, Sarah Tisdale is living with her sister, Emily Louck and her daughter Helen Louck, in the house on Union Street, Homer, in Cortland. There is no mention of Bessie or of Abbie Card.

According to the terms of James Tisdale's will, Abbie should have been still living with his wife Sarah. Instead we later found that around 1905 Abbie had gone to work, as a servant, for another family. So what happened? And what happened to the thousand dollars she was bequeathed? Abbie remained with her new employers until she died, in her bed, age seventy two. It was stated that she had been with them for over thirty years.

We had previously found a B. Tisdale in a street directory in Forth Worth, Texas, listed as a 27 year old student in 1907. Could Bessie be attending college or university as a mature student?

There is no further mention of Bessie Tisdale until Sarah Tisdale dies in 1918. The death announcement states that she is survived by her step-daughter, Miss Bessie Tisdale of Fort Worth, Texas. Bessie, of course, was not her step-daughter but her adopted daughter.

Sarah Tisdale's obituary states that she and her sister, Emily Louck, had long been widows and they had lived together in Sarah's house on Union Street, Homer for many years. Sarah had died in the County Hospital in Cortland, aged eighty six years, and her sister, Emily, had died just seven hours before in their house on Union Street. Emily had been ill for several months after suffering a paralytic shock. The report says that it was worry about her sister which had caused Sarah to become ill. Both of their funerals were to take place from their house on Union Street.

So now the mystery was why was Bessie Tisdale (Robina Delaney) living so far away? She is not married and she would now be thirty eight years old. What was she doing in Fort Worth? We found a Bessie Tisdale in a Fort Worth Street Directory of 1907. She is listed as a student. If this is our Bessie then she would be twenty seven years old, so quite old for a student.

Rosalind Newlands continued to search for Robina but it seemed as if the trail had gone old. She searched for a Robina Delaney, a Bessie Whitehead and a Bessie Tisdale but no trace could be found of her.

The years passed and we had given up hope of finding an ending for the last of our lost children.

Then, out of the blue, in April 2024, I received an e-mail from Blake Downes, in the USA. His family research had made a DNA link to Mary Mowat, the lost children's mother, who had died in childbed precipitating the tragedy that befell Arthur Delaney and their children. We started to share information and I learned that Blake had read my book -'*The Delaneys of* Edinburgh'- and he was particularly interested in what had become of Robina Delaney (Bessie Tisdale) after 1918. We continued to correspond and just before I was going off on holiday, in May 2024, he e-mailed to say that he had found a census return for a Laverne Tisdale and wondered if there was an outside chance this could be our Robina? He had read Mr Tisdale's Will in which it was noted that the couple had given Bessie Tisdale a middle name of Laverne. The Will was handwritten and myself and Team Delaney had transcribed the middle name as Lauraine. In this 1900 census for Elmira ward 2 Chemung, New York, Blake Downes had found a Laverne Tisdale. She is a servant living in the house of a Carl Heughan who is a grocer. Laverne is nineteen years old and born in Scotland to Scottish parents. These were the facts that caught Blake's eye and made him wonder if this could be Robina Delaney.

Blake Downes next find was a 1920 census for Oklahoma, Texas, where a Laverne Tisdale is listed as living with Mrs Lou Noland who is a widow. Oddly, she is stated to be Mrs Noland's 'foster-daughter', age 40, born in Scotland and she is a teacher. Her father's birthplace is given as Ireland and her mother's Scotland. In spite of these anomalies we felt certain that this was our Robina.

Given I was off on holiday the next day I e-mailed Rosalind Newlands with the information and she was off and running! We had only just arrived in our hotel next day when the e-mails started pinging in - I knew she would not be able to resist it – she had always felt particularly drawn to Robina's story.

Rosalind did some more digging and found a marriage certificate dated 3 March 1920 for Laverne R. Tisdale to David C. Walker in

Oklahoma, Texas. The C. in his name stood for Crockett. Could the initial R in Laverne's name be Robina? Interestingly, Mrs Lou Noland had been born in Arkansas and so had David C. Walker.

Their only child, David Crockett Walker, Junior was born on 2 September 1921 in Carter County Wilson Oklahoma. Interestingly, Robina raised her son as a Catholic in spite of Emma Stirling and the Tisdales's efforts to wipe out her Catholic heritage.

Rosalind found the family again in a 1930 census for Elsboro Pottawatomie, Carter County, Oklahoma, Texas. David Crockett Walker is 40 years old and was an Oil Worker. His wife, Laverne R. Walker is age 39 and born Scotland and she is still a teacher and their son David Crockett Walker, Junior is eight years old. It is obvious that Laverne (Robina) lied about her age she was not 39, she was 49! In all the descriptions of her, as a child, Robina was described as very good-looking so she must have got away with the deception! Presumably, her age was the reason the couple only had one child.

The family moved to Huntsville, Texas, where her husband continued to work in the Oil Field Industry. Tragically, in 1934, he was killed after falling from a derrick and fracturing his skull. Their son, David Crockett Walker, Junior, was just 13 years old.

Robina's time of happiness and good fortune had again run out.

Her son David Crockett, Junior served in the army in WWII.

On 19th December 1942 he married Orvietta Miller Chance.

On 15th September, 1943 his mother dies in Hutchins, Dallas, Texas.

Rosalind Newlands traced her death certificate confirming that she had indeed found our Robina.

It states that Mrs Robena Laverne Walker had been a resident at 711 Graham, Dallas, Texas, for eight years. She was a widow and a retired housewife born Scotland, 12 August 1880. Rosalind had found Arthur Delaney and Mary Mowat's wee daughter from Edinburgh. Robina appears to have been unwell for many years. Her cause of death was Paralysis Agitans (Parkinson's disease) and General Debility.

She was buried in Itasca Cemetery, Dallas, beside her husband David Crockett Walker.

Rosalind Newlands even found their gravestone with the inscription – *Together Forever* – sounds like, in spite of all the tragedy of her life, at least she was blessed with a happy marriage. Sadly, like her sister Annie Delaney, Robina is not buried under her own name. The inscription reads Laverne Lourena Walker. The girl who had borne so many different names throughout her life – Robina Delaney – Bessie Delaney – Bessie Whitehead – Bessie - Tisdale and Laverne Walker. but there is no doubt she is the last of our lost children.

Sadly, she didn't live long enough to see her three grandsons born. David Crockett Walker III was born in 1944, Johnny Walker in 1945 and Tommy Walker in 1949.

Back when 'Team Delaney' had uncovered what happened to our lost boy James Delaney and Sarah Ryan-Frost had connected me to Michael Delaney in Florida we were hopeful that perhaps we might see a photograph of our James.

Michael Delaney got in touch with his Auntie Sandi. She was able to give him the name of another family member that Michael had not known about. Her name was Beatrice O'Hora and she had actually known James Delaney! Beatrice had married Bill O'Hora who was the son of Anna Robina Delaney (James's daughter) and William O'Hora. Beatrice had known James and Frances Delaney when she was dating their grandson Bill. We knew, from the census, that James and his wife Frances were living with Anna and William and their children at that time.

Our lost James died in 1958, aged eighty one years, and his wife Frances two years later. They are both buried in Lakeside Cemetery, Auburn. Also buried there are James and Frances' daughter, June Delaney and her husband Clarence Wilbur. They both died young - in their twenties. Sarah Ryan-Frost also found, online, photographs of all their gravestones. This was a very poignant moment for me as I thought of James lying there far from his father Arthur's grave in Mount Vernon Cemetery, in Edinburgh. But it was a consolation to know he was beside those who loved him.

Michael had e-mailed to say that Beatrice was happy for me to contact her. When I did I asked her if she had any photographs of our James Delaney.

To my great joy, and gratitude, Beatrice O'Hora, sent me a photograph which showed James and Frances surrounded by their surviving children – Allan, Anna, Marie, Agnes and Arthur Burton

Delaney. Another showed them with their grandchildren - Ellen and Bill O'Hora, Anna Robina Delaney's children, and Agnes Delaney's children Joyce, June, Doris, Harold and Leonard Moll, and Ronald Delaney, Arthur Burton Delaney's son.

James Delaney has a face full of character and humour. In spite of all he suffered he won through and, with Frances, built a lovely family. We can see our Grandfather, Patrick Delaney, his half-brother, in him.

Our family will be forever grateful to Beatrice O'Hora for taking the trouble to do this for us. She had read my book, *The Delaneys of Edinburgh*, and said she enjoyed it and found it interesting reading her husband's family history. It just seems fated that we should connect.

In more recent times we have obtained a lovely family group photograph of Beatrice and William (Bill) O'Hora with their children and grandchildren. Every time I look at it my heart lifts!

In spite of Emma Stirling's attempt to ruin young James Delaney's life he won through. She didn't win. He always knew who he really was and told the Cayuga Children's Home that his real name was James Delaney. He never saw his father again, but he never forgot him, and named one of his sons, Arthur, in his honour, and he never forgot his 'lost' sisters, naming one of his daughters Anna Robina after them. We know that young Annie had no children. Thanks to Rosalind Newland's most recent research we now know that Robina Delaney did marry and had a son and that three grandsons survived her.

It is Arthur Delaney, of Edinburgh, who fought so hard to get his children back, who went searching for them in Canada, who never saw James, Annie or Robina again and who died bereft, in 'Little Ireland' whose genes continue to cascade down through his descendants in America today.

It is of some consolation to us to know that, through telling this story, James Delaney's great-great grand-children know that his father never forgot him, or his sisters, and did his best to find them.

His brave spirit lives on!

Emma Maitland Stirling leaves no trace of herself behind.

CONCLUSION

Researching and writing this book has been a fascinating, but often heart-breaking, journey. So much sadness, so much tragedy, so much hardship. But it has also shown how the human spirit can transcend that and rise triumphant above it all. The Delaneys are both a unique family, with unique experiences, while also being a typical family living in 'Little Ireland' in the nineteenth century. This book is a social history of the times that they and their neighbours lived through as much as it is a family history. It is also a lesson in the extreme prejudice that the immigrant Irish community was subject to and, hopefully, will hold up a mirror to how we treat immigrants to our country today. Because, sadly, we are governed by politicians who view 'incomers' as 'other' – as the enemy – instead of just human beings, like ourselves, hoping to make a better life for themselves and their families. If they are allowed to, new immigrants will enrich our society as the descendants of our Irish ancestors continue to do to this day.

Since beginning to research this story, almost thirty years ago, technology has changed our world almost beyond belief. Whereas my mother, my brother, Michael, and myself pored for hours over handwritten, heavy, leather-bound volumes of births, deaths and marriages, in churches and Register Offices now information can be found at the click of a mouse! It is quite astonishing the details of the lives and times of our families that can now be accessed online. Some may ask - so what? – does any of it really matter? It does because, like it or not, they tell us where we came from – who we are. It does not, of course, tell us what we can become – that is in our own hands. Programmes like '*Who do you think you are?*' and '*A House through Time*' are hugely popular, showing that many people are interested in genealogy even when it is not their own. Why is this? I think it is because it tells us stories – and who doesn't love a good story? That is what 'Little Ireland' is – it is a storybook.

Another amazing discovery of our times is the knowledge of our DNA that has made it possible to connect with people we would never otherwise have known were blood-relations. My sister, Frances

Connolly (nee Delaney) had her DNA tested and posted on *Ancestry*. This opened up a treasure trove of family, from around the world, she never knew existed let alone that she was related to. It was through DNA that we heard the stories of what became of family members after they left 'Little Ireland'. They told us their 'stories'.

Technology linked us to our Delaney cousins in London through an online post from them picked up by my brother, Michael, and then Frances' DNA confirmed the blood relationship. A photograph posted online by Beth and Chuck Barry, in Canada, linked us to our lost Tregilgas cousins, and then Frances' DNA confirmed Beth's husband Chuck's blood-line to us. Frances' DNA connected us to our cousin Maureen McNeill (nee Martin) in Canada. I had been at school in Edinburgh with Maureen, who was a year younger, and we must have passed each other hundreds of times in the corridors without knowing we were blood-related. After leaving school she had emigrated to Canada and had been living there for more than fifty years when her DNA 'pinged' with Frances and she was able to tell us her Martin family story.

It was through technology, in the form of online research, that I was able to speak on the phone to our 'lost boy' James Delaney's great-great-grandson, Michael Delaney, some one hundred and thirty years after James was abducted from Edinburgh. Michael was able to tell us what had become of our lost James – it brought such comfort because now we know he and his sisters survived, against all the odds. Through DNA my sister Frances made contact with James' great-grand-daughter, Shelley, and now she knows that her great-grandfather, Arthur Delaney, fought so hard to get his children back and that he never forgot them.

Emma Maitland Stirling tried to destroy Arthur and ruined his children's lives but the blood lives on and the blood is strong!

ACKNOWLEDGEMENTS

It is said that it takes a whole village to raise a child. In the same way it has taken many, many people, family, friends and perfect strangers to produce this book. My thanks go to them all.

I first began the journey into this story in company with my late brother, Michael Delaney, and my late mother, Liz Delaney. The book is very much in their memory. My gratitude also goes to my sister, Frances Connolly (nee Delaney) – online genealogist extraordinaire – who followed in their footsteps, discovering so much about the Delaney family and confirming our Granny Coyle's view that she was the nosiest person in the family!

Along the way we made contact with so many generous minded people who shared information with us. This began with Seamus McCluskey, author and historian of Emyvale in County Monaghan, a lovely, talented man who became a good friend to the Delaney family. He introduced us to Leah O'Grady, in Prince Edward Island, a descendent of the Emyvale Delaneys who had emigrated to the island in the middle of the nineteenth century. Leah had already begun her journey into our shared heritage and generously shared her research with us.

Huge thanks go to our cousin, Janet Croome (nee Delaney), a gifted genealogist who shared her extensive research into her branch of the Delaney family in London. She became a good friend on the journey and we had such fun! Thanks also to our cousin, Terry Delaney, who has faithfully kept the Delaney family archive begun by his father, Desmond Delaney. I could not have written that part of the book without his generous sharing of material and photographs from the archive. Gratitude also to him and his wife, Kathy, for the support and hospitality they showed to my brother, Michael, on the way. In recent times, our cousin, Nick Delaney, has generously shared his research into the tragic death of his uncle, Luke Sylvestre Delaney, in the Second World War and his account of his, and his wife Pauline's, trip to Albania in search of Luke's and his crew's last resting place. My thanks also to Don Clark, creator of the amazing RAF 211 Squadron website which enabled me to tell Luke Sylvestre's war story.

The chapter on the Hibernian Football Club would not have been possible without permission from the late Alan Lugton. His incredible book - 'The Making of Hibernian'- is not just the best book about the team ever written, it is also a social history of 'Little Ireland' – he knew he had my grateful thanks.

The chapter on 'The Tregilgas Sisters' was made possible by the online skills of my sister, Frances Connolly, who made contact with Matt Lunn. Matt was one of the 'perfect strangers' who became a friend and not only shared his own research into the Tregilgas family, but searched and found for us additional information on our family and, in particular, their war records. Thank you Matt.

Frances' skills also led to contact with Beth and Chuck Barry in Canada. Chuck is descended, like us, from the Delaney family of County Monaghan. My thanks to Beth and Chuck for sharing their research into Pierre Paul Auther and for sharing their priceless family photographs. We also appreciated their memories of Chuck's 'firecracker' mother, Jeanne Auther! My special thanks go to Beth Barry for helping with the proof-reading of this book – you deserve a medal! All mistakes are, of course, my own. In the process of this sharing we have all become fond friends.

The wonders of DNA (Frances again!) have united us with our cousin Maureen McNeil (nee Martin) in Canada. Maureen kindly shared with us her research into the Martin family and she found, and had restored, the priceless Skiffington/Delaney Family Bible from 1847. We have now met up and become good friends.

The chapter on 'Searching for the Lost Children' was only possible because of the generosity, commitment and skills of 'Team Delaney' – Rosalind Newlands, Lorna Wallace, Sarah Ryan-Frost and Isabella Lennie - myself and the whole family, owe a huge debt of gratitude to them for finding our 'Lost Children'.

Last, but by no means least, my gratitude goes to my husband, Brian Dishon, without whom this book would never have been written. My thanks to him for his love and support over all these years, for his patience, guidance, chauffeuring, photography, editing and amazing computer skills!

ERIN GO BRAGH!

LIST OF ILLUSTRATIONS

Fig.1.   Tombstone of Arthur Delaney in Old Donagh
           Graveyard, Emyvale, Co. Monaghan.   181

                        Inscription
                        ERECTED
                     By Arthur Delaney
                     of Emyvale in memory
                    of his Father Arthur Delaney
                    who Departed This Life
                     January 9th 1849
                     AGED 88 YEARS
                    may he rest in peace
                        AMEN

Fig.2   Emyvale village in 1910. The Delaney house is
           the first on the right with the bay windows.   182

Fig.3   These are the first Guards (Garda Siochana) assigned to
           Emyvale in 1923 standing outside their new barracks.
           The previous barracks had been burned down during the
           Irish War of Independence (1919 – 1921). This building
           belonged to the Delaney/Neeson family and was rented
           out to the new police force when the new "Irish
           Free State" was set up.   183

Fig.4   Brown Square, Edinburgh, from 'The Society'
           early 19th. Cent. This was where the Priest's
           House of the original St. Patrick's Church in Lothian
           Street (later St. Francis Church) was located.
           Arthur Delaney and Helen Collins were married in the
           house in 1839. Brown Square was swept away
           when Chambers Street was built.   184

Fig.5   St. Mary's Wynd, Old Town Edinburgh, looking up
           towards the Netherbow. Painting by Thomas Hosmer
           Shephard. Arthur Delaney settled here around 1838.   185

Fig.6   St. Mary's Wynd where it joined the Cowgate.
           The church steeple in the background is St. Patrick's
           Church in the Cowgate.   186

Fig.7   St. Mary's Wynd where it joined The Netherbow.
Philip Boylan's tailor's shop on right. He married
Helen Delaney (nee Collins) in 1850 and she
and her three sons James, Thomas and John
Sylvester Delaney moved into Philip's large
house above the shop at No.17.   187

Fig.8   Illustration from the London Illustrated News
showing the collapse of Paisley Close on Edinburgh's
Royal Mile in November 1851. Thirty-seven people
were killed. The building on the left was Sarah Delaney
and John Skiffington's five-storey house and shop.
Their 'Wholesale Rag Merchant' sign can be
clearly seen. The building and shop was inherited
by Sarah's sister, Jane Murray (nee Delaney) and
her family lived there until
about 1901. The building and shop still survive
though reduced to three stories.   188

Fig.9   The Boylan Monument in the Graveyard of the
Canongate Kirk on the Royal Mile erected by
Eleanor Lennon (nee Boylan). She, her father, Philip
Boylan, her mother, Dorothy Warrick, her son,
John Lennon, her half-brother, Luke Joseph Boylan
(Helen Delaney's son), his wife, Patricia Campsie,
and other members of the Boylan family are
buried in the plot surrounding the Monument
but not Helen (Delaney) Boylan.   189

Fig.10   Tregilgas/Barry group. L-R – Sarah Skiffington
Murray (grand-daughter of Jane Delaney and John
Murray) daughter of Ellen Murray and Joseph
Tregilgas – she was later known as Constance
Tregilgas – she married Dr. Joseph Lussier in Canada.
Next to her is her daughter, Gabrielle Lussier, then
Emma Harvey Tregilgas (grand-daughter of Jane
Delaney and John Murray) and daughter of Ellen
Murray and Joseph Tregilgas – she became a nun
(Sister Saint Elphege) in Canada. In front of her,
the little boy is Michael Barry and beside her is his
father Charles Barry. The new mother in bed is

Jeanne Barry (nee Auther) She is the great grand-
daughter of Jane Delaney and John Murray, the grand-
daughter of Ellen Murray and Joseph Tregilgas and
the daughter of Ellen Clarke Tregilgas and Pierre
Paul Auther. The new baby is Charles (Chuck) Barry.   190

Fig.11   Ellen Clarke Tregilgas (grand-daughter of
Jane Delaney and John Murray) – daughter of
Ellen Murray and Joseph Tregilgas. Later known as
Blanche Tregilgas. She became a nurse in New York
and later volunteered to serve in WWI. She served
on the battlefields of France and Belgium earning
a medal from the King. She was invalided out of the
Canadian army and returned to New York where
she met Pierre Paul Auther. They married in 1918 and
their daughter Jeanne Auther was born in 1919.   191

Fig.12   John Sylvester Delaney the actor. Son of Arthur
Delaney and Helen Collins born in 1848. Married
Elizabeth Mc Alpine in London in 1878. Probably
taken in Plymouth in 1879 the year his son Luke
Terence Delaney was born when we know John was
appearing to rave notices in the theatre there.   192

Fig.13   Elizabeth Mc Alpine born in 1857 married
John Sylvester Delaney in London in 1878. Mother of
Luke Terence Delaney, Kathleen Delaney and
John William Delaney. She was twenty-six years
old when this photograph was taken and we think
recently widowed. John Sylvester died in Oldham in
December 1884.   193

Fig.14   Luke Terence Delaney son of John Sylvester Delaney
and Elizabeth McAlpine born in Plymouth in 1879. In
March 1884, when he was just over four years old, his
mother took him to Edinburgh and left him in 'Little
Ireland' to be brought up by his grandmother, Helen
Delaney Boylan and his father's family. He did
not return to live with his mother and his younger
brother, John William Delaney, in London, until his
grandmother died in 1990.   194

Fig.15   Luke Terence Delaney starting off in the infamous
          Paris to Madrid Road Race in 1903, aged twenty-
          four and the car after he crashed!   195

Fig.16   Luke Terence Delaney (first on left) on a
          buying trip to the Paris Motor Show.   196

Fig.17   Luke Terence Delaney with his son Desmond
          and his daughter Dorothy (Dosh).   197

Fig.18   Luke Terence Delaney driving his family Tourer.   198

Fig.19   Luke Terence and his wife, Amy Farquhar,
          with their children - back row L - R Eric, Tom,
          Desmond and Dorothy - front Luke Sylvestre
          and Connie.   199

Fig.20   Luke Terence Delaney setting off by plane for
          the Paris Motor Show.   200

Fig.21   Luke Sylvestre Delaney, son of Luke Terence and
          Amy, enlisted in RAF in 1838 died in 1941,
          aged 21, when the plane he was piloting was
          damaged by enemy fire and he crash-
          landed in Albania.   201

Fig.22   Arthur Philip Delaney, son of James Delaney
          the artist, and Anne Maloney. First married
          Mary Mowat (mother of the 'Lost Children')
          then, after her death, Cecilia Clifford.   202

Fig.23   James Delaney (one of our 'Lost Children'),
          son of Arthur Delaney and Mary Mowat, his wife,
          Frances Metosh, and their surviving children –
          back row L – R Agnes, Arthur, Anna Robina
          and Marie – front Alan.   203

Fig.24   My great-grandmother, Cecilia Clifford,
          wife of Arthur Delaney and mother of Arthur,
          Bernard, Cecilia, John, Patrick, Mary,
          Helen (Nellie) Cecilia (2) and Edward.   204

FAMILY TREES

ARTHUR DELANEY
b 1761 | d1845

JAMES DELANEY m MARY HUGHES

ARTHUR DELANEY
b 1816   d 1850

ARTHUR DELANEY
b 1761 | d 1845

JAMES DELANEY m MARY HUGHES

ARTHUR DELANEY m 1839 HELEN COLLINS
b 1816 d 1850 | b 1820 d 1890

JAMES	MARY		ROSEANNA		THOMAS	JOHN
b 1840	b 1843	d 1844	b 1843	d 1844	b 1845	b 1848

ARTHUR DELANEY
b 1761   d 1845

JAMES DELANEY m MARY HUGHES

ARTHUR DELANEY m 1839 HELEN COLLINS
b 1816 d 1850   b 1820 d 1890

JAMES DELANEY m 1859 ANN MALONEY
b 1840 d 1888   b 1840 d 1902

ARTHUR PHILIP	ELLEN	ANN	JAMES
b 1860 d 1907	b 1862	b 1863 d 1866	b 1865

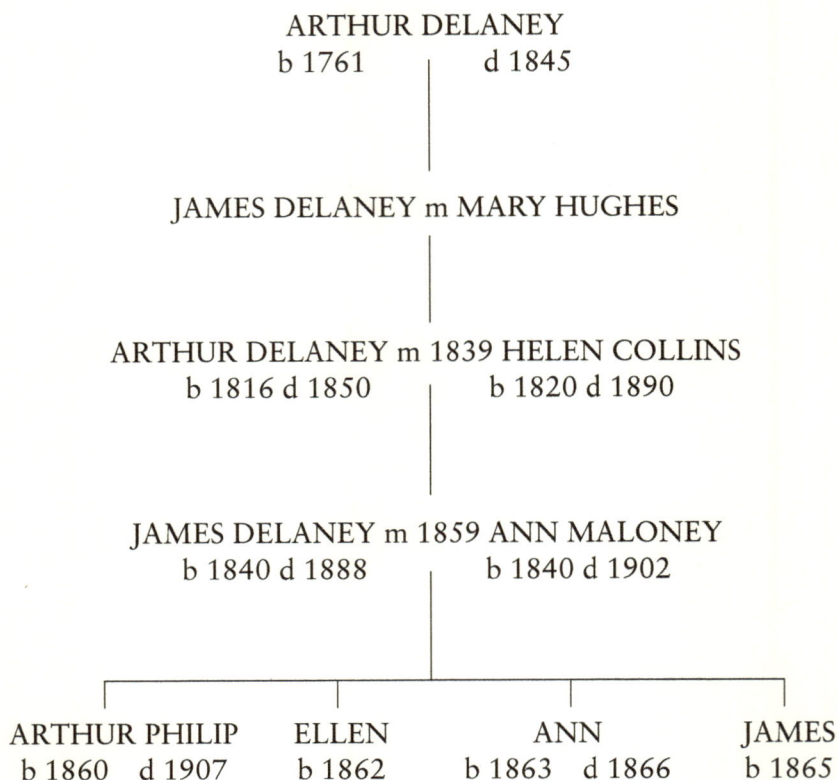

Their daughter Ellen Delaney died unmarried as did their son James Delaney.

Only their son Arthur Philip Delaney's line continues unbroken to the present day both in Scotland and the USA.

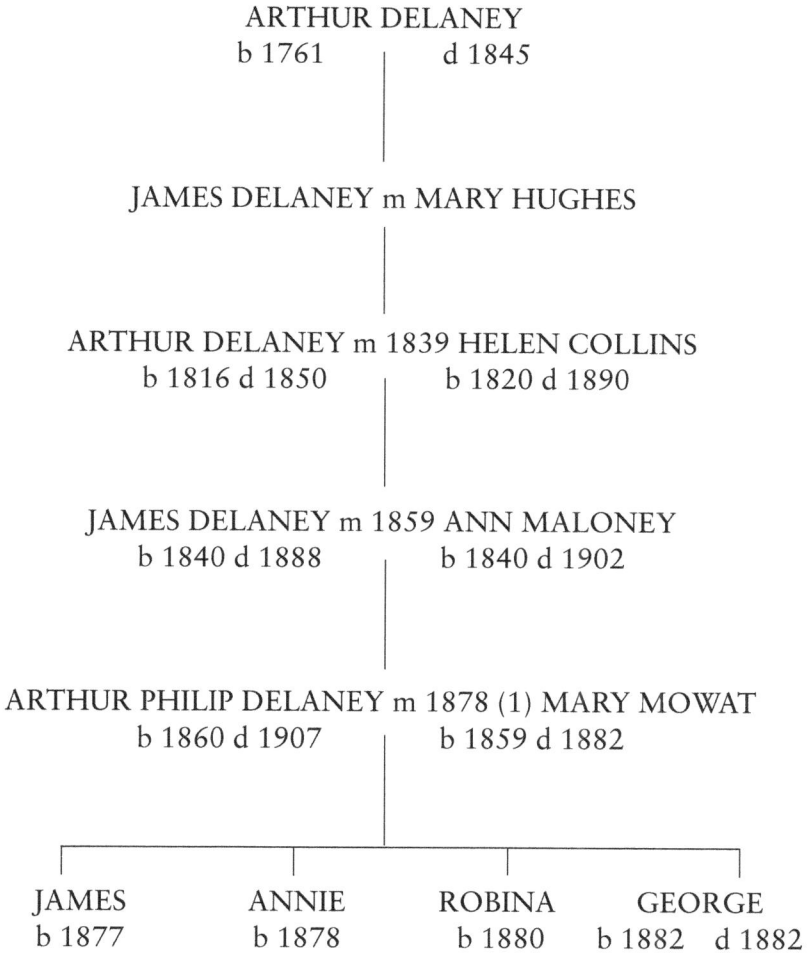

ARTHUR DELANEY
b 1761 | d 1845

JAMES DELANEY m MARY HUGHES

ARTHUR DELANEY m 1839 HELEN COLLINS
b 1816 d 1850 | b 1820 d 1890

JAMES DELANEY m 1859 ANN MALONEY
b 1840 d 1888 | b 1840 d 1902

ARTHUR PHILIP DELANEY m 1878 (1) MARY MOWAT
b 1860 d 1907 | b 1859 d 1882

JAMES	ANNIE	ROBINA	GEORGE
b 1877	b 1878	b 1880	b 1882 d 1882

ARTHUR DELANEY
b 1761 | d 1845

JAMES DELANEY m MARY HUGHES

ARTHUR DELANEY m 1839 HELEN COLLINS
b 1816   d 1850 | b 1820   d 1890

JAMES DELANEY m 1859 ANN MALONEY
b 1840   d 1888 | b 1840   d 1902

ARTHUR PHILIP DELANEY m 1878 (1) MARY MOWAT
b 1860   d 1907 | b 1859   d 1882

JAMES DELANEY m 1906 FRANCES METOSH
b 1877 | b 1880

ALLAN J	ANNA	AGNES	ALMA	MARIE	ARTHUR	JUNE
b 1906	ROBINA	b 1908	b 1910	b 1911	b 1913	1916
	b 1907					

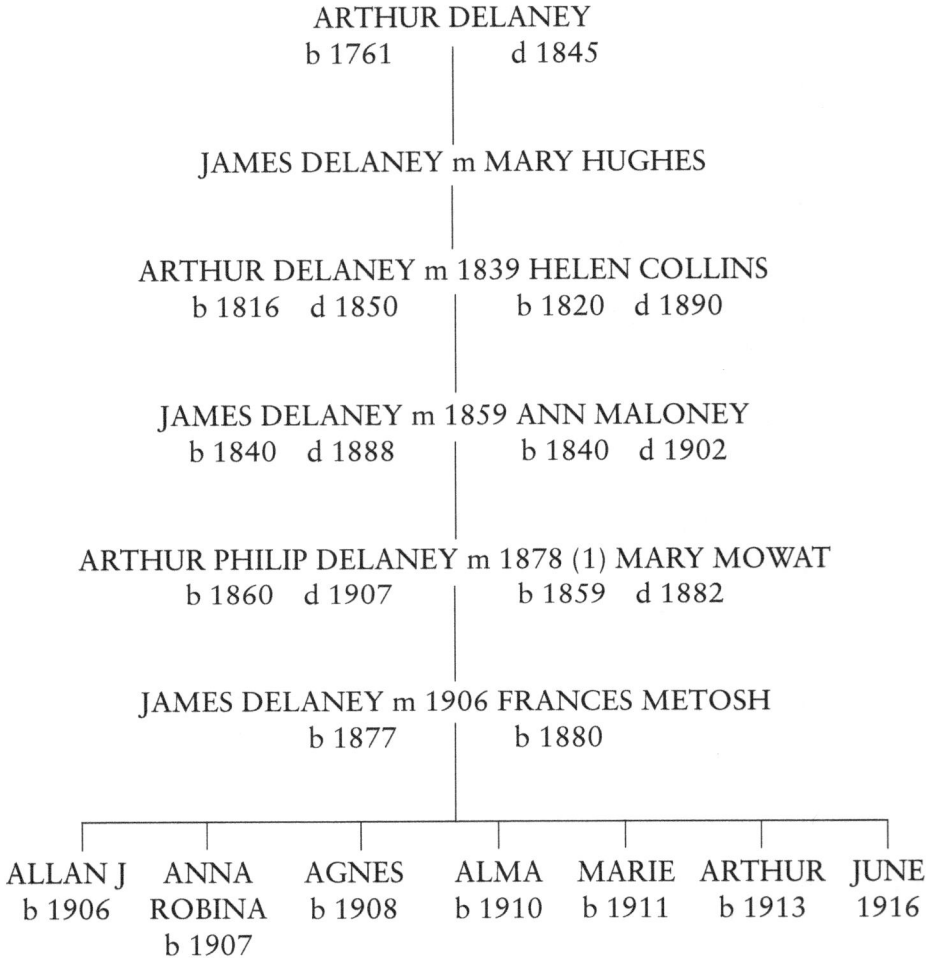

Anna Robina Delaney had two children – Ellen and Bill O'Hora.
Agnes Delaney had five children – Joyce, June, Doris, Harold and
Leonard Moll.
Arthur Burton Delaney had a son, Ronald Delaney.

340

ARTHUR DELANEY
b 1761 | d 1845

JAMES DELANEY m MARY HUGHES

ARTHUR DELANEY m 1839 HELEN COLLINS
b 1816   d 1850 | b 1820   d 1890

JAMES DELANEY m 1859 ANN MALONEY
b 1840   d 1888 | b 1840   d 1902

ARTHUR PHILIP DELANEY m 1878 (1) MARY MOWAT
b 1860   d 1907 | b 1859   d 1882

ANNIE DELANEY
b 1878   d 1895

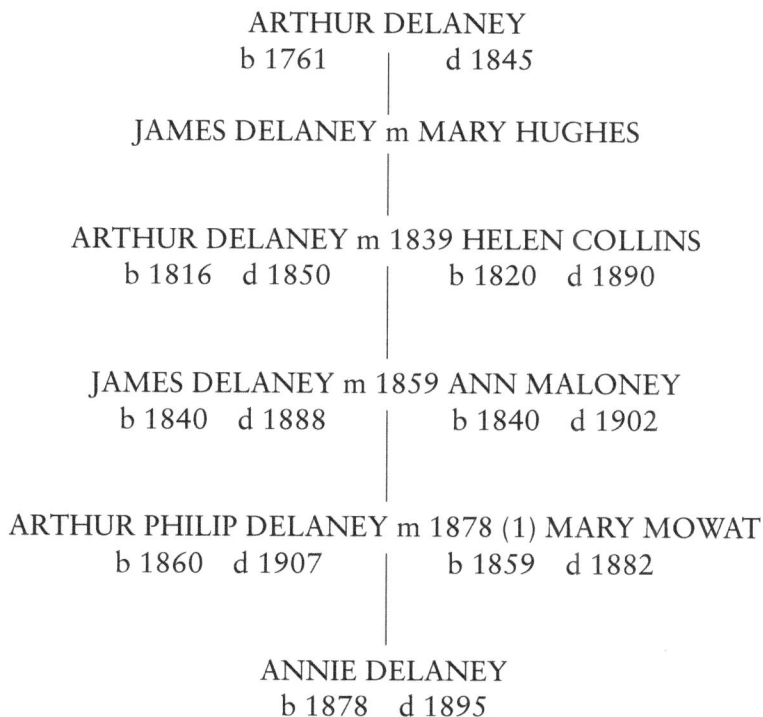

Annie Delaney died, aged 17, in the Cayuga Children's Home, Cayuga, New York State, USA.

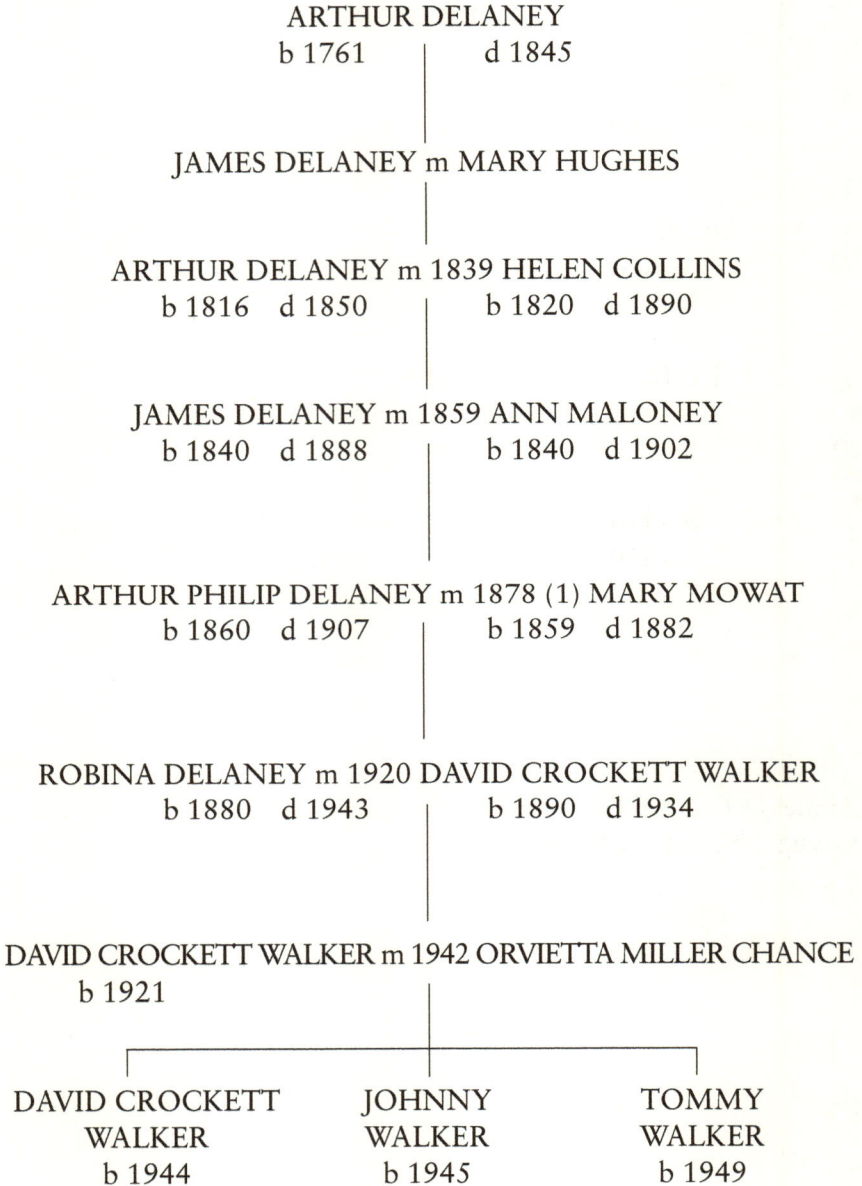

ARTHUR DELANEY
b 1761   d 1845

JAMES DELANEY m MARY HUGHES

ARTHUR DELANEY m 1839 HELEN COLLINS
b 1816   d 1850   b 1820   d 1890

JAMES DELANEY m 1859 ANN MALONEY
b 1840   d 1888   b 1840   d 1902

ARTHUR PHILIP DELANEY m 1878 (1) MARY MOWAT
b 1860   d 1907   b 1859   d 1882

ROBINA DELANEY m 1920 DAVID CROCKETT WALKER
b 1880   d 1943   b 1890   d 1934

DAVID CROCKETT WALKER m 1942 ORVIETTA MILLER CHANCE
b 1921

DAVID CROCKETT WALKER b 1944	JOHNNY WALKER b 1945	TOMMY WALKER b 1949

ARTHUR DELANEY
b 1761   d 1845

JAMES DELANEY m MARY HUGHES

ARTHUR DELANEY m 1839 HELEN COLLINS
b 1816   d 1850   b 1820   d 1890

JAMES DELANEY m 1859 ANN MALONEY
b 1840   d 1888   b 1840   d 1902

ARTHUR PHILIP DELANEY m 1886 (2) CECILIA CLIFFORD
b 1860   d 1907   b 1863   d 1923

ARTHUR BERNARD CECILIA JOHN PATRICK MARY HELEN CECILIA EDWARD

ARTHUR DELANEY
b 1761   d 1845

JAMES DELANEY m MARY HUGHES

ARTHUR DELANEY m 1839 HELEN COLLINS
b 1816   d 1850   b 1820   d 1890

THOMAS JOSEPH DELANEY m 1869 MARGARET McGUIRE
b 1847   d 1917

MARY MARGARET CATHERINE JOAN CHRISTINA ARTHUR PATRICK
HELEN   ANN   d 1880   d 1880   b 1890
b 1869 b 1871 d 1882

THOMAS JOSEPH DELANEY also had an illegitimate son JAMES
to HELEN McINTOSH in 1868.

ARTHUR DELANEY
b 1761 | d 1845

JAMES DELANEY m MARY HUGHES

ARTHUR DELANEY m 1839 HELEN COLLINS
b 1816   d 1850 | b 1820   d 1890

JOHN SYLVESTER DELANEY m 1878 ELIZABETH McALPINE
b 1848 | d 1884

LUKE TERENCE	KATHLEEN	JOHN WILLIAM
	b 1882 d 1884	b 1883

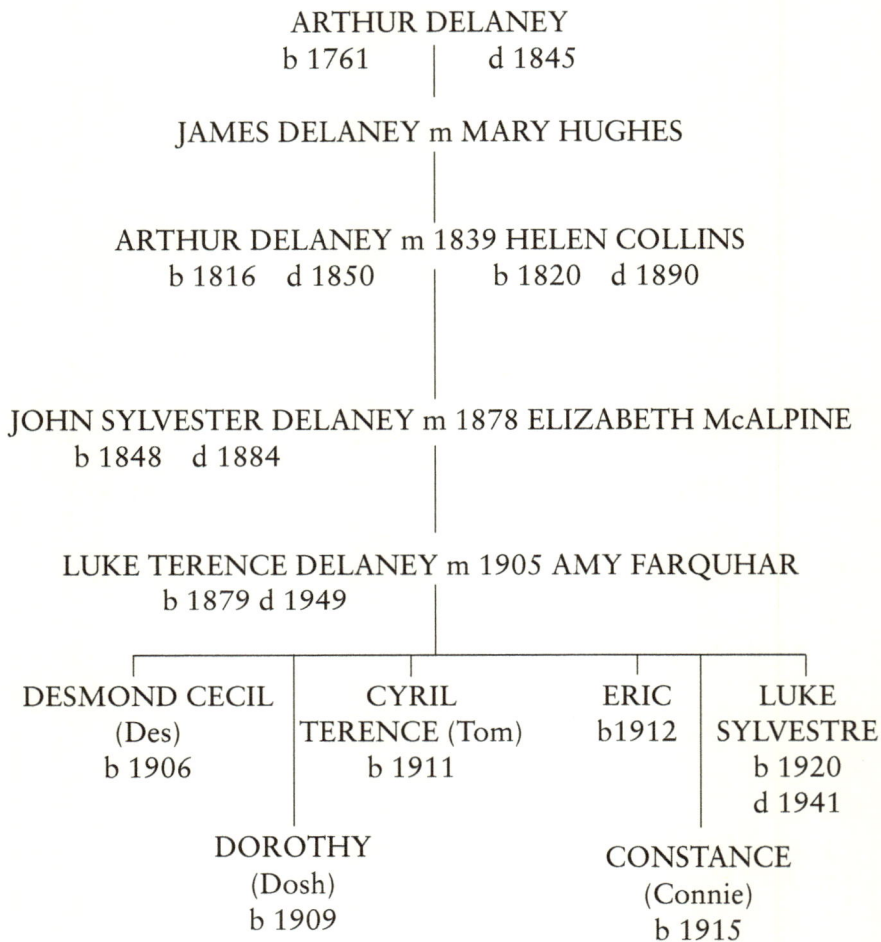

ARTHUR DELANEY
b 1761 | d 1845

JAMES DELANEY m MARY HUGHES

ARTHUR DELANEY m 1839 HELEN COLLINS
b 1816   d 1850 | b 1820   d 1890

JOHN SYLVESTER DELANEY m 1878 ELIZABETH McALPINE
b 1848   d 1884

LUKE TERENCE DELANEY m 1905 AMY FARQUHAR
b 1879 d 1949

DESMOND CECIL
(Des)
b 1906

CYRIL
TERENCE (Tom)
b 1911

ERIC
b1912

LUKE
SYLVESTRE
b 1920
d 1941

DOROTHY
(Dosh)
b 1909

CONSTANCE
(Connie)
b 1915

ARTHUR DELANEY
b 1761 | d 1845

JAMES DELANEY m MARY HUGHES

ARTHUR DELANEY m 1839 HELEN COLLINS
b 1816 d 1850 | b 1820 d 1890

JOHN SYLVESTER DELANEY m 1878 ELIZABETH McALPINE
b 1848   d 1884

JOHN WILLIAM DELANEY m 1910 ADA WEEKS
b 1884 d 1963

Janet Croome (nee Delaney) can find no evidence that the couple divorced but ADA WEEKS using the name ADA WIGG (her real name) appears to have married a Harry Richter in 1914.

JOHN WILLIAM DELANEY has a daughter EILEEN MADORA DELANEY to a woman named ALICE MAUD DELANEY (nee Neal) in 1915 and a daughter named PHYLLIS JOAN DELANEY to the same woman in 1919. Janet can find no marriage certicate for John William Delaney and Alice Maud Neal so it is possible that both the daughters were illegitimate. Neither of the daughters had children so that Delaney line did not continue.

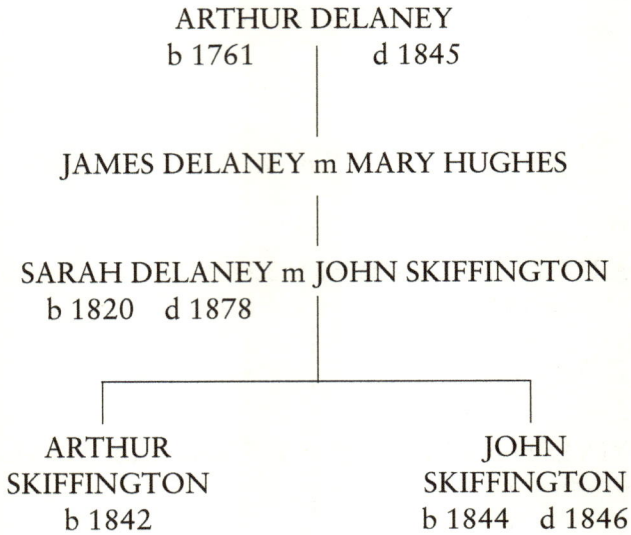

ARTHUR DELANEY
b 1761   d 1845

JAMES DELANEY m MARY HUGHES

SARAH DELANEY m JOHN SKIFFINGTON
b 1820   d 1878

ARTHUR
SKIFFINGTON
b 1842

JOHN
SKIFFINGTON
b 1844   d 1846

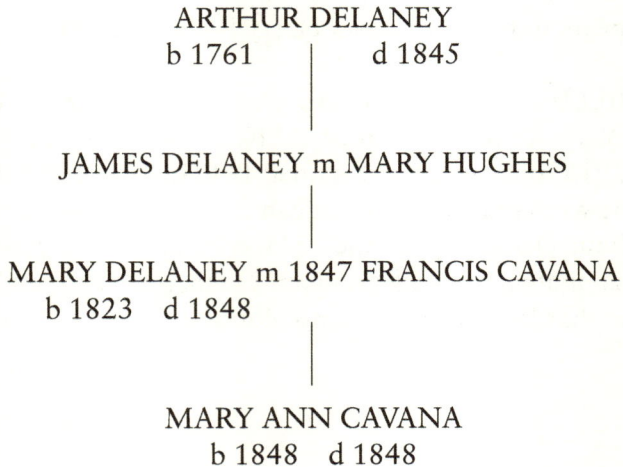

ARTHUR DELANEY
b 1761   d 1845

JAMES DELANEY m MARY HUGHES

MARY DELANEY m 1847 FRANCIS CAVANA
b 1823   d 1848

MARY ANN CAVANA
b 1848   d 1848

ARTHUR DELANEY
b 1761 | d 1845

JAMES DELANEY m MARY HUGHES

ANNE DELANEY
b 1831

JOHN DELANEY (illegitimate)
b 1856   d 1856

ANNE DELANEY married JOSEPH DALY in 1864. They had no children.

We can find no death record for ANNE DALY (nee DELANEY) in the Scottish Registers.

ARTHUR DELANEY
b 1761 | d 1845

JAMES DELANEY m MARY HUGHES

JANE DELANEY m 1855 JOHN MURRAY
b 1833   d 1883 | b 1833   d 1874

ELLEN	JOHN	SARAH	MARY	ARTHUR	JAMES	JANE
b 1856	b 1860	b 1863	b 1865	b 1867	CHARLES b 1869	b 1872

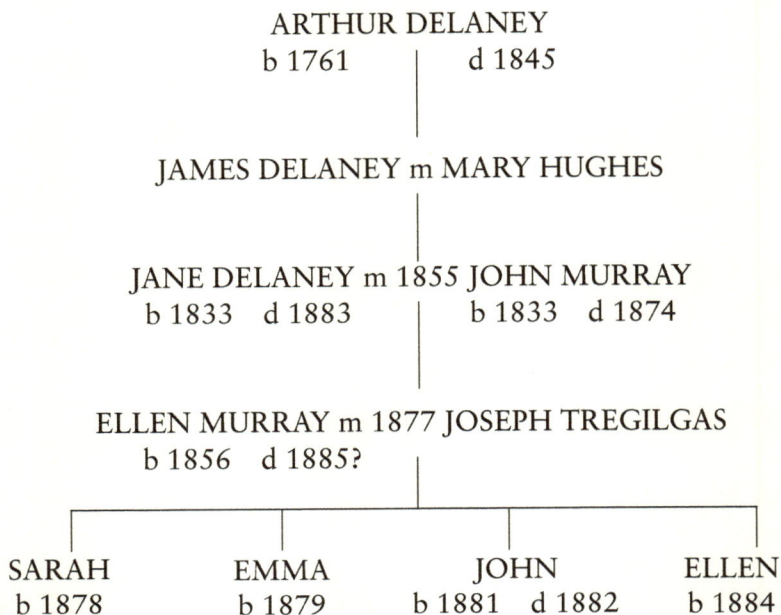

ARTHUR DELANEY
b 1761 | d 1845

JAMES DELANEY m MARY HUGHES

JANE DELANEY m 1855 JOHN MURRAY
b 1833 d 1883 | b 1833 d 1874

ELLEN MURRAY m 1877 JOSEPH TREGILGAS
b 1856 d 1885?

SARAH	EMMA	JOHN	ELLEN
b 1878	b 1879	b 1881 d 1882	b 1884

ARTHUR DELANEY
b 1761 | d 1845

|

JAMES DELANEY m MARY HUGHES

|

JANE DELANEY m 1855 JOHN MURRAY
b 1833   d 1883 | b 1833   d 1874

|

ELLEN MURRAY m 1877 JOSEPH TREGILGAS
b 1856   d 1885?

|

SARAH (CONSTANCE) TREGILGAS m 1914 JOSEPH LUSSIER
b 1878 d 1968

MARIE FERNANDE
HELENE LUSSIER
b 1915

GABRIELLE LUSSIER
b 1918

ARTHUR DELANEY
b 1761 | d 1845

JAMES DELANEY m MARY HUGHES

JANE DELANEY m 1855 JOHN MURRAY
b 1833 d 1883 | b 1833 d 1874

ELLEN MURRAY m 1877 JOSEPH TREGILGAS
b 1856 d 1885?

EMMA TREGILGAS (Sister St-Elphege)
b 1879 d 1953

ARTHUR DELANEY
b 1761 | d 1845

JAMES DELANEY m MARY HUGHES

JANE DELANEY m 1855 JOHN MURRAY
b 1833   d 1883 | b 1833   d 1874

ELLEN MURRAY m 1877 JOSEPH TREGILGAS
b 1856   d 1885?

ELLEN (BLANCHE) TREGILGAS m 1918 PIERRE PAUL AUTHER
b 1884 d 1927

JEANNE AUTHER m CHARLES BARRY
b 1919

ARTHUR DELANEY
b 1761   d 1845

JAMES DELANEY m MARY HUGHES

JANE DELANEY m 1855 JOHN MURRAY
b 1833 d 1883   b 1833 d 1874

JOHN MURRAY m 1884 JESSIE McGEE
b 1860 d 1907

| ARTHUR MURRAY b 1887 | MARY JANE MURRAY b 1891 | MAGGIE MURRAY |

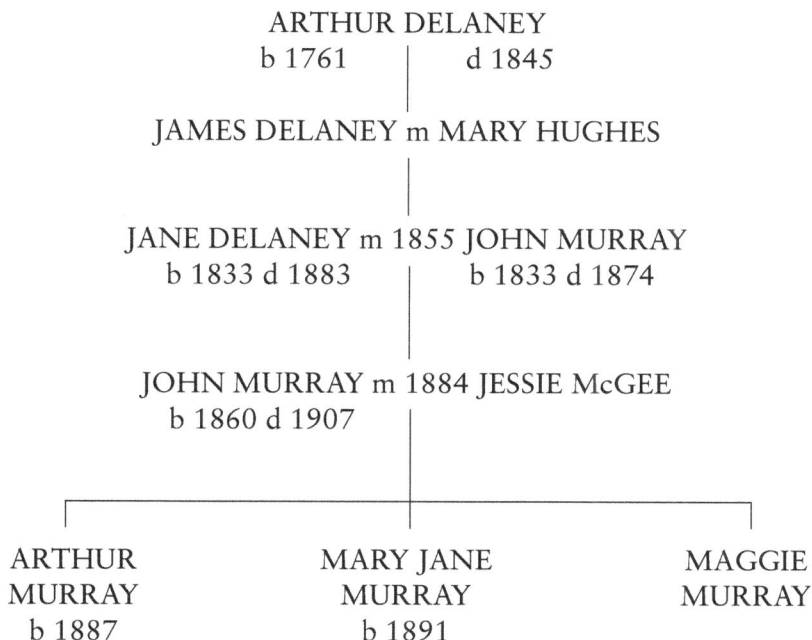

John Murray and Jessie McGee also adopted a boy named George Lavin born in 1894. His father was dead at the time of his birth and his mother Maggie Lavin appears to have died when George was six years old.

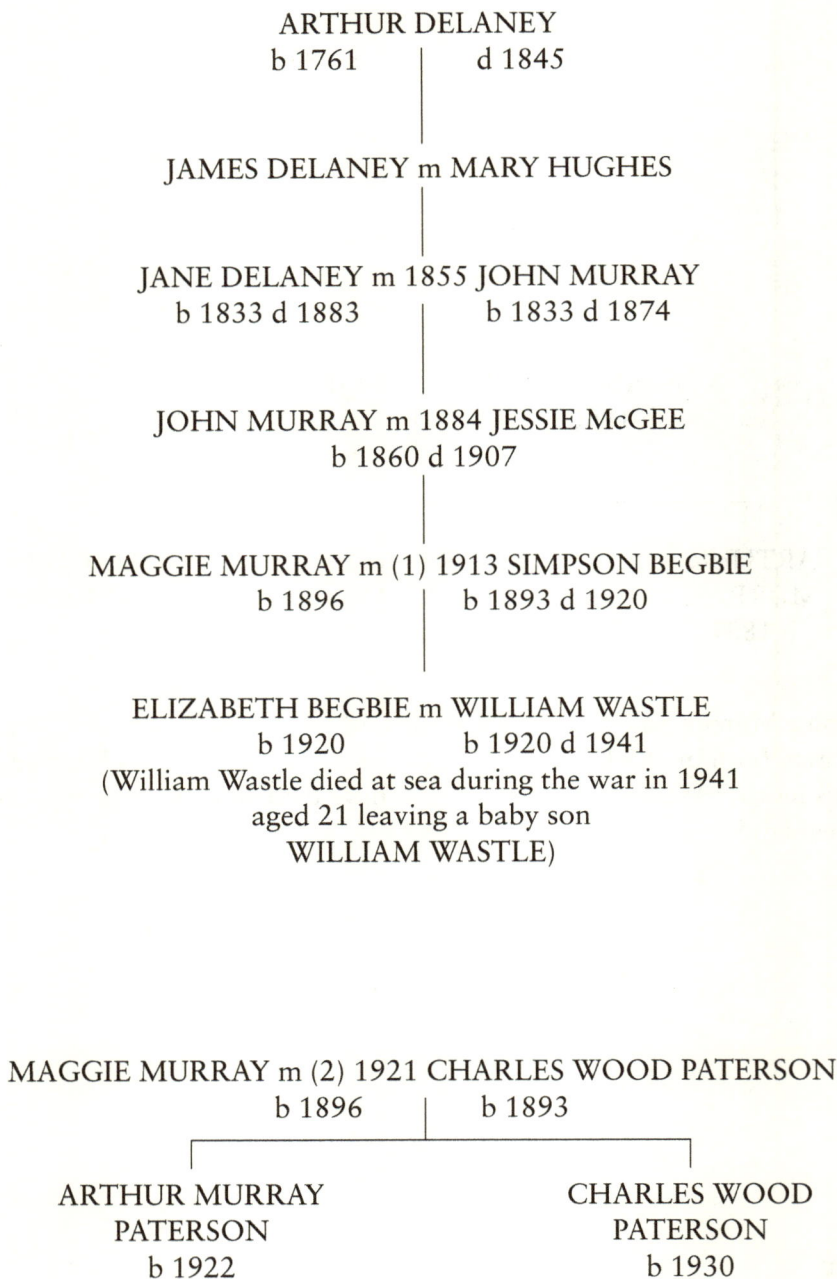

ARTHUR DELANEY
b 1761 | d 1845

JAMES DELANEY m MARY HUGHES

JANE DELANEY m 1855 JOHN MURRAY
b 1833 d 1883 | b 1833 d 1874

JOHN MURRAY m 1884 JESSIE McGEE
b 1860 d 1907

MAGGIE MURRAY m (1) 1913 SIMPSON BEGBIE
b 1896 | b 1893 d 1920

ELIZABETH BEGBIE m WILLIAM WASTLE
b 1920   b 1920 d 1941
(William Wastle died at sea during the war in 1941
aged 21 leaving a baby son
WILLIAM WASTLE)

MAGGIE MURRAY m (2) 1921 CHARLES WOOD PATERSON
b 1896 | b 1893

ARTHUR MURRAY
PATERSON
b 1922

CHARLES WOOD
PATERSON
b 1930

ARTHUR DELANEY
b 1761 | d 1845

JAMES DELANEY m MARY HUGHES

JANE DELANEY m 1855 JOHN MURRAY
b 1833 d 1883 | b 1833 d 1874

SARAH MURRAY m 1884 JAMES JOSEPH MacMAHON
b 1863 d 1901

JANE
MacMAHON

ROBERT
MacMAHON

SARAH
MacMAHON

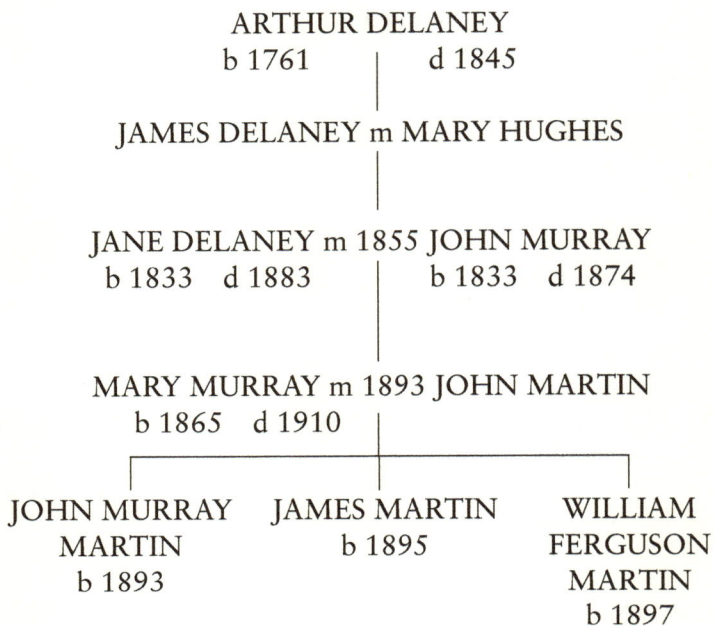

ARTHUR DELANEY
b 1761 | d 1845

JAMES DELANEY m MARY HUGHES

JANE DELANEY m 1855 JOHN MURRAY
b 1833   d 1883 | b 1833   d 1874

MARY MURRAY m 1893 JOHN MARTIN
b 1865   d 1910

JOHN MURRAY
MARTIN
b 1893

JAMES MARTIN
b 1895

WILLIAM
FERGUSON
MARTIN
b 1897

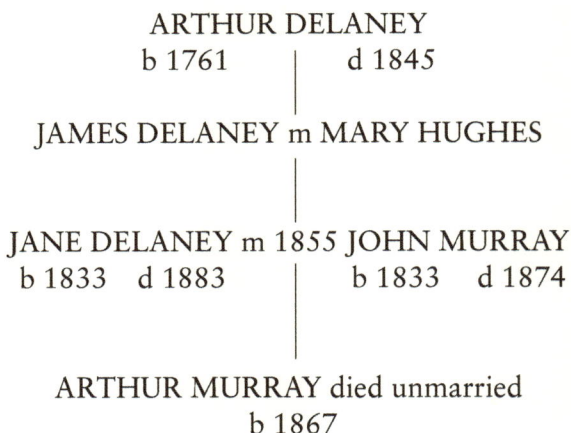

ARTHUR DELANEY
b 1761 | d 1845

JAMES DELANEY m MARY HUGHES

JANE DELANEY m 1855 JOHN MURRAY
b 1833   d 1883 | b 1833   d 1874

ARTHUR MURRAY died unmarried
b 1867

ARTHUR DELANEY
b 1761   d 1845

JAMES DELANEY m MARY HUGHES

JANE DELANEY m 1855 JOHN MURRAY
b 1833   d 1883   b 1833   d 1874

JAMES CHARLES MURRAY
b 1869

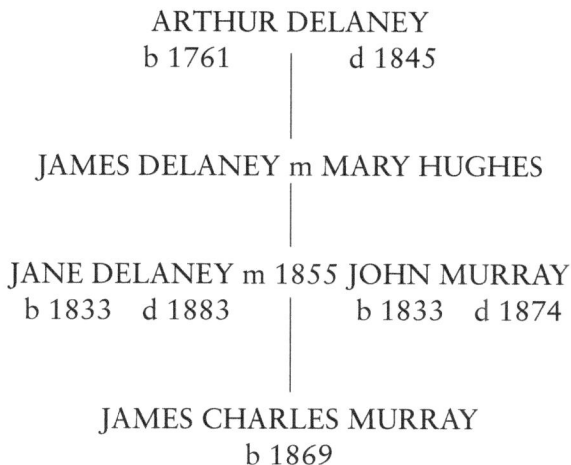

James Charles Murray appears in the 1891 census living at 7 Hill Place, Edinburgh with his sister Sarah Murray and her husband James McMahon. We can find no other information about him.

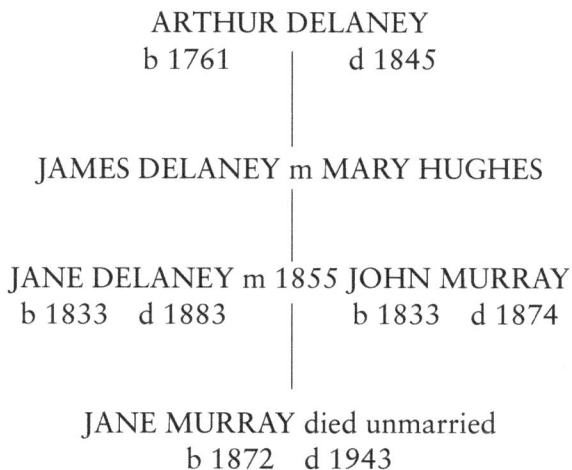

ARTHUR DELANEY
b 1761   d 1845

JAMES DELANEY m MARY HUGHES

JANE DELANEY m 1855 JOHN MURRAY
b 1833   d 1883   b 1833   d 1874

JANE MURRAY died unmarried
b 1872   d 1943

HELEN DELANEY (nee COLLINS) m 1850 PHILIP BOYLAN

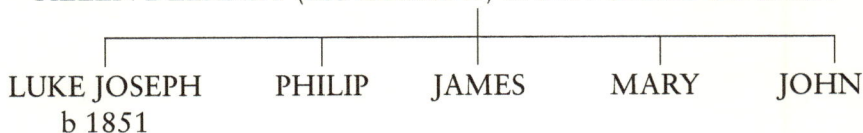

LUKE JOSEPH   PHILIP   JAMES   MARY   JOHN
b 1851

HELEN DELANEY (nee COLLINS) m 1850 (2) PHILIP BOYLAN

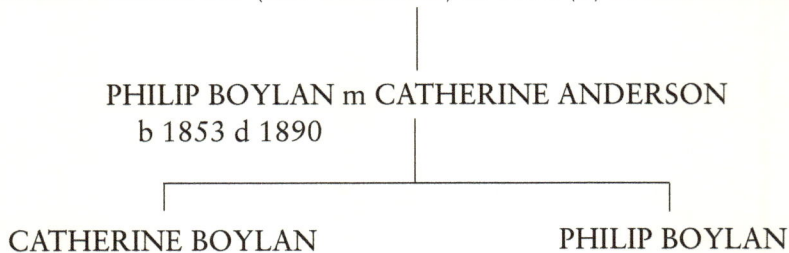

LUKE JOSEPH BOYLAN m 1881 PATRICIA CAMPSIE
b 1851

They had no children.

HELEN DELANEY (nee COLLINS) m 1850 (2) PHILIP BOYLAN

PHILIP BOYLAN m CATHERINE ANDERSON
b 1853 d 1890

CATHERINE BOYLAN   PHILIP BOYLAN

HELEN DELANEY (nee COLLINS) m 1850 (2) PHILIP BOYLAN

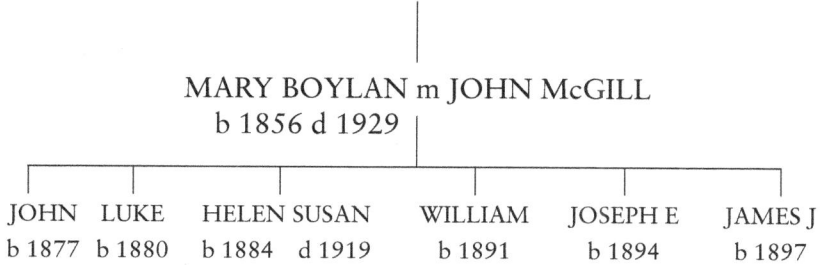

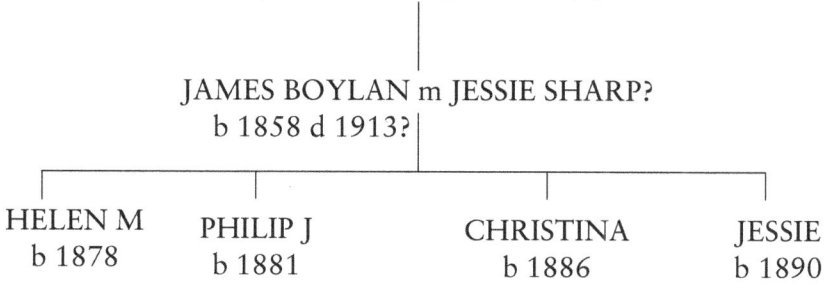

MARY BOYLAN m JOHN McGILL
b 1856 d 1929

JOHN	LUKE	HELEN	SUSAN	WILLIAM	JOSEPH E	JAMES J
b 1877	b 1880	b 1884	d 1919	b 1891	b 1894	b 1897

HELEN DELANEY (nee COLLINS) m 1850 (2) PHILIP BOYLAN

JAMES BOYLAN m JESSIE SHARP?
b 1858 d 1913?

HELEN M	PHILIP J	CHRISTINA	JESSIE
b 1878	b 1881	b 1886	b 1890

BIBLIOGRAPHY

Copies of the Custody Case, Court of Session Records, Edinburgh

Copies of the Custody Case Supreme Court of Nova Scotia records

Copies of Slander Case, Court of Session Records, Edinburgh

Emyvale, Sweet Emyvale – by Seamus McCluskey

St. Patrick's Church, Edinburgh, Archive

Burial Records of Greyfriar's Churchyard held at Mortonhall Cemetery, Edinburgh

Our Children in Old Scotland and Nova Scotia – by Emma Maitland Stirling

The Making of Hibernian - by Alan Lugton – published by John Donald – 1995

THE REPUBLIC - by Charles Townshend – The Penguin Group – 2013

The Life and Times of James Connolly – by Desmond Graves

The Uneasy Peace – by Tom Gallagher

The Scotsman Newspaper Archive

211 Squadron RAF website - www.211squadron.org – by Don Clark

Article on Luke Sylvestre Delaney – by Nick Delaney

General Registers Scotland/Scotland's People

The London Delaney Family Archive – in custody of Terry Delaney

Goodbye to All That – A Memoir of Life on the Western Front – by Robert Graves

En-route to Flanders Field. The Canadians at Shorncliffe During the Great War – by Diane Beaupre of Canterbury Christchurch University – published by Saltwooid Village.

Wikipedia – Profile of Canon Edward Hannan from Hibernian History Society

Wikipedia – Information on troopship requisitions in WWI

Wikipedia – Profiles of Dr John Macrae and the No3 Canadian General Hospital (McGill)

Wikipedia – Profile of Arthur Mignault and the No4 Canadian Stationary Hospital (Laval)

Wikipedia – Profile of Charles Stewart Parnell

Wikipedia – Article on Rhon-Rossitten Gesellschaft

Wikipedia – Profile of Wolf Hirth

Veteran Motor Cars – by Steve Lanham – Shire Publications 2020

Article in *The Auto Journal* – 'Between Ourselves' – by 'Iolaus' – July 1921

Article in *'The Aeroplane Magazine'* – 16 April 1919

Article in *Autoweek Magazine* – by John Matras – 4 March 1993